CHILDREN OF THE MILL

Midwestern History and Culture

GENERAL EDITORS
James H. Madison and Thomas J. Schlereth

Nature study at Froebel School, ca. 1914

CHILDREN OF THE MILL

Schooling and Society
in Gary, Indiana,
1906–1960

RONALD D. COHEN

INDIANA UNIVERSITY PRESS

Bloomington and Indianapolis

Manufactured in the United States of America

Library of Congress Cataloging-in-Publication Data

Cohen, Ronald D.,
Children of the mill : schooling and society in Gary, Indiana,
1906–1960 / Ronald D. Cohen.
p. cm. — (Midwestern history and culture)
Includes index.
ISBN 0-253-31377-5
1. Public schools—Indiana—Gary—History—20th century.
2. Education—Indiana—Gary—History—20th century.   3. Educational
sociology—Indiana—Gary—History—20th century.   I. Title.
II. Series.
LA285.G2C65   1990
371′.01′0977299—dc20   89-45477
                                                              CIP

1 2 3 4 5   94 93 92 91 90

TO
The late Raymond J. Sontag, who had faith in me
when it counted.
And Nancy, who still does.

CONTENTS

Illustrations follow chapter IV.

PREFACE

In 1970 and shortly thereafter two significant events converged, leading me to break from my established scholarly interest and embark instead on what would turn out to be an almost twenty-year odyssey. I arrived at Indiana University Northwest, in Gary, Indiana, as the new decade began to teach American history, and more specifically American colonial history, my focus in graduate school and in my research. I had no thoughts of starting along a new historical road. I happened to read Lawrence Cremin's *The Transformation of the School* (1961) soon after arriving in the city, however, and was struck by his discussion of progressive education, particularly of William A. Wirt and the Gary Plan. Finding myself in the home of what had been, perhaps, the most exciting and famous of progressive era educational experiments, I was quickly lured to abandon my labored study of seventeenth-century Virginia society and begin not only a new project, but a fresh scholarly bent, the history of education in the United States. The early fruits of my research appeared in (with Raymond A. Mohl) *The Paradox of Progressive Education: The Gary Plan and Urban Schooling* (Port Washington, N. Y., 1979). In its topical and chronological chapters Mohl and I attempted to explore a variety of themes, fixing our understanding of the work-study-play plan in Gary and New York City during Wirt's tenure (1906–38) somewhere within, and beyond, the spectrum of current revisionist interpretations.

Cremin depicted the Gary Plan as an exemplary manifestation of John Dewey's concept of progressive education: "Wirt's notion was not only to afford each child vastly extended educational opportunity—in playgrounds, gardens, libraries, gymnasiums and swimming pools, art and music rooms, science laboratories, machine shops, and assembly halls—but to make the school the true center of the artistic and intellectual life of the neighborhood. Open all day, twelve months a year, and to all the age groups, the Wirt school would be the heart of all effort toward long-range community improvement, ultimately the most important single lever of social progress." Cremin's depiction was most positive, coinciding with his overall view that "progressive education began as part of a vast humanitarian effort to apply the promise of American life . . . to the puzzling new urban-industrial civilization that came into being during the latter half of the nineteenth century."

Some years before Ellwood P. Cubberley, dean of educational historians, had been almost as effusive, believing the Gary plan "represents one of the most original pieces of constructive thinking ever attempted in American education, and one that, in its various adaptations, has profoundly modified school organization in this country."[1]

A different interpretation of the Gary schools appeared in 1962 in Raymond Callahan's *Education and the Cult of Efficiency*. Anxious "to explore the origin and development of the adoption of business values and practices in educational administration," Callahan discovered that the Gary schools epitomized the "manifestation of the principles of scientific management in the schools." Indeed, he named the chapter "The 'Factory System' in Education—The Platoon School." Callahan was interested in the organizational influence of business leaders and did not investigate the larger topic of the meaning and influence of corporate capitalism in American life. But his study broke sharply with Cremin's "romantic" view and paved the way for the soon-to-appear, more critical "revisionist" interpretations; and his approach has tended to prevail. Most recently, Herbert Kliebard, in his sweeping *The Struggle for the American Curriculum, 1893–1958*, has argued that "the platoon system was clearly more managerial than curriculum as an educational innovation" and an important aspect of scientific curriculum-making.[2]

My goal is not to put the Gary schools, 1906–60, in an ideological straitjacket, but to explore them in considerable detail, emphasizing two central themes that are crucial to understand the rise of urban schooling in the twentieth century. First, the Gary schools exemplified the rise of a system of mass education in a multiracial, multiethnic, class-structured urban setting. In this context, public schools, in Gary and throughout the country, manifested an expanding mission to provide a plethora of services to the community, many positive, some, perhaps, negative. Schools did not just offer curricular and extracurricular choices to children, but also provided medical care, baby sitting, social welfare services, recreation for the entire family, adult programs (particularly during the early decades), facilities for the handicapped, and employment opportunities, and served as an anchor for the community. The work-study-play school plan incorporated a large variety of programs and services, as befit progressive education; but, even with its lingering demise after 1940, the schools did not abandon their broader mission. Americans have long been suspicious of increasing government programs, but have generally accepted proliferating school services.

Second, because of their important and visible public role, schools have served as a magnet for the views and interests of a complex of organizations, interest groups, and individuals, whether local, state, or national. While historians have concentrated on exploring the ideas and actions of school boards and administrators, teachers, state and national educational policy makers, professional groups, and the experts, it is vital also to examine the role of others: business interests, labor unions, civil rights organizations, parents, politicians, writers, churches, voluntary organizations, and even the students, to name but a few. Some of these interests have been continually involved, others surfaced at a particular time depending on other factors. For example, during the two world wars the role of the federal government temporarily increased, then subsided following peace. Economic exigencies, say during the Great Depression, thrust other interests to the fore. And the cold war created a different set of concerns and interested parties. A study of the Gary schools, spanning the first six decades of the century, will bring into sharp focus the intersection of these two central aspects of public schooling—the involvement of a large number of groups and individuals in shaping the schools' manifold programs.

Certainly, the early Gary school plan was also unique. William A. Wirt was justly famous for his work-study-play plan, which combined an enriched curriculum and an interesting school organization. The superintendent was not particularly original, but he had his finger on the progressive pulse. He fit together various existing pieces to form a captivating, and controversial, mosaic. The system was widely copied, but never exactly, and even generated excitement in other countries. I have tried to explore the meaning and substance of the plan as well as its rise and fall in Gary and nationally, rooting my study in a large variety of primary sources and incorporating the most recent secondary interpretations.

Captivated by the intricacies of progressive education, particularly the connection between the rise of urban schooling and the development of industrial capitalism, historians have tended to concentrate on the early decades of the century. While I have devoted much attention to this period, I, perhaps, have found it more intriguing to explore the 1930s through the 1950s, when the schools had to cope with the depression, political changes, war and peace, contraction and gross expansion, anticommunism, personnel changes, racial upheavals, labor unrest, and newer educational theories. I was able to depend on a vast secondary literature for the early chapters, but often found myself in uncharted waters once into the depression years. In connecting the earlier with the later decades, I attempt to illustrate both continuities and changes.

I have been greatly influenced by the revisionist studies of Michael Katz, Marvin Lazerson, Joel Spring, and so many others, as well as the contrary work of Diane Ravitch, and the books and articles of those who find themselves somewhere along the political path from right to left. While my inclination is to veer leftward, perhaps interpreting the schools as conscious or unconscious tools of the corporate hierarchy, I have rather an ambivalent view of what happened in Gary. Surely William Wirt and his successors, as well as the school board members, were closely connected to the business community and held rather conservative political ideas. Moreover, the schools did sort and channel the students, distinguishing between black and white, rich and poor, academic and nonacademic, the winners and the losers.

The business community also had inordinate influence over school (and civic) affairs. Still, there was not necessarily a unified business class, but one divided between U.S. Steel and its supporters on the one hand and many professionals and small businessmen on the other. Moreover, there were various other influences, ranging from the students and their parents, many of them businesspeople, to labor unions, educational experts, politicians, and ethnic organizations. Schools have not always worked the way they are supposed to. And there was significant change over time.

The schools became a battleground because they were taken very seriously, offering to many the vision, if not the reality, of an open, equitable, democratic society, perhaps not for themselves but at least for their children. The aspirations and expectations of the majority, not just the power of the few, must be explored in reaching a fuller understanding of the history of urban schooling. Of course, most of the boys in Gary were destined for jobs in the steel mills or some such employment, and the girls would become wives and mothers. Schooling, however, could still be intellectually, culturally, and socially stimulating, and perhaps for many it was in the old Wirt system (and even afterwards).[3]

Most simply, I do not believe that pluralism has been the guiding premise of American society. Rather, it seems to me that the Gary schools and their counterparts throughout the country have operated within the rather narrow framework of developing corporate capitalism. Yet, within this limited economic, political, intellectual, and social structure there has been a general give and take among various and competing individuals, groups, and organizations. And, perhaps, children have, occasionally, reaped the benefits. The Gary schools thus mirrored and reaffirmed the dominant ethos.

I want, above all, to tell the story—the historian's prime responsibility—of the Gary schools during the first half of the twentieth century in all of its manifest complexity. My emphasis on the dual themes of educational expansion and multifarious influences is designed to tie the narrative together over the decades, as well as to link the Gary schools to other urban systems, where similar conditions surely prevailed. My thematic schema was developed after much wheedling and battering by my two close friends, Ed McClellan and Bill Reese of Indiana University, perhaps the finest critics in our profession. They have also been scrupulous in giving the most minute criticism and advice. I have occasionally rejected their views, stubbornly and at my own peril.

Ray Mohl, Jim Lane, Jeff Mirel, Lewis Ciminillo, and Jim Madison have also given valuable criticism and assistance over the years. Don Warren was a most astute critic, whose support I gratefully acknowledge. I have got much inspiration from Wayne Fuller, whose spirited writing style, particularly in leading off each chapter with a telling anecdote, as well as his thorough documentation, has established a very high standard that I have attempted to reach. Steve McShane of the Calumet Regional Archives has always been exceedingly helpful, as have Cynthia Bauer Szymanski, Tim Sutherland, Lois White, and the rest of the staff of the IUN library. Rosalie Zak, over the years, and Margaret Wheeler, more recently, have provided their valuable office skills. Andrew Biancardi drew the map and Gary Wilk helped with the illustrations. I have regularly received important financial support from Indiana University Northwest in the form of research grants, summer faculty fellowships, and two sabbaticals. I would also like to thank the staffs of various research libraries and archives, particularly the Lilly Library at Indiana University, the Library of Congress, the National Archives, and the Gary Public Library. Numerous individuals in and around Gary have been most generous with sharing their records and memories, and I value their friendship and assistance: Sherwood Wirt, Mark Roser, YJean Chambers, Clifford Minton, Haron Battle, and many others too numerous to list separately. And, finally, I thank Nancy for her fortitude, critical judgment, and support.

I end my narrative in 1960. This is not an arbitrary date. The Wirt system had finally died after a protracted illness, and the schools would hereafter more closely resemble the mainstream. So, I have chosen to discuss the rise and fall, in all of its complexities, of a notable school system. Moreover, new problems and issues emerged in the 1960s, particularly regarding racial matters, curricular changes, and the role of the federal government in school affairs. The enrollment would move from predominately white to heavily black within only a few years. A new superintendent would shake up the curriculum, prodded by national reforms and governmental pressures. The sixties and their aftermath into the 1980s constitute a complicated and fascinating story, one that needs a separate telling. That job I will leave to others.

The reader may inquire what connection the past has to the present. Does an understanding of the Gary schools thirty or sixty years ago help us to fathom current educational matters? Yes, in a variety of ways. For one, we can gain some insight into what it is possible for (particularly elementary) schools to do—not just to offer a limited variety of academic subjects, but also to provide public speaking, nature study, crafts, music, manual training, athletics, and a whole host of other activities. We need a richer, not a more constricted, curriculum and a more exciting school atmosphere, despite the current mania for testing generated by the academic skills scare. We also need to understand how schools operate through appreciating the plethora of organizations and pressure groups that continue to work their will within the broader socioeconomic-political context. Public schools are not restricted institutions, but public responsibilities, although they should be protected from the overzealous who would prefer to abolish Constitutional safeguards. Schools should, above all, provide an enlightened intellectual, cultural, so-

cial, and physical experience for our children, stimulating them to be thinking, creative, energetic citizens. And perhaps, within limits, they have
occasionally accomplished this.

I hope *Children of the Mill* will appeal to my fellow historians, helping
guide them through the thicket of the history of modern urban schooling, as
well as to professional educators, school reformers, and education policy
analysts and planners. I also hope those who experienced the schools first
hand—as students, teachers, parents, or administrators—will find it enjoya-
ble and informative. Perhaps none will agree with me, but I expect to excite
and challenge their thinking.

CHILDREN OF THE MILL

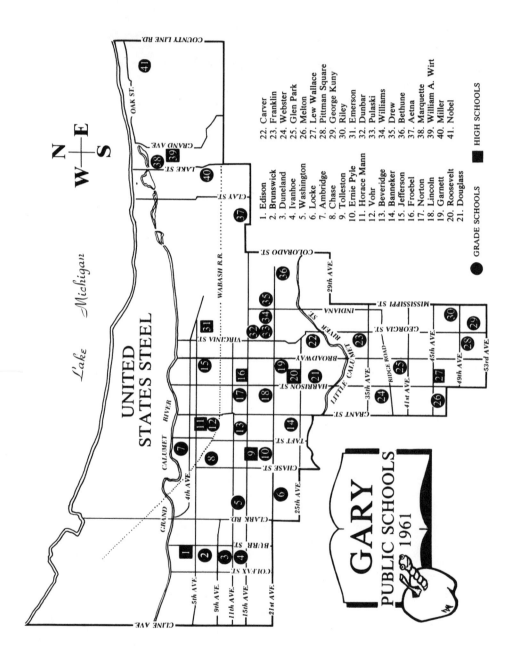

Lake Michigan

UNITED STATES STEEL

GARY PUBLIC SCHOOLS 1961

1. Edison
2. Brunswick
3. Duneland
4. Ivanhoe
5. Washington
6. Locke
7. Ambridge
8. Chase
9. Tolleston
10. Ernie Pyle
11. Horace Mann
12. Vohr
13. Beveridge
14. Banneker
15. Jefferson
16. Froebel
17. Norton
18. Lincoln
19. Garnett
20. Roosevelt
21. Douglass

22. Carver
23. Franklin
24. Webster
25. Glen Park
26. Melton
27. Lew Wallace
28. Pittman Square
29. George Kuny
30. Riley
31. Emerson
32. Dunbar
33. Pulaski
34. Williams
35. Drew
36. Bethune
37. Aetna
38. Marquette
39. William A. Wirt
40. Miller
41. Nobel

● GRADE SCHOOLS

■ HIGH SCHOOLS

I

ESTABLISHING THE SYSTEM, 1906–1910

Gary's third winter held few comforts for the thousands of foreign construction and mill workers crowded together in the makeshift boarding houses on the town's southside. Work days were long, and frigid temperatures and blowing sand made life difficult. The thirty single men who called the boarding house at Massachusetts Street and Eighteenth Avenue home welcomed the services of fourteen-year-old Katie Kordich, who did their cooking and housework for four months. Her two dollars a week also came in handy for her family while her father was temporarily too sick to work. The police, however, had other ideas. Following state law, they ordered the father to enroll the girl in school; but, when he entered the boarding house, the boarders refused to let her leave and shot at him. She was finally rescued by the police and placed in the local school on June 1, 1909. "She is well along in the grades and is exceptionally bright considering her training in a foreign home," the local paper commented.[1]

Katie Kordich quickly faded from the historical record. But the schools, in the opinion of educators like the famed William A. Wirt, had rescued her from an alien, destructive environment. Wirt soon emerged as one of the world's leading school innovators, and the Gary school plan became synonymous with progressive education, even though Wirt's beginnings were as inauspicious as Katie's. He was born in 1874 near Markle on Indiana's eastern border, the son of Emanuel and Mary Elick Wirt, middling farmers. Like those of so many people born in the Middle Border, his childhood memories were of school hours filled with play and tramping the countryside. The teachers neglected many important subjects, however, and "something more than study out of books and wholesome games on the playground were wanted." Sounding like the early John Dewey, Wirt recalled that "the only nature study laboratories were the brooks, the river, the fields and the woods. I do not remember any teacher ever calling my attention to a flower, a bird or a tree. No teacher ever discussed the work on the farm. However, to live so close to Nature that you were unconscious of her had some advantages. Besides I had my father and mother as teachers in Nature and in the practical arts." Wirt's first years in the high school in nearby Bluffton were highly regimented. Partial relief came with a new superintendent, "a young man who was a natural science enthusiast, a lover of music and art and a strong believer in the value of the high school assembly periods." Weekend work on the farm provided the recreation absent at school, but education still held much promise.[2]

Young Wirt entered DePauw University in Greencastle, Indiana, during the fall of 1892 and attended intermittently until 1899, taking two years off to become the principal of the high school and then superintendent in the small town of Redkey, somewhat south of Bluffton. His traditional ideas of school curriculum and student regimentation soon became modified. Summer classes at the University of Chicago exposed Wirt to John Dewey's school innovations, as well as to the public playground at Hull House, and to English reformer William Morris's ideas of the dignity of work. He introduced dramatics, natural science, drawing, music, calisthenics, medical inspection, and a public library in the Redkey schools. He then returned to complete the undergraduate program and one year of graduate work at DePauw. Somewhat older than the other students, Wirt filled his time outside of class as president of his fraternity, mathematics teacher in the public high school, Sunday school teacher, and protector of those urban classmates who got into social trouble. "I could not help but become interested in understanding the why of the city boy's view of life," he later wrote. "I finally saw that the principal occupation of these lads was to kill time, and that killing time was about all they ever had done in life." Why? "It was apparent that the lack of taste for worth while [sic] things was the reason why the average college boy could not use his leisure time profitably. He had never had any training in developing skill as well as appreciation in art, music, dramatics, literature, nature, wholesome sports, outdoor recreation, current events. Besides he had never worked." Wirt was also influenced by the eclectic, searching mind of Professor James Riley Weaver, who combined the teaching of anthropology, sociology, political science, economics, and constitutional history.[3]

A mature and widely read Wirt returned to Bluffton as superintendent of schools in 1899, eagerly awaiting the challenge of shaping a school system. "I did not then have any idea concerning the multiple use of school facilities or the frame work [sic] of the Platoon School," he later recalled. "When I went to Bluffton in 1899 I only knew that children should want to go to school, that it was natural for them to learn to want to work, and that they should find happiness in school and in work and that the school should meet its responsibilities." Bluffton was no metropolis—although with forty-five hundred inhabitants, it surpassed Greencastle, Redkey, and particularly tiny Markle— but it had a large enough system to present a challenge. There were three elementary schools and one high school, Wirt's alma mater.[4]

Starting slowly, the new superintendent managed over the next seven years to put his stamp on Bluffton's schools and students, numbering over one thousand in 1906. He concentrated on three areas—diversifying the curriculum, making the schedule more flexible, and improving school facilities. Schooling should be pleasant and instructive, for children had few positive influences in their lives, he would argue for the next thirty years. Family, church, work, and community—traditional institutions controlling and guiding children—had been steadily declining in influence. Creative schooling had to fill the breach. In Bluffton, Wirt inherited four shabby schools; over the years he modernized their heating systems, installed flush toilets, running water, and drinking fountains, replaced old desks, added playgrounds and educational equipment, and decorated the schools with paintings and other works of art. He was particularly proud of the purchase of an Edison kinetoscope and an expensive telescope. The school day was lengthened, and the manual-training shops were open on Saturdays. Students and adults could use some facilities, including the playgrounds, at night. The school year of eleven months was divided into four terms, with one month off in August. Students could select any three of the four terms, and by 1906 nearly half were enrolled in the summer term. The expanded schedule, more efficient and flexible, was designed to relieve the overcrowding and allow the students extended work or sick leave, as well as broaden the schools' influence. "In every way the school tries to help in finding profitable employment for the children and to interest the entire family, if possible," he reported at the time.[5]

Comfortable schools and elastic schedules created the right climate for the central thrust of Wirt's educational agenda—a greatly diversified curriculum. During his last year in Bluffton he reported to the State Superintendent of Public Instruction on the "industrial work" in the schools, but his curricular additions were broader than the term seemed to imply. In the high school he instituted wood-working, sheet-metal work, book-binding, pattern-making, printing, and pottery for boys and domestic science for girls. Younger students were not excluded from manual training, however. First- and second-grade students did construction work; for the next six years the boys had various manual-training classes, while the girls took domestic science and art. Wood-working began in the sixth grade, basketry and weaving started in the third, and work with clay occupied all ages.

Drawing on the latest curriculum theories, Wirt emphasized that manual classes should be correlated with the academic subjects; for example, clay contour maps were used for geology lessons. Students applied their manual skills to keep the schools in repair and construct needed equipment. Moreover, there were expanded academic offerings in the primary schools, with a departmentalized format starting in the sixth grade—physical culture, music, arithmetic, history, reading and literature, spelling, writing, geography, physiology, nature study, elementary science, and current events. Special teachers handled elementary industrial work, music, drawing, physical culture, and science. "A broad general culture foundation must by all means be provided for the child, but it can not be done by isolating him from the real life and work of the world," Wirt argued in his report. "The harmonious working together of culture and industrial work in the school will be the surest preparation for the continuation of the right education of the child when he leaves the school. . . . It is not our purpose to make carpenters or cooks, but men and women." Here were the stirrings of the later work-study-play system.[6]

By 1906, with strong local support, Wirt had transformed the Bluffton schools. He was now prepared for a greater challenge. To his north and west, on the southern tip of Lake Michigan, a new city was emerging out of the sand dunes and sloughs—Gary, Indiana, named after Elbert H. Gary (1846–1927), chairman of the board of U.S. Steel Corporation. Wirt was attracted by the prospect of shaping a new school system. Despite the existence of scattered settlements in the area with their own schools, a new economic order would surely require novel educational arrangements. The city fathers boasted of a future multiethnic, multiracial industrial city, with an expanding population and the world's largest steel mill.

During the spring of 1906 U.S. Steel began to design its new lakefront mill and adjoining city on nine thousand acres of Lake Michigan coastline. Construction was well advanced by early fall. In September the town board named a three-man school board, composed of C. Oliver Holmes, Edward Jewell, and Thomas H. Cutler. Holmes, in his mid-twenties, was the town clerk and secretary to A. F. Knotts, agent of the Gary Land Company (a subsidiary of U.S. Steel); Cutler, also in his twenties, was a contractor and later a civil engineer for the steel company; and Jewell worked for the mill as well. At their first meeting on September 14, they hired Ora L. Wildermuth, a lawyer, who began teaching on October 1 in a one-room frame school just south of the mill site. "The first day he rang the school bell from a stump, for the schoolhouse had not yet been completed," he later recalled in a now familiar story. "Next day at noon the roof was on and the floor laid. He helped the carpenter put in rough seats, and started in to train the youth. Scholars came from tents and camps all around." Built for thirty-six, enrollment soon reached fifty. By October the school board had authorized construction of an adjoining building. The original schoolhouse initially accommodated the first four grades, and the addition, under R. R. Quillen, grades five through eight. There were also two existing schools in outlying areas, one with fourteen pupils and the other with twenty. Lake County School Superintendent Wilbur Curtis furnished the schoolbooks and some sage advice: "The Report Cards must be printed especially. . . . I mention such details as report cards etc., believing that it will aspire [sic] confidence on the part of the patrons of your school to have matters thoroughly systematized from the very outset." System and order slowly left their imprint on the local schools.[7]

Wirt may have begun considering working in Gary in the spring of 1906, then met with Town Board president Thomas Knotts that fall. He signed a contract with the school board on October 17, 1906 for the princely sum of $2,500, with further increases tied to the growth in student population. Still, in early November Wirt was in some doubt concerning the job, and had to be reassured by Holmes that he indeed was hired. Wirt responded that the Bluffton school board had accepted his resignation, to take effect on or before July 1, 1907: "I have never taken hold of any work with more enthusiasm than I shall take hold of the school proposition in your city. It is a field of work for which I know that I am especially fitted and in which I shall be right at home." The Bluffton *Evening News* congratulated the superintendent, recognizing "he has ability of the biggest nature for such work. . . . During his eight years in Bluffton he has always had the welfare of the city and the schools at heart and to the schools has given his untiring and constant efforts." (After his departure the Bluffton schools quickly reverted to a traditional organization and curriculum.)[8]

Wirt epitomized the new breed of urban superintendents—white, male, Protestant, Republican, small town—who believed in individual and civic virtue. He and many others were lured to the city where they found decent pay, power, prestige, and a challenge. They were also influenced by the new science of school administration, pioneered by Wirt's contemporaries, particularly Ellwood P. Cubberley at Stanford, George Strayer at Teachers College, Columbia University, Charles Judd at the University of Chicago, and Paul Hanus at Harvard. Here Wirt's background somewhat diverged from the norm, for he had only fleeting contact with the University of Chicago; otherwise, he fit the mold. And he was more creative than most.[9]

Even before his arrival in the Steel City, Wirt began organizing the new system. Of utmost concern was the employment of qualified, experienced teachers at a competitive salary with some job security and a meritocratic promotion system. Soon he began hiring teachers, even some from Bluffton. A school system needed students, teachers, and, of course, buildings. In December, while acknowledging that "it is too early to begin the erection of buildings," he advised the school board that "several months should be given to the careful investigation of a desirable plan for school buildings." School board president Holmes responded that he and his boss, A. F. Knotts (manager of the Gary Land Company) had discussed possible school sites within the company's subdivision in the northern part of the city. Anticipating a public school population in this area of forty-eight hundred, with another twenty-four hundred attending parochial schools—there might be four elementary schools and one high school, plus a new school in the city's unplanned south side. In January 1907, Wirt selected an architect for the proposed schools, William B. Ittner, a prophetic choice.[10]

William Ittner had been appointed building commissioner for the St. Louis schools in 1898 and soon began to change the face of the city's schools. A journalist well described Ittner's perspective on school architecture: "He

conceived the modern school as a splendid civic monument, to become a
potent factor in the aesthetic development of the community, as well as a
practical building to answer the present-day educational demands." Ittner
would eventually design over five hundred schools throughout the country,
mostly brick, with an English Renaissance influence. Massive, efficient,
multipurpose, and sensitive to lighting and sanitary needs, Ittner's schools
always set an exceedingly high standard. Wirt called upon him to design all of
Gary's large schools, and they built a professional friendship that lasted over
two decades.[11]

Since Ittner could not immediately begin work, the problem of preparing
for the school year was very serious. There were two solutions—more portable buildings would be ordered, and the Gary Land Company initiated plans
to erect its own building. Learning of the company's scheme, Wirt complained that the structure would be too costly and have inadequate facilities,
but he was ignored. The Jefferson School, after disappointing delays, was
opened in 1908, and for a few years was rented to the school board, causing
numerous problems. Yet it would serve its purpose. By early spring 1907
Wirt, having accomplished much, was planning a trip to Europe before
moving to Gary. Holmes assured him that "I have never entered into a
contract before concerning which I felt so sanguine as to the far reaching
effects as this one. I trust that nothing will occur for as long as you are able to
carry on the work to hinder you in your progress here, and hope that this may
indeed be a life work. It is a work for a master-mind and we are convinced
that we have found the mind." He would not be disappointed.[12]

Wirt took a few months to tour Western Europe, inspecting schools and
discussing educational matters with various officials. He picked up a few
ideas from the German system on industrial education and returned by late
summer to begin his Gary experiment. The threads of this thought were
coming together. Led by C. Oliver Holmes, the school board was most
supportive; as the local paper commented, "he certainly is not handicapped
by the board. They are with him in every effort that will mean good for Gary
schools." And he was gathering a loyal staff. From Berlin he had urged
Holmes to sign Guy Wulfing, a manual-training teacher who had been with
Wirt since his first year in Bluffton. Wulfing later recalled that in the fall of
1906, "Wirt called me into his office and showed me a newspaper clipping
about the new steel mills in Gary. Wirt said, 'Here's our chance to put our
school plans into operation.' " When called, Wulfing came, and he stayed for
thirty-eight years. He was joined by a twenty-nine-year-old science and music
teacher, Melvin Snyder, who had been in Bluffton since 1904. Arriving in a
raw city hard-pressed for living space, Snyder moved in with another
Bluffton teacher, S. J. Brickley, and his wife. Eleven teachers were present
for the first staff meeting with Wirt, who closed with "a brief prayer for the
success of the undertaking." There were now four school locations—the
original buildings on Broadway, one on the far west side, another at Twenty-

first and Adams, and a group of six portables on Fourteenth Avenue. Snyder split his time between the southside and northside schools, trudging through the sand from one to the other, teaching literature, physiology, geography, and singing. "There were many distractions—trains—crowds of workmen passing—grading and paving of Broadway from 4th Ave. to the Mill Gates—grading and laying the tracks of the South Shore just outside our windows and occasionally a dog fight," he remembered. At the end of the first year he married, and soon bought a house. As music supervisor he retired, finally, in 1951.[13]

Of the approximately five hundred students now enrolled, only a handful were of high-school age, but their needs were not neglected. Soon after arriving Wirt met Charles Hyman's mother and asked her if her son "would attend high school if he organized one." Charles and nine others began classes in Wirt's two room office in the Phillips Building on Fifth and Broadway with two teachers, Gertrude Ogg and Nell Whitfield. With housing so limited, particularly for single women, Ogg was forced to room temporarily with the Wirts, taking her meals at the Delaware Hotel. Despite such limited school facilities, she and Whitfield still managed to teach English, algebra, geometry, physical geography, ancient history, botany, and physics. Ogg would also stay for many years. Wirt had an uncanny ability to generate a fierce loyalty to himself and his programs. The long tenure of the superintendent, as well as key administrators and teachers, assured continuity and stability. Yet few, if any, became personally close. Synder, who worked with Wirt for thirty-four years, admitted "my association with Dr. Wirt was in no sense a personal one. I called at his home occasionally, usually on some errand for we were both very busy men. . . . Once or twice, we attended the Opera in Chicago. . . . When our first Gary Track Team entered the County Track Meet at Crown Point [1908], Dr. Wirt and I pitched in and helped massage our Gary entries both before and after the events." Even Wulfing, Wirt's right hand for almost forty years, seems always to have called him Dr. Wirt. He was aloof and rigorous, a combination that produced loyalty, not friendships.[14]

The superintendent's first year was occupied with planning for the future. The nature of the first major buildings was, perhaps, somewhat in doubt, with the school board pushing for the construction of a separate manual-training school on the city's south side. Word spread that the board looked to the Chicago schools for a suitable model, such as the Crane Manual Training High School—one of the city's specialized technical schools—rather than to the Saint Louis system. According to the *Chicago Tribune* in late January 1908, "the Gary trustees, it was learned yesterday, were much impressed by certain features of the Chicago schools. It is manual training that the Gary people want, and Chicago's manual training equipment was found to be really excellent. St. Louis? Why, it would hardly be delicate to make direct comparisons, but the Chicago buildings have many points that Gary people want." Whatever the school board's thinking, Wirt went ahead with his plans to draw more on the Saint Louis system and had Ittner design a $200,000 school to be located on land purchased from the Gary Land Company east of Broadway. While it had little inkling of what Wirt had in mind, the local paper touted the virtues of the proposed Emerson school as "one of the finest school houses in this or any other country." By the end of the school year the 530 students, fifteen teachers, and fifteen portable buildings were only a hint of what would shortly occur, with thousands of pupils housed in the Jefferson school, Emerson school, and another large school on the south side. The only jarring note was the resignation of board member Edward Jewell to become the schools' head janitor, which "nearly caused the members of that august body to faint. His ambition is to run the scrubbing, window-washing and boiler firing divisions." As the paper editorialized, "Brother Jewell is a man of simple tastes." He was replaced by Gary's town engineer, A. P. Melton, a Democrat.[15]

Many of the over six hundred students who appeared in early September 1908 found welcome room in the newly opened Jefferson school, which could hold seven hundred, as well as in additional portables on the south side; attendance would quickly be over eight hundred. The high-school class, soon to swell to fifty, moved into the Jefferson school. Greater specialization, sometimes leading to racial segregation, seemed to be called for. The thirty or so black children, except for two in the high school, for example, by year's end were to be transferred to rented facilities in a Baptist Church. "This move of the school board, which has always been included in its plans, has met with the favor of the better element of the negro residents of this city," noted the *Gary Daily Tribune,* although there was some opposition to segregation. What bothered the "better element" was the church's proximity to Dave Johnson's saloon. Within a year a segregated portable was erected a discreet distance from the evil influence, and a black teacher hired. For Wirt, "we believe that it is only in justice to the negro children that they be segregated. There is naturally a feeling between the negroes and the whites in the lower grades and we are sure the colored children will be better cared for in schools of their own, and they will take a pride in their work and will consequently get better grades." The children and their families would also benefit from having a black teacher. Alluding to Booker T. Washington, the *Gary Daily Tribune* argued "it is certain that as soon as they become accustomed to the new situation the [black] school children will become friendly rivals of the other children in their school work." Hereafter, black and white would be separate in the Gary schools, but hardly "friendly rivals." While legal under the "separate but equal" laws then common in Indiana (adopted in 1877) and other northern states, school segregation was not automatic. Northern cities experienced various degrees of racial separation at the time, although most were moving in the direction of explicit segregation. Gary, somewhat early in joining the movement, was hardly different.[16]

Whether in common or separate schools, one-room frame portables or the three-story Jefferson school, Gary's children had to be enrolled. Those who were not were rounded up. In Indiana school attendance was compulsory from eight to fourteen, according to a 1897 state law, which also mandated at least one truant officer per county. By 1913 children seven to sixteen were expected to fill the state's classrooms. Often depicted as a comic figure, the attendance officer was yet a necessary evil with a difficult task. The man Lake County's truants loved to hate was J. A. Muzzall, who was initially responsible for Gary and adjoining cities. School Board president Holmes requested Muzzall's services in December 1906, since "there are a number of children who are attending irregularly, in fact come not at all and we would like your assistance very much in bringing them in."[17]

Two years later Muzzall, who split his time between Gary, East Chicago, and Hammond, cautioned the board that there were many truants throughout the town. Although it would take time—he could spend only one day a week in Gary—"arrangements will be made to find every child who is not in school this fall." There was now enough room for all the students. Gary quickly obtained its own truant officer, P. R. Ray, which "will probably come as a shock to the youthful scholars of this city, many of whom have been allowed to roam unmolested over the sand dunes and along the lake shore during school hours," the *Gary Daily Tribune* editorialized. "Those happy days 'laying out' of school will now come to an end if the new appointee does his full duty under the terms of the law." Perhaps there were two or three hundred slackers, with another twelve hundred children attending classes. "It is probably that the majority of truancy cases in the Gary schools is caused by the lack of interest taken in education by the foreign born residents of the city," the paper continued. "The foreigner and his wife in the larger number of cases have never known what the inside of a school house looks like," but "thanks to the laws of the country, the foreigner or the native who disregards the education of his children is not allowed to continue disregarding it." Culpable parents could be fined by the county court. In early 1909, Wirt requested that Muzzall return to the city to "take care of these cases, and unless something is done at once our whole truancy problem over here will be a farce."[18]

Truant officers helped link local schools to youth who faced difficult personal and family situations. Leo Vogler, a stubborn thirteen-year-old, was first sent to the state reform school, then ordered to check in every evening at the police station with a report from his teacher. He was a chronic runaway whose parents and the truant officer decided belonged in the state reformatory. Leo's parents were very cooperative, unlike nine-year-old Edna Starkovich's guardian George Starkovich, who kept her from school and forced her to work dressed in rags. Fines proved inadequate, and finally Muzzall threatened to prosecute Starkovich and remove the girl. "Several foreigners were not sending their children to school," the paper commented, "but when the law was explained to them, they placed their children in the school immediately. Starkovich is the only man that has been fined."[19]

Edna was not alone in suffering parental neglect, however, which was becoming a serious problem. Tonie Obir from Poland followed in Starkovich's footsteps, for he kept his two small children out of school after being warned by Officer Ray and was arrested. Ignorance, stubborness, and particularly poverty were all contributing factors. As the population increased in 1909, conditions worsened. "Got-a seven kid. Anglo have got shoe, Rosie no got-a shirt. Michelo got-a da breeches, Pete no got-a shirt. Can no buy. I'm work dollar feefty cent day." This was the sole defense that Mike Tajeo, an Italian laborer, offered this afternoon when arraigned before Justice P. L. Fitzgerald on a charge of not allowing his children to attend school." He and three other families in similar circumstances, threatened with fines, agreed to cooperate. The *Gary Daily Tribune,* despite its nativist overtones, understood that the authorities would attempt "to keep the children in schools, even though many hard working parents may not be fined." They were too poor. The paper believed the township trustee, the heart of Indiana's welfare system, such as it was, should provide clothing to needy children so they could attend school. During the winter, while investigating children with contagious diseases, Ray found "the homes of the children in a fearful filthy condition—ill ventilated and crowded. It seems to me that before they can be cured & made fit to return to school along with *decent* children their home conditions need to be improved."[20]

In July 1910 Ray reported that during the previous term he had investigated 289 cases of children attending irregularly or not at all—out of a school enrollment of some fifteen hundred—the majority of whom lived in the immigrant and black neighborhoods on the city's south side. Only twenty-four parents were brought to court, one fine was paid and six suspended, and six boys were sent to the state reform school. He made 134 visits to the schools and 514 to delinquents' homes. "I have labored to create a sentiment favorable to the Schools," he shrewdly assured Wirt, "have the people send their children to school through an *appreciation of its merits,* rather than from a *fear of the law*—in this effort I have been most loyally supported by teachers." Tellingly, he added praise for the police department, which "helped me very much espetially *[sic]* among the foreign people." The truant officer was particularly sensitive to environmental factors that might keep children out of school. Support, not punishment, was the answer. Certainly the vast majority of the city's children occupied their school chairs each day, yet Wirt was never confident that all was well. For some years truancy and its solutions would occupy his thoughts. Society and its authorities had decided children had to attend school. Some parents, through ignorance, willfullness, or both, acted otherwise. They would, however, lose out, for their children more and more arrived at the schoolhouse door.[21]

Enrollments were increasing daily, continually overtaxing facilities, yet the superintendent vigorously added programs to extend the schools' reach. Compulsory attendance laws were set for age seven, but public kindergartens might attract even younger children. Prior to 1890, kindergartens, which had become popular following the Civil War, were privately funded and often located in settlement houses. Primarily urban institutions supplying poor preschool children with food, clothing, and education, as well as a "healthy" environment, kindergartens were based on romantic as well as the latest scientific theories of childhood. Financial strains, combined with the growing problem of urban poverty, encouraged the free kindergartens to look to the public schools for a home. By 1915 there were 8,463 public kindergartens, serving approximately 12 percent of the country's children. Kindergartens were now part and parcel of the expanding role of public schooling, and the Gary schools would not be left behind.[22]

A free kindergarten for twenty-three five-year-olds was opened in the Jefferson school in September 1908. Soon a mother's club was formed. Although "a regular department of the public school system," as Wirt announced, because the budget was very limited, the teachers were privately paid by Jane and and Katheryn Williams of Lima, Indiana. The next year a separate kindergarten was started at Twenty-fourth and Adams, with the sisters contributing $100 for the two teachers' salaries. By early 1910, despite a temporary threat of closing, there were four centers, six teachers, and about 135 pupils. "There is a particular need of kindergartens in Gary, however," the *Gary Daily Tribune* editorialized, "for here the large body of foreign people will gain their first instructions in the English language and in American customs." While the kindergartens were eventually funded exclusively by the schools, the Williams sisters remained close to the system. Wirt informed the school principals in early 1914 to treat them cordially, for "these ladies are a part of the Gary School organization and are not visitors." Successfully combining the older style of private philanthropy and the newer public commitment to kindergartens, Wirt early managed to bring in at least some of the city's five-year-olds for three hours a day. Later he would also include four-year-olds.[23]

An important thrust of the kindergarten was to Americanize the preschool immigrant children by exposing them to English and in general weaning them from the perceived cultural limitations of their family environment. If youngsters needed uplift, their elders were similarly deserving. Evening schools, dating back to the 1860s, were springing up throughout the country, particularly in the burgeoning industrial cities. In late 1908, the Gary school board established a class in English to be offered in the public library. "That the foreign born citizens who are so deeply desirous of learning the English language, will be given an opportunity in the night school, is one of the best things we have heard for a long time," the *Gary Daily Tribune* editorialized. Children can learn English in school, "but for men and women, who do not know English, the opportunities for learning are exceedingly limited, particularly when large masses of the same nationality are bunched as they are in Gary." Twenty-five students appeared on January 6, 1909, the first night that classes were held. Soon history, geography, and other subjects were added. Classes ended in mid-April, then resumed the following November; those under twenty-one attended for free, others were charged one dollar a month. The *Gary Evening Post,* highly enthusiastic, believed "the night school system is almost as important in cities which have a large foreign born population as are the day schools for children, and the institution of this Gary night school shows that our city government and our school officials are keenly alive to the situation."[24]

During the 1910 winter term, however, with classes having moved to the Emerson school, a broader curriculum was introduced. Any course would be taught if there was a great enough demand, including mathematics, commercial law, and other business subjects, and, "the attendance will be largely American, although the elementary classes in English will still be kept up." By fall a greatly expanded schedule with a vocational bent was available: chemistry, physics, mechanical drawing, architecture, drafting, typing, bookkeeping, commercial arithmetic, designing, and German. The gymnasium and swimming pool could also be used. Of course, "the foreigners will also be taken in the schools and will be treated the same as Americans," the paper assured its readers. "English will be taught the foreigners and those who expect to remain in this country are anxious to attend." This was the start of a program that would mushroom in coming years, as the evening classes transcended their initial Americanizing function.[25]

As Gary rapidly developed in size and composition, the schools struggled to keep pace, and Wirt continued to find new uses for them. In Bluffton he had tried to blur the distinction between work and play. The role of the latter now began to absorb more of his time. In June 1909, he addressed twenty-five women who were meeting in the Jefferson school to begin a playground association. Within a month, the women of the Gary playgrounds association were actively seeking sites because "cities are coming to realize that it does not pay to turn the boys and girls loose, not only for the summer but even after school hours and on Saturdays, with no place to play except the street, alleys, railroad yards, docks and other places." Organized playgrounds were necessary "for the formation of good habits and the development of character." Wirt, particularly concerned about boys, advised the group that "by the supervision of play . . . the obscene language and other vices boys learn on the street are eliminated and they are directed better morally, mentally and physically," although there was yet no talk of linking the playgrounds and the schools. The thriving organization was soon headed by Mrs. Bertha (Koch) Wirt (they were married in 1900), with school board members Melton as third vice president and Holmes as treasurer. Frustrated by half-hearted local interest, Superintendent Wirt requested "literature, suggestions and assistance" from the Playground Association of America. In November, however, at the new Emerson school, two-and-one-half acres were set aside at the rear of the school for a playground, with the boys on one side and the girls on the other. There was no room for a baseball diamond or football field, which with luck would be located in a nearby public park donated by the Gary Land Company.[26]

Hereafter, while parks would be scattered around the city, children's playgrounds would be linked with the schools. This followed the latest thinking. In *Constructive and Preventive Philanthropy* (1902), Joseph Lee listed the "great practical advantages in having the playground adjoin a public school." The children could go outside for their recess, "the school is situated near where the children live and is a place to which they are in the habit of going, and . . . the school building supplied many things that the playground ought to have." In the late nineteenth century reformers had become more concerned with the physical and moral well-being (and control) of urban children. In 1887 sand gardens adjoined to public schools were started in Boston; they were soon followed by summer school playgrounds. Early in the twentieth century playgrounds were scattered around many major cities, mostly located in poor neighborhoods, and were first privately, then publicly funded. Often a drab affair with some equipment and space for team games the playground was designed to keep the children off the streets and under professional supervision. The movement came together in 1906 with the founding of the Playground Association of America, the brainchild of Henry S. Curtis, which gave it drive and coherence. Linking playgrounds and schools assured funding, accessibility, and trained play directors.[27]

By late 1909, Wirt was expanding his vision of Gary's playground needs. In a meeting with the Gary Playgrounds Association, the mayor, city council, and school board, the superintendent argued that "the best playgrounds now contain from 60 to 80 acres. This statement rather took the breath out of the mayor and the members of the city council, but Superintendent Wirt explained that he did not mean the Gary schools should begin with playgrounds of that class." The *Gary Daily Tribune* reminded its readers that the city could not afford such space, "but those few acres we ought to have next to the public school building." The following spring, gardening began for many students, particularly at the Emerson school, because "it is Superintendent Wirt's idea that the planting of flowers and shrubbery should become play and it will be treated as such." This would become part of the schools' nature study program. While gardening could be masked as play, there was a growing urgency to provide more playgrounds, especially for the working-class children on the city's south side.[28]

Piecemeal, Wirt was constructing what would soon be called the work-study-play system. Much of his philosophy had been previously formed, as

expressed in his report on industrial work in the Bluffton schools, but as
Gary expanded and school facilities improved, his plans remained fluid. By
late 1908 he could summarize the obstacles as well as accomplishments.
State and local funding was woefully inadequate because the rapid enrollment increase always ran ahead of revenues, he wrote in his first (and only)
annual report. Land was very expensive, and "the lack of appreciation of the
magnitude of the school problem and the necessity of at least securing
suitable sites now before the town is compactly built up" was frustrating,
although "we are not urging that an industrial paradise be created in Gary."
Economic stringency had forced him to a greater emphasis on economy and
efficiency. The Emerson school, then under construction, unlike the Jefferson school, would combine great efficiency and elaborate facilities for two
thousand students. In use night and day, functioning essentially as a social
center, the school would allow both children and adults to take advantage of
"the manual training, technical, commercial and industrial course, and physical culture classes," as well as the "gymnasia, swimming pool, shower
baths, play ground [sic], auditorium, lecture rooms, outdoor gymnasia,
branch station of the public library and industrial rooms." Including all
grades, kindergarten through grade twelve (K–12), would increase manual-
training classes for the elementary students, as well as smooth the transition
from elementary to high school because the students would stay in the same
building. Students under sixteen would have a general course and those over
sixteen a more specific vocational program all under one roof: "our secondary school will, in fact, be a technical college, or polytechnic school, and will
give the opportunity to every young man and woman in Gary to secure a
practical training for life's work in any commercial, professional or industrial
line." Wirt continued to stress the connection between school and life.[29]

As construction proceeded on the elaborate Emerson school in early 1909,
there was already talk of erecting a similar school on the city's south side.
The *Gary Daily Tribune,* however, urged the school board to proceed with
caution, for "the children of the new city require smaller school houses in
their immediate neighborhoods far more than they do magnificent buildings
like the Emerson school." Wirt countered that planning was necessary
because the lack of recreational space would become acute. "By building
schools of the Emerson type, the playground would be at the site of the
school and the gymnasiums, libraries and recreation rooms in the basements
of the buildings could be used by both children and adults," he explained to
the Ladies' Aid Society of the Methodist Church. With more small schools,
"it would be impossible to bring the system to the point at which it would be
most effective." Wirt had decided that the unit school would be the focus of
his system. The graduation of the first three high-school students at the
Jefferson school in June offered him the chance to expound on his dream,
which now included adding college-level courses as an extension of the high-
school program.[30]

School opened in mid-September 1909 with much excitement: "At 8:30 o'clock the streets were filled with crowds of children hurrying toward the several schools in different parts of the city for the beginning of the term." With fifty-five teachers and twelve hundred students in the half dozen public schools, and another two hundred in two parochial schools, as well as the opening of the still unfinished Emerson school, there was cause for excitement. A pressing problem was the hiring of new teachers to fill the proliferating classrooms. The school board had already decided that grade-school teachers had to have a high-school diploma, seventy-two weeks of scholastic and professional training, and preferably teaching experience; high-school teachers must have a four-year college degree and teaching experience. Married women were not eligible, although an exception was made in the case of Mrs. Elizabeth Lytle, who would be the second teacher in the school for black children.[31]

Teachers volunteered and were recruited, many from Indiana. While superintendent in Redkey, Wirt had encouraged a young worker in the glass factory to continue his schooling. After attending college, Charles Coons joined Wirt in Bluffton. He arrived in Gary in 1911 and soon became principal of the Froebel school. Emerson's first principal, Edward Sargent, with nine-years experience as a school principal in Wisconsin, Michigan, and Illinois, applied for the job as high-school principal in 1908 because of the "salary consideration alone." He was not completely honest, since his interest also stemmed from the fact that he had already resigned from his current job because of another prospect, which had fallen through. He was currently jobless. S. J. Brickley, Froebel's first principal, born in Markel and a teacher under Wirt in Bluffton, had little trouble moving to Gary as principal of the Fourteenth Street school. Orra Faxon, from Akron, Ohio, was asked to come to Gary for an interview before being hired; she was soon teaching first grade for $81.50 a month under Principal Brickley.[32]

Some applied personally, others through a teachers' agency. In July 1909, the Thurston Teachers' Agency in Chicago recommended four women for the position of grade supervisor, including Annie Klingensmith, with a college degree and credits from Harvard, New York University, and the University of Chicago, and teaching experience. Hired in 1909, she looked forward to "no school traditions, no poor buildings, and no disaffected people." She later became an assistant superintendent. Some stayed for years, such as Keziah Stright, who started teaching second grade in 1908, served as head of the child-welfare department from 1920 to 1941, then retired as a teacher in 1946. Others had less success. Ross Netherton, still a student at Indiana University, but with football and teaching experience, applied for the job of athletic director in 1909. He undoubtedly believed that being a fraternity brother of Wirt—he addressed his letter "Dear brother Wirt"—would be of some help. He was hired, but did not last long. Within two years he was out, having been informed by Wirt at one point that "the college coach spirit has been dominant in your work which has prevented you from securing the expected appreciation of your efforts." Netherton's female counterpart, Annette Wahl, was also dismissed because she was "not adapted to the position." Another, who had resigned in 1908 and "given up teaching for all time," complained of the difficult living conditions and poor pay; however, she found "Mr. Wirt a splendid man to work for. I liked him better than any other Supt. I ever had." All in all, experienced teachers, overwhelmingly female, seemed to be plentiful, and many were interested in coming to this community with its innovative superintendent and expanding school system.[33]

The opening of the Emerson school increased national curiosity about the nature of the steel city's schools. Wirt had already lengthened the school year to ten months, with all pupils attending at least forty weeks and possibly forty-eight, if they chose to go to all six terms; teachers had a similar option. "The plan offers great elasticity both from the stand point [sic] of the teachers as well as the pupils and does not necessitate a radical reorganization of the school system and practically not increased expense to give the plan a trial," he informed one correspondent. Redesigning the calendar was part of Wirt's aim to expand the schools' reach. To an inquiry concerning the Emerson school, Wirt described its numerous facilities, including various laboratories, sound construction, and pleasing appearance. Ittner schools, he explained, "are models for convenience, durable construction, artistic design and perfect lighting, heating and ventilation"—and they cost two-thirds what similar school buildings in other cities cost. The *Gary Evening Post* argued that the Emerson school "is a home and not an edifice. The corridors, rooms, offices, gymnasiums and auditorium are all roomy, airy, well lighted, cheerful and decorated and furnished in excellent taste." "There is none of the loafing and idling that is so noticeable in so many schools." In early 1910, word circulated that Ittner would design a similar school on the city's south side, where there were currently over five hundred students enrolled, with another five hundred projected in the near future. Now, however, enough property would be purchased to provide ample playground space. In May the city council authorized purchase of a ten-acre site—later increased to fifteen—to include both playgrounds and an adult park. Ittner revealed his new plan the following month.[34]

The extravagant south-side Froebel school, described by a proud Wirt as a true "social and recreation center," would not be open until 1912. Meanwhile, the system developed incrementally. Stirrings of what would later be the auditorium program, the center of the Wirt plan, were evident in late 1909 when the two student literary societies in the high school, now at Emerson, began presenting monthly "programs consisting of music, recitations, debates, or other entertainments along literary lines." Soon there were seven special nature-study teachers, and the students began learning more than just gardening. By October 1910, there were also twelve physical education teachers, employed for twelve months, who also supervised the playgrounds.

In the first five grades students had forty-five minutes of physical culture and play in the morning and another forty-five minutes in the afternoon; while older children had about one hour a day. Playgrounds were also open after school and on Saturdays. Adults could use the swimming pool and gymnasium in the Emerson school at night and even during the day.[35]

Moreover, a new summer program offered mostly practical subjects for interested students: sewing, drawing, cooking, botany, chemistry, physics, zoology, commercial arithmetic, commercial geography, bookkeeping, stenography and typewriting, manual training, and music at the Emerson school; drawing, music, elementary science, and manual training at the Jefferson school. The playgrounds would also be open. Wirt was confident he was in the vanguard of school reform. As he informed William Bruce of the *American School Board Journal,* which had run photos of the Emerson school, "when the tax payers understand that adding social centers and recreation center facilities, playgrounds and physical culture, nature study and school gardens, industrial training, drawing, etc. to the school curriculum does not increase the first cost of the school plant or its annual maintenance, but actually reduces the per capita cost, the objection of the tax payers to these departments will cease." Professional educators will also accept the new schools' "Scientific Management."[36]

A central component of the national expansion of school services was the development of manual-training classes for the younger children and vocational programs for high-school students. The *Gary Evening Post* remarked on "the deep interest that is taken by Gary boys in the manual training department of our public schools in this city. . . . The great majority of children must earn a livelihood and the opportunity offered by manual training to develop skill and taste for industrial pursuits must lead in the right direction." Handwork for younger children and specific vocational-skills training for teenagers had begun in public schools in the nineteenth century, partly to meet students' perceived needs and partly to connect the schools more directly to rapidly changing social and economic conditions. In his report on the Bluffton schools, Wirt had argued that the manual programs were designed to produce men and women, not narrowly trained workers. Without directly citing the source, he was partly drawing on John Dewey's view of the psychology of occupations. "By occupation I mean a mode of activity on the part of the child which reproduces, or runs parallel to, some form of work carried on in social life," Dewey wrote in *The School and Society* (1915). "Occupation as thus conceived must, therefore, be carefully distinguished from work which educates primarily for a trade. It differs because its end is in itself; in the growth that comes from the continual interplay of ideas and their embodiment in action, not in external utility."[37]

The introduction of manual and vocational courses was becoming commonplace, much to Wirt's satisfaction. He later recalled the pleasure of hearing Colonel Francis Parker, an educational innovator and Dewey's fore-

runner at the Chicago Normal School, at a meeting of the National Superintendent Association "urge the furthering of nature study, manual training and
other practical subjects in the schools without being held up to derision and
labeled a traitor to real culture and an advocate of merely a bread and butter
education." The struggle was developing not over the teaching of such
courses, but whether they should be part of a comprehensive school curriculum or detached in separate curricula and technical schools. In Chicago the
battle lines were drawn in the late nineteenth century between business
leaders and their school board allies who desired the latter and the labor
movement (and its allies) which fought simple vocationalism. Similar struggles occurred throughout the country. As part of the mainstream, Wirt
stressed the democratic and practical nature of the comprehensive school,
despite initial local pressure to establish a dual system. Later the issue of
specific skills training would become controversial in Gary; for now Wirt's
emphasis on a well-rounded education—Dewey's notion of schools as "an
embryonic community life"—held its ground.[38]

Because the Emerson school had vocational courses, but not vocational
training for regular pupils, other institutions emerged in the city to furnish
specific skills training, particularly for adults. The night school somewhat
served this purpose. Apprenticeship classes were initiated by U. S. Steel, and
Gary Business College opened to teach office skills. The YMCA also began
to fill the gap with both day and night classes. Within a year it would offer
mechanical drawing, practical mechanics, and the study of heating, metals,
and the chemistry of oils; there were also business courses, foreign languages, arithmetic, and English for foreigners. Further cementing the tie
between the schools and the YMCA, which were not rivals, was Wirt's role
as its first president.[39]

Writing to Wirt in early 1910, E. J. Buffington, president of the Gary Land
Company, now headquartered in Chicago, assured him that he was highly
qualified to be the YMCA's president. "The starting of this organization I
regard as among the most important activities yet undertaken in Gary,"
Buffington confessed. Wirt was flattered, particularly because of Buffington's
seeming approval of the city's schools. He had to decline the honor, however,
because of his exceedingly busy schedule, including directing the night
school, attending library board and school board meetings, and handling
delinquent children. He then summarized some of his pressing concerns to
Buffington:

> My success in Gary depends upon my being able to keep the schools out of
> factional, political and religious squabbles, to create favorable public senti-
> ment, and to meet successfully the attacks of influence that consider public
> work and position only as an opportunity for graft. The simple matter of
> securing honest construction work according to plans and specifications by
> local contractors is not only a contest with the contractors personally, but is a
> community contest at large with the combined influences of the local archi-

tects, contractors, material men and labor unions. I am not even hoping to win out in this contest for I know that they will get me through the political machine sooner or later.

Self-interest was surely widespread, but fledgling Gary was "exceptional because of the large number of unscrupulous adventurers that have been attracted here and because the better element of the community has not as yet been able to form a crystalized public opinion concerning civic affairs." As for Wirt, "school work is for me purely an unselfish occupation"; and he admitted, "I consider the public schools a much greater factor in the intellectual, social, civic and industrial life of the community, than will be granted." So, he could not possibly accept the added burden of heading the YMCA. Two weeks later, however, he was elected president, with the paper noting he "accepted his position reluctantly."[40]

Wirt's relationship with Buffington was most cordial, as it was with other steel company executives and the Gary business community in general. Perhaps it was even somewhat deferential—he assured Buffington disingenuously that the selection of an architect and plan for the proposed Froebel school "are held in abeyance until you can inspect the work done so far and give us the benefit of your judgement." U. S. Steel and lesser business interests, with some struggle, early gained the upper hand in Gary. The school board, for example, would long be controlled by kindred spirits; in 1910 William Cain, a street contractor and businessman, replaced banker Holmes. Wirt was still not a tool of Buffington and his cohorts. Rather, he represented one of the new breed of "educational entrepreneurs" who believed they were above politics and just objective administrators protecting the public's well-being. Nonetheless, Wirt and Gary's (big and small) business community shared much in common, not only in religion, politics (Republican), and general interests, but also because he was a businessman. Soon after arriving in the city he had opened a hotel; over the years he would have investments in real-estate development, a car agency, a bank, a planning firm, and a golf course. Business and school interests, personified by the superintendent, smoothly merged in the steel city.[41]

School clashes were rare in the first few years, but a few emerged. One complication was the Gary Land Company's continued ownership of the Jefferson school. While outsiders assumed that the schools were blessed by U.S. Steel's beneficence, there was little evidence at the time that the company was particularly generous. Wirt continually complained of financial distress because tax collections were always a year behind; current expenditures and building plans were tied to future revenue. Local school innovations, with the emphasis on efficiency, were partially designed to correct this problem. The Jefferson school was another matter. In late 1909 the *Gary Evening Post,* creature of antimill mayoral candidate Tom Knotts, a Democrat, attacked the Gary Land Company for taking credit for hiring Wirt when

Knotts had been responsible. Moreover, "there exists an erroneous impression in the minds of some Gary people that the Gary Land Company is donating the Jefferson school building to the town, while as a matter of record the school board pays the Gary Land Company $7,000 a year rental for the use of the building." The company's asking price for the school was $89,000, while similar buildings in other cities cost less than half this figure. Land for the Emerson school was no gift, but was purchased from the company for $24,000, the going rate. "That the Gary Land Company has even co-operated with the school board is refuted by its record of opposition to the work accomplished by that board," the paper concluded in a fit of partisan rhetoric. Countering this slur, the *Gary Daily Tribune,* backing Republican candidate John Brennan, downplayed Knotts's role and averred Brennan "has announced publicly that he is in favor of continuing the system as it now is. In this he will have the aid of the school board and of Prof. Wirt." Fulfilling the superintendent's wish, the schools had quickly become nonpartisan. The Jefferson school would continue to be a thorn, however.[42]

With strong local backing, shaky but increasing funding, and growing confidence in his ability to shape an eclectic educational system, Wirt's plans began to take on more definite contours by the summer of 1910. Renovation of the Jefferson school, for Wirt an inadequate structure, marked the beginning of the mature system. Expanding the third floor into a playroom and equipping the basement for manual training allowed the superintendent for the first time to initiate fully his system in this elementary school. "By the new arrangement the board will be able to use the platoon system in the school, which means that it will have the use of nine rooms for double capacity or eighteen rooms," the *Gary Daily Tribune* commented, for the first time using the soon-tc-be-famous designation "platoon system." Simply, the students would be divided into two platoons; while one group was in the classrooms, the other would be in the playroom, the outside playground, or perhaps in the basement. During the day they would change places, thus utilizing all of the space all of the time. A rudimentary beginning, the plan would take on heightened importance in the Emerson school and other unit buildings, although to some extent it was usable in all the schools.[43]

When the children returned to their classrooms in September 1910, most were probably unaware that they were launching what would soon be broadcast to the world as the most exciting school system in the country. Wirt's years of toiling in the educational vineyards had prepared him for this moment. Step by step he had built the programs, added the buildings—particularly the Emerson school and soon-to-open Froebel school—garnered the support, and began to develop an educational philosophy that would link past to present, children's needs with social and economic imperatives, and small town values with urban realities, all the while exuding an optimism tinged with caution. Urban blight and turmoil could be countered by all-inclusive schools, attracting and influencing children and their parents, natives and immigrants, and workers and housewives. The young could be made whole, while developing skills necessary for success in the marketplace and development as productive citizens. Hardly an original thinker, Wirt was particularly adept at borrowing a program here, a concept there, and fitting them together into a coherent whole that captured both pedagogical innovations and the latest administrative developments, set within the most modern physical plant. He was fortunate that he avoided problems common elsewhere. Starting from scratch, he was not involved in the consolidation and shrinking of the school board, one of the central developments in most cities starting in the late nineteenth century that marked the success of administrative progressives. The three-man Gary school board, ostensibly representing the entire community, was pliable and supportive. Factional school politics had little popularity.[44]

Although a new town, Gary soon had much of the look of a typical older industrial community as well as of a frontier town—squalid shacks, overcrowded neighborhoods, ragged children, open sewers, dirt, and violence. Giving it uniqueness, however, was the world's largest, most modern steel mill and the start of an extravagant school system. Gary's schools were not all modern, to be sure—the teacher of the older, isolated one-room Clarke school complained to Wirt in September 1910 that the outhouse was falling apart, the clock did not work, and the windows and floors needed cleaning—yet they would become among the most modern and elaborate in the country.[45]

Wirt had arrived in Gary in the summer of 1907 with much promise and an eclectic mind. Within a few years he had begun to fashion a complex school system incorporating the latest in educational thinking and having the full support of the community. He would soon extend his stage, making his mark on the country. In the fall of 1910 he was poised on the edge of greatness. Hereafter, Gary's children and adults would experience a unique educational system that captured their imagination and for some years the attention of the nation. With fame, however, also came controversy.

II

IN THE SCHOOLS, 1910–1915

In early October 1911, truant officer W. P. Ray happily reported to Superintendent Wirt that he had found perfect attendance among the twenty-three "*very* nice children" in the one-room school on Gary's far west side. As the children flocked about him, the girls politely requested that he "ask Mr. Wirt to put us up a swing and the boys supplemented this petition with [a] request for *2 balls.*" Looking around, he "noticed two girls trying to *see saw* on a rough 2X4 over a saw horse." Ray could have been describing conditions at any one of the hundreds of poor, rural schools still scattered around Indiana and throughout the Midwest. Instead, he had just visited one of the schools in what was fast becoming the country's most celebrated educational system noted for its efficient management, elaborate facilities, and lucky children. Gary's schools were becoming justly famous, yet all of the city's children were not necessarily benefiting from Wirt's accomplishments. The system was more complex than most were willing to acknowledge. It continued to mature during the decade, however, adding curricular and extracurricular programs and generating considerable national controversy, and most in the city seemed content. They were proud of their celebrated superintendent and showpiece schools.[1]

During the summer of 1910, Wirt announced two significant innovations for the coming year—vivid reflections of the superintendent's persistent and growing commitment to the progressive ideal of an expanded, quasi-academic school environment catering to the perceived needs and interests of the rapidly swelling urban population. First, the Emerson and Jefferson schools and the recently annexed Beveridge school in the Tolleston neighborhood were being converted to the platoon system. While half the children would be working in the academic rooms, the other half would be on the playground under the supervision of special teachers. Wirt explained what this would entail at the Emerson school: "Each child will have a steel locker for his wraps, books and equipment. . . . With this plan no school desk belongs exclusively to any child, but may be used by other children during the day school period, and the school plant can be made to accommodate practically double the customary number of children." He expected eventually from eighteen hundred to two thousand children at the day school, with fifteen hundred adults attending at night and using the same desks and facilities. The night program would be modeled on the YMCA and the German continuation schools. Second, the manual-training department for boys would be expanded and a printing press added to the Emerson school; girls would receive additional commercial courses—bookkeeping, shorthand, and typing. "All the schools start in their fourth year under the best outlook for effective work," the *Gary Daily Tribune* announced, then gave its own emphasis to this point: "They are meeting the peculiar demands of a city with a large foreign population in a consistent and broad manner. In the Americanization of the foreign-born, the schools are doing the work which wide statesmanship demands." Americanization did not mean a narrow indoctrination, but a broad educational experience, including an emphasis on good health.[2]

Urban expansion in the late nineteenth century stimulated various reform movements, including public health and child welfare. They converged in 1894 with the introduction of medical exams in the Boston schools; the following year school physicians were appointed in Chicago, and by 1911 over four hundred cities had school medical inspections. Doctors as well as nurses were on the school payroll. The goals were to prevent contagious diseases, partially through compulsory vaccination, as well as to detect and sometimes correct obvious physical defects. Immigrant children were particularly suspect of harboring infections. Members of Gary's board of health were thereby following standard practice in the spring of 1910 when they recommended frequent inspections of schoolchildren. Health inspections were initiated the next fall with an emphasis on sight, hearing, the teeth, and the body. Daily screening of students was done by the playground teachers, and those children with signs of disease or other problems were sent to the board-of-health physician. "A dozen children, each with a sore finger, a mysterious abrasion or a suspicious looking abrasion on the face or hands, appeared yesterday afternoon in the office of Dr. H. F. Walsh," according to the *Gary Daily Tribune* on September 23. "It was one of the daily delegations that are sent from the schools by the teachers for a thorough inspection and the inspection was an example of how contagious diseases are prevented in the schools where all classes and nationalities come together." The children were sent back to school with a note for their parents to have them looked at by the family doctor.[3]

During the next winter, fearing a greater incidence of illness due to the weather, board-of-health doctors began to visit the schools. At one portable school Dr. Millstone discovered children with defective eyes, enlarged tonsils, adenoids, and skin disease. He found the school sanitary and lectured the boys on the evils of tobacco, for "the majority of school boys are smooking [sic] cigarettes." Students in the Glen Park school, which was kept clean and well ventilated, seemed particularly healthy. Decent conditions were found at the other schools. Children continued to stream into the office as well, where their wounds were dressed, prescriptions handed out, and notes written to the parents. Housing conditions were also checked on the south side, where they were "very sad and deplorable." Mrs. R. M. Charlton, the inspector, was particularly concerned "that many of the children are sent to school half clad as well as unwashed." She encouraged the mothers to correct these problems. Passage of a state medical inspection law in March 1911 reinforced a move to appoint a full-time medical staff, which came at year's end with the hiring of two doctors, Dr. Charles Yarrington for the boys and Dr. Carolina Lawrence for the girls. They were to inspect, not treat, the children, thereby preventing competition with private doctors. The hope was that healthier children would do better in school, for "it has been found that a large percentage of children who do not get along well in school are afflicted physically in some way that keeps them back." This was the beginning of an expanding health service; two years later the city's dentists generously donated their time to inspect the students' teeth and even correct defects for those too poor to afford a private dentist.[4]

Good health came from an active body as well as medical intervention. At the Emerson school greater stress was placed on "corrective gymnastics and knowledge of the care of the body," thereby downplaying competitive athletics and leading to the replacement of Coach Ross Netherton. The school even opened a store for selling athletic goods to the students, which incidentally offered practical experience for those enrolled in the math classes who worked in the store. When the Gary Park Board desired to obtain four acres adjoining the Froebel school, now under construction, for an adult park to offer some greenery for the "workmen who live in that vicinity," the Playgrounds Association protested. They wanted the land kept as a playground for children and were backed by an editorial in the daily paper. In matters of mental and physical health children should come first.[5]

Truancy was also decreasing, thanks to the "fact that our schools have been made so pleasant that the children enjoy the work," according to officer Ray. Children begged to attend school every day, but there was a hard core of families, about fifty, who continued to keep the children out. If they moved out of the district, Ray suggested, the problem would be solved. By the end of the school year no parents were brought to court, Ray preferring the personal approach. Nonetheless, with the opening of school in September 1911, potential truants were warned by the press that better record keeping would insure that none would escape detection; by year's end, perhaps because of the new system, eleven were brought to juvenile court. Truancy had been steadily declining, according to the *Gary Daily Tribune,* because "the foreigners were gradually brought to realize that they must keep their children in school." Instead of rounding up truants, Ray occupied more of his time with uncovering parental neglect and searching for delinquents, although there were few cases of either. In his 1911 report, Ray noted the "marked improvement in the personal appearance of the children and the interest of parents in the work of their children in the schools." There seemed little cause for worry.[6]

Nonetheless, when Judge Willis Brown arrived in Gary in September 1910, he received a warm welcome. Appearing before the school board, Brown suggested establishing Boyville, a boy's government paralleling the established system, as well as a separate school with moral training for troubled children. The latter would also have its own doctor "to correct the diseases of children who are thought to be bad," for Brown believed "wrongdoing among children" was "in most cases due to sickness of some kind"—a sentiment sure to appeal to Wirt. Within a month after he had moved to Gary, Brown was the unpaid head of the schools' new Department of Civic and Moral Education and had immediate plans to launch Boyville. "The field here, being new, is considered the most favorable place in the country for beginning the movement," the *Gary Daily Tribune* commented, "which may at some time become a part of every school system in the country." Optimism was rampant.[7]

Born in Chicago, the son of a north-side minister, Willis Brown had been involved in child-saving activities in Salt Lake City, Winona Lake, Indiana, and Charlevoix, Michigan. With a secure base in the school system and Wirt's support, Brown quickly organized Boyville, a citywide boy's republic. Boyville was designed to train productive citizens. Those boys who resisted authority were brought before the parental court, run by Brown, and a few were even sent to the new parental farm located east of the city. Brown's stay in Gary was brief, however, and he had left by the summer of 1912. He moved around the country and even promoted a Boy City in Florida in the late 1920s.[8]

Brown's legacy to the city was mixed. Perhaps the level of morality among boys was raised. At least the *Gary Evening Post* believed that "from a moral standpoint the school children of Gary are being regenerated"; both smoking and swearing appeared to be declining by early 1912, "and theft—well, it is becoming a lost art among school children." The Boyville Bank, renamed the Emerson School Bank, continued to pay its 3 percent interest and issue checks. Members of the defunct Boyville Band reformed into a YMCA band. Gary's boys had a number of new diversions, which certainly sparked their interest and temporarily redirected their energies, surely pleasing to Wirt, who shared the broad progressive spectrum with Judge Brown.[9]

With Brown's departure the parental court was abolished, but its role had never been clear, since it had not replaced the work of the county juvenile court judge and truant officer, both of whom had carried on as usual. For example, Ray brought Mike Andros and his son to the county court for truancy in February 1912, as well as Louis Balinski and his son, the first miscreants to appear in some time. Andros was sentenced to the county jail and his son to the White Training School in Wabash, while Balinski's son was sent home "upon good behavior." Mike Andros did not serve his sentence, but was forced to pay $2.10 a week for his son's support. Perhaps feeling some competition from the parental court, Juvenile Court Judge McMahan "stated that he is ready to cooperate with the Gary school authorities in all cases where parents do not take proper care of their children and will force them to support the children in some state school," thereby relieving the school system of the burden. In April five boys, aged seven to fourteen, were arrested for robbing a jewelry store and also seemed headed to the juvenile court. Andrew Kollus appeared in the city police court on the charge of allowing his son to work in his south-side saloon before he was sixteen. The young Kollus appeared to be sixteen, but Judge Brown, "a citizen who wished to save boys from the evil association of the south side saloons," testified that the boy had been working there the past year. Interestingly, young Kollus had also lived at the Parental Farm "for some time prior to his becoming 16 years old and was said to be a good boy."[10]

Lacking the parental court, Wirt "did not see any reason why the Special School [Parental Farm] cannot be operated in harmony with our Juvenile Court procedure." Unable to obtain such cooperation, the following year Wirt transformed the Parental Farm into an agricultural training center for Gary students supervised by Purdue University. For the school year ending in June 1912, Ray reported that of the thirty-six cases he brought to the juvenile court, sixteen boys were transferred to one of the three state institutions, while the other twenty were sent home on probation. And, he concluded, "with one exception all the 20 children sent home . . . have made good record and parents made reasonable efforts to improve home conditions." In his report there is no mention of the parental court or farm, which Ray studiously ignored. Thus, with or without Judge Willis Brown, the juvenile justice system continued to operate as usual. With an increasing case load, in January 1914 Circuit Court Judge Willis McMahan agreed to move the juvenile court to Gary on Saturday afternoons.[11]

Despite Brown's ultimately ill-fated sojourn in Gary, his connection with the schools added somewhat to their growing national reputation. Early praise appeared in *The Iron Age,* the voice of the steel industry. In March 1910 it lauded a school system "which appeals with peculiar force to the merchant or workingman who wants his children to grow up with educational advantages." The article noted the Emerson school's superior facilities: theatre, gymnasiums and swimming pool, shops, and drinking fountains. "The citizen of to-morrow has been made the center of the civic development of Gary," the magazine happily concluded. Similar sentiments appeared shortly thereafter in a German educational publication, *Das Schulzimmer,* which printed a picture and diagrams of the Emerson school. Educational news quickly crossed the Atlantic.[12]

More important, an insightful, though no less effusive, discussion appeared in *Hampton's Magazine,* a popular monthly, in July 1911. Rheta Childe Dorr, one of the leading muckraking journalists, later boasted "I wrote the first authorized article on the wonderful public schools of William Wirt, in Gary, Indiana." She gathered her information by briefly visiting the city and corresponding with the superintendent. Wirt informed her that the children were not in school "from morning until close to bedtime," but they were kept busy all day, including Saturday, with academic, manual, and physical training and other courses. The only new feature, he stressed, was the schools' efficient organization; "by correlating all of the school departments we are able to offer a school plant of this type without increasing the per capita cost for public school education." Wirt also stressed the value of the unit school, arguing that "we consider it nothing less than criminal to place primary children in a school by themselves, where they are deprived of the right sort of educational environment." In her article Dorr repeated Wirt's views, stressing particularly that the schools "operated on the same principles of scientific management that animate the ten miles of steel works on the lake front." She praised the close cooperation between the schools and the business community, which insured jobs for many adolescents. Dorr was particularly impressed by the schools' Americanization program. "You would never know, to visit the Gary schools that the pupils, or most of them, are children of immigrants, most primitive in type, illiterate, non-English speaking," she wrote. "The Gary school children, with few exceptions, look like American children, act like American children, and to all intents and purposes they are American children. They are getting a kind of education which is more American, or at least more democratic, than any other children in the country." Both city papers hailed the article, with the *Gary Daily Tribune* reprinting it word-for-word.[13]

The Dorr article, as Wirt pointed out to journalist Lewis Edwin Theiss, included a few inaccuracies, such as misstating the size of classes. Theiss was conducting his own research, which would appear in the June 1912 issue of *Pictorial Review*. To Theiss, Wirt again stressed the importance of the schools' organization "through which real educational work can be done." With "each teacher teaching only the things that they [sic] can teach, and teaching these things in a perfectly natural way so that both pupils and teachers can enjoy their work, we are able to operate the school plant eight and ten hours per day and everyday [sic] in the calendar year, without crowding the school curriculum and over burdening the teacher." And the costs were no greater than in a traditional system. In "A School Built on Play: How They Solved the Public School Problem in Gary, Indiana," Theiss emphasized how meaningful the instruction was rather than the schools' organizational features. "The system in Gary is probably the most elastic in the world, for here they have reversed the usual order—they have made the system to fit the child," he argued. Work was turned into play, and it was made "real, vital, related to life." By mid-1912 the schools appeared to be getting praise from all quarters.[14]

Such positive national attention prompted P. P. Claxton, United States Commissioner of Education, to instruct Dr. Harlan Updegraff, chief of the Division of School Administration in the Bureau of Education, to investigate the new educational wonder. While visiting the city, Updergraff praised Wirt before the school board and noted surprise at "the thirty different nationalities that are attending school here and the rapidity with which they are becoming Americanized." His favorable report, never published, encouraged Claxton to visit Gary twice. In 1913 Claxton commissioned a second study, which was done by Dr. William P. Burris, dean of the Teachers' College of the University of Cincinnati and Wirt's predecessor in Bluffton, and was published as a Bulletin of the Bureau of Education the following year. Impressed by the schools' efficiency, practical vocational program, and use of specialized teachers, Burris nonetheless noted the difficulty of finding teachers "properly trained with reference to the team work and the spirit demanded by a school system organized as this is." Most important, "the common people believe in their schools at Gary" because of the combination of cultural, recreational, and vocational programs. While attending the high school graduation, Burris was struck by Wirt's reference to diplomas as "work certificates," "a significant reminder to the graduates of the purpose of the school. And this is the final word of a school program which begins with play," he concluded. During various speaking engagements throughout the country, Burris reported favorably on the Gary schools; he assured Wirt, "you may count on me at any time to assist you in promoting the good work. It is sound philosophically, and in time will fully justify itself in practice." He also assisted the superintendent in obtaining suitable teachers. Because of the Burris and other encouraging reports, the Bureau would later become an unofficial sponsor of the platoon plan.[15]

Growing national curiosity and active self-promotion increased the number of visitors to the schools, which would reach floodtide proportions within a few years. Over thirty high-school teachers from Indiana and Illinois toured the Emerson high school in late 1911; a few months later a group of superintendents and principals from Chicago and Cook County inspected the Emerson and Jefferson schools. "Scarcely a day passes that someone does not come from a distance to visit the Gary schools," the *Gary Daily Tribune* remarked in January 1912. "Noted educators from other cities are frequent guests, drawn by the wonderful stories they have heard." By April, twenty to thirty visitors a day were trooping through the Emerson school. In the fall of 1913 the crush of visitors convinced the school board to restrict tours to a total of four weeks, one in November, March, June and July. Still, by year's end as many as five hundred were arriving each week; for Wirt, "the visitors loom up as a menace to the model system." To avoid confusion, school officials distributed a pamphlet, "Notes to Visitors," describing the schools' organization. The pamphlet stressed that "the entire school curriculum is planned to gradually but effectively transfer the play impulse of the child into a work impulse so that as he grows to manhood he will take the same pleasure in his work that as a child he took in his play." Simultaneously, Wirt and the school board visited the schools, and the superintendent lectured in various Eastern cities, including Cleveland, Philadelphia, and New York. New school board member William Flynn, foreman of the rail mill at U. S. Steel who had replaced A. P. Melton, returned from the trip encouraged by the evident superiority of the Gary system.[16]

Flynn's enthusiasm was shared by school administrators in other, particularly working-class, cities who early decided to adopt the Gary plan and its emphasis on curricular expansion and efficiency. Superintendent S. O. Hartwell in Kalamazoo, Michigan, led the move in late 1911 by converting one of the city's elementary schools to the platoon plan and two more in 1912; within a few years nine of the city's schools had copied aspects of the Gary system. Hazletown, Pennsylvania, in the anthracite region, was the next to be convinced, with its first platoon school organized in 1913. The *Gary Daily Tribune* announced in early 1912 that Bellingham, Washington, and tiny Hermiston, Oregon, following visits by Willis Brown, were also convinced to convert their schools, but this is doubtful. Nonetheless, platoon schools were becoming fashionable.[17]

Wirt was not shy in both publicizing his creature and encouraging others to promote the system. His election as president of the department of school administration of the National Education Association in mid-1911 assured him some national exposure. He was particularly proud of his article, "The Place of the Public School in a Community Program for Child Welfare," appearing in *The Child* (July 1912). Following William Morris and John Dewey, he envisioned a school in which "the play impulse is transformed into a work impulse so that real pleasure is experienced in work." It should be multipurpose, thereby securing "the highest possible efficiency from buildings, grounds and equipment, and the time and energy of teachers and pupils. It gives the child, not a shop, not a playground, but a life." As he reported the following year to Lake County school superintendent Frank Heighway, the Gary schools were accomplishing these goals: "It is the conviction of the Gary school management that not only is the wholesome character building of the child inseparably linked with his work and his play, but that for the great majority of children the mastery of the academic school subjects cannot be separated from work and play." Burton Hendrick's positive article in the popular *McClure's Magazine* stressed "the element of purposefullness" in the schools' manual training. "Everything the boys and girls do has a definite end," he concluded, much to Wirt's delight.[18]

The superintendent had some advice for Albert Jay Nock after reading a draft of his article on the Gary schools to appear in *American Magazine* in early 1914. While generally pleased, he advised that "your paragraph concerning living conditions in Gary should not be published, in my opinion. The local people would be very much incensed to have their city heralded everywhere as the worst place in the country to live." Journalists commonly contrasted the city's forbidding environment with the schools' amenities. But for Wirt, "Gary is a much better place to live than any other steel town of my knowledge." Nock admitted, "when I went to Gary . . . I expected to see a 'vocational school' of purely instrumental knowledge, with perhaps a ghost or larva of formative knowledge lurking in the background for the sake of appearances. I looked for a school that should be busily turning out 'useful citizens' in the cant sense, but doing very little for the diffusion of sweetness and light; and in this I was wholly wrong and prejudiced." His surprise was heightened when he realized that Gary was "a city of foreigners—that is, a city of poor workingmen who came here from other countries. . . . It would be very good for our provincial and insular ideas of foreigners—that they won't wash, enjoy illiteracy, practice assassination as a pastime and are radically dishonest—if we could all make a pilgrimage to the Gary schools." While delighted with such praise, Wirt was piqued by the supposed "misrepresentation[s]" of other "poorly informed magazine and newspaper writers," even if they were few. Most would agree with the *Gary Evening Post* that Wirt was the "wizard of the educational world" and the city had "the greatest educational plant on this continent."[19]

The fame of the city's "educational plant" was commonly linked in the public mind with its justly famous industrial plant. Indeed, Wirt was dependent upon Judge Gary and U.S. Steel for much more than just publicity, and mill personnel were heavily represented on the small school board; the company even contributed $5,000 in 1914 for a Gary schools exhibition at the Panama-Pacific Exposition in San Francisco. Yet, relations between the company and the schools were not always cordial. One sticking point was the shaky status of the Jefferson school, originally built by the company and rented to the school board. In June 1911, school board member W. A. Cain, an independent businessman, recommended that the school be abandoned and portable buildings erected in the neighborhood rather than continue to pay the $8,000 yearly rental in addition to repair costs. The board voted, instead, to attempt to negotiate a lower fee with E. J. Buffington, president of the Gary Land Company. Finally meeting with Buffington in September, the board attempted unsuccessfully to arrange new terms. They now learned, however, that part of the rental was being applied to the purchase price. "The Gary Land Company was really extending favorable terms to the schools and the upshot of the matter will undoubtedly be that the board will soon come into ownership of the property," the pro-mill *Gary Daily Tribune* editorialized. "Taking all its subsidary companies in Gary into the accounting, the corporation pays 90 per cent of the taxes in Gary, which puts another color on the proposition."[20]

New rental arrangements were agreed upon early the next year, but the dispute over the purchase price continued into the summer. As rumors circulated that the building might be abandoned, doctors at the General

Hospital considered purchasing it for use as a hospital. Soon after the lease expired on July 1, 1912, the Gary Land Company took over the school, now guarded by a deputy sheriff. Incensed, Cain urged court action to recover the building or at least its contents. Summer classes were temporarily halted, but were resumed in early August as the board began to reach agreement with Buffington on a purchase price if repairs were made. Final terms were arranged in September, with the board consenting to pay a total of $145,000, which included a large tract of land on the city's west side. The school's one thousand or so pupils could now return to their familiar classrooms. A thorny issue had finally been settled. Wirt's relations with the company throughout had remained most cordial. A year earlier Judge Gary had visited the Emerson School and had come "away amazed at the perfectness of the system of education." "You certainly have achieved great results through your administration of the Schools," Buffington wrote the superintendent in late 1913, "and all who are interested in any way in the community of Gary should be truly grateful to you." And, he added, "I know that this is the sentiment of the Officers of the United States Steel Corporation and its Subsidiary Companies which have interests in Gary." The company could heartily support Wirt without compromising its business scruples by donating valuable property.[21]

Steel corporation officials were excited by the schools because they served a multitude of purposes. Adults as well as children found them increasingly hospitable, following modern trends. "The twentieth century public school has begun to discard its individualism for a broader principle of socialization," Edward Ward argued in *The Social Center* (1913). "It has begun to extend the boundaries of its sovereignty so as to include not only the whole of the territory of childhood, but that of adulthood as well." Educational expansion was in the air. Starting in September 1910, the Emerson night school offered chemistry, physics, mechanical drawing, freehand drawing, architecture, drafting, merchant English, typewriting, bookkeeping, commercial law, commercial arithmetic, designing, and German. Additional courses were added as necessary.[22]

Particularly important was the Americanization of the foreign born. Much of the burden was undertaken by the YMCA and the churches, which were beginning to establish settlement houses in the immigrant neighborhoods, but the schools were in the forefront of the movement. After all, noted the *Gary Daily Tribune,* "when they have found the work which brought them from the huts of poverty and want in Eastern Europe, it is certainly the bounden duty of the native-born to put forth a helping hand in their Americanization." Community groups initially attempted to use the night schools for their own purposes—the Polish community to teach Polish and the Socialist party to teach English along with "liberal doses of Socialism"—but they were unsuccessful. The schools became reserved for inculcating the English language, American history, and other aspects of becoming an American, particularly among the large population of foreign born living on the south side.[23]

Because of a change in the state law, the small night-school tuition was waived for those under thirty beginning in September 1911. A cluster of portable buildings on Fourteenth Avenue was devoted exclusively to the teaching of English, while the Emerson school offered a greater variety of night classes, such as mechanical drawing and business courses. Classes were now held four nights a week from 7:00P.M. to 9:00P.M. During the year 1911–12 the Emerson night enrollment was over eleven hundred, of whom two-thirds were men clustered in the English, arithmetic, mechanical drawing, and manual-training courses and using the gym. Women were scattered among most of the classes, but avoided physics, mechanical drawing, music, and manual training. Twenty-three classes were offered, in addition to use of the gyms and swimming pool.

Wirt and the school board, anxious to connect the schools with other community institutions, encouraged close coordination between the YMCA and the night school. Wirt became chairman of the YMCA's education department, with George W. Swartz, formerly superintendent of the Chippewa Falls, Wisconsin, schools, as the director. With only men attending, emphasis was put on practical mechanics, mechanical drawing, and other industrial subjects, along with business courses, foreign languages, and English. To further cement the tie between the YMCA and the schools, in July 1912 Swartz, while continuing his former work, was also named superintendent of the night schools. Having a strong vocational bent, he had "been spending much of his time in the industries of the city, seeking positions that may be filled by men who are taking up social work and fitting themselves for that alone." Now, "this work will be extended, looking out for positions for the boys who are taking special training in the public or continuation schools of the city." Simultaneously, the YMCA was initiating classes for the foreign-born "in the rear of saloons or at any place where a group of men can be gotten together."[24]

Night classes were flooding the city. Twenty people, after petitioning the school board, could demand classes in their neighborhood. In early 1913 Swartz announced that "the schools will be thrown open to the communities as club rooms and meetings may be held as often as is desired, and entertainments of all kinds which will furnish social intercourse in every part of the city." The opening program at the Beveridge school on the west side was well attended; there were games, music, recitations, spelling matches, as well as a talk on children's health. "The night schools of Gary are the saving grace of Gary," remarked the *Gary Evening Post* in October. "Without them the leavening process by which twenty-nine different nationalities are being leavened into perfect American citizenship, would be impossible." By the end of 1913, over three thousand students were enrolled, about two-thirds men, with nineteen academic teachers and seventeen for vocational work.

The day school enrollment was about forty-three hundred. Most popular were the classes at the newly opened Froebel school located in the heart of the immigrant community, which enrolled about half of the total, with the rest attending the Emerson, Jefferson, Beveridge, and Glen Park schools.[25]

The public school and YMCA night programs served three educational purposes—Americanizing the foreign born, offering academic courses such as government and sociology, and teaching industrial skills to young men—as well as their social functions. While the students certainly profited in many ways, the steel mill was also greatly pleased with the results. "Officials of the steel corporation in Gary are standing back of the work of the night schools and the Y.M.C.A.," commented the local paper in February 1914. "Young men who are serving as instructors are being let off from work so that they can teach an hour or two at the Y.M.C.A. . . . One of the mill heads . . . has brought fifty of his men over to Mr. Schwartz's *[sic]* English classes. None of these men could read or speak English—that was what they came for." Within a month Swartz left the YMCA, becoming Wirt's full-time assistant superintendent for $4,000 a year. His organizational skills and faith in promoting Americanization and industrial efficiency were highly prized by the superintendent—Swartz had earlier spoken "of the great work being done in Gary by transforming ore into steel, and assimilating foreign races into good American citizenship." Into 1915 the night enrollment continued to increase, reaching over seven thousand, although the year was reduced from ten to fewer than seven months because of financial problems. Despite their close cooperation, some board members of the YMCA believed the schools were deliberately offering competing night classes. Negotiations were necessary to prevent friction.[26]

With the opening of the Froebel school in September 1912, the night-school program, as well as the other essential features of the school system, were materially and symbolically heightened. Apprised of the school's construction in early 1911, the nativist *Gary Daily Tribune* believed the "new building will be of much greater assistance in the Americanization of the foreigners than will ever come to Gary." Certainly the school "will be in a position to carry on a work of the greatest import to all who see in the Americanization of the foreign-born the cure for most of the ills that have come from the large immigration to American manufacturing centers in recent years." Six months later, with the school far from completed, the school board increased the salaries for teachers in the southside portables because of difficult working conditions: "sand fleas, sand storms, hot rooms, cold lunches and many other objections were raised against education in portable buildings." According to Wirt, the "teachers were accomplishing wonders with the little foreigners." Finally opened in September 1912, although not yet finished, the building included a large auditorium, two swimming pools, numerous academic and vocational classrooms, spacious playground and gardening areas, and even a minature three-room apartment for practice homemaking. Planned to accommodate grades K–12—the unique unit concept Wirt instituted in all of the major schools—it was perhaps the finest school building in the country. There was even a day nursery, opened early the following year under the direction of a trained nurse paid by the Women's Home Mission Society of the First Methodist Church. "Women espousing the cause of equality of the sexes should find the building just exactly to their fancy as the girls have been provided with every attraction and accommodations as have the boys," noted the *Gary Evening Post*.[27]

The Froebel school's Americanization program took a variety of forms. Emphasis was placed on cleanliness; "this will mean that when the young foreigner comes to school with unwashed face and hand, that he will be sent to the lavatory to complete the toilet that was neglected at home." Sinks, showers, and soap were readily available, but "if he does not succeed in expunging the earmarks of the home neglect there the instructor in charge will finish the task in accordance with the latest and most up to date methods." The hope was that parents would soon get the message. Froebel's students of foreign stock—over 80 percent of the total in 1914, with 740 of the 1,850 foreign-born—were also assumed to be more vocationally oriented, so the school "will emphasize the trade branches even more than the Emerson does."[28]

As Wirt, the school board, and their supporters had hoped, Froebel quickly became a magnet, attracting both children and adults to the school's superior and convenient facilities. Happily, "the foreign men who are attending the Froebel night school have been bringing their wives and children with them with the result that the Froebel building at night resembles a big family clubroom." In December 1914 enrollment was over two thousand, out of a total city-wide total of almost five thousand. "The clock is just striking seven when a queer little group hurries into the Froebel School at Gary, Indiana," began one description.

> First there comes the man whose name appears on the pay-roll of the steel mill as Mike Evans. His name isn't Evans, but the timekeeper can't spell—or even pronounce—the strange Slavic name that Mike brought from the old country; and Mike isn't able to tell him how. . . . With Mike is his son, Joe, whom another timekeeper has dubbed Jackson. Behind the two men comes Anna, Joe's wife, and hanging to her hands are little Stephen, aged five, and solemn Marja, two years his senior. They are all on their way to the evening classes, held nightly in the big school building. There Mike and Joe are learning English. . . . Anna is going to the room on the third floor, where a smiling lady will teach her to make a stylish black velvet sailor to take the place of the gay kerchief she wore when she reached Gary, tired and homesick, six months ago. And while their father and grandfather wrestle with the strange English words that all sound so much alike, and their mother drives an unwilling needle through a stiff buckram frame, Marja and Stephen will be in the manual

training room, where a young man in an apron made of blue-and-white ticking
will show them how to cut with scroll-saws fascinating wooden rabbits and
squirrels—strange, flat beasties that they may take home with them, if they
like. Three generations of them—and all on their way to school. But in Gary
such sights are common.[29]

For a few years there was a rather large night enrollment of children, who
were already also attending day classes. Although in 1914 this was discouraged, it continued on a smaller scale—over one thousand, most listed as
"foreign-born," were still attending. For Swartz, "there is danger of over-
stimulation, both physical and nervous, by duplicating in the evening,
whether in school or in other child welfare community agencies, those
mental, recreational and physical practices that characterize the long day of
the Gary schools." Despite his fears and the overcrowded facilities, whole
families continued to attend at night. He was particularly proud of the
involvement of women: "No discrimination has been made against any
woman or any class of women. . . . The remarkable showing made by the
Gary women this year in the industrial, the commercial, and the cultural
studies easily sets a new mark for work of this kind in American public
evening schools." Less than two thousand women enrolled during 1914–15
(compared to almost five thousand men), but only 114 were listed as foreign
born, with another ninety-eight designated as "colored." Despite the publicity, few immigrant women actually enrolled, although many others, perhaps, accompanied their husbands and participated in the social activities.[30]

As evening school attendance continued to grow at the Froebel school and
throughout the city, there was increasing evidence that a need was being met.
Over thirty different classes were offered, ranging from basketry, leather-
working, shoe repairing, and telegraphy to English, Latin, and music.
Froebel's principal Charles S. Coons was particularly optimistic, describing
the school's evening program as "the great melting pot of Gary." And, he
continued, "When we look into the future we hope to see no foreign quarter
for Gary, but we do hope to see a community, although composed of various
nationalities, yet speaking a common language and having a common interest
in and respect for American laws and institutions." Swartz was even more
confident. "I have found nothing but the best kind of co-operation upon the
part of local citizens," he informed Wirt in the spring of 1915. "This spirit has
been manifest from the humblest foreign day laborer who directs his newly-
arrived brother from the Old World to an English class in the great Froebel
school to and including the heads of Gary's great industrial plants, all of
whom demonstrated their friendly attitude towards our work in multitudes of
ways throughout the year." Confirming Wirt's expectations, the schools did
indeed appear to bring civilization to the urban wilderness, transcending
class and ethnic barriers. Particularly gratifying was the "pageant of nations"
during closing ceremonies of the Froebel night school. "The climax of the

pageant—a salute to the American flag and the chorus 'America' brought a wave of patriotic cherring [sic] from the men and women of all nations in the audience."[31]

Race, however, was another matter. Black children continued to be crowded into their separate school on Twelfth Avenue. An adjoining portable building erected in November 1910 soon housed the lower grades taught by a second teacher, Mrs. Elizabeth Lytle. By spring, with seventy students, the school was offering a variety of activities, including plays, musicals, concerts, and drills; Saturday classes were started in October 1911. Lacking the proper equipment, the students were transported to the Emerson school one hour a day for manual-training classes. The impending opening of the Froebel school in the same neighborhood caused a shift in thinking among school officials. "While the school authorities wish to give the colored children every educational advantage that other children have," reported the *Gary Daily Tribune,* "the segregation arrangement must be kept up. The children cannot be left in the portable buildings when other children are accommodated in fine new buildings and unless some arrangements are made to place them in the new buildings, the construction of a small building would be necessary and even in this the children would not have the advantage of a large school." As a compromise, Wirt proposed to segregate the black students in two rooms, but they would be allowed to use the manual-training room, gymnasiums, and playgrounds. With Froebel's opening a few were transferred, but the majority remained in the portables for another year. Enrollment reached almost 140 in April 1913, who were wedged into the two small buildings.[32]

Finally, in July during the summer session, the portables were abandoned and all of the students transferred to Froebel. But segregation continued, as Wirt had planned, with the black pupils "placed in separate classes in charge of two colored teachers and taught in the old way." As understood by W. P. Burris in his report to the Bureau of Education, "this is not due to the preference of the colored children themselves or their parents. The other patrons of the school, most of whom are foreigners, strenuously object to mixing colored children with the others." This, at least, was Wirt's explanation to Burris, although there is scant evidence that the immigrant parents had called for segregation. While sharing some of the facilities, the black students were deemed unfit to benefit fully from the system. They tried to make the best of the situation, however, by forming a school club: "The social and school spirit will be encouraged and an effort made to inculcate a premium upon being a school boy or school girl in Gary." The adults were treated similarly. A class in electricity for men was initiated at the Twelfth Avenue school in late 1912, and parents were urged to attend meetings to discuss school problems. More telling were the classes begun two years later at the Froebel school. As the *Gary Evening Post* proudly announced in late 1914, "Few of our citizens know anything of the revolutionary work that has been done in our schools and training classes for adults. . . . Some thing *[sic]* is now being done for the colored people. Two vocations are specially attractive and open to these people, that of cookery and automobile driving. To help them classes have been organized in these callings and they are thus given a chance to fit themselves for scientific work along these lines." During the school year 173 blacks attended night classes, with twenty listed separately in their own academic course. Continuing to follow national trends, the Gary schools attempted to maintain strict racial barriers among both children and adults.[33]

The commoness of the schools was breached in other ways as well. While all children were expected to attend classes and sample the wide variety of courses and activities offered in many of the schools, experiences nonetheless differed. The smaller schools had limited facilities, handicapping their students, compared to those in the Emerson, Jefferson, and Froebel buildings. More important was the introduction of a diversified curriculum, separating vocational from academic students, particularly in the secondary grades. Wirt followed John Dewey and others in justifying manual-training courses for younger children on pedagogical grounds—connecting hand and mind enriched learning experiences and created a more interesting educational environment.

Vocational courses, however, were a different matter, for they were directly connected with theories of differential abilities and interests, as well as future employment opportunities. "In utilizing the school plant as a laboratory for vocational training, it is first essential that we recognize the fact that the school is intended for the pupil and that the program must be arranged accordingly," Guy Wulfing, director of vocational work, argued. "We must have a flexible program. There must be more freedom in election." Starting in the seventh grade, each student was expected to devote one period a day to vocational work. "During the eleventh and twelfth years he gives less attention to shop work and emphasizes the technical side of any line of work he wishes to follow," Wulfing explained. "If he cares for more shop work we advise him to get out in the industries and give half time to shop and half time to school." Shopwork in the Emerson school early concentrated on iron-work, with a forge, machine shop, and foundry installed in 1912, as well as a tinsmithing shop and a clay-modeling department. Cabinetmaking, pat-ternmaking, carpentry, blacksmithing, electrical work, plumbing, painting, printing, and other skills were also taught. And additional courses were offered at the Froebel school. Most of the instructors were union workers, not professional teachers. "Of course we will not attempt to turn out skilled workmen for the mills," Wirt explained, "but we will give the boys a foundation which will be valuable to any of them that engage in that sort of work after leaving school." Putting a slightly different emphasis on the situation, the Republican *Gary Daily Tribune* argued that, since the education of workmen is so important, "if a portion of that troublesome problem can be taken off the hands of manufacturers and be done by the schools, it is a great step forward in the way of practical education." For the paper, at least, the shadow of the mill loomed large over the schools.[34]

Training in heavy work was reserved for the boys, with time spent on building and repairing school property, but the girls were not slighted. Domestic science was stressed, and a restaurant existed at the Emerson school so that the girls could prepare and serve lunch to the students and teachers. The cafeteria was self-supporting. Business and secretarial skills were also stressed. In late 1912 Wulfing informed the superintendent that at the Emerson school 229 students were "pursuing work of a vocational nature," from painting, printing, and drafting to cooking and bookkeeping. Following the national trend, most of the upper-grade vocational students were girls clustered in the homemaking and secretarial courses. "There are special courses in business training and qualifying boys and girls for general office work at the steel plant," the *Gary Daily Tribune* noted in the spring of 1913. It could now be admitted that the Emerson school curriculum was aimed at "supplying fairly skilled labor for the big mills in the steel town of Indiana." Soon shops were established at the elementary schools.[35]

The Gary schools were attempting to present a practical curriculum that would not only prepare the older students for a job, but also prove an efficient way of maintaining the schools through using student labor. Skilled workers were "hired to do the work that is needed to be done in the manufacture of school equipment and the repair work throughout the school plants," Swartz later explained. "They are employed with the understanding that they will allow the boys to act as apprentices and to give them special attention." Indeed, Wufling was the building superintendent as well as director of vocational education. When queried whether the shop instructors were certified teachers, and they were not, Wirt responded that "I do not see that it makes any difference whether the shop work that the boys do is in school repair shops, or in regularly established commercial shops in the community." While efficiency was the goal, it was difficult to achieve. In early 1914 Wulfing reported to Wirt that some of the shop instructors were allowing the students "to loiter and kill time. Others would be found slovenly in the care of their shops." Conditions at the Emerson school were improving, but at "Froebel, conditions are bad, and not improving." "I want to bring the whole vocational situation up to the highest possible standard of efficiency as rapidly as possible," he pledged, "and will thank you for advice and criticism at any time."[36]

Although unstated by Wufling, another problem was the small vocational enrollment of boys, particularly in the upper grades. Before the opening of the Froebel school, all high-school students in the city attended Emerson. Of the 717 attending the high school in May 1911, twenty would graduate; a year later the number increased to twenty-five, with twenty-six receiving their diplomas in 1913. Within another two years the Emerson class numbered forty, and five graduated in 1915 from Froebel, its first senior class. Most students, anxious to work, saw little reason to prolong their schooling. Of the eighty-nine students who had graduated by the summer of 1913, forty-six girls and forty-three boys, seventeen of the former continued in a two-year postgraduate course in the Gary schools designed to equal a normal school program. In addition, four others "entered commercial lines," one became a public school teacher, another entered journalism, nine chose college, and the rest married or did something else. Among the boys, twenty-two selected higher education, eight worked in the mills, and the rest were scattered in various businesses. Graduation was for the select few who could afford to extend their schooling with hopes of a more professional future.[37]

While school officials were concerned with the students' future, they were also becoming more involved in their present. The students were expected to promote health and sanitation, for example. In the spring of 1913, as a sticky summer approached, students were recruited by school and city officials in a war on flies. "The big task in Gary is to make a big part of the foreign element understand the necessity of keeping their premises clean, in bringing about a spread of the knowledge of the great evils that come from the presence of the fly and then inciting enough interest to eradicate the conditions that make the presence of the fly possible," argued the *Gary Evening Post*. Sanitation was public, but sex hygiene was considered a private matter. Instead of class discussions, Wirt preferred individual discussions between the doctors and students. The hiring of Dr. O. B. Nesbit, the author of numerous studies of hygiene, in October 1913 was a significant step. He soon discovered that of the 3,334 pupils given dental examinations, only 342 were without cavities. For decades he would head an expanding medical department. The schools' practical bent was well illustrated with the appointment of science supervisor S. G. Engle as city chemist; he established a public health laboratory in the Emerson school, using the students to do the laboratory work. In a variety of ways, the schools were working for the improved health of all in this immigrant, swampy city.[38]

Program expansion continued in various directions. Saturday classes, begun in 1911, were briefly suspended the following year until their legality was clarified by the state Department of Instruction. Only employed teachers were hired to teach Saturday classes, and they were paid extra. Saturday classes would soon become very popular. Even Sunday was not sacred, as the Emerson playgrounds, gymnasiums, and pool were opened under supervision for both children and adults beginning in 1913. Academic, vocational, and recreational programs were also offered during the summer, and by 1914 over fifty teachers were supplementing their incomes as well as keeping children busy and off the streets.[39]

Wirt was concerned about saving not only the students' minds and bodies, but also their souls. In late 1913 he initiated a potentially controversial yet widely popular program of connecting the schools with the city's churches, a natural extension of his crusade to make the public schools civilization's anchor in the corrupt city. "This year we have sixty minutes each day for free application of all sorts of school activities," Wirt informed Albert Nock in October 1913. "We have religious instruction by churches in the immediate neighborhoods of the schools. The children who bring written requests from parents are excused during this sixty minutes of free application work to go to their respective churches for definite religious instruction under trained religious teachers provided by the church." Wirt met with the Gary Ministerial Association, and soon after the Reformed, United Presbyterian, Episcopal, and Reformed Jewish congregations opened their doors to the city's students. During their released time children could also go to the YMCA, public library, or obtain music lessons. "The entire system is designed to eliminate evening work of this kind from the routine of children," remarked the *Gary Daily Tribune*, "in order that they may spend their evenings at home." Wirt would later be concerned about the separation of church and state, but in November 1913 he allowed eight ministers—Methodist Episcopal, English Lutheran, First Congregational, Central Christian, United Presbyterian, First Baptist, Christ Episcopal, and First Presbyterian—to give talks each week at the four largest schools.[40]

Because religious instruction soon became a burden on the ministers, during the following spring the churches began to bring in full-time teachers, starting with the Methodists and quickly followed by the Christian Chruch. Attendance was now limited to four periods—before school, before lunch, after lunch, or at the end of the day—and to those in the primary grades. The fledgling Hebrew Education Alliance, also included, was quite pleased with the new arrangement. "Their purpose seems to be to have their children feel that the work they are doing in the religious school is recognized as valuable by the public schools," Wirt informed Froebel principal S. J. Brickley. "I am sure that they would be very appreciative of any visits that you may make them and any recognition that may be given to the work that they are doing."[41]

Starting in the fall of 1914, ten congregations were offering religious instruction, but as yet there was little cooperation among them. Most advanced was the work of the Central Christian Church, whose early enrollment of eighty pupils necessitated converting the second floor for the religious school, with each student attending two hours a week. There was even talk of the students receiving credit for their work. This pioneering effort by the schools to cooperate with the Protestant and Reformed Jewish communities would soon be widely copied by school systems throughout the country. It was another example of the expanding role of the schools in community life.[42]

Wirt's success in continually adding programs and activities, as well as artfully rearranging the daily and yearly schedule, was quickly recognized. Less understood, however, was the role of individuals—teachers, administrators, parents, businessmen, citizens, as well as the students—in influencing daily practices. And because of this personal element, as well as ongoing monetary and space problems, the schools did not always run perfectly. The continual addition of programs and the lengthening of the school day created a more complex situation, with great potential for difficulties. A laundry list of school problems that reached Wirt sometime in 1913, probably prepared by Assistant Superintendent Annie Klingensmith, hints at many of the difficulties, great and small. In the Emerson school she found excessive corporal punishment, confusion in the classrooms, high school girls dressing immodestly, and, perhaps most imporant, in "taking up complaints with Mr. [E. A.] Spaulding [the principal] [I] do not receive comfortable satisfaction, treated as 'rank outsider.' " At the Jefferson school conditions were "deplorable": children sat in classrooms wearing their rubbers and sweaters, apparently because the teachers took little interest in them. The teachers used excessive punishments and were very unpopular. Classes were too large, hours too long, and the platoon system did not give teachers enough time with individual students. There were similar problems at the smaller Twenty-fifth Avenue school, where the "mixing of colored and white children is a bad influence." Overall, there was the "general complaint with few exceptions of the lack of interest shown by teachers in the child, particularly younger children," and the younger children, perhaps up to grade six, should not be moved from room to room. Surprisingly, it "seems to be that the system is all right if carried out right. Teachers not loyal to [the] Wirt System and are not sympathetically carrying out the Wirt System. Lack of co-operation. Not enough supervision. Incompetent teachers." Only the night schools and the high-school students received favorable comments.[43]

Like all human institutions, Gary's public schools were imperfect. Problems surfaced at various schools, for example, because of local conditions and interests. T. E. Englehart, president of the South Broadway Land Company, complained continually about problems at the older Glen Park school. In late August 1912 he notified the school board about the school's filthy appearance; he also suggested replacing the teachers, who were too well known by the older boys. Wirt soon responded that the school would be cleaned and that there was a new teacher for the lower grades, but it was too late to replace the upper-grade teacher. The next year Englehart demanded more seats for the school. More serious was the school board dispute over hiring E. A. Spaulding to replace Emerson principal Sargent during the Summer of 1912. Two of the board members supported Sargent despite Wirt's having offered the position to Spaulding. Wirt threatened to resign, stating "that he would not feel like carrying on his work here unless the instructors would work in unison with the plans laid down." Board treasurer Flynn countered "that a number of prominent men had interceded with him for Mr. Sargent asking that he be re-employed." After more behind-the-scenes maneuvering, Spaulding was confirmed at the July 3 meeting, a position he would hold for the next forty years. Perhaps angered over the defeat, board member Cain then fruitlessly opposed funding of the night and Saturday schools. This was a rare attack on Wirt's judgment. But Spaulding was not out of the woods. Two years later he was charged by two members of the Humane Society with severely punishing Carl Wheelock, a sixth-grade student. Believing that the case should be settled in court, Wirt reminded the school board that school policy mandated that the parents be notified and their consent given before corporal punishment was inflicted on a student; but if "the board should tell the teachers not to whip the children, it would demoralize school discipline." City Judge William Dunn dismissed the case, finding that Wheelock was a chronic truant who seemed to deserve his punishment. Spaulding admitted, however, that he had used the standard paddle.[44]

Other controversies occasionally surfaced. Class differences were rarely discussed, but the *Gary Daily Tribune* gave a peculiar twist to the issue in mid-1913 when it complained of the lack of park facilities for the more favored children on the city's north side, while the Froebel school had ample grounds and another park was planned on the west side. "The Tribune has no desire to hold back in this great work of caring for and Americanizing the foreign-born people," an editorial proclaimed, "but it must insist that the NATIVE-BORN CHILDREN IN THE CITY OF GARY HAVE SOME RIGHTS AS WELL. We are losing sight of the American children to some extent in our plans for benevolent assimilation." The complaint did not reappear.[45]

Feeling the need for greater solidarity, another interest group also soon emerged—the teachers. In early 1914, seventy teachers organized a teachers' club in order to "promote cooperation among the teachers and the officials of the public schools." It would also promote social activities, "to create a better spirit of unity among the teachers." Within two months the club had visionary plans to have each of the city's 130 teachers contribute $100 to build a cooperative apartment building, then every teacher would have "a substantial and paying investment in Gary." Unlke the older Chicago Teachers Federation, which consciously fought for increased benefits, the (now titled) Gary Teachers' Federation was initially busy with welcoming new teachers and holding picnics. Soon, however, it would cultivate a greater labor orientation.[46]

A few voices of dissent, a hint of factionalism, could not hinder the local (or national) momentum of the Gary Plan. New programs continued to be introduced. Before the start of the 1913 fall term the auditorium period, a key program, was launched. This would soon become the heart of the Platoon Plan. Starting in the Emerson school, the students would spend one hour each day in the auditorium, with the program varying "from music and expression to talks on scientific lines." Special auditorium teachers would supervise the hundred or more students. Ministers were soon lecturing once a week during the auditorium period in the four largest schools. The eight-hour school day allowed for such activities as released time for religious instruction and the auditorium period. Because some parents complained of the long day, Wirt announced that the hours were flexible—children could arrive late or leave early. Indeed, "if any mother wishes to take out her child for an hour or two a day to help at home, to take a music lesson, to peddle papers, or for any other reason, a personal interview or a signed note to the principal will secure it, because it is possible to eliminate or change an auditorium or other period for which no credit is given." Of course, "in the majority of cases the children prefer to spend their time here than to play outside the school," the superintendent confidently added.[47]

Visitors continued to flood the halls and inspect the facilities, but all were not necessarily welcome. After a critical article appeared in a Cleveland newspaper, Wirt informed Superintendent E. A. Hotchkiss in early 1914 that he would not permit a special tour for a team from that city. There was much literature already available, and he did "not see any necessity for our making the necessary sacrifices to turn the schools over to other investigators, particularly when their minds are already made up." When New York City Mayor John P. Mitchel, Board of Education President Thomas W. Churchill, and other dignitaries arrived in June, however, following on the heels of previous visitors from the city, they were well received. Within the month Wirt had accepted an offer to spend part of his time in New York, soon to be one week a month, reconstructing a few elementary schools along platoon school lines. He had already written that if "there is a fair chance to give New York a municipal institution that will make the city a good place for the rearing of children, I will be delighted to help get the thing done." The *Gary Tribune* calmed fears that the superintendent was resigning, reminding its readers that he still had a binding contract and was only leaving for the summer. Although he did remain in Gary for another twenty-four years, his frequent trips to New York for the next three years would occupy much of his time and energy. The school board approved the arrangement in September, showing little surprise that the Superintendent would be collecting $10,000 in New York for part-time work, considerably more than his $6,000 annual salary in Gary. Realizing his financial potential, businessman Wirt next proposed opening a school in Gary to teach platoon-school principles. For $250 the students would spend one month listening to lectures and another assisting in the schools. The idea was apparently stillborn.[48]

From the outside the schools looked very good, at least to most visitors, but those on the inside knew better. There were flaws. If a study were done, Wulfing cautioned Wirt, "a few teachers would be found conscienceless, a few lazy, and a few over zealous." A week later, in early February 1914, he was complaining of the distribution of supplies. More distrubing, perhaps, "for the enumeration work, Miss Hess has been assigned the worst 'Red Light' district in the city. She has very few pupils from the district, and naturally hesitates to send pupils or to go herself, into such houses as are found there." Most zealous in her reports was Assistant Superintendent Klingensmith, who was now responsible for the Froebel district, while Swartz inspected the schools on the north side. Her reports to Wirt were most complete. At the Beveridge school, for example, she found Miss Graham, the teacher, giving the "appearance of a person who has just waked up *[sic]* and feels like yawning and stretching." Others were better, but Klingensmith found herself conducting math lessons because some of the teachers were not prepared. She was very impressed with conditions at the older Glen Park school, and she did not "believe we are likely to ever achieve schools where it is much better for children to be, than it is there, however much we might add of facilities for teaching." Even Miss Greenslade, whose "teaching shows very plainly the crudeness of the beginner," had "that unclassified power of holding children's attention with little apparent effort."[49]

Wirt assured one correspondent that "our children of foreign born parents advance so *[sic]* rapidly as any other children in our schools," but Klingensmith had another view. While the immigrant children at the Froebel school were sent into lower grades for their reading, she believed they became discouraged if forced to be with younger children. "Some pupils here made such a noisy disturbance in the rooms about it, that the teacher had to either send them out or give up having a lesson with them in there." She preferred the practice, begun by school principal Julia Richman in New York City, of placing the students with their own age group and letting them learn English on their own. Klingensmith later asked the superintendent to add more Saturday teachers. "There are especailly *[sic]* the foreigners of any age from about ten to sixteen, scattered along thourgh *[sic]* these grades that I mention who come constantly to their teachers and ask not to be sent to the playground, saying that they want to work. These would come into such a Saturday class and receive great benefit from it." Additional Saturday work was particularly needed at the Glen Park school, for the "children seem to run wild out there." There was also a difficulty in finding enough teachers, for some were paid more to teach at night than on Saturday, or more at one school than at another. Part of the problem was tension betwen Swartz, who headed the night program and recruited his own teachers, and Klingensmith, who was responsible for filling the teching slots on Saturday. On one of her letters to Wirt complaining of Saturday conditions, Swartz scrawled "This letter is a tissue of misrepresentations from beginning to end."[50]

A rivalry between the two assistant superintendents mounted, fueled by Wirt's monthly trips to New York City. In late November 1914, Swartz asked Wirt to "make clear to the entire teaching force and other employees of the school just what my relations to the schools are during your absence," then complained of the poor supervision of the Saturday schools. A few weeks later Wirt formally delegated authority to Swartz during his absences. Quick to assert his power, the acting superintendent became very critical of Froebel principal S. J. Brickley, who informed Swartz that "My position as principal in dealing with you two assis't Supt's throughout the year has been rather difficult. You feel that I have not given you sufficient consideration; the other [Klingensmith] feels that I have given you too much and have been a big factor in crowding her down or back." Then, Swartz transferred a teacher from Saturday to night work without informing Klingensmith. With the superintendent's iron hand periodically missing, there was some decline in administrative efficiency.[51]

As war descended upon Europe, Wirt and the Gary schools were poised to experience increasing popularity as well as critical scrutiny. The superintendent was most confident, reporting to the school board in August 1914 that "pupils go to school longer in Gary, the cost per capita is lower, the average daily attendance is larger and the school property is more valuable than that of any city in the country." City leaders swelled with pride that their superintendent was being paid $10,000 to advise the New York schools one week a month. "The schools will not suffer any neglect," acknowledged the *Gary Evening Post,* "for the superintendent is not the man who neglects anything he starts to do. Besides, after this when some glib New Yorker is indulging in his usual self-satisfaction it will be a pleasure to crush him by telling him that Gary is making over his schools." What could bring more honor to the city and its schools? The death of longtime truant officer W. P. Ray in early 1915 was an occasion to honor his memory. He worked to the end, having furnished ninety-seven poor children the previous fall with clothing so they could attend school. "[G]iving personal attention to so many indigent cases has caused frequent delays in handling truancy and delinquent claims—have in past four months filed but twenty cases in Juvenile Court," he informed Wirt soon after Christmas. "To give more prompt attention to my official duties [I] should be relieved from relief work but I have grown up in it so we can't [sic] for a time at least, get apart." To the end Ray saw his job as helping students. He was succeeded by J. B. Sleezer, now called the attendance officer, who was "no longer to be feared but is considered an advisor and an aid to the parents of school children."[52]

Increasing economic difficulties in late 1914 caused severe problems for the schools and students, however. With heavy unemployment in the steel industry, school revenues declined, and Wirt was forced to postpone building construction and soon tighten the belt in other ways. Poor children on the south side were increasingly absent because they did not have adequate shoes during the cold weather. The W. P. Ray shoe fund was established at Froebel to collect money for leather, thread, and nails for shoe repair, a project previously suggested by Ray. The children could either use the materials to repair their own shoes under expert supervision, or borrow money from the fund to pay for the repair, to be repaid later with a one-cent interest charge. The scheme exemplified the practical side of the Wirt system, with the children learning a skill and economics; the older students ran the fund. Assisted by the Campbell settlement house, teachers at the Twenty-fourth Avenue school furnished lunches to the students for three cents or less. It was a rough winter in the steel town with a famous school system and many distraught children.[53]

As Wirt began to leave the city on his frequent trips to New York, the system he had initiated eight years before was substantially in place. There would be changes over the years, of course, but nothing drastic until the 1930s. The Gary Plan had yet to prove itself on the national stage, however, and local circumstances continually forced a reshaping of programs and personnel. It would also remain to be seen if the work-study-play system benefited all in Gary—rich and poor, black and white, native and immigrant—equally. And how would the system stand up to external criticism, war, labor disputes, economic crises, and the like? The next five years would be a rigorous testing period.

III

TIME OF TROUBLES, 1915–1920

In the spring of 1916 during a driving snow storm, Assistant Superintendent Annie Klingensmith discovered Katie Poppaditch, "a lame child, without coat, mittens or head covering, falling repeatenly [sic] on snow covered ice, crying and rubbing her face with freezing wet hands what time she was not on hands and feet trying to get up with bare hands in snow above the elbow." She took the child home, which was located up a narrow passage between a saloon and barber shop on Washington Street between Thirteenth and Fourteenth Avenues. Frightened because of the rough neighborhood, Klingensmith was surprised to find in the "shacks and flats a great collection of Froebel School children." She also discovered that many of the children in the predominantly male neighborhood—composed of pool rooms, barber shops, boarding houses, and saloons—were unregistered because the teachers were afraid to go there. "The larger girls in Froebel beg the women not to go into certain districts, out of which they have been warned by their parents." The children living in the heavily immigrant, overcrowded south side had wretched home conditions. But, Klingensmith and many others considered those children lucky to have the opportunity of attending the Froebel school, the linchpin of the increasingly famous Gary school system.[1]

The schools experienced steady growth during the war years, increasing their hold on the city's children and demonstrating their vital, expanding role in civic affairs. The approximately six thousand students enrolled in 1915 mushroomed to nine thousand within five years, mostly elementary school increases. High-school enrollment, centered at the Emerson school, was over seven hundred in 1920. Emerson and Froebel high-school graduates numbered forty-five in 1915 and peaked at around eighty by the end of the decade (in 1918, fifty-five graduated from Emerson and twenty-four from Froebel). Over 60 percent of the students were foreign-born or the children of immigrants, with the majority attending the Froebel school (over 80 percent from Eastern Europe), which also had the largest enrollment, with about two thousand in 1919. The Emerson school, attended by native whites, had about five hundred fewer, followed by the Jefferson school with one thousand in the elementary grades. Trailing far behind were the tiny Clark Road school with sixty-six and the even smaller West Gary building with thrity-three, out of the thirteen schools at the time. The teaching staff increased accordingly, from about 130 in 1915 to well over two hundred by 1920.[2]

While the students were commonly from working-class, non-English-speaking homes, the schools were in the safe hands of native white teachers and school board members. When an opening on the board appeared in May 1915, the Gary Civic Service Club, a women's suffrage organization, demanded that the city council appoint a woman. This strategy—women on school boards—was a common opening to an expanded female political role before the Nineteenth Amendment was enacted. Two years later a night-school class was initiated at the Jefferson school "to instruct the women in everything pertaining to elections, primaries . . . [etc.]. The idea of the school authorities is that with this instruction, the women who will cast their first vote will not become confused by awkwardly answered questions from varied sources." The women were temporarily frustrated, as the council named Henry Hay, president of the Gary State Bank, who served until 1929. He was soon joined by George Hunter, general manager of the American Bridge Works, a subsidiary of U.S. Steel; Hunter resigned in 1917 and was replaced by A. R. McArthur, resident engineer of the tin mills, who also lasted until 1929. The third member, Tolleston attorney E. Miles Norton, was followed by Herman Uecker, cashier of the First State Bank of Tolleston, in January 1919. Uecker's tenure was surprisingly short, for he was innocently killed during a bank robbery in June. The council then named Adele M. (Mrs. Charles W.) Chase, a Democrat and wife of the president of the Gary Street Railway Company, the board's first woman, who served until 1932. The board managed to remain firmly in the hands of the city's elite, mostly male but now including a woman. Yet it exercised little power, preferring instead to trust explicitly in the managerial abilities and administrative decisions of Superintendent Wirt.[3]

Entering his second decade at the helm of the schools, William Wirt was filled with confidence and energy even in the face of staggering family adversity. One problem was his oldest son, William Franz, who, ironically, adjusted poorly to public school, perhaps because of the family connection as well as difficult home conditions. Wirt was an aloof, domineering father who demanded strict formality at home as well as in his public life. In mid-1916, Wirt wrote to the Interlaken School in Rolling Prarie, Indiana, inquiring about their program. Established by Edward A. Rumely, a LaPorte industrialist and current publisher of the New York *Evening Mail,* Interlaken was a rural school committed to training boys in manual skills and physical survival in a "democratic" environment: "All this means rigorous living in plenty. But it is natural, outdoor living, normal primitive life—work and play in the sun and wind and rain, the hand in the soil. And the boys, many of them puny lads when they first come, get the vigor of the original savage." Wirt held off sending Franz, but not for long.[4]

Emerson school principal E. A. Spaulding complained about Franz to the superintendent in early 1917, "we feel that we are at the limit of our means of controlling him, the only thing left being to suspend him from school if he continues as he has been doing." Wirt encouraged Spaulding to "administer any form of punishment that you think is necessary in your judgment," and promised "I shall punish him myself severely." A month later Franz and three friends tried to run away, but did not get far. He was soon enrolled at Interlaken. Then Mrs. Wirt died suddenly in July 1917. Wirt had married Bertha Ann Koch seventeen years before, and they had three children, Franz, now fifteen, Sherwood, six, and Eleanor, four. For the next few years after Mrs. Wirt's death the children were sent to live with relatives in the East, and Franz was enrolled at Raymond Riordan's school in Highland, New York, which was even more rustic and physically demanding than Interlaken. Wirt attempted to have Franz return to Interlaken the following year, now under new control since Rumely, charged with pro-German sympathies, had resigned. But the school was making plans to become a training camp for the War Department and had suspended its regular work. Unable to cope with his loneliness, Wirt married his secretary, Martha Ruth Jacques, an Emerson graduate and barely half his age, in July 1919. Three months later Franz joined the navy.[5]

Heavily distracted by family difficulties, the superintendent continued to manage the Gary schools while actively promoting the work-study-play plan throughout the country. In March 1915, local economic difficulties diminished school revenues, necessitating the reduction of day classes by one month (to nine months), night classes by two months (to six months), and the virtual elimination of Saturday and summer programs. During the summer building maintenance was greatly limited, and fifteen teaching positions were dropped. In September, however, the steel industry revived, the deficit disappeared, as revenues caught up with expenditures, and programs were reinstated. Plans were resumed to build a new unit school in the Tolleston neighborhood (temporarily named the Pestalozzi school) or on West Fifth Avenue, and new teachers were hired. Construction was delayed; then, in May 1917, with the outbreak of war, the governor halted all school expansion. Only portable buildings were erected for the remainder of the decade, necessitated by the swelling enrollment generated by war workers, but Wirt managed to squeeze additional classes into the existing buildings.[6]

Despite this temporary economic crisis, to most outsiders the work-study-play system—an efficient school organization combined with an enriched program—exemplified the illusive search for order, cost savings, as well as expanded municipal services during the Progressive Period. Platoon schools in some form were adopted in four cities in 1915, eight in 1916, and an average of about four a year until the end of the decade; by 1920, thirty-two cities had instituted the system in 117 elementary schools. There was certainly controversy, exemplified by the protracted debate in New York City over Garyizing its elementary schools that continued through the municipal elections in the fall of 1917, but generally the reaction was favorable. Wirt was a paid consultant to a few systems, in addition to the New York City schools, which he continued to visit into 1917. The rhetoric was heated in Chicago, Cleveland, and Minneapolis. There were scores of published articles and pamphlets, mostly favorable. "The Gary plan, though not on the program, is the subject of constant burning discussion among delegates" at the National Education Association, Department of Superintendence, convention, the *Gary Tribune* reported in early 1916. Wirt announced to a score or so of city superintendents and other school officials the following year, "I have always personally deplored any semblance of propaganda to make the Gary Schools model schools for the rest of the country and for this reason I have never written a book or other publications upon the Gary Schools." Nonetheless, he suggested that they "secure a dozen or more leading school men cooperating together in an effort to assist each other" in promoting the use of "playgrounds, gymnasiums, swimming pools, gardens, laboratories, libraries, music and drawing studios and well equipped auditoriums as well as good class rooms for all the children of our cities." Within a few months he had positive replies from a dozen or so, and the skeleton of an organization was formed.[7]

Throngs of curious observers passed through the schools, often disrupting classes. The local paper, for instance, complained in late 1917 that "the continuous stream of visitors through our schools in the past has tended to lessen attention to the pupils themselves." There were also assorted delegations from other nations. Professor Yaezo Wada of Tokyo's First National College arrived in June 1916, since Japanese school overcrowding had attracted the interest of educators to the Gary Plan. Subsequently, various male visitors from Japan reported favorably to the emperor, and in April 1918 a female delegation arrived "to see if the men have not exaggerated in the praise which they have bestowed on Mr. Wirt's achievements." The following year John Dewey, then in Asia, informed Wirt that P. C. Chen and a Chinese Educational Commission were visiting American schools and were most interested in Gary. "China has a greater opportunity than any country in the world for cooperation between schools and the local development of industries," Dewey added, and this cooperation was "carried on in immense variety in the homes. The social work of assemblies etc, will also Im [*sic*] sure appeal to them."[8]

English school officials were particularly impressed, as the war had produced increasing social and economic strains. One notable article praised Gary in London's *Teachers' World* in mid-1916. The Gary Plan was also discussed at the 1918 Conference of Educational Associations by John Adams, who romanticized the social side of the reform: "The school is not a hugh classificatory box with a pigeon-hole for each pupil. It is rather a social institution in which each pupil must find what he most needs." Four years later, in his popular study *Modern Developments in Educational Practice,*

Adams wrote that "it would be perhaps too much to say that the system has a communistic basis, but it certainly suggests communistic ideals. Its promoters would rather express its aim as a training in citizenship, and they maintain that this training demands some sort of communal work." On the other side, the Canadian J. H. Putnam, writing in the English *Educational Review,* emphasized economic issues and was most critical: "But in spite of the fact that the plan on a superficial survey seems feasible and economical, I am convinced that it can not provide an education equal to that now given in the best elementary schools in Canada and the United States which are organized on the orthodox plan. . . . The Gary plan (as practised in Gary) has two weaknesses, of which both can not be cured. It either overworks the teacher or neglects the child." In early 1917, Wirt traveled to Ottawa and presented his views to the Canadian Education Association. Upon the request of a third party, Wirt even sent material to A. S. Neill, soon to be the controversial founder of the Summerhill school. The debate in Great Britain and Canada paralleled that within the United States, some emphasizing structures, some curriculum, and others efficiency. Reformers continually saw different things in the enigmatic Gary Plan.[9]

The position of advocates abroad as well as at home ranged across the political spectrum, but the most vociferous defense appeared to come from those on the left—social activist, prolaborites, some outright socialists. They emphasized the system's humane, democratic elements. Scott Nearing, a professor of economics, a socialist, and an antiwar activist, was charmed by what he found in Gary: "There, perhaps more consistently than anywhere else in the United States, the school authorities are providing for the whole child in their schools." He quickly jumped from the general to the specific: "During his school day, John has played, used his head and his hands, and alternated the work in such a way that no one part of it ever became irksome. . . . John, in the schools of Gary, is John Frena, with all of John Frena's limitations and possibilities. The Gary school seeks to bridge the limitations, expand the possibilities, and give John Frena a thousand and one reasons for believing that if there is any place in the world where he can grow into a complete man, that place is the Gary school."[10]

Equally enthusiastic was John Dewey, the country's leading theorist of one brand of progressive education and a strong influence on Wirt's thinking. Dewey's daughter Evelyn briefly visited Gary in 1914 to inspect the schools, then returned home to coauthor with her father *Schools of To-Morrow* (1915), a collection of essays on school reforms throughout the country. Dewey had already praised Gary (along with Chicago and Cincinnati) for "adapting industry to educational ends. . . . In these places the aim has not been to turn schools into preliminary factories supported at public expense, but to borrow from shops the resources and motives which make teaching more effective and wider in reach." He extended his discussion in the chapters "The Relation of the School to the Community" and "Education through

Industry," dwelling on his belief in connecting mind and hand and schooling with citizenship and the world of work.[11]

Dewey was quick to stress that the schools "were not instituted to turn out good workers for the steel company, nor to save the factories the expense of training their own workers, but for the educational value of the work they involved. In the same way it would be a mistake to consider the Gary schools simply as an attempt to take the unpromising immigrant child and turn him into a self-supporting immigrant, or as an attempt to meet the demand of an industrial class for a certain sort of training." Rather, through the enriched curriculum and unique organization, the schools "are doing everything possible, in cooperation with church and home, to use to the best educational purpose every resource of money, organization and neighborhood influence." Specifically through manual and industrial training, the children are given "the same sort of things to do that occupy their parents and call for muscular skill and find coordination in the business of everyday life." The schools' practical side definitely appealed to Dewey.[12]

A more detailed study was published by Randolph Bourne, a brilliant, acerbic social critic, then engaged in blowing away the cobwebs of Victorian gentility. After touring the schools, Bourne published a series of very favorable articles, particularly in *The New Republic* in 1915, followed by a book in 1916. In Gary he found, agreeing with Dewey, "a school which does reflect all the healthy interests of the community, and where the child does become familiar with its life and with his own interests and vocational opportunities through practical doing of work." The book was quite detailed, with toned-down rhetoric compared to that of the articles, and an introduction by Wirt. Indeed, Bourne sent the manuscript to Wirt for his approval, as required by the publisher, and assured the superintendent, "I should not think of publishing it if you did not think it would aid the public in getting a clear idea of your remarkable school." He particularly aimed at influencing the debate over the Gary Plan then raging in New York, since he was closely allied with the pro-Gary forces. "The visitor to the Gary school finds everywhere little groups of busy children, absorbedly interested, working on the different needs of the school, under kindly and intelligent teacher-workmen," Bourne discovered. The program was organized around the idea of "the school community life." Any relationship between Bourne, the spokesman for youth and rebellion, and Wirt, representing the establishment, seems highly incongruous, yet they combined to promote the system.[13]

Perhaps most radical in his defense of the Gary Plan was the author and socialist Floyd Dell. Angered by the downfall of the system in New York with the defeat of Mayor John Purroy Mitchel in late 1917, he warned that education "will either fall into the hands of capitalist reformers, who will make it a training school for wage slaves, as they are already planning quite definitely to do; or it will be made the instrument of a democratic culture which accepts the present but foresees the future. There is no doubt on which side all revolutionary minded people will find themselves in the coming struggle." The Gary schools, for Dell, epitomized the latter.[14]

Most commentators were content with reading the relevant literature and briefly visiting the city, viewing a few classrooms, getting the official tour, and, perhaps, even meeting with the superintendent. Elsa Ueland and Elisabeth Roemer, however, decided to experience the system firsthand. Born in Minneapolis, with advanced degrees from the University of Minnesota and Columbia University, Ueland was connected with the Vocational Education Survey in New York City. Roemer was born in Denmark, attended universities in her native country and in France, moved to New York in 1901, and soon became the head worker at the Richmond Hill Settlement House, where she met Ueland. She also worked on the Vocational Education Survey under the direction of Alice Barrows. Having passed through Gary going to and from Minneapolis, both women became interested in the schools. "We have always wanted to be a part of your organization in order to learn the *how* of the whole Gary scheme," Ueland wrote to Wirt in August 1914, "for it is the Gary idea as it is actually worked out in concrete detail that is of value to the country, and not mere magazine enthusiasm." They would accept any sort of work and "want to come at any salary."[15]

The following month, as the new school year opened, Ueland found herself teaching arithmetic, geography, and history in the fifth, sixth, and seventh grades in the Jefferson school. The next spring she was transferred to the Emerson school, where she headed the English department and supervised two auditorium periods. Roemer was also teaching in the middle grades. In early 1916, Roemer became director of registering children, keeping the school census, and monitoring home conditions (which she did for two years), and Ueland became Wirt's special secretary—both paid out of funds donated by Judge Gary. Ueland was instructed to collect, edit, and publish information relating to the schools, shepherd visitors, and possibly contribute a volume to a projected series on the Gary Plan. She moved to Philadelphia in September 1916.

Years later, Ueland remembered "Gary was a very wonderful experience" and recalled her "association with Mr. Wirt with thankfulness." At the time her feelings were equally positive. As a feminist, she was particularly struck by the schools' attempt at gender equality: "But the main point about the Gary system is its refusal to stifle the girl's physical development out of deference to convention. You know a girl is sentenced by nature to feel human impulses very much like a boy's. She is not taught here that she should be ashamed of them. . . . As a consequence she grows strong and hardy, becomes efficient and accomplished, is able to bear great strains, has a speaking acquaintance with the word robustness, and best of all is permitted a joyous, spontaneous childhood free from the tyranny of false notions of feminity. I tell you the Gary system is superb for the development of the girl." She also stressed the close ties between teachers and students and teachers and the community: "each teacher seeks to adapt her subject to the children of the neighborhood she had learned to know. One is studying the history of Serbia because she wants her children to understand Americanism by knowing their own background first." The entire community profited from the enriched curriculum and specialized teachers. Because of her firsthand experiences and social activist credentials, Ueland was in a unique position to comment on the system. She added another voice to the swelling chorus of praise.[16]

Perceptions of the Gary Plan, whether positive or negative, were based on essentially subjective views. But it became apparent to some that a more "objective" study, a survey, was necessary to clarify both the schools' strengths and weaknesses. The first professional school survey was of the Boise, Idaho, schools in 1910, followed by studies of Montclair and East Orange, New Jersey; there were hundreds more during the next two decades. According to survey expert Jesse Sears, "a survey is a scientific inquiry which obtains facts about the present efficiency of a school system and on the basis of these facts offers constructive proposals for desirable improvements," part and parcel of the increasing emphasis on science and professionalism at the time. Private foundations, such as Rockefeller and Russell Sage, sponsored many of the early surveys.[17]

Abraham Flexner was born in Louisville, Kentucky, in 1866, attended Johns Hopkins University, then returned to teach in his hometown's high school. In 1890, he opened a private school, which he operated until 1905, when he continued his education at Harvard University. After heading a study of medical education for the Carnegie Foundation and another on prostitution in Europe for the Bureau of Social Hygiene, he joined the Rockefeller-funded General Education Board (GEB) in 1913, initially organized in 1903 to study and finance black and white schooling in the South. Flexner was responsible for state-wide school surveys, first in Maryland and later in Delaware, North Carolina, Kentucky, and Indiana. In *A Modern School* published by the GEB in 1916, Flexner expressed the general view that schools should "give children the knowledge they need, and to develop in them the power to handle themselves in our own world." His ideas were put into operation with the establishment of the elite Lincoln School in 1917, sponsored by the GEB and Teachers College, Columbia University. Simultaneously, he was a member of the New York City Board of Education, then in the throes of implementing the Gary Plan, and appeared to be leaning in its favor.[18]

Casting his eye on the controversial Gary schools, Flexner arrived in the city in May 1915 to get a firsthand impression. "I have spent a most interesting day in the Gary schools," he enthusiastically informed his daughter Jean. "I wish you & Eleanor & Willie & Jimmie might have some of the opportunities that all these children have. . . . They are all as happy and as busy as bees." He was particularly impressed by the shops, gardens, gyms, and swimming pools. Encouraged by the GEB, the following month he expressed to Wirt "my great interest in your work in the Gary Schools. It seems to me that a thoroughly scientific study of these schools from every legitimate point of view would be of very great value at this time." The school board, under Wirt's direction, quickly invited the GEB to conduct a survey. Searching for someone to head a survey team, Flexner focused on Stanford University's Ellwood P. Cubberley, an experienced surveyor. Others involved were most sensitive to the peculiar nature of the study. "In conducting most school surveys it is as though we were deciding how to bring up our children and how to feed and clothe them," school expert Leonard Ayres, then heading the Cleveland survey, wrote to Flexner. "In conducting a Gary survey, we are scrutinizing an orphan child in order to find out whether or not to adopt him into the family. It is a national rather than a local matter and the report will be read with a critical interest that has been accorded to no previous piece of work in this field." Flexner agreed. Cubberley spent a few days in Gary in late September, but decided he could not put much time into the project and, with Flexner's prodding, reluctantly resigned a month later.[19]

Flexner quickly stepped into the breach to head the investigation, with Frank Bachman, his assistant in the Maryland study, serving in the same capacity in Gary. The new director promised "to make a cold-blooded study of the whole thing." He soon assembled a talented team—C. R. Richards, director of Cooper Union, for industrial work; Eva White, director of Extended Use of Public Schools of Boston, for household arts; Lee Hanmer, director of the Department of Recreation of the Russell Sage Foundation, for physical training; Otis Caldwell, head of the Lincoln School, on science teaching; George Strayer of Teachers College for organization and administration; Stuart A. Courtis, supervisor of Educational Research for the Detroit Schools, on testing and measurement. Team members soon descended on the city. "I understand now why able school men come away from Gary with such absolutely different views about Supt. Wirt's plan," Hanmer reported to Flexner in early February 1916. "Each school has a system of its own which is determined by the character of the building, the equipment, the neighborhood, the numbers to be handled, the cooperating facilities available, the funds, the personal factor in principals and teachers, etc."[20]

Flexner arrived in Gary in early March with overblown confidence in his ability to do a first-rate survey of this educational enigma. The freezing city seemed an "unspeakably dreary environment. [F]or Gary is the godforsakenest hole I ever tarried in," he confided to his wife. "That schools representing an intelligent effort to embody modern ideas should spring up & obtain support here is a miracle—just such a miracle as the origin of Christ or Abraham Lincoln. The ways of Providence are indeed inscrutable." And he ended, "we are keeping our minds open, not driving ourselves in the matter of speed, but just working ahead in the hope not only of describing Gary, but of striking a blow—felt round the world—for modern education." While school authorities and the teachers were most cooperative, there were some problems. Rumors circulated among school officials that the survey would not be impartial, which stung Flexner; and the testing of school children, conducted by Courtis, was not going smoothly. During his May trip to the city, Flexner discovered that "the testing work was just about to run wild or mad, & I have had to bring it back to earth." A month later, wrapping up the project in Gary and with a feeling of relief, he wrote to his wife: "Such a mixture of good & bad, of sense & nonsense, of intelligence & childishness, one would scarcely find again in a lifetime!" He sent copies of Bourne's book to the team members in mid-May, explaining "it is for us, of course, to see and describe the Gary schools, as they actually are; but we want also in a cautious spirit to compass their possibilities and the possibilities of the underlying ideas." The fieldwork was completed in late June.[21]

It took until the end of the year for the various team members to sort through their data and compose their preliminary studies. Courtis, overly fussy and nervous, felt pressure early on from Detroit school superintendent Charles Chadsey to release some of his findings because of local discussions over adapting the Gary Plan (which occurred in 1918). Flexner could commiserate, since, as a member of the New York school board (he resigned in May 1917), he was in a similar situation. "You will perceive at once the forces impelling me to drop a hint now and then as to the outcome of our Gary studies," he responded to Courtis in August. *"I have never said a word to a soul. . . .* I am a surveyor,—a detached, impersonal agent." Courtis, sending drafts of the summary volume being composed by Bachman, worried that it would be too favorable to the Gary Plan. Surprised, Flexner reminded him "that I have absolutely no desire whatsoever to 'boost' the Gary system." Yet he also believed "you are absolutely wrong in saying that Gary is stimulating in interest and effort only to people who hypnotize themselves."[22]

In March Flexner began sending Wirt copies of the drafts of the summary volume, soliciting his comments and suggestions. The superintendent's first response was favorable. As the more detailed sections arrived he became more critical, which Flexner welcomed, and Wirt forwarded selected portions to his staff for their comments. Compiling a detailed criticism, Assistant Superintendent Klingensmith informed Bachman that those in Gary considered the schools "frankly experimental." Because of the report's criticisms, people in the city "will not think of the fact that they feel distinguished to have an experimental school which has the eyes of the world fixed in [sic] it. They will just think if you found the results poor when you came shortly after the final great step of the great experiment was inaugurated, that it is because the people who do the work are poor school people, unless you state the facts right along with your estimate of results at that time." Consequently, morale would decline along with local support. Here was the sticking point—whether any documented problems were inherent in the system or were the result of inadequate administration—a dilemma that would plague all surveys.[23]

The new year arrived with still no published report. With the defeat in New York of pro-Gary Plan Mayor John Mitchel in November 1917, public clamor diminished, but curiosity was still running high. Flexner stuck to his game plan. "We are anxious to make this the most scientific piece of survey work that had yet been done," he wrote in early 1918, "and indeed, our slowness in doing it would be unexcusable[*sic*] if we did otherwise." Wirt's criticisms became more strident. He was particularly disturbed by Bachman's report on instruction and Courtis's on testing, labeling them "the poorest attempts at a criticism of school work that I have ever read and I am not able to understand them at all." Flexner urged the superintendent to come to New York to iron out any differences, but was rebuffed. "I do not hold you personally to blame in any respect regarding the unfortunate conditions of this survey and consider the unfortunate results as unavoidable," Wirt assured Flexner. "I consider it important, however, that I use what little time I have to make preparation[s] for meeting the situation that will arise when your report is published." Disappointed, Flexner reminded Wirt that their "relations have been so intimate and delightful that I know you will agree with me that they must be continued on this basis." Weakened over the summer by illness, the superintendent finally met in New York with Courtis, Bachman, Flexner, and Frank Ballou, Assistant Superintendent of the Boston schools, to seek a compromise; but by October, as he notified Alice Barrows, I "have my fighting spirit again [and] I regret that I have attempted to secure a revision of the report."[24]

After much delay, indecision, and perusal by selected school experts, the first of the series, *The Gary Schools: A General Account,* by Flexner and Bachman, was issued in November 1918, followed by the seven highly detailed topical volumes over the next few months covering organization and administration, costs, industrial work, household arts, physical training and play, science teaching, and measurement of classroom products. The *General Account* mixed praise with pointed criticism: "The Gary school plant is not indeed by any means of uniform excellence; but every part of it shows even amidst most unfavorable conditions a distinct effort to make possible something in the way of an expanded curriculum, while two of the nine schools— the Emerson and the Froebel—belong to the very best type of modern school construction and can hardly be paralleled outside our largest and richest communities." As for the teaching, "the modern attitude is indeed encountered here and there in almost every subject, but, while heartily encouraged, it is still exceptional and individual rather than characteristic and general. . . . In the main, therefore, the teaching is of ordinary type, ineffectually controlled." The relatively low scores on specific skills tests, "the essential tools of learning," demonstrated inadequate supervision. The system got high marks for efficiency, for "the advantages offered by the Gary schools at their best probably cost less than the same advantages on a more conventional plan of school organization." And "the schools are rich in color and movement, they are places where children live as well as learn, places where children obtain educational values, not only through books, but through genuine life activities." But, "it remains to be admitted that in respect to administration and instruction Gary might fairly have been expected to make a better showing. Fundamentally, the defect is one of administration." Overall, Flexner and Bachman applauded Wirt's "courage, liberality, and imagination to 'try things.' . . . Disappointment was inevitable, but it is disappointment that does not necessarily imply fundamental error. . . . Gary's experience up to this time means merely that further efforts, at Gary and elsewhere, more clearly defined, more effectively controlled, must be made in order, if possible, to accomplish Gary's avowed object—the making of our schools adequate to the needs and conditions of current life." The theory was sound, the practice (administration) somewhat faulty.[25]

The survey's apparent balance was generally welcomed in the reviews. Julius Sachs, writing in the *Columbia University Quarterly,* believed the Gary Plan "is a reform that calls not for overthrow, but for patient evolution." Harvard's Henry Holmes congratulated Flexner because the "report presents more clearly than anything I know the problem of modernizing education." Meeting with a group of city superintendents, Bachman assured Flexner in June 1919 that "they have gotten more stimulation and ideas from Gary than from any other single source, and, I am almost inclined to say, from all other sources combined. . . . I am increasingly grateful that the General Education Board made possible our Gary study." Some years later, according to his autobiography, Flexner's view was more jaundiced. "The general effect of the report was disastrous to the exploitation of the Gary system," he recalled in *I Remember.* "Education is far too complicated a process to be advertised on the basis of inadequate supervision and without definite accounting—mental, moral, and financial. With the publication of the report the school world was relieved, and the Gary system ceased to be an object of excitement. It disappeared from discussion as suddenly as it had arisen." In 1919 he was more positive. Nonetheless, sometime after 1915 his enthusiasm had waned; perhaps the struggle in New York wore him down, perhaps he took more seriously his role as "objective" scientist, or perhaps he was persuaded by the negative thrust of Courtis and others.[26]

Among the system's defenders, particularly in Gary, the reaction was generally hostile, although the *Gary Evening Post* believed that "to perfect the great system and make it adequate needs stronger pressure of repressive and executive power." Former school board member A. P. Melton confided to Wirt, "the animus pervading the whole series is so apparent that the documents could hardly be called a 'Report' but could be better named an 'Attack'." The superintendent considered publishing a rebuttal, perhaps a pamphlet, but changed his mind. Because of the increasing interest in the platoon-school concept, in early 1920 he assured Bessie Stern, a loyal supporter, that the report "has not made any difference any way [sic] or the other in my estimation." But he was wounded. A few months later he complained, "these really fine men [Flexner and Bachman] misrepresent entirely the conditions in the Gary Schools and the flexibile program idea itself because they have only the viewpoint of the traditional school forcing education upon children." While not going public with his complaints, Wirt did circulate locally a lengthy manuscript, focusing on Courtis's tables and findings. "Eight or ten years ago it was the common practice with many professional educators to label the Gary School Plan as a joke," he began. "Judging from the survey report it is now the practice among some professional educators to admit the value of the Gary School Plan but to label the people responsible for its development as jokes." As for himself, "I am not very much concerned with the effect of this report upon my own reputation. It has been blasted so many times that a blast more or less does not make very much difference. But as to the effect upon the many teachers and principals in the Gary Public Schools who have labored zealously in this experiment I am concerned." In the midst of his point-by-point refutation of Courtis's findings, he made a fratricidal attack: "No wonder the quack Doctors of Pedagogy see red when they look at a Gary school. These schools not only refuse to take their nostrums but proclaim from the house tops that variability in class attainments is a sign of health and that the real disease is the condition created by the quack Doctors of Pedagogy themselves,— uniform class attainments." Here was the heart of Wirt's defense (and educational philosophy)—what he was doing could not be measured by standard tests or traditional assumptions, although he surely would have preferred higher scores.[27]

Wirt and his supporters in Gary (and elsewhere) initially welcomed the study, awaited its publication with some trepidation, then dismissed it as just another comment on their popular school plan. Perhaps controversy was endemic to any new educational program. Take the example of the program of released time for religious instruction pioneered in Gary and one of the prime fears among Jewish parents in New York who opposed the Gary Plan. Wirt was most sensitive to the charges and suspicions that the schools were promoting religion. When the steel city's Hebrew Educational Alliance complained in late 1915 about religious (Christian) songs being taught during auditorium periods, the superintendent responded that "religious songs of all kinds are discouraged in the public schools on account of the varied nationalities." State law, conforming to the First Amendment, provided that the schools could neither prohibit nor promote religion. But Wirt went further, noting that the "schools try to deemphasize Christmas and Easter and instead emphasize national holidays like Thanksgiving and birthdays of Washington and Lincoln"; nothing in the schoolwork "could offend any sect or creed." And he assured one correspondent, "in no instance is religious instruction permitted in the school building and by school teachers." (Yet, in late 1919, Father John DeVille thanked the superintendent for allowing use of a classroom in a south-side school for the teaching of catechism to Catholic pupils.) Instead, the students were allowed to leave the schools to attend church schools.[28]

Initially begun in late 1913, the program escalated within the next few years. Because of the long school day, students were able to attend religious classes two hours a week in the morning or afternoon during their play hours. Parental approval was necessary, since attendance was strictly voluntary. There were eight or more separate religious schools operating by late 1916, including those by the First Methodist Church, Episcopal Church, Orthodox and Reformed Jewish Congregations, First Baptist Church, Neighborhood House(Presbyterian), and Campbell Friendship House (Methodist). Having first been discussed the previous year, in August 1917 a coordinating Board of Religious Education was established by the mainline Protestant denominations, with each congregation making a donation supplied by its parent body. A principal, Mary E. Abernethy, and two teachers were hired. Classes were offered at the Neighborhood House for Froebel students (there were no Protestant churches in the neighborhood), at the Central Christian Church for Jefferson students, and in a new building on land donated by the Gary Land Company erected across from the Emerson school. Within a year, pupils at Glen Park school were meeting at the Christian church, Tolleston students at the Presbyterian church, and those from Ambridge school in the Red Cross room. The Hebrew Educational Alliance opened its own building in 1918 "to the strains of 'The Star Spangled Banner' as played by the excellent Emerson school orchestra. . . . Mayor Hodges delivered a stirring patriotic address and was received with thunderous applause." The teachers circulated among the Christian schools, teaching about 750 students by the end of 1917; within two years there were five teachers for two thousand pupils, with another two hundred students at the separate Episcopal and Baptist schools and over one hundred at the Jewish school. Students now attended from seven public schools, the smallest number coming from the Froebel school.[29]

The schools served various purposes other than just teaching knowledge of the Bible. There was much testimony of the schools' effect on student conduct. "Superintendent Wirt says that the superior moral fiber of the pupils who attend the church school classes is quite noticeable," one study reported. "For a city 75% foreign-born and having 8000 negroes many of them just come from the densely peopled 'Black Belt' of the South, Gary does not seem to have a high percentage of juvenile delinquency. It is easy to believe that if it were not for the religious education agencies of the city, conditions would be far worse than they are." A principal found "a difference in the pupils in regard to lying and stealing. . . . She lays it chiefly to the

work of the Church School which the majority of the children are attending."
More telling were the personal anecdotes:

> A boy who had never been to Church or Sunday School, and who had had the
> reputation of being the "toughest" boy in school, but who never had missed
> Church School since he had entered several weeks before, came up to his
> teacher after class one day and said quietly—"Yesterday a guy put some stones
> in the ball bearings of my cart, and I was so mad that I was going to smash in
> his face, then I remembered the story we had about forgiving and I forgave him
> instead."

> A little hot blooded Italian girl with snapping black eyes hurried up to her
> church school teacher and said, "Teacher, when Mary slapped me yesterday I
> didn't slap her back, I forgave her." Johnny is a Polish boy who lives with his
> father and mother in two tiny back rooms. He came breathlessly into the
> Church School room one day, ahead of his class. "Teacher, I've got a gang and
> we meet in a cave." "What do you do with your gang?" "I teach 'em to pray
> and to sing 'Jesus Loves Me,' another kid has a gang and he is teaching them to
> swear and to fight, but I won't let my gang do that."

The winning of immigrant children to Protestantism, part of the larger Americanization movement, was emphasized, particularly during the war. Only a
small percentage of the Froebel students were attending, about 25 percent,
but this was considered significant. And church officials argued that many of
the parents were afraid to sign the consent cards because they could not
understand English. "Many of them have come in tears to the church school
teachers to say that their parents would not sign the card; others have gone a
step farther and have said: 'My father said I could not come any more, but I
"snuk" away.'" According to the publicity, the church schools were a decided success in Gary; and by the end of the decade, because of Wirt's lead, it
was estimated that around 300,000 children nationwide were enrolled in
similar programs.[30]

Consensus existed in Gary regarding the church schools. On other issues
there was disagreement. There was some friction between Wirt and the
teachers, for example, when teachers began to organize in a labor union. The
superintendent attempted publicly to hold the middle ground in the ongoing
struggle between capital and labor, but his personal inclination was to closely
identify with the former. In addition to his various capital ventures, such as
ownership (with his brother Chester) of the National Bank of America, which
would increase during the next decade, he continued to depend on the steel
corporation's largess. Judge Gary doled out $10,000 to Wirt in 1916 to be
used at the superintendent's discretion; the grant paid the salaries of Alice
Barrows, Elsa Ueland, and Elisabeth Roemer, three special teachers in the
Emerson school, platoon-school promoter Dr. Edward Jewell in Fayetteville,
Arkansas, and various office expenses. Wirt assured the steel magnate,
"these arrangements which have been made possible by you will help tre-

mendously in furthering the work that we are trying to accomplish." Judge Gary's concern was fueled by the schools' seeming influence on the workers and their vocational bent. As he wrote to William Randolph Hearst, the powerful newspaper publisher, in introducing Wirt, "I have been very much interested in the schools at Gary because of their practical effect upon the boys and girls of our workmen and consequently upon the workmen themselves." Judge Gary's contribution was repeated in 1917, but when Wirt applied for a continuation of funds during 1918 he was turned down, for the chairman had more pressing interests. Nonetheless, Judge Gary's moral support continued. And the platoon system was adopted in schools on the Minnesota Iron Range, with the help of Assistant Superintendent Swartz (using Judge Gary's money), in communities dominated by the corporation. "It is believed here that steel men, having seen the value of the Gary schools, have recommended the adoption of the plan in Eveleth [Minnesota]," the *Gary Daily Tribune* reported in early 1916.[31]

Despite his capitalist inclinations and ties, Wirt relished his ability to attract labor's support. In some circles, the Flexner report's critical tone would be proof of the Gary Plan's democratic inclination; Upton Sinclair, the outspoken socialist, claimed that "the Rockefeller General Education Board is without doubt the most powerful single agency now engaged in keeping our schools subservient to special privilege." In New York City organized labor was generally hostile to the scheme, indeed the New York State Federation of Labor officially opposed the system, but in Gary the unions were supportive. To the charge from Charles Burns, secretary of the Long Island Building Trades, "that the Gary School League [in New York City] is partially financed by John D. Rockefeller, Morgan, Cleveland H. Dodge, and Geo. W. Perkins, and men of that type, who have accummulated [sic] their vast amount of wealth by exploiting labor," Gary union leader George Sheehan willingly responded that "the system is fair to Organized Labor to date."[32]

In early 1916, seemingly to offset the GEB survey, the American Federation of Labor (AFL) planned its own study. The Gary schools have "frequently been brought to the attention of organized labor, because the workers themselves are more vitally interested than are any other group of citizens," President Samuel Gompers informed Wirt. "The workers desire to secure the best kind of education for our children and we do not wish to take any official position upon so important a matter without having given it fullest consideration." The superintendent welcomed such an investigation, then paraded his own labor credentials: "I first became interested in the labor movement when at Redkey. I there met Mr. Gompers for the first time and saw a great deal of the labor troubles in the glass factories. I was a member of the American Federation of Labor while at Bluffton, Indiana, and have wished for a great many years that the American Federation of Labor would investigate our schools at Gary."[33]

Although inviting the study, Wirt was nonetheless troubled that his dealings with organized labor would be misconstrued or, perhaps, rankle Judge Gary. "While I appreciate the difficulty of securing an endorsement from the American Federation of Labor for a work that is especially credited to the United States Steel Corporation," he wrote to Judge Gary in trying to placate him, "yet I believe we have a fighting chance to secure a favorable report." There is no evidence that the AFL study was launched, but its promise caused mixed feelings for Wirt, who worked to obtain universal support. As he assured E. J. Buffington, president of the Illinois Steel Company (U.S. Steel), "it seems very difficult to have our work understood as a cooperative effort between the employees and the employers."[34]

Wirt welcomed labor backing, but had some difficulty in dealing with the formation of a teachers' union in his own backyard. The teachers organized a local federation in 1914, reorganized in mid-1915, and affiliated with the AFL after gaining Wirt's approval: "I am heartily in favor of organizations of teachers and it is entirely immaterial to me whether they are federated with National organizations, or not." Organization and affiliation he would publicly support, but not partisanship. "I would not hesitate to oppose any Federation of Teachers or any Affiliation if they were inimacal [sic] to the highest welfare of the public schools," he confided to one conservative correspondent in Chicago, then in the midst of a teachers' union–school board battle. "I think the principles of teachers alligning [sic] themselves with one element in society is unfortunate. . . . An affiliation with any one class of society for the selfish interest of the teachers as a group or of this one particular class of society is unfortunate and will eventually weaken the influence of teachers and labor representatives."[35]

In order to strengthen its hand, the Gary teachers' federation joined with three of Chicago's teacher unions and four other city federations in May 1916 to form the fledgling American Federation of Teachers (AFT), which quickly affiliated with the AFL. Anxious to cooperate with the superintendent—he was honored at a union dinner the following October—Local No. 4 nonetheless pursued an agenda designed to increase teacher benefits in various ways. Soon after affiliation, the federation asked the school board for a general wage increase; the board voted a compromise increment. Coincident with the board's vote, the federation was addressed by Margaret Haley, the flamboyant president of the Chicago Teachers' Federation then opposing the Gary Plan in Chicago, who announced "the entire school world is watching the Gary teachers fight for higher pay. . . . If the system is adopted in other schools, teachers everywhere will be interested in the salary paid in Gary." A year later, in April 1917, the union requested another raise, this time of 20 percent. After the outbreak of war prices increased; teachers were expected to contribute to the Red Cross, YMCA, and other patriotic organizations; the salaries of other workers rose; and teachers were lured to more lucrative positions. "There should be no occasion for saying that Gary seems to be able to 'go over the top' in everything but in the matter of paying her teachers a living wage," the union declared, using the new battle jargon. The school board complied, but again voted less than requested. At the end of the war the teachers returned to the well one more time because of the high cost of living, and once more received a small increase.[36]

The union's main goal was to increase wages, but there were other issues of concern. Individual grievances were taken up when necessary. In mid-1916, the federation questioned the long school day for teachers and recommended that any work from 3:30 P.M. to 5:00 P.M. be paid as overtime; extra duties, such as acting as an enumerator or visiting nurse, were to be curtailed in order to enhance teaching efficiency. On December 31, 1918, the union bitterly complained about having to work on New Year's Day in order to make up time lost in the fall because of the flu epidemic. And, during the next Thanksgiving holiday, paychecks were not issued because the state tax board ruled the city was broke. Within a few days the tax board allowed the city to issue $205,000 in bonds to raise money. The teachers, particularly through the union, constantly worked to protect their collective rights, increase their benefits, and gain some leverage with the school board. They maintained a professional identity, yet often acted as a labor union. Disagreements with Wirt and the school board were sporadic, but denoted a continuing clash of interests. George Sheehan, AFL leader in Gary, however, reported that the "teachers Federation in Gary has a membership of 160 [in September 1917] and other shop men and mechanics, even down to the laborers carry union cards," and asked how anyone could "honestly say the Gary Schools are unfair to organized labor." During the next decade the union would disintegrate.[37]

Part of the teachers' economic problems stemmed from the inflationary pressures of World War I, which also pulled some teachers to more lucrative jobs. More broadly, the nation's schools were recruited as the first line of defense to promote democracy, patriotism, and militarism among children as well as adults. Programs were initiated in Washington by the United States Commissioner of Education through curriculum revision, and the War Department through establishing military training in the schools. Mobilization was widespread. Wirt, despite his many commitments and distractions during these years, enlisted in the effort as a member of the state advisory committee of the Boys' Working Reserve, headed the city's War Savings Committee, and served briefly as chairman of the county Thrift Savings Campaign.[38]

Considering the war's impact on society, it is surprising that the public schools managed to conduct business without much disruption or alteration. One innovation was the introduction of military training. First discussed in the spring of 1916, nothing was done for a year. Then, on March 30, 1917, a few days before the declaration of war (April 2), boys at the Emerson high school met in the auditorium to hear from Lieutenants Ord and Conrad about establishing a military training corps. When the state board of education announced soon after that senior boys would be granted their diploma if they enlisted, Emerson's boys discussed forming their own company. Coach Jack Gilroy planned drill exercises with wooden guns. "The entire school is in a patriotic fevor. The discussions in English are all on the war and daily talks are given on the war in the different auditoriums. The students are called upon to voice their opinions and to the man they are all willing to fight. There have been several pacifists in the student body," the *Gary Tribune* announced, "but they are rapidly decreasing in number." Earlier, social worker Lillian Wald had asked Wirt to join with John Dewey, Max Eastman, and others to appear before the Senate Military Affairs Committee to work against universal military training because "the most modern spirit in Education must be represented." He declined.[39]

Boys enlisted and training continued, but a formal military course was delayed until September 1918 (the war ended in early November), when fifteen-hundred boys joined the program established as part of the physical culture department at the Emerson, Froebel, and Jefferson schools. Boys above the fourth grade were now eligible for training four hours a week, which replaced their gymnastic work. Wirt had doubts that military training was "a good thing for the boys personally," and earlier argued that the schools' physical-training program was sufficient. But he eventually succumbed. As he wrote to the War Department in early 1919, "at present our physical training teachers are doing work of this kind with wooden guns. The efficiency of this work can be increased very much by proper equipment and with the trained army officer in charge." The teachers also advocated hiring a regular army officer to professionalize the program. By the spring, boys in and beyond the second grade received some military training during their gym classes. Major Meade took over in early May, bringing a more regular army organization to the program, the war's legacy to the schools.[40]

Both day and evening students were involved in other war-related activities. School authorities supervised student gardening beginning in the summer of 1917, and a select group of "strapping boys" were selected to move to outlying farms, receiving a wage as well as free room and board. There is little evidence of the war's impact on the regular curriculum, but during the summer of 1918, in addition to gardening, students were enrolled in mathematics, telegraphy, and commercial courses, all considered valuable military skills.

Girls were heavily involved in Red Cross sewing. The summer night program, initiated in 1918, was more oriented to "help win the war," with an emphasis on shop and technical courses, as well as "soldier's French." Women were encouraged to attend, doing "their 'bit' for the 'boys over there' and for those who are preparing to go." There were soon commercial classes for women, fitting them to replace men in industrial jobs; the American Bridge Company (U.S. Steel) promised to hire all women who completed the courses. Time during the auditorium periods was devoted to presentations by the Red Cross, the Boys Working Reserve, the YMCA, and the Thrift Stamp Campaign. Schools were active in selling Thrift and War Savings stamps and Liberty Bonds. Teachers were busy securing bond and stamp subscriptions, as well as donating their time working at the draft boards, and even requested from the superintendent one hour during the day to allow for this work.[41]

Most important, the Americanization campaign with its emphasis on patriotism led to an attack on the teaching of German. "Gary's night schools are the best endorsement of how Gary stands on the war," the daily paper crowed in October 1917. "Since the schools were opened nearly a month ago, there has not been a single application from a person who wants to study German while the teachers are being overwhelmed with demands for French." By the following spring there was an undercurrent of pressure to eliminate German and "other class work considered 'pro-German' " from the day program. The school board, encouraged by Wirt, agreed in May 1918 to gradually faze out the teaching of German and substitute Spanish. Students currently enrolled would be allowed to finish. The superintendent also noted that "attempts had been made to criticise the Germans and their claims to superiority in order that students would be given the proper attitude toward the country." But he had to defend German teacher Mrs. Childs. Her parents had immigrated from Germany before the Civil War, and he had "not been able to find a single instance of pro-German sentiment promulgated or encouraged" by her. Certainly he would "not hesitate a moment to discharge any teacher who is not actively loyal in support of American interests."[42]

The Americanization program was central to the schools' mission and had taken a variety of forms. When the night program was cut short in the spring of 1915, the "foreigners of the south side, who have been learning the English language at Froebel school and who desire to continue this work" moved to the Neighborhood House for free day or evening classes. A citizens' club of five hundred foreigners, who were enrolled in the night program at Froebel, was formed to discuss American laws, problems, and customs over the summer; and during the closing ceremonies for the year there was a pageant of nations, climaxing in a "salute to the American flag and the chorus 'America' [which] brought a wave of patriotic cherring [sic] from the men and women of all nations in the audience."[43]

As American entry into war approached, the program went into high gear, encouraged by federal pressure. "Men of every nationality jammed the Froebel school auditorium to the doors last night to hear the program arranged by the schools at the request of the United States government, designed to encourage the naturalization and Americanization of the foreign speaking people in the country," the *Gary Tribune* happily announced in January 1917. They were treated to a rousing speech by Superintendent Wirt. Assistant Superintendent Swartz encouraged increased night-school attendance, currently over four thousand. School officials discussed adding to the evening program, offering more academic subjects to enable adults to obtain a high-school diploma, but concentrated on expanding the citizenship program. By September 1918, the course included "elementary English, letter writing, the history of the American flag, its government and presidents. . . . A feature of the course is the 'citizen's laboratory.' The idea of which is to have the students elect a community mayor, judges and all regularly elected officials. . . . The housewife is taught the ways of the American housekeeper, how to cook, feed her children and many other maternal duties." The program was free, supported by state and federal subsidies.[44]

The schools shared the city's adult Americanization effort with a variety of other community organizations. School authorities cooperated with the YMCA to conduct "community sings," using slides to teach patriotic as well as popular songs. The YMCA conducted its own English and citizenship classes, as did the Neighborhood House; the Welfare Committee of Illinois Steel ran its own night school, teaching technical subjects as well as English. And even the Knights of Columbus, eager to "combat socialism, bolshevism, and other outlawed principles and doctrines," would somehow become involved. Wirt and his colleagues running the other programs bragged about their effectiveness—in one letter he boasted of the immigrants' general quiesence during the 1919 steel strike—yet one critic noted their relative unpopularity. Only about one thousand, mostly immigrants, were enrolled in the public schools' evening courses in 1919 (which probably excluded those attending the auditorium programs and using the gyms and swimming pools), reported Estelle Sternberger, a strong proponent of Americanization, and the other programs were much smaller. Why? "The close and sympathetic interest with which the foreigner, in many instances, follows the developments across the sea undoubtedly engrosses his attention to the exclusion of any desire to accommodate himself to American institutions and interests," she argued. "We must also reckon with the general problem of illiteracy that prevails among many of the foreign groups. . . . They have not yet come to appreciate the benefits that come from educational opportunities, and so they are indifferent to any educational effort." Moreover, men were surely tired after working a twelve-hour day in the steel mill, while women were busy raising children and doing domestic chores. The Americanization thrust continued into 1919 because of the Red Scare, steel strike, and other disruptions that increased the nervousness among the school officials and the city's dominant class, despite their seemingly limited success.[45]

In addition to focusing on Americanization of adults, there were increased programs to indoctrinate the immigrant children in the schools. The summer program in 1918 "helps in the Americanization of this element and in the consequent unification of the city's forces and therefore of the nation's energies and morale, in two ways," Swartz announced.

First, by teaching the children of the alien peoples the things which they will carry home to their parents, tending to make them follow American ways of doing and thinking, and creating in them a love and patriotism of the land of their adoption. And then, too, the summer session helps to boil the 'melting pot' by actually coming in contact with the foreign born themselves. Not only with the aliens does this influence work, but as between the white and colored, between the low in social position and the high.

Swartz readily admitted that the children and their parents were divided by class, race, and ethnic differences, but could be united through continued interaction. And through the children, the adults could be melded—one ostensible goal of Americanization. Estelle Sternberger questioned the effectiveness of the program, but Wirt's and his subordinates' faith continued. The Froebel school was at the center of the effort, not only in the classrooms, but also in the swimming pools, at drinking fountains, and in lavatories, where the immigrant children were cleaned up and exposed to modern sanitation. "From kindergarten on through school, loyalty to our country and flag is taught without abatement. . . . When they leave school it is with a definite knowledge of what our country has given them, in opportunity, freedom and blessing which their parents were denied." And perhaps this was so.[46]

While the announced goals was to increase the "melting pot," the reality was continued class, ethnic, and racial divisions because of persisting religious and nationality identities, economic discrepancies, prejudices, and deliberate policies in the city to perpetuate school and neighborhood segregation. Particularly affected were the black children and their families. By 1915, all of the black children were attending the Froebel school, which was internally segregated; black children had their own teachers and were excluded from many activities, including shop work. A portable was erected at Twenty-first and Adams, somewhat south of Froebel, in September 1916 to accommodate two classes of sixteen black children. Representatives of the recently formed Gary Branch of the National Association for the Advancement of Colored People (NAACP) protested to the school board that the school "would cause race prejudice and that it looked like segragation [sic]. . . . [The students] were required to drink out of the same bucket, that the toilet there was unsanitary and that conditions there are very bad." Because of the protest, few children initially appeared. Wirt agreed about the poor conditions, pointed out they were no better at the Clark school, and promised something would be done. He also argued that the parents wanted a school closer to their homes and that they could always transfer their children back to Froebel. The superintendent willingly replied to a query from the NAACP's national office that the schools would continue their segregation. "No wonder the Gary schools are considered as models throughout the land," quipped the editor of *Crisis,* the NAACP journal.[47]

With the outbreak of war the black population of Gary rapidly increased, rising to over five thousand by 1920, with the number of children aged six to twenty-one going from 267 in 1916 to 1,125 in 1920, heightening friction in the Froebel school and neighborhood. A handful or more of white parents, expressing their feelings of being treated as second-class citizens, petitioned the school board in late 1917 to remove the black children from the school as "has been a customary rule in the past and is still practised in the schools of the north side." Nothing happened. Considerably more serious was a revolt among the white teachers, largely female, in March 1918. Led by J. W. Lester, forty-two of the fifty-four teachers petitioned Principal Charles S. Coons, recently appointed, complaining of "the frequent disturbances, innumerable cases of insubordination, and other ill effects of mixing the white and colored children." The black students, rapidly increasing in number, "now constitute a positive menace to the moral and physical welfare of both pupils and teachers." The petition contained eighteen separate complaints, ranging from the general to the most detailed:

> I object to colored children in classes, because of poor attendance, deficient work and resistance in cases of discipline.

> I find that it is dangerous to pass up and down stairs when a class of colored children are dismissed. They act like a pack of wild animals let loose.

> For the last year we have had many colored children enter the beginning first grade class of the Infant School. Many of them are over age, any where from eight to twelve years and have never been to school. I have found that many of the colored boys must be held in line by forceful means. They are a source of much trouble and confusion in the corridors. On one occasion a large colored boy attacked me with his fists when I ordered him to put in order a pile of books which he had disarranged.

> Upon asking a colored girl for the third time to be silent, her answer was, 'I won't.' Immediately I slapped her, and she returned the slap and refused to be quiet.

> The promiscuous association of the white and colored pupils is a terrible thing. It should not be allowed, particularly in a school with the large number of foreign pupils. They will soon lose sight of the color line.

Their complaints focused on disruptions often caused by overage black students, with limited skills and from rural backgrounds, mixing with immigrant white students who were either upset or becoming too friendly.[48]

Principal Coons dismissed the grievances, believing that the black children "with few exceptions are orderly and well behaved, but they probably have a feeling of being out of place, or more properly, distinctive, among so many white children. They readily sense any feeling of race hatred in [a] teacher." But in a letter to Wirt he admitted that, while in the previous year when asked by the superintendent he had rejected the notion of transferring the black students out of the school, "the time may now be at hand when it would be possible for the Board of Education to establish a separate school for these children." He admitted there were problems, perhaps because the Gary Plan created more mixing of students in various classes and activities; and many of the overaged black students were in the lower grades, increasing the teachers' burdens. Whatever the board's decision, he would "do everything possible to maintain harmony and to secure the best possible working conditions for these children, if left in this school." The matter was dropped, probably because there was nowhere to send the students.[49]

Assistant Superintendent Swartz publicly announced in July 1918 that "the Gary schools are doing more for the colored people, both children and adults, than is any other public school system in America," but he knew there were problems. The NAACP chapter continued to discuss school segregation; a mass meeting was held in September 1918 when information circulated that a new black school would open on the east side, amid the city's first all-black neighborhood being constructed by the Gary Land Company on Virginia Street. Swartz regretted in a memo to Wirt that the word was out, for "all manner of surmises, suspicions, and open charges have already gained circulation." But in a letter to J. E. McCoughtry, vice president of the NAACP, he stressed "that the Gary Schools are doing for the colored children what they are doing for the white children in providing school conditions near their homes." Black children and adults had the same use of their schools as did the whites. The issue was convenience, not segregation, "a question that has not been considered by the school authorities up to the present time, but which easily might be made an issue because of premature agitation." He hoped that McCoughtry "will heartily co-operate with the schools in their efforts to help the children in the day schools and to get out larger numbers of the colored people to the evening schools." The portable building opened the following January, on the corner of Maryland and Fifteenth, "a site that is accessible by their little ones without any track-crossing or automobile thoroughfares to cause apprehension." Enrollment jumped from thirty-five to ninety-four by September 1919 in the first eight grades.[50]

There were more difficulties. Conditions were poor at the Twenty-first Avenue school, and Swartz reported "they rightfully feel that in some respects they are neglected." There was no playground equipment; a shortage of supplies—stove pokers and shakers, coal scuttles, ink bottles and their stoppers, clocks—; lavatory facilities were inadequate; the kindergarten needed soft balls, gift beads with shoe strings, soap-bubble pipes and cups; the auditorium was barren; and there were sparse supplies for the cooking classes. The teachers were willing to buy a Victrola, if the school board ordered it. Most supplies were available, if requested, Wirt quickly responded. The auditorium was to be converted to a manual-training shop for boys, and another portable would be moved to the site from the Twenty-fourth Avenue school to serve as the auditorium. "We wish to do everything that we can for this school," the superintendent assured his subordinate, "and are very glad indeed to have our attention called to failure to provide supplies, etc." But he suspected the teachers did not know how to order supplies. Although severely overcrowded, over 250 students and growing, in September 1919 the school opened with "its regular study and recitation periods," the *Gary Tribune* reported. "The teachers are taking particular credit for this record as this is the colored school of that section and the students gave every assistance in getting down to work quickly." Cooperation was not enough. By December "the deplorable situation" necessitated renting the basement of a nearby black church to use as the auditorium, the school board furnishing the chairs and paying for the heat and janitor services; and Wirt promised "the room will not be used by us in any matter objectionable to your church authorities."[51]

Another difficulty, as the population mounted, was securing qualified black teachers. The four in 1917 increased to sixteen in 1920. Guy Wulfing, director of the industrial department, inquired of the county superintendent of schools regarding the propriety of hiring Cree Chiles, who had attended Tuskegee Institute for three years, as a manual-training teacher since he lacked a teacher's license. E. D. Simpson, the schools' first black teacher and principal of the new east-side school, projected in early 1919 that "the number of Colored Teachers has had a sudden growth and . . . there shall be a still larger force necessary to handle the many children in our schools." He was "anxious that each of these teachers shall acquit himself with credit; that he shall give to the children an Inspiration; to the patrons Service; and to the community a noble life." To that end he recommended that Wirt hire A. Velma Strickland, "an excellent young lady." Despite the difficulties, additional black teachers soon found themselves joining colleagues in the classrooms of the portables on the east side and Twenty-first Avenue, with a few remaining at Froebel. The schools were segregated, over protests, but nonetheless secured the support of the black population.[52]

The majority of children under sixteen—black and white, native and immigrant, rich and poor—continued to attend their neighborhood schools. But what of the few who shunned the classroom, for whatever reason, or got into trouble? They were still a problem. Attendance Officer W. P. Ray, a combination truant officer and social worker, died in mid-January 1915 and was replaced by J. B. Sleezer. In keeping track of the children and their home conditions he would be assisted by the teachers, who would each be assigned about twenty families to visit and continually monitor their needs; the teachers would also take part in the spring child census. "The attendance officer is no longer to be feared but is considered an advisor and an aid to the parents of school children," Wirt declared. In Ray's honor, the Ray Shoe Fund was started at the Froebel School in conjunction with a shoe-repair department. During the cold winter many poor children were unable to attend school because their parents could not afford to have their shoes repaired or buy new ones. School janitor Charlie Skolak, a trained cobbler, began repairing shoes on his own, then was appointed head of a new shoe-repair department. Supplies were purchased from contributions, and the children either did the work under Skolak's supervision or paid him from a loan from the Ray fund.[53]

After four months on the job, attendance officer Sleezer, personally insecure, issued his first report. There were 164 cases of truancy, relief and nonattendance that he recorded, and he had visited 595 homes, schools, and stores. He had directed relief cases to the Associated Charities, Neighborhood House, or Presbyterian Church, and happily reported that the Froebel shoe shop was making money as well as providing a valuable service. He had dealt infrequently with the county courts, preferring to turn delinquency cases over to the county probation officer or the Board of Children's Guardians. When Sleezer requested a raise in September, Wirt was critical and, in fact, argued that the position should be held by a woman who could more easily "go into the homes and teach the care of children and urge their attendance at school." He preferred to stress the social-work side of the position. But Sleezer stayed.[54]

In his June 1916 annual report, Sleezer noted that truancy seemed to be on the upswing. This was, perhaps, due to the zealous attendance work organized by Elisabeth Roemer. There were 291 reported cases of truancy. He responded to reports from individuals and haunted the streets and alleys. Certainly, "the indifference of parents, their desire to put their children to work, bad home conditions, imorality [sic], filth, and improper food, all of which are largely due to the drink habit, are causes of truancy which are always with us, and can only be eliminated by educational means and the strong arm of the law," he believed. But the schools were also to blame: the students were free to come and go during play period, and nonpayment of the book rental—Indiana public schools did not supply free texts—caused problems, discouraging pupils from attending. He wanted control over issuing work permits to keep track of employed children over fourteen and tried to keep boys under sixteen out of the bowling alleys. He had made two thousand visits during the year, mostly friendly, and "esteem[ed] greatly the friendship of the children who greet me with a nod and 'hello's' and rarely try to evade me." Eight boys had been brought to court for truancy, some others for various acts of delinquency, and eighteen parents for contributing to truancy. The GEB survey reported that in 1916 few children under fourteen were out of school, but the numbers climbed thereafter, with about half the fifteen-year-olds attending, but only about 30 percent of those aged sixteen. The figures were disturbing, but not unusual in the national context.[55]

When the attendance officer in May 1917 used his discretion in excusing the attendance of underage children to tend cows at home, Wirt reprimanded him. Although Sleezer was reappointed, the superintendent was also dissatisfied with his ability to corral truants: "I think the difficulty is largely due to too much lost motion by giving children probationary periods all along the line in place of classifying parents negligent concerning their childrens' attendance and going at the matter in a straightforward businesslike way and having them change their viewpoint of this matter." Sleezer agreed, with reservations. Without a car, he was unable to move very fast; besides, "everyone knows me and children often hide from me." Assistant Superintendent Swartz cruised the south side and west side in his car, however, rounding up truants and dropping most at the Froebel school. Sleezer could pick up children on the street, but could not take them out of their homes without parental consent or court order. He was reluctant to take the parents to the justice court because of the lengthy postponements, and if they were fined by the juvenile court, the fine was remitted under probation. But he was taking more parents to court, admitting to Wirt "I think perhaps I have been too easy and this reminder will help to correct this tendency." In his report the following month he noted "a marked improvement in the attendance." He had investigated 364 regular truancy reports as well as assorted others and brought in many children from the streets and alleys. He still complained about the play period, particularly at the Froebel school, suggesting that the younger children be under more strict supervision. A large number of parents had been taken to court, and eleven boys and one girl had been sentenced to various institutions as confirmed truants by the Juvenile Court. There were additional delinquency cases.[56]

The war increased some of the difficulties. Job opportunities attracted many children, and Sleezer reported that "children [are] employed in most of our leading stores without certificates and sometimes even under age and [I] have fixed them up, but have decided to take a more strenuous course in future, i.e. to prosecute all offenders." Not only were jobs available, but parents seemed to have less control over their children. Police Chief Glenn Rambo announced in April 1918 that the "war has had no effect in increasing crime among Gary's juvenile boys and girls," but truancy seemed to be on the rise. There was hope with the passage of the Keating-Owen Act in late 1916, which controlled the employment of children under sixteen, that child labor would be restricted. But the law was struck down by the Supreme Court two years later; "this relieves the school officials from administering the Compulsory Education Law in such a way as to conform to Federal requirements," State Superintendent Horace Ellis informed Wirt. "The schools should assist the employers in establishing the ages of children, in factories, but they are not really responsible for the children except during school days." Job opportunities, family values, and economic needs combined with reduced policing powers led to increased youth employment as the war wound down.[57]

Following the war's end and with the ensuing flu epidemic, which forced the closing of the schools, there was a push to increase attendance. "During the war there has been a tendency to evade the school law both by parents and employers," Sleezer publicly announced in January 1919. "In accordance with the recommendation of President Wilson and in compliance with the state primary school law, we shall endeavor to secure the attendance of all children at once. It is the duty of the parents not only to send their children to school but to see that they arrive there. . . . Proprietors of all stores, restaurants, laundries or other places employing children are warned to comply with the law and all cases of violations will be prosecuted without further notice." Within two weeks the local paper warned the public of the increased activity of the truant officer, with three recent convictions of fathers for truancy violations. Wirt secured a truck for Sleezer, for "so many children are out on the streets and it is practically impossible to pick them up in any [other] way." The superintendent also appointed a second truant officer, Miss Keziah Stright, to work with Sleezer, adding the needed woman's touch. Simultaneously, a "Stay in School" campaign was launched in the city.[58]

By spring the problem was still troubling. "Despite threatened prosecution parents are persisting in assisting the delinquency," the *Gary Tribune* reported in mid-April. "Where references were made to special cases it was found by the truancy officer, J. B. Sleezer, that in most instances the child was used in helping to support the family. Then there were others who, due to lack of clothing and shoes were literally detained from attendance—sometimes from 10 to 15 days." The township trustee, publicly responsible for helping the truly needy, provided some assistance to the poor, but not enough. School authorities and their allies tried both the carrot and stick approach to increase attendance, assisting those families in economic need and punishing those who were recalcitrant. To facilitate the latter, they desired to have the juvenile court moved to Gary. And in September a part-time school was opened for those employed students, perhaps nine hundred, aged fourteen to sixteen, whose work permit would mandate that they attend classes at least five hours a week; only 109 permits were actually issued in late 1918 (seventy-eight to boys, thirty-one to girls), down from 235 issued the previous year. They would have two hours of academic work (trade mathematics, English, citizenship, and trade science) in separate classes at the Binzenhof Hall, then go to Emerson or Froebel for vocational training. Thus, by decade's end a variety of programs and strategies were in place to increase the schools' hold over the city's children, at least those under sixteen, and possibly those older as well (and their parents). During the next decade they would have the desired effect, for a variety of reasons.[59]

Through the war years the schools' role in the community extended beyond capturing the bodies and minds of the young as well as their elders, coordinating activities among the various social service organizations, and attempting to increase community understanding—all of which continued the established trend that would stretch into succeeding decades and marked the schools' dominant role in society. "It is the earnest desire of the Gary school system to co-operate with the community in every way," the superintendent explained to the school board in early 1919. Soon thereafter, the city council announced its own investigation of the schools. Simultaneously, Coach Jack Gilroy organized a banquet for teachers and business leaders to allow them to become better acquainted. The Gary Commercial Club, sparked by the GEB report, planned its own study of the schools. And the superintendent began speaking throughout the community, beginning at the First Presbyterian Church: "This is the first time during his residence in Gary that he has ever honored the city with a talk on education, his life work," the *Gary Tribune* noted. "During the past year he has been able to spend more time in Gary, than at any other one time, and his presence here has helped much in all activities." Wirt was anxious to repair any damage done at home by the criticisms of the Flexner study, thus securing his base.[60]

Wirt championed the system as epitomizing the modern school program, and he had worked hard to keep it up-to-date. For example, the school board ordered 264 individual chair-desks in 1917 to begin to replace the fixed desks. "They are not fastened to the floor and allow for freedom of arrangement in the class room—the students can slide the chair anywhere he [sic] desires: of course, at the discretion of the teacher." A year later, a class for "subnormal children" was opened at the Froebel school, requiring a special teacher "to attempt to give them the help which they require." And in early 1919, Wirt wrote to the Division of Psychology in the War Department, requesting copies of the Alpha and Beta tests recently developed for army recruits, which paved the way for the greatly expanded use of IQ testing in public schools.[61]

While the schools represented education modernization in numerous ways, they remained materially deficient in many areas. Assistant Superintendents Klingensmith and Swartz prowled the schools, checking on both physical conditions and classroom activities and keeping Wirt minutely informed. The tiny Clarke Station and West Gary schools remained dirty and lacked adequate facilities and materials; other portables needed new roofs, playground equipment, and much else. When Marvin Fuller complained that his son had to use an outside toilet at the Glen Park School—a "dingy, dirty looking, repulsive . . . little building"—Industrial Education director Guy Wulfing responded that all but three of the schools (Emerson, Froebel, and Jefferson) had outside toilets. The father of four school children himself, Wulfing believed "it is a very fine thing for the children to be taken from the school room in to [sic] the open air as often as possible." There were continual organizational and other problems. Klingensmith complained in November 1916, "the grades in Froebel are greatly retarded and mostly so along about the second and third grades. Much of it comes from the frequent disruption of classes by putting in a considerable mass of pupils who cannot work with the class." Another difficulty was sporadic attendance. Klingensmith also worked hard to place teachers in the grades in which they were the most effective. Some, such as Helen Gorrey, were unsuited to the lower grades, because the students were "slow of speech, some of them almost drawling, and of a withdrawn, contemplative expression of countenance." Consequently, "the pupils become sluggish and heavy and seem not to have energy enough even for mischief." But Gorrey and others functioned better with older, more academic children. There was also much discussion and activity about attempting to place the children at the proper grade and ability level, where they could adequately perform. To better organize administrative responsibilities, in September 1918 Klingensmith was put in charge of supervising kindergarten through third grade and Swartz all grades above the fourth. Building principals worried about teacher and student behavior and the smooth running of the schools day and night.[62]

There had been considerable jurisdictional disputes, personality clashes, and backbiting between Swartz and Klingensmith and between them and Emerson principal E. A. Spaulding and Froebel principal Charles Coons over the years, and each complained to Wirt. The turmoil reached a head in July 1919. Wirt had sided with Swartz and demoted Klingensmith to his assistant, supervising instruction in the lower grades; and he informed Klingensmith, "I regret very much that I urged your re-employment at the last meeting of the Board of Education." Needing allies, Klingensmith promised to cooperate with Spaulding, hoping "to have this stigma removed." Next, she implored school board member Henry Hay to save her job and was appropriately subservient to Swartz, to little positive effect. She continued in her job, ever nervous about Swartz's criticism and Wirt's silence. She was fired in 1921. The infighting among top administrators surely caused some confusion among the teachers, who had little direct contact with the superintendent.[63]

In most matters Superintendent Wirt had ultimate authority, but occasionally higher powers would intervene, as occurred with funding problems or federal government intervention during the war. State power rarely intruded, as long as the schools followed the law. An issue emerged in late 1917, however, which caused some local grumbling. While there were high-school classes at both Emerson and Froebel, their athletic teams had been combined. Receiving complaints that this was illegal, the state high-school athletic association suspended the team from organized competition. Coach Gilroy officially protested, noting the small size of the high schools, particularly at Froebel, and the lack of a centralized high school because of the nature of the Gary Plan in erecting neighborhood unit schools. Local feelings ran high, but the teams were soon separated according to state mandate. However unique, the schools had to conform to some extent.

There were many distractions during the years 1915–1920—the GEB survey, national popularity, Wirt's public and private activities, the rise of the AFT, World War I, continuing segregation, economic problems—but the schools continued to operate, the teachers to teach, the students to learn, the parents to be involved, and the community to be concerned and proud. Below the rhetoric and publicity, the classrooms functioned, trying to connect the students with the outside world. "In my eighth grade English class, we studied the industries of the community which we could visit easily and used these as topics for composition work," Froebel teacher Nora Lockridge proudly informed Wirt, countering the criticisms of the Flexner report. "An example is a visit to the Pearl Laundry where a guide took us through the plant and explained the work to the class from the time the soiled clothes came in, until they were delivered to the homes. . . . Another time, later in the year, when Dr. Lawrence was starting a campaign on flies, we worked out an Auditorium program. The children visited alleys and made reports of conditions found there." Laundries and flies—these would remain in the students' minds long after Flexner was forgotten, Swartz and Klingensmith had moved on, and even after Wirt was in his grave. The next decade would underscore this point, as the schools faced internal and external pressures and changes. They would persist, however, in clinging to their central purpose—to offer a wide array of courses, facilities, and services to an increasing segment of the city's multiracial, multiethnic, class-structured population, within a basically stable social-economic-political system.[64]

IV

FLUSH TIMES, 1920–1930

Mrs. Staples and her five-year-old daughter YJean proudly entered the office of Longfellow/Roosevelt school principal J. W. Standley, near Twenty-fifth and Jackson in September 1927, anxious to get his permission for YJean to enter the first grade, rather than kindergarten. Her mother mentioned that she could already read and write, which little YJean readily demonstrated. Surprised and pleased, Standley admitted that she certainly qualified for the first grade and directed them across the sand dune to the all-black Roosevelt Annex school. YJean could not attend the mostly white Longfellow school, her mother was informed, because it would soon be closed. According to Standley, who was white, "your leaders have requested their own schools. This entire center will be for Negro children." Mrs. Staples was astonished, declaring that she had left the south because of segregation and was not about to accept it now. But she had no choice.[1]

The pride of the city and gaining popularity throughout the country, the Gary schools continued to be divided along racial lines, to the dismay of many black families. They epitomized in many ways modern urban schooling into the century's third decade—offering increasing programs and services, yet with different facilities and purposes, with some children and adults benefiting more than others, for a variety of reasons. Congeries of organizations, personalities, institutions, and power blocks somewhat influenced the schools, although Superintendent Wirt, strongly supported by the school board and the city's elite, generally kept his iron grip on the system.

During the twenties the school system was marked by stability as well as growth. As an example of the former, the school board until 1929 was controlled by holdovers A. R. McArthur, Henry Hay, and Adele Chase, except for three years when Harry Hall, a contractor and real estate operator, temporarily replaced Hay. They were comfortable working with the superintendent and the business community. Wirt settled into his role with increasing confidence and familiarity prepared to continue his tenure in Gary with little thought of moving on, while he expanded his business ventures and promoted the spread of the Platoon System nationally. His family life was not without its ups and downs, however. He married his young secretary Martha Ruth Jacques in July 1919 and his two youngest children remained at home. Franz, the oldest, attended college, then returned to Gary to work for his father in his various business ventures, such as managing the Franklin-Nash-Wirt Motor company and assisting in the surveying of Dune Acres, a six hundred tract along the lake shore east of Gary planned as an exclusive residential area. Wirt also formed a planning and construction company with William Ittner and A. P. Melton, both longtime colleagues, and continued as president (until 1929) of the National Bank of America, among whose directors was school board member Hay. His life took another twist in August 1926 with his divorce, due to incompatibility because of the thirty-year difference in their ages, according to the petition of Mrs. Wirt. One year later he remarried; he wed Mildred Harter, the auditorium director, who had been a Gary school employee since 1919.

The superintendent also plunged into civic activities, somewhat resembling his fictional contemporary George Babbitt. He was appointed to the city's new planning commission by Mayor W. F. Hodges in 1921, served as a director of the YMCA, and was a member of the council of the Gary Boy Scouts and (reluctantly) the state board of education, but he declined appointment as director of the Gary Chamber of Commerce. His old friend U. S. Lesh, Indiana attorney general, speaking before the Gary Rotary, compared Wirt favorably to Judge Gary: "Judge Gary typifies industry, while William A. Wirt typifies education. One represents capital; the other represents culture. Capital builds railroads and steel mills; culture builds school houses and parks and boulevards. They should go hand in hand, the speaker declared."[2]

Straddling the fence between public and private service, the superintendent increasingly stressed the schools' socializing and controlling role in the community. For example, he cautioned one Rotary official about the limitations of private agencies: "What I have in mind is that in the average city most of the public spirited citizens are giving a great amount of time and backing to all sorts of institutions and movements that are alright [sic] in themselves but can never do the work that the schools can do." Voluntary agencies, he argued, used most of their money for administrative costs, while the schools had considerably more funds for direct child work. Yet, "the very fact that so many other agencies are trying unsuccessfully to meet the leisure time problem of our young people makes it difficult for the only institution that can successfully meet these problems, the school, to actively enter the field." As an example, in the mid-1920s he encouraged the incorporation of the Boy Scouts into the school program, to be managed by Coach Gilroy. He stressed the school-home-church axis, because until "better schools, better teachers, better parents, more aggressive church leadership tackles [sic] the problem of youth's training, America cannot be builded [sic] upon a safe foundation. All other agencies but scratch the surface, and really get nowhere."[3]

Through numerous speeches and articles, Wirt continued to refine his concerns about the role and meaning of schooling and "flayed organizations seeking to reform the boy and girl, saying there are 60 such associations in the country doing more harm than good." Throughout the decade he spoke before various groups in the city, including the Central Christian Church, the school supervisors, Rotary Club, Elks Club, and at a 1928 meeting jointly sponsored by the Gary Women's Club, Rotary, Kiwanis, Optimists, and Lions, among others. He periodically addressed his fellow administrators at the annual meeting of the National Education Association (NEA), as well as other professional organizations—his contract, renewed in 1922, included permission to speak to educational groups throughout the country. And he published in professional journals. Over and over again, mixing nostalgia and hard-headed realism, he repeated his attack on the proliferating child-welfare service agencies and organizations, which were increasing threats to his power base. He lamented that "the three primary institutions, the home, church, and school, [are] without proper support because even their own salaried employees are drafted away from their real jobs where they might do something for children to give time and energy to well intentioned, but fruitless effort in fourth agencies." Emphasizing Gary's low level of delin-quency, he asserted that "it doesn't make any difference whether a city has Y.M.C.A. or Boy Scouts, etc. so far as juvenile crime is concerned, but the minute you get into towns where platoon schools have been functioning for some time, you find that the per cent of juvenile crime is cut in half." With the publication of the *Platoon School* magazine in 1927, launched by the Na-tional Association for the Study of the Platoon or Work-Study-Play School Organization, he had a ready-made forum for his views, and he generously used its pages.[4]

With or without Wirt's promotional activities, the work-study-play plan advanced during the decade, made attractive by its mix of financial efficiency and program expansion. There was much publicity, as well as organized activity. Starting slowly, only eight cities adopted the plan in 1920 and a few dozen others by 1925. But, twenty-eight adopted it in 1925 and were soon followed by another seventy-five or so; by 1929, 202 cities had over one thousand platoon schools. The system proved most popular in Michigan, Pennsylvania, New Jersey, Texas, and Alabama; the leading cities were Detroit and Pittsburgh. According to Roscoe Case, in *The Platoon School in America* (1931), "about two-thirds of the platoon schools in the United States were organized in order that a better educational program might be provided, while about one-third of the platoon schools were organized to save money or to relieve congestion." In his lengthy study, Case emphasizes that the platoon system was a plan of elementary-school organization and not a method of teaching. Following the Gary model, most cities divided instruc-tion into two categories: fundamentals—reading, arithmetic, writing, spell-ing, and history, etc.—and special subjects—art, music, physical education, auditorium, library, nature study, home economics, and manual arts. The students would move from activity to activity. Classroom hours, the range of activities, architectural styles, and other particulars varied from city to city, and the class scheduling could get quite complicated. Most important was the enriched curriculum and ability to deal with student differences. When the Milwaukee committee to study platoon schools queried 175 platoon school teachers in Pittsburgh, Akron, and Detroit, 167 responded that they preferred to teach in the new system.[5]

Publications about the platoon plan proliferated, with many focusing on the miracle in the steel city, "a flat, far-flung town, scattered over forty square miles. Blocks of vacant lots. Telegraph poles and trolley poles and electric-light poles. A dozen different languages on the sidewalks. At night the sky lurid with an angry glare from great blast furnaces: Gary, Ind. A rather sever [sic], heavy-set man, slightly past middle age, graying a little, with stubby-toed shoes. A level, noncommital eye, square jaw, and firm mouth, relieved at intervals by a quick, kindly smile: William A. Wirt, Superintendent of Schools." Praise came from many corners, as educators searched for promising concepts and programs. Carleton Washburne, the prominent superintendent of schools in Winnetka, Illinois, who stressed individualized instruction, praised the platoon plan for putting "additional emphasis on out-of-door work and shopwork and social gatherings. . . . It alternates mental and manual work, classroom work and shopwork. The monotony is broken. School becomes less of a prison and more of a playground."[6]

The platoon schools' biggest boost came from the United States Bureau of Education, spearheaded by Alice Barrows, who had joined the Bureau in 1918 after leaving Wirt's ill-fated New York City campaign. From 1922 to 1925 she organized platoon school conferences coincident with the winter meetings of the Department of Superintendence of the NEA. The conferences were designed for those already implementing the system or considering doing so, and were not to be forums for debate. In planning the second meeting, Commissioner of Education John Tigert informed Wirt that the interested superintendents "want *constructive suggestions* in regard to the organization of auditorium work, play and special work, detailed descriptions of how the public was educated on the plan, how building programs were carried out, etc." In preparation for the third meeting in 1924, which over five hundred attended, various committees were appointed to discuss the issues and make a report, thus establishing a more formal structure; later the Bureau issued bulletins on the subject. But Tigert emphasized, when informing Wirt about the 1925 conference, that the "Bureau of Education is not interested in promotion of, or propaganda for or against, the Work-study-play or Platoon plan." A platoon-schools conference was also held at Teachers College, Columbia University, during the 1924 summer session. Out of this increasing demand for information came the formation of a promotional association with the unwieldly name the National Association for the Study of the Platoon or Work-Study-Play School Organization in 1925.[7]

Wirt played little official role in the new organization aside from serving on the advisory council, but was very much involved in giving advice. Gary's Assistant Superintendent John G. Rossman became the first treasurer, Alice Barrows was secretary, and Gary administrators John Gilroy and Guy Wulfing were on the Executive Committee. Charles Spain, Deputy Superintendent of the Detroit schools, was president during the first year and leading platoon-school advocates held the other offices. It quickly attracted a membership of three thousand and had over four thousand within a year (334 were teachers in Gary), including individuals from Canada, England, and Holland. Its first conference was held in 1926. Spain had some reservations, fearing the organization might "savor of too much propaganda," but plunged in nevertheless. Various standing committees were appointed, involving many others in organizational matters. Discussions were initiated early about publishing a magazine, and the first issue of the quarterly *The Platoon School* appeared in January 1927, edited by Barrows, with Wirt's lead-off article "Creating a Child World." The superintendent was most pleased, writing Barrows in his usual laconic fashion, "I wish to congradulate [sic] you most hear[t]ily and to say that I am much more than delighted with the entire proposition." She was ecstatic, answering Wirt, "you, more than any one else in the world except perhaps Elsa [Ueland], know what it means to me to have a chance to try my hand at this magazine. And to know that *you* like it! Well, I am ready to go on now!"[8]

In early 1927, Barrows rented an office for the organization, secured better cooperation from the Bureau of Education to allow her to edit the magazine and publicize the work-study-play plan (Wirt's preferred term), and juggled the finances, including those involving memberships and advertisements. She increasingly relied on Wirt for support and advice. But by mid-year the commissioner was again limiting her outside activities: "I get less and less chance of advancement in the Bureau, and the conditions under which I work make it almost impossible to make a success of this magazine work which I care about more than anything else in the world." The magazine continued to appear, with articles on platoon schools in various cities, theoretical pieces, suggestions for auditorium programs, and other bits of practical information. Wirt was supportive, assuring Barrows "I have never had the slightest thought that the Work-Study-Play school movement could keep going without your help." When she became the Bureau's "School Building Expert," she was able to more directly advocate her ideas, particularly after platoon-school advocate W. John Cooper became commissioner of education in early 1929. She returned to Gary in March, "her annual pilgrimage," inspecting the new buildings and facilities and reporting on the continuing spread of the plan throughout the country. As the decade ended and the depression crept closer, there continued to be financial problems for the magazine; Wirt offered more advice, but cautioned Barrows "I am not in close touch with the situation outside of Gary." Still optimistic, Barrows wished Wirt a happy New Year—"I think as I look over all the new years of the past decade, the thing that has meant most to me has been my wonderful luck in meeting you and having the chance to work with you. *What would life have been without that?"*9

The enthusiastic support of the platoon system given by Barrows, prominent schoolmen throughout the country, and even the Bureau of Education and its widespread adoption marked the high point of Wirt's popularity and optimism. There was adequate vindication of his ideas and accomplishments in Gary. Simultaneously, however, there were dissenting voices, introducing a persistent sour note. The stigma of capitalist hegemony, personified by Judge Gary, clung to the plan. Some believed the system was suitable only in cities with large immigrant populations. Most controversial was the attempt at adaptation in Chicago advocated by newly appointed Superintendent William McAndrew. Previously an associate superintendent in New York City and strong supporter of the Gary Plan, McAndrew was eager to promote its implementation. Wirt, always sensitive, cautioned him upon his Chicago appointment in January 1924, "it is not wise for you to continue to use the name 'Gary System.' I have urged my friends in Chicago to not mention the 'Gary System' but to talk of the 'Detroit Platoon Plan' or the 'Pittsburgh Platoon Plan.' . . . Since it is not desirable in Chicago for you to associate yourself with anything under the name of the 'Gary System,' I expect to deny myself the very great pleasure of visiting you occasionally." But there could be no hiding the connection.[10]

Opposition to the Gary Plan was led by the Chicago Teachers' Federation (CTF) and the Chicago Federation of Labor, one of a number of their battles with the school board and school administration lasting over a decade. CTF spokesperson Margaret Haley later recalled, "educationally the platoon schools are frightfully destructive. Even under the best physical conditions, they are evil. The schools, which had been successful in Gary, a completely industrialized town, were being advocated in Chicago by the industrialists and their minions." In her article "The Factory System," in *The New Republic,* she remarked that "to a nation that is fed on machines, eats, drinks and sleeps by their assistance, the evils of this mechanicalized system of education, the platoon schools, are too subtle to be seen and understood. . . . They fail to recognize what the educator sees—the factory system carried into the public school, which needs only the closing-time whistle to make complete its identification with the great industrial plants." Upton Sinclair was even more extreme. Angered by the Chicago situation, he wrote in *The Goslings: A Study of the American Schools,* "when this new scheme has been set up in all our schools, big and little—and it won't take them but a few years—it will be possible for Judge Gary or Mr. [J. P.] Morgan to press a button at nine o'clock in the morning, and by twelve o'clock noon every child of our twenty-three million will be ready to go out and kill the 'Reds.' " Nonetheless, McAndrew continued the experiment in selected schools during his few years as superintendent.[11]

Somewhat distracted by the national publicity, Wirt nonetheless concentrated on the situation at home where the schools rapidly expanded and new programs were implemented, all part of the booster spirit of the decade. As the steel mill and other factories mushroomed and retail businesses proliferated, the city's population shot up from fifty-five thousand in 1920 to one hundred thousand ten years later, caused heavily by black and white migration from the South. The school population climbed accordingly, from about nine thousand at the beginning of the decade to about twenty-two thousand in 1930, over a 50 percent increase (compared to less than 25 percent nationally). The teaching staff more than doubled, reaching 615, and numerous administrators were added. Most impressive was the high-school enrollment, increasing from eight hundred to about forty-five hundred, with over five hundred (three-fifths girls) graduating in 1930.[12]

With the schools continually overflowing and new neighborhoods springing up throughout the city, there was a pressing demand during the decade for additional buildings, both large and small. Extensive construction, long postponed, was not begun until 1922 when the Jefferson school was finally paid off. Under a new plan smaller brick buildings, with a capacity of eight hundred and designed to be enlarged as necessary, were erected at various locations throughout the city, in addition to new portables. The new school on the east side in a predominantly Polish neighborhood was named after Casimir Pulaski, a Polish patriot. Finally opened in 1923, the Horace Mann building was erected on the north side, the (Albert) Beveridge school on the west side, the (Theodore) Roosevelt school at Twenty-fifth and Jackson, and another farther south in the Glen Park neighborhood, correcting the overcrowding and promoting greater efficiency. Additional construction at both old and new sites continued throughout the decade. There were nineteen separate schools by 1929, ranging from the Froebel and Emerson schools with about three thousand day pupils each, Horace Mann with a slightly smaller student body, down to the three hundred students at the Riley school and the twenty-seven at still tiny Clarke school. The work-study-play system—an enriched elementary curriculum with the platoon organizational structure—was in place in all except the smallest buildings.[13]

Despite overcrowded buildings, school officials continued to worry about truancy and keeping older students in high school. Under state law, children under fourteen could not be employed except in farm or domestic work; those between fourteen and sixteen could not work more than forty-eight hours a week, only during the daytime, and must have passed the eighth grade; females between sixteen and eighteen could not work more than sixty hours a week. Offending employers could be fined. Children between fourteen and sixteen were required to obtain a work permit and to attend the public continuation school at least four hours a week during working hours. Originally in the Binzenhof, all continuation classes were moved to Emerson and Froebel in early 1920. In his report for 1920–21, Attendance Officer J. B.

Sleezer believed "the attendance at Continuation School has been all that could have been expected," but cautioned that work permits should not be issued without meeting the requirements. Of the 241 enrolled in February 1921, most of the girls worked as domestics or in sales, with others scattered in laundries, restaurants, and other small businesses; the boys served as delivery boys, store clerks, messengers, factory helpers, and in a variety of capacities in shops and offices. Because of federal law and company policies, the steel mills and other large factories did not employ children. Over half worked for financial reasons, others because of choice, health reasons, or dislike of school. In general, truancy seemed high, however, because of economic problems—working mothers, lack of shoes and clothing, boys doing farm work. Thirty-seven children (thirty-one boys, six girls) were brought to court with their parents for truancy, with seven boys sent to state reformatories—Plymouth, White's Institute, Plainfield, or the Girls' School. Sleezer made 2,465 visits. "The laws for working children were always hard to understand and now with the radical changes will have to be *pounded* into people again," he complained.[14]

Economic problems continued through 1921, but as conditions improved so did attendance, according to Sleezer's next report. He publicized the more restrictive attendance laws, now mandating that children fourteen to seventeen had to have work permits and attend the continuation school; those under sixteen, the compulsory attendance age, had to be brought to school by their parents, if necessary. His patience wearing thin, Sleezer reported "now that conditions have changed and all should know the law I shall make much fewer visits before ordering to court." At that, he had brought thirty-five cases to the juvenile court. But parents still had difficulty understanding the tighter rules. D. G. Madera was fined $10 for keeping his son home to protest the rule that children had to either eat lunch at school or go directly home for the noon meal. Many had apparently been stopping at ice cream parlors and stores, "encouraged in bad habits by unscrupulous merchants, who sold pupils cigarets [sic] and allowed them to gamble in their places. The pupils also often purchased unwholesome food." Young Madera had been caught in a store near the Emerson school by Principal Spaulding. In another case, Helen Wassel, not quite sixteen, forced to stay at home to take care of younger siblings because her mother worked and the father was in the "insane asylum," was ordered to attend the continuation school.[15]

In his June 1923 report, Sleezer believed conditions continued to improve, after making 3,438 visits during the year. He advised that parents should be made more responsible for their children's attendance. Keziah Stright, Sleezer's colleague, complained that many cases of delinquency and truancy were handled by the police and never reported to the attendance officers, causing confusion. Another problem was that the juvenile court was held in Crown Point, a few miles south of the city. Both Sleezer and the local paper argued that a court in Gary would help considerably: "Within a few years the child problem has grown to be one of the biggest problems in this county. Indeed, we dare go further and say it is the biggest problem this county must solve," editorialized the *Gary Post-Tribune*. If the court were in Gary, the judge would "quickly learn the facts about parents and environment that create the child problem. Then he would be in a position to go to the root of the evil." Particularly troublesome were the recently arrived black and immigrant parents, who still seemed unaware of the school and work laws.[16]

Neither truancy nor delinquency were particularly serious problems, but they continued to cause concern. School and civic authorities believed the basic answer centered on the family working with the school. At a meeting of school officials with the city police matrons in late 1923, "the various causes of delinquency were discussed and attention was called to the importance of good food, sufficient clothing, the right home life and their bearing on the conduct of the child." Still, school officials took credit for the apparent low delinquency rate. Certainly the vast majority under sixteen were in school, but even most of those from sixteen to twenty-one were connected with the day schools, night schools, the continuation school, or were attending college, leaving only about 12 percent beyond the long reach of the educational establishment. "It is in this way that the boys and girls of the community are kept away from the crime school of the street and alley," Assistant Superintendent John Rossman boasted in 1925. "A rather extraordinary substantiation of this claim is that in the criminal court records of both the city and the county less than five per cent of the Gary entries are names of Gary boys and girls under twenty-one years of age." So, whatever success was due to the schools, the failures were attributed to the families. As Keziah Stright argued the next year, "the parents are very much to blame. . . . More delinquency and petty crimes of the young boys and girls . . . are the results of keeping late hours, roaming the streets . . . or lax morals on the part of the parents." And, of course, there was the curse of idleness, the street time so feared by Wirt.[17]

Schooling was generally designed for children under eighteen, but in Gary (and other industrial centers) there was strong encouragement for adults to make use of school facilities. Night enrollment grew from ten thousand in 1921 to over sixteen thousand by the decade's end, at one point (1922–23) surpassing the day enrollment by a few hundred. Moreover, beginning in March 1920, the day continuation school at the Binzenhof was used only by adults (the children having been transferred to the Emerson and Froebel schools), with classes in commercial work (shorthand, typing, bookkeeping), millinery, dressmaking, and home decoration, as well as in business English—classes designed especially for women. As the enrollment grew, classes were also held at the YMCA and public library. By mid-decade the enrollment was over three thousand, with most in the vocational classes, followed by English for immigrants, and a few taking other academic subjects.

Most adults, however, crowded into the night-school programs. As the decade began, Assistant Superintendent Swartz, former coordinator of night programs, reported that "as a whole the evening schools have gone to pieces. . . . An occasional class is still alive and comparatively prosperous, but the figures clearly show that the number of cases of this kind is not sufficient to affect the result as a whole." The movie, social, and physical programs, except for women, seemed to be healthy, but the academic classes were poorly attended. He accused night school director Arthur Smith (who soon resigned) and someone from the YMCA of conducting Americanization classes in pool halls on the south side, mixing religion with the course work, and offering other classes in private homes. All classes should be conducted in the public schools, he believed. Moreover, some teachers were not qualified, there was a lack of adequate supervision, and children were to be encouraged to accompany their parents, as had previously been the case. There was also competition from the educational programs of the steel mill, YMCA, International Institute, and even the Knights of Columbus. [18]

Swartz returned as night-school director and quickly worked to turn the program around. He prodded the principals, particularly Coons of Froebel and Spaulding of Emerson, to promote the classes; the former reported about announcements during Wednesday evening auditorium meetings as well as about notices sent through the Boy Scouts about the English classes. Meeting with business leaders and the directors of private organizations, which had their own adult classes at the Commercial Club, in September 1921, Swartz was able to get their commitment to support the public schools' program, "the backbone of Gary's fight against the ills of unemployment." The poor could learn manual skills, cooking, thrift, plus be kept busy. "It was a revelation, the speakers said, to hear of the things accomplished in the classes of the schools. The articles the adults can make by giving a little time to night school work, curtailling [sic] their expenses thereby." Very popular were the weekly auditorium nights at the schools, which featured movies; one evening the Froebel program included "one reel of Americanization, two reels of animal studies, a two reel comedy . . . and an animated cartoon," plus "Goldilocks and the Three Bears" for the children. With the return of prosperity, emphasis focused on the vocational and academic classes at twelve school centers (twenty by 1929) throughout the city. [19]

The community was enrolled in the cause. A Citizens' Evening School Committee, a blue ribbon group chaired by W. P. Gleason, superintendent of U.S. Steel's Gary Works, was established, and each school principal was encouraged to organize a neighborhood citizens' committee. Members visited the evening schools and hopefully gave their support. Although the *Gary Post-Tribune* noted that ten thousand attended night classes in 1922 and another twenty-five thousand used the showers, playgrounds, and auditoriums, this was not enough. New classes were continually introduced, such as a sales course for chain-store clerks (at the Woolworth and Mc-

Clelland stores) and another for prospective bankers. Courses ranged from elementary reading, writing, and arithmetic to history and government, a variety of academic and commercial courses, as well as manual training— machine shops and foundries, auto mechanics, cabinetmaking, and drafting for men, millinery, sewing, cooking, home decoration, china painting, basketry, and knitting for women. Social activities included piano recitals, radio concerts, dances, parties, class exhibits, plays, and club meetings; the physical-training program was extensive. Generally,the physical-training and vocational classes enrolled the bulk of the students, about eighty percent. Adult education director Albert Fertsch reported to the NEA meeting in 1928, the multifaceted program "makes provision for the cultivation and stimulation of intellectual interests, not for a few years only, but as a permanent, necessary and inspirational aspect of citizenship." And a few received their high-school diplomas.[20]

Most important were the programs at the Froebel school, the only evening center offering classes five nights a week by 1929, rather than the usual two or three, because of the Americanization effort. "It is my personal opinion that the Americanization work done in the public night schools of Gary is by far the most important phase of our work," Wirt wrote early in the decade. "Of course, the [Americanization] workers outside of the public schools would probably not endorse this opinion. But I am not able to see how large groups can be reached in any other way." Gary's elite, having survived the 1919 labor uprising and fear of radicalism, rededicated themselves to the campaign. Both society and the individual would prosper. "An alien who comes to enjoy the privileges of America and who persistently refuses or neglects to learn the language and is trimmed by sharpers deserves no more sympathy than the man who got fooled at the grand opera," the *Gary Tribune* editorialized in early 1921. "Thousands of aliens in Gary are already using them [the night schools] and are reaping a deserved reward in being readily accepted as a first-class citizen by all Americans. Those who do not show enough interest to learn the language and customs of their own accord cannot expect to enjoy the privileges their more energetic fellows receive." Stressing patriotism, the schools also shielded the immigrants from any exposure to radical ideas. A meeting for the relief of "Soviet Russia" scheduled for a Sunday afternoon at the Froebel school was cancelled because "the school auditoriums could not be used for any sort of Bolsheviki propaganda."[21]

Two years later F. J. Broche, assistant educational director of the Federal Bureau of Naturalization, gave the seventeen English classes in the program, five at Froebel, his blessing. Director Albert Fertsch worked diligently to expand the work by adding new courses, seeking students, and welcoming instructional materials from patriotic organizations. In the spring of 1924, over nine hundred students received certificates of attendance, with another two hundred accepting government diplomas for completing the required advanced courses. There were now twenty English classes. When immigrants applied for their first citizenship papers, the Department of Labor invited them to enroll in the schools' English and citizenship classes. "The romance of Americanization is being written in Gary night schools this year in 25 classes of English and government which are attended by 753 students in 12 educational centers," the local paper announced in November 1927. Assistance was provided by various patriotic organizations. A reprint of Lincoln's Gettysburg Address was distributed to the students by the Women's Relief Corps, an auxiliary of the Grand Army of the Republic (GAR), and Wirt welcomed the American Legion's donation of equipment to show the patriotic "Chronicles of America" film series. While proud of the schools' Americanization effort, Wirt was aware that only a fraction of the city's immigrants were enrolled. Certainly, others were attending classes at the various settlement houses, YMCA, the International Institute, and other private organizations. But it is doubtful that a large number was involved. Despite the strenuous efforts of Wirt, Fertsch, and the other Americanizers, a strong current of pluralism (but not anti-Americanism) continued in the steel city. The immigrants were considerably more interested in using the swimming pools and gyms, taking vocational courses, and attending the auditorium programs, which had a heavy patriotic content.[22]

"In essence the [night-school] system is manipulated to provide an educational opportunity for all persons from the unlettered to the graduate of a university." Wirt believed the schools should offer programs for students of all ages and levels of ability and training, from the illiterate to high-school graduates, who were encouraged to continue their education. In 1918 Assistant Superintendent Swartz had bragged that a majority of the latter continued their schooling in normal schools, colleges, technical schools, or universities. But to do so, they had to leave home. Beginning in 1919, Wirt explored the possibility of Indiana University (IU) offering an extension program in the city, paid for by the school board. Implementation of this plan was postponed, but the university established a teachers-training school for night-school teachers who were unfamiliar with "the pedagogy of adult instruction."[23]

Convinced by Wirt of its need, in October 1921 IU began its extension program by offering four university courses at the Jefferson night school—sociology, educational psychology, English composition, and advanced English—taught by professors from Chicago. College credit was granted to those with a high-school diploma, and there was a nominal charge. Any course would be taught if at least twenty students enrolled. The Lions club soon organized its own psychology class, but allowed others to attend. Occasionally prominent professors from Chicago were involved, such as the sociologist Frederick Thrasher, who offered a course in modern social problems. As more Gary students began attending college outside the city, a total of almost 150 in September 1922 (two-thirds graduates of Emerson), Wirt began advocating the construction of a separate university building in the city, possibly a state normal college to serve the county—a dream frustrated by the state legislature's refusal to pass a funding bill and a ruling by the state superintendent that "it would be strictly illegal to establish a separate school, known as a Junior College for the training of any group or groups of individuals."[24]

Extension enrollment edged upward, with 304 attending twelve courses in early 1923. A wide range of courses was offered, including American history, real estate, Spanish, vocational psychology, industrial arts, and dramatic arts. A full two-year program was begun in September sponsored by IU, with additional courses offered by Purdue University, including "Heat Treatment of Iron and Steel" and industrial teacher training. High-school graduates, teachers, and business people enrolled in the academic courses as well as in salesmanship, public speaking, and journalism. Enrollment reached 559 in 1925, with classes now offered at the YMCA, the public library, as well as the Jefferson and Froebel schools. By 1927 students could get full credit for the first two years of normal school work, allowing them to teach, fulfill the requirements for the first semester of Purdue's engineering degree, or complete their degree after having taken the first two years at another college. In order to broaden the appeal, courses were continually added, including one on pets of the Victorian era. Until the end of the decade the extension enrollment hovered around five hundred, allowing many in the city the opportunity to obtain college credits while saving money, living at home, and working locally. While not as independent or extensive as Wirt envisioned, the program remained a vital part of his cradle-to-grave concept of community schooling and promoted the flowering of higher education during the decade.[25]

Educational expansion was only one aspect of the booster spirit so pervasive at the time which infused the school programs and their community supporters. Strong backing continued to come from the city's business and corporate leadership. The Gary Commercial Club, the right arm of U.S. Steel, in September 1921 voted to establish a committee (which later included two representatives from the Gary Woman's Club) to investigate the schools and to collect information as well as grievances from citizens and school officials alike. Six months later, the committee's report included substantial praise for the Wirt system, encouraged closer ties between parents and school authorities, and waxed enthusiastic over the night program. "We believe the school authorities here are endeavoring to conduct the schools along the line of meeting the requirements of an industrial city like Gary," it laconically concluded.[26]

Indeed, throughout the decade businesses happily paid their school taxes and believed the schools were serving their needs—synonymous with the community's needs. U.S. Steel even attempted a pale copy of the schools' program for its employees, arguing that "the work-study-play ideal of the Gary schools could well be adopted by all men as a standard by which to live." Workers were encouraged to work hard, attend evening classes in the mill, and join the Gary Works Athletic Association. And the schools reciprocated. Following on the heels of the Commercial Club report, the schools organized an educational week with exhibits in the storefronts along Broadway in the heart of the business district. Over eight thousand students participated. "In some windows one found a group of students doing mechanical drawing, in another a history lesson, in another demonstrating as living pictures the stories in the classics read in the English classes." When Judge Gary arrived the next month for one of his rare visits, the Emerson students "waved flags, recited the creed and cheered the founder of Gary." The three thousand Froebel students "recited the creed in unison," while five hundred black children at the Virginia Street park "cheered the visitor and sang the songs so dear to their race and color. Judge Gary was visibly impressed," the local paper reported.[27]

Harold Detrick, Froebel class valedictorian, in 1920 spoke to his eighteen fellow graduates and their families on the topic of teamwork, suggesting "that the profiteers and laborers get together in the spirit of teamwork used in the high school games." He had struck the right chord. Cooperation was the order of the day in the schools and throughout society. Wirt, an educational capitalist—"probably the most important single industry in Gary is that of educating the children of this community. The manager of this great industry is William E. [sic] Wirt," the *Post-Tribune* editorialized in 1925—sought a harmonious relationship with his laborers, the teachers, and in this succeeded. As the decade opened, the teachers' union, American Federation of Teachers (AFT) Local No. 4, petitioned the school board for a raise and quickly gained new members. "Teachers here feel that their petition is not receiving prompt attention, said an instructor. . . .'I remember,' this teacher said, 'that when the painters in the vocational department of the schools asked [for] an increase in salary, it was at first denied them. However, a ten-minute strike brought them the desired increase.'" Supported by Wirt and the local power structure, and without a strike, the teachers soon received their raise.[28]

The teachers' union limped along for a few more years with hardly an outcry, paralleling the slump of the national parent union, then virtually disappeared. There were apparently few issues or complaints. In January 1922, the union was concerned that the teachers were not paid for Christmas Day. And a year later, just before its demise,the union presented a petition to Wirt asking for a vacation between the end of regular classes and the start of summer school. When the school board changed the method of rating teachers, which controlled and limited salary increases, there was no outcry; Froebel principal Charles Coons warned Wirt, however, "it seems to me you are headed for a lot of trouble when you arbitrarily limit the number of teachers who can get into the upper group to 25% of the teaching force." The decade's economic prosperity provided a sufficient tax base, but the teachers were divided among themselves and at the mercy of the administrators for their annual raises. Abandoning any idea of identifying with labor, they now fully embraced an alliance with capital (not that the two were particularly incompatible). At a general meeting in late 1923 the teachers were addressed by Gary Rotary president A. M. Fisher and A. H. Keller of International Harvester, who emphasized the business orientation of the schools.[29]

Nationally, organized labor supported the platoon plan, although it was opposed in some cities, such as Chicago. After studying the platoon system in its own city in 1924, the Detroit Federation of Labor found the plan excelled in health, efficiency, flexibility, training for citizenship, and lower costs and that the schools were not "factorized and militarized." The American Federation of Labor (AFL), having earlier abandoned its study of the Gary schools, continued to be interested in Wirt and his system. In early 1925, Mathew Woll, chairman of the AFL Committee on Education, in an "effort to realize Labor's educational program" asked Wirt to submit his definition of education. The superintendent happily obliged, assuring Woll "the public school belongs to labor more than to any other group. Also it will only be through the active efforts of labor that the public schools can be brought to perform their mission." His definition was short and direct: "Education for all of our children through good books and teachers supplemented by real experiences in school shops, laboratories, studios, and playgrounds." The Committee on Education also began a study of the platoon plan. At the AFL convention later in the year an attempt to pass a resolution supporting the system was defeated by Chicago's labor leaders, but a neutral statement was adopted until more information could be collected. Four years later Wirt, still in the union's good graces, was asked by union president William Green to review a book on the community uses of schools for the *American Federationist,* which he readily accepted. The superintendent always sought support from labor as well as capital and easily obtained it during this period of cooperation.[30]

The 1920s were a decade of growth and continuity, when the schools extended and elaborated upon earlier structures, thereby reinforcing the status quo. Part of the process was to continue segregated facilities. Segregation, fueled by rampant white racism and reinforced by a separationist strain within the black community, was barely challenged by black integrationists and their few white allies. The number of black children (aged six to twenty-one) shot up from eleven hundred in 1920 to over four thousand ten years later, about 15 percent of the total child census; those attending school increased from 634 to 2,759 in 1930, over 90 percent of all black children between the ages of seven and seventeen, and were initially concentrated in the Froebel school and the two small all-black schools. Black teachers increased from fourteen to over eighty at the end of the decade; virtually all taught in the black schools.[31]

Segregation was a controversial issue within the black community. When in

January 1921 a committee from the (black) Odd Fellows' lodge countered charges that two community stalwarts, Dr. James Garnett and the Reverend Charles Hawkins, supported segregated schools, John H. Smith wrote the local paper defending separation. "I am sorry to hear that my friends, Dr. Garnett and Rev. Hawkins, were not instrumental in bringing about colored schools in Gary as well as they were in colored banks and colored churches to be controlled and operated by colored people and for the benefit of colored people," Smith argued, summarizing a position most forcefully articulated by Marcus Garvey and the Universal Negro Improvement Association (UNIA). Recently founded, the UNIA chapter in Gary was a strong voice for racial pride and voluntary separation, particularly as the population grew. The National Association for the Advancement of Colored People (NAACP), racially mixed and strongly integrationist, still existed, but had a feeble voice. When Dean William Pickens, associate field secretary for the NAACP, visited the city to promote integration a few months later, the *Gary Tribune* pointed with pride to the "statements of Superintendent Wirt . . . and Capt. H. S. Norton of the Gary Land company on what has already been done for the advancement of colored people in Gary." Battle lines, although fuzzy, were now drawn—between black separationists, black integrationists, and the white power structure eager to defend benign segregation.[32]

Strongly committed to improved schooling for their children, the black community continued to demand good facilities and teachers. For example, in the spring of 1921 one parent complained of the "fighting, thieving, vulgarity and general roughness" at the Twenty-first Avenue school. Part of the problem was the removal of longtime teacher Elizabeth Lytle. After the Twenty-first Avenue portables were moved a few blocks south and west, to Twenty-third and Harrison (adjoining the white elementary school on Twenty-fifth Avenue), a "Peoples' Committee," composed of black professionals, complained to Wirt and the school board of various discriminatory practices—arbitrarily transferring black pupils from the Froebel school to the segregated and inferior Virginia Street and Twenty-third Avenue schools and putting black students in vocational classes. But when seventy-five black teachers, attending summer school at the University of Chicago, toured the schools in July, Swartz assured them "we recognize no difference in race, color, or creed, and we at all times put extra effort forth to meet the needs of our young people."[33]

Segregation took various shapes and forms. The "Colored YMCA" began offering night classes, the first in business and salesmanship, for those "whose needs are not met in the public night schools." There was a separate "colored center" at Froebel on Monday and Thursday nights. The evening program at the Virginia Street school offered shorthand, sewing, woodwork, reading, arithmetic, gymnasium, and lamp-shade making. School personnel stressed manual training for black day pupils, and to further this end a trade school was opened at the Twenty-fifth Avenue school center. Boys were taught the building trades and constructed a four-room building, and the girls learned home economics. The white students seemingly did not prefer racial segregation—a Chamber of Commerce poll among high school students in 1922 found only one-third wanted segregation, perhaps because most were not particularly threatened by the presence of only sixty-eight black students out of a total high school enrollment of 1,035 in November—but they got it anyway.[34]

The NAACP chapter pursued its assault on the segregated facilities, which continued when the separate white and black schools near Twenty-fifth Avenue were combined under one white principal in 1923, the former named the Roosevelt school, the latter the Roosevelt Annex. Lewis Campbell, former NAACP secretary, attempted to go over Wirt's head by submitting a petition to Benjamin Burris, state superintendent, complaining about "unsatisfactory school conditions," and met with state school officials shortly thereafter. Black children were academically behind, he argued, and short of textbooks because of the "gross neglect" of school administrators. The local paper scoffed that most of the signatures on the petition were of school children. And state officials referred Campbell back to Wirt. The next year, 1924, activist black attorney W. C. Hueston complained to Wirt that when black children were turned away from the heavily Polish Pulaski school and sent to the Virginia Street school, the "new coming Americans" were educated "in an incorrect way as to their attitude toward my race." Besides, while many in the black community might choose to send their children to the all-black Virginia Street school, as did Hueston, "it is the pride of the Negroes here that we do not, at least in policy, have a separate school system." Wirt rejoined, "in order to prevent serious race conditions in the schools it is the policy to offer, if possible, opportunities for determined individuals to escape conditions that conflict seriously with their prejudices. We have, therefore, one separate school for whites [Pulaski], two for colored [Virginia Street and Roosevelt Annex], and fifteen for both." That is, most schools drew from the surrounding neighborhood, but most neighborhoods had no (or very few) black residents. Wirt took no credit, or blame, for the prevailing segregation.[35]

Campbell was also writing to the NAACP national office, fearing the establishment of a separate black high school. In response, James Weldon Johnson reminded local president T. J. Wilson, "there is a seemingly general campaign at this time towards the establishment of segregated high schools in our northern cities. This campaign our branches must consistently oppose." As the rumor continued into 1925, Walter White, national executive secretary, wrote William Smith, Gary NAACP recording secretary, "it is quite certain that you have a situation which must be met for it is almost inevitable that you will suffer complete segregation of all colored schools unless the present attempt is defeated." Then, two years later, the anticipated happened, but came from an unexpected source.[36]

In the fall of 1927, the black students were divided among several schools. There was a large concentration at the Froebel school (about one thousand), fifteen hundred at the brick Roosevelt Annex (including one hundred in the secondary grades), two hundred at the adjoining Roosevelt and Longfellow schools, and another 750 at the Virginia Street school. There were also six black students in the upper grades at the Emerson school. Because of limited high-school facilities at the Virginia Street school, eighteen black students were transferred by the administration to the north-side school at the start of classes in September. On Monday, September 26, more than six hundred white Emerson students walked out of school to protest the presence of the additional black students. After two-thirds returned to the classrooms, about two hundred paraded through the streets, "painting signs on sidewalks and buildings which read, in substance: 'We won't go back until Emerson's white.'" School officials threatened the remaining strikers with expulsion. But the next day eight hundred were out, despite Wirt's stand that "there can be no segregation of white and colored students in Emerson school this year, next year and perhaps never." Possibly when a new black school was erected on the east side, Emerson would be again segregated, he hinted, but it would have to be equal to the white schools according to state law.[37]

On Wednesday, September 28, about half of the twenty-eight hundred students were out, including three-fourths of the high-school students. Mass rallies were held in the school auditorium and at the local park. Black council-man A. B. Whitlock later argued that the strikers "were of the poorer element, not far removed from serfdom," who were influenced by "ignorant parents" and had limited contact with blacks. Strike support seemed considerably more widespread, however. By Friday a settlement was reached and the strike was called off. No students were punished, all except three of the black students, who were seniors, were transferred out (but not immediately), and a new black school was planned at Twenty-fifth and Georgia, first some portables followed by a permanent high-school center. Resolution came when the city council, at the mayor's urging and despite opposition from the three black councilmen, appropriated $15,000 for construction of the portables. School officials seem to have been slightly involved in the settlement.[38]

During the strike the NAACP national office, pleased with Wirt's position, sent him a telegram stating, "we trust that no amount of mob bluster and bluff will budge you from the position which you have taken." The local black community quickly united in its opposition to the strike. A mass meeting was held and a petition circulated declaring the action of the mayor and city council "discriminatory, un-American, prejudicial, unfair and unjust," and certainly unconstitutional. Support came from around the country, including offers of money and legal talent. "Granting that it is Gary's business whether or not it should segregate well-behaved Negro students in its schools," ran an editorial in the *Chicago Daily News,* "it is nevertheless a matter for national concern that the governing body of a municipality has permitted itself to be dictated to by school pupils who take the high hand and lay down the law to their teachers and the agencies of local government. Surely any further spread of contempt for duly constituted authority presages evil for this country, the historic upholder of democratic ideals."[39]

Summarizing the press response, an article in *School and Society* noted that "the northern papers naturally enough view this incident as a surrender to prejudice, and fear that it may lead to similar action in other communities above the Mason and Dixon line." Southern papers, on the other hand, "adopt an attitude of friendly interest in the attempt of the North to grapple with a problem that they themselves have settled, so far as settlement is possible, by segregation of the two races." Blame was heaped on the Ku Klux Klan and prejudiced parents. But G. Victor Cools, also writing in *School and Society,* believed "the Gary situation is the direct result of the demand for and the acceptance of segregated schools by the southern blacks. . . . They are reaping with bitterness what they so thoughtlessly sowed."[40]

Far from taking credit for the strike and subsequent settlement, the black community led by the NAACP brought suit against the city council. The sum of $15,000 was thought to be too little to build a proper school and, besides, the city government could not spend money on school matters. When Porter County Judge Grant Crumpacker issued a temporary injunction in mid-November, *The Sun,* representing the UNIA chapter, was jubilant: "In its both righteous and indignant war on segregation Gary's colored population triumphed again. . . . The erection of a pigsty, which is to be misnamed for a school, somewhere in no-man's land is to wait." With the prodding of Mayor Floyd Williams, the council rescinded its motion to raise the $15,000, which was illegal; the case was then dismissed. The school board continued to plan a four-room school on the east side, in addition to a large black high school in the central district south of the Froebel school. "Never before in any crisis that has arisen in the 'steel city' have negroes been so united," announced the *Gary Colored American,* voice of the NAACP. "Never before in the history of segregation in America has the public been so consistently bitter in its criticism against a great wrong, such as the plan proposed, by the city and the school board, but defeated by the race, aided by its true Caucasian friends."[41]

The NAACP tried working with the superintendent to improve school conditions, particularly the high-school offerings for black children. After a meeting with Wirt in mid-December, attorney Edward Bacoyn informed the national office that he was not anxious to remove the black students from Emerson, but was pushing ahead with plans to erect the portable on the east side. "I've got the goods on this man Wirt," Bacoyn reported, "he is as clever as they come and as cunning as they make them. This is my own way of saying that there is nothing to him. I am convinced he has no more idea of giving the school children a square deal than he has of going to heaven without prayer." Optimistic, he recommended that the NAACP should lead the fight to prevent the new segregated portable, but "no attempt should be made to stop the erection [of] the shack until it is about completed. It would enable us to make a better case."[42]

A new issue, and a second law suit, emerged in January 1928 after Wirt finally transferred eight black high-school students to the Virginia Street school. According to Bacoyn, the school "has inferior equipment, no library, no laboratories, a dump heap, which, Mr. Wirt himself admits, should have been condemned and torn down, four or five years ago." The parents of Alberta and Earline Cheeks and Alberteen Marsh, representing all of those transferred, filed suit (in four different courts) to have their daughters reinstated at Emerson. Wirt, having escaped criticism during the strike, was now the target of the attack. In addition to the "general atmosphere of squalor" at the Virginia Street school, neither French nor Spanish were taught, and the boys and girls were forced to use the gym together, which was "not only improper and revolting, but . . . would affect the sense of decency of any person." Rumors circulated that Froebel's black students, along with sympathetic whites, would stage a sympathy strike. The *Gary Colored American* announced it "has obtained documentary evidence revealing startling conditions in the school system, which it may publish next week for the benefit of those who wish to know the truth—quick—of the Gary school situation." Citing the provision for separate but equal schools in the 1877 Indiana law, which defined segregated schooling throughout most of the state, the paper stated that if the parents "allow the school city of Gary and Superintendent Wirt to deprive them of their legal rights by relegating them to the sewer of the school system, then they might as well give up the good fight for equality of opportunity, forget the Emancipation Proclamation, and spend the rest of the years in 'come day, go day. God send Sunday' fashion."[43]

The case dragged on until the fall of 1928, when Judge Crumpacker ruled that the school-city had legally transferred the black students out of the Emerson school because the Virginia Street school, as an extension of the Froebel high school, was a separate but equal facility. The NAACP then appealed to the state Supreme Court, where they finally lost in 1931. Meanwhile, three of the black girls, given free transportation, were attending high school in Chicago. When prospects seemed dim in July 1928, the NAACP attorneys came under attack. Soon, however, conditions brightened when the school board decided to demolish the Virginia Street school and move the students to better facilities adjoining the Pulaski school. "I am writing to report that the local situation in regard to school matters show very distinct signs of improvement," attorney Bacoyn wrote the national NAACP office in August.[44]

The black community was united in opposing forced segregation and in criticizing the shabby Virginia Street school until it was demolished and reincarnated as East Pulaski, but at the same time it demonstrated pride in having its own schools, teachers, and administrators. Virginia school principal H. Theo Tatum epitomized the mixture of racial pride and integrationist principles. Raised in Beaumont, Texas, Tatum received his BA from Wiley College and a MA from Teachers College, Columbia; he had taught in the Hampton College Summer School and at McDonough High School in New Orleans before arriving in Gary in 1925. Upon his appointment to principal, "straightway every department of the school was galvanized into action and began working to capacity," as he later wrote. He worked to instill pride in the students through "the organization of 'Good Citizens Clubs' in a number of register rooms, the stimulation of inter-class competition, the organization and operation of a Student Self-Government Council, and the enlisting of student help and participation wherever appropriate." Teachers were closely supervised, and parents were encouraged to visit the school and join the Parent-Teacher association, he reported in 1927.[45]

Attendance increased the next year to about eight hundred, particularly in the junior-high grades, which Tatum attributed to the addition of new courses in commercial work, Latin, Spanish and orchestra—probably resulting from the Emerson strike,. An adjustment class was added for "the atypical child or the child who needs special coaching," which was separate from the two classes for "mentally retarded pupils." He mentioned, somewhat apologetically, the need for a new building because of public pressure; "However puerile and artificial may seem the attitude of the parent in this matter, it does have its unwelcome effect on the pupil. Aside from the fact of the actual inconveniences encountered, the constant invidious comparisons of his school environment serves to weaken materially in the child, the attitude bases for loyalty, pride, self-respect and wholehearted cooperation." Then he added in his report to Wirt in June 1928, two months before the building was torn down, "no specific suggestion is made in this connection because the superior wisdom of the school authorities most probably anticipated and analyzed this problem long before this tardy presentation is made." He optimistically concluded, perhaps surprisingly in light of public criticisms of the school, "it may be truthfully stated that there is a real and definite progress being made in the work at Virginia School. Despite certain obvious handicaps, the main objectives of instructional activity are being realized."[46]

Tatum, characteristically, was anxious to please the superintendent, but he also represented pride within the black community. Teachers were the backbone of the community's middle class and occupied one of the few professional careers open to blacks, particularly women. "Too much importance can hardly be attached to the part played both individually and collectively by Gary's colored school teachers," editorialized the *Gary American* in September 1928. "Those who condemn separate schools for Negro children and who seek to criticize Negro school teachers as a whole should ponder for a moment and they would see . . . that the community would be a dead and prosaic place were it not for the altruistic interests of our teachers here in our social, religious and educational welfare." It was obvious that black teachers could only teach black students in all-black schools. There were only three black teachers at the Froebel school, in charge of "ungraded, unfortunate children,—children over age, unkempt *[sic]*, with lice in their heads, from the south who need getting adjusted." Many in the black community, even NAACP members, thus accepted separate schools as cornerstones of power and prestige. But as the Reverend A. C. Bailey, president of the local NAACP, was reminded by the national office, "the Association does not recognize the right of the school city to segregate Negro children no matter how excellent the accommodations for Negro children are. This is the crux of the entire Gary school case and is the principle for which we are fighting."[47]

Countering the NAACP's position was the separationist stance of the UNIA, personified by Frederick C. McFarlane. Born in the Virgin Islands, he was schooled in Denmark, returned to teach in the Virgin Islands, attended Teachers College as a fellow of the General Education Board, then arrived in Gary in 1927, and was soon principal of the two buildings of the Roosevelt Annex school (with over sixteen hundred students in 1929), now independent from the adjoining (white) Roosevelt school. "His philosophy for educating the Negro child was simple," according to his friend Jacob Reddix: "The public schools are already segregated throughout the nation. Would it not be better to have good black schools, completely segregated for the present, than to sit in the back of white classes, or to attend segregated classes in a white school?" In separate schools "Negro children could develop dignity, pride, and self-respect." Despite a rather small membership through most of the 1920s, the UNIA had a strong presence in the black community, educational leadership, and a voice through *The Sun*. During the Emerson strike controversy the paper lauded the Virginia school, "despite its inferior facilities . . . the very essence and symbol of this remarkable scholastic organization." It reserved its highest praise for the Roosevelt Annex school, which with thirteen hundred students was "one of the most active and creative in the Gary system," and had "the most elaborate form of student government of any school in the country." The Square Deal club supervised most of the extra-curricular activities, including a student detective agency which arrested school-law breakers, who were tried before a student court. In praising the Gary schools' "world wide reputation for scholarly efficiency and the progressive use of modern educational methods," the paper singled out "the colored school teacher [as] an indispensible part of this splendid system."[48]

By the end of the decade the city's black citizens were forced to accept, willingly or not, predominantly segregated schools. They extracted as much solace as possible from the situation. But some incidents, such as the Emerson strike, were particularly galling. In June 1929, the black students at the Froebel school (little noted in the black press), having protested segre-

gated social activities, attempted to have an integrated dance for the graduating seniors, but the principal and the white teachers kept the white students
out, according to the *Gary American*. Some of the black students complained
that the paper was too critical of the school principal. The editor rejoined:
"The young high school boys and girls who promoted a jim-crow school
prom after being flattered by their white teachers will have something to be
ashamed of in [the] after life should they make any progress in the affairs of
the world. . . . We want the high school students to enjoy themselves, but if
it necessitates official discrimination and segregation for them to do so, we
are opposed." Integration was an elusive reality in the steel city's famous
schools. Some fought the system, others preferred separation with dignity,
but the power lay with the superintendent and school board. Segregation was
the order of the day, soon to take on more visual form with the erection of a
grand all-black unit school on the south side.[49]

Just as Wirt maintained the separation of the races, hoping to satisfy both
whites and blacks, he also continued the weekday church schools so as to
draw a thin line between schooling and religion. Balance was his watchword.
Having begun before World War I and soon adopted nationally, the program
of released time for religious instruction was well established in Gary by
1920. The Board of Religious Instruction supervised a network of teachers
and facilities; there were also separate Catholic, Lutheran, and Jewish week-
day classes. If the public schools could not teach religion, Wirt also believed
that the full-time parochial schools should not offer secular education. "I am
convinced that when public schools are re-organized to give the churches
every opportunity for week-day religious instruction that the churches will
voluntarily abandon the effort to control the secular education of their
children," he wrote in 1920. "The leaders of the parochial schools may not
favor the transfer of their secular instruction to the public schools, but their
people will force this change." Anxious to extend the public schools' reach,
Wirt indeed had little to worry about. The scattered parochial schools—
German Catholic, Irish Catholic, Polish Catholic, Lithuanian Catholic,
Slovak Catholic, Croatian Catholic, Hungarian Catholic, and German
Lutheran—only attracted about 15 percent of the city's students.[50]

Through mid-decade the part-time church schools accommodated a
healthy number of students, mainly immigrants. Director Mary Abernethy
reported an enrollment of thirty-seven hundred in 1923, with almost half
attending no other church or Sunday school. The children provided food and
clothing for the needy in Gary and sent contributions to Near East Relief and
the Japanese relief fund, indicating "that the Church School is trying to teach
good citizenship, neighborliness, and world friendship as well as to give
instruction in the Bible, in morals and right conduct." Funding came from the
parent bodies of the participating denominations, local industries—"because
they will reap the benefits in more reliable, trustworthy employees"—and the
parents. Almost five thousand students were enrolled in 1926, then the

population began to decline because of funding problems. The depression severely crippled the program, reducing the faculty, shortening the length of the terms, and limiting instruction to four schools at a time.[51]

In 1931 for financial reasons the classes were also moved to the public schools. "The Wirt [reorganization] plan places church school classes on the same footing with other courses offered in the public schools curriculum," the *Gary Post-Tribune* reported. "The pupil does not have to forfeit a play period in order to attend classes. The church school board of education, however, still has full charge of the teaching staff and preparation of the curriculum." This appeared to be a break with past policy, for Wirt had always insisted that the schools could not directly become involved with religious matters, but the dividing line had never been rigidly maintained. Assistant Superintendent Swartz reported to the superintendent in 1923 that a few teachers in the Ambridge school opened the morning with a prayer. Seemingly an uncommon practice, he concluded that "this report is not submitted in any critical sense but merely by way of information for which you may possibly have some use." There is no record of Wirt's response. A few months later Wirt granted permission for Abernethy to use space in the newly erected Horace Mann portable for the neighborhood church's school, surely a break with past practice. And a few of the smaller schools were used for Presbyterian Sunday-school services by the Gary Neighborhood House. Two years later, during the Scopes trial in Dayton, Tennessee, Wirt announced that evolution would not be taught in the schools—but "that's not a confession that the heads of the city's public schools are aligned with William Jennings Bryan and his Tennessee fundamentalists," the local paper cautioned its readers. "It's a declaration, if you please, that the Gary schools are conducted on a tolerant basis, not guided by the rigid rules of an extremist of either sort, fundamentalist or evolutionist." But evolution as a scientific theory was offered in the high-school science classes.[52]

The line between church and school was growing thinner. But it still remained in November 1926, when Assistant Superintendent John Rossman reminded the teachers of school policy:

> The subject of Christmas should not be taken as a basis for work the weeks preceding that holiday; but a reasonable number of simple Christmas songs, stories, and games not involving the religious element, may be used. Also, some handwork, that might be classified as Christman handwork, may be done if it is not to the exclusion of other manual activities. There should not be a Christmas tree or a Christmas party.
>
> Room decorations should not be exclusively Christmas decorations. The governing idea should be common sense acceptance and use of the children's interest without using it to the exclusion of all other interests.

Wirt desired to broaden the schools' role in the community as much as possible, even into religious affairs. But in the 1920s limits remained. All were still not pleased, however. Gary Klan No. 123 of the Knights of the Ku Klux Klan protested school holidays on Good Friday and Easter Monday in 1927, obviously Catholic celebrations.[53]

Despite his numerous concerns and activities in public and private life, Wirt always returned to his first love, the schools' classes and programs. The heart of the work-study-play system was, after all, the child's school day connected to the larger world. Ties between school and society were many and varied. The ROTC program was continued, for example, because "of unquestioned great value in the moral and physical development of our students," as the superintendent wrote in defense of the program. "Also it is by far our best Americanization agency." The boys were learning the prime values of order and obedience. "They are ceasing to 'hesitate,' the besetting sin of Young America," the *Gary Tribune* added. Good citizenship was also promoted through installing savings machines in the schools, begun at Emerson in 1922. Students would insert their pennies, nickles, dimes, and quarters "instead of spending them foolishly, as is usually done." They received savings stamps in return, pasted the stamps on cards, and once the cards were full they were deposited in the students' accounts at Wirt's National Bank of America. Cash prizes were awarded to those with the most savings. Connecting frugality, patriotism, and capitalism marked the decade. A sign of the schools' success was the participation of thousands of students in the 1923 Loyalty Day parade—"fifty different nationalities and races were included in the parade but all were Americans. They were young Americans of the type that are not influenced by May Day uprisings of Communists, that believe America is a land with a constitution and law and freedom. . . . The Froebel school contingent particularly was alive with pep, banners and enthusiasm."[54]

Early in the decade there was considerable emphasis on the practical side of the students' education, that is, the connection between school and work. "Many parents do not know of the opportunities offered their children in the Gary schools for learning a trade," noted the local paper. "There are several hundred boys and girls in the trade and vocational classes at Froebel school." Learning the rudiments of a trade in the schools gave the students a general knowledge "to aid in counteracting the tendency mechanical operations connected with modern industrial work have of deadening the mental alertness and appreciation of its workers." During Boy's Week in May 1923, a Boy's Day in industry was initiated, with the boys visiting the city's plants and factories. Part of the purpose was "to demonstrate to the boy the necessity for being not only well educated but also for being trained for the work he expects to follow throughout his life." For boys, work was life; for girls, work was the step before marriage. The paper boasted that over four thousand pupils were receiving vocational training, almost twice the number than in the much larger Indianapolis school system. "Co-operation of tradesmen and mechanics, business men and leaders of finance in Gary has always been accorded the departments in the Gary school system where an obvious ideal of service has always been the motivating spirit," according to Wirt. "The need for men who will work with their hands rather than for more to rush into the overflowing tide of youth headed for the 'white collar' jobs was recognized here 20 years ago." With industrial jobs plentiful, although hardly lucrative, many boys, particularly from the immigrant and black neighborhoods, were naturally attracted to blue-collar work. This was expected by their family, and there was little choice. Few boys, however, learned much of practical consequence in school, most dropping out when possible, while the girls' clerical program continued to be a steppingstone to the store and office.[55]

While vocational work remained important, it took a different twist from that of earlier years. Originally, the students not only learned manual skills, but applied them in practical and economical ways. Working with union craftsmen, the boys built and repaired school furniture, painted the walls, and fixed the equipment. By mid-decade, however, licensed teachers had replaced the unionized workers, who always had difficulty receiving certification. Little practical work was now done by the students, except in the cabinet and printing shops at Emerson. "The rapid growth of our school enrollment forced each year a larger number of pupils into these special shops," vocational director Guy Wulfing explained to Wirt. "Since these shop rooms were necessarily small with a small amount of equipment and larger classes had to be taken care of it was practically impossible to continue such shops on a productive basis." Wirt's belief in learning by doing had to take a back seat to the practical matters of certification and overcrowding.[56]

As initially conceived, vocational education was designed to accomplish many purposes, including attracting students who lacked a scholarly bent. This goal was reinforced during the 1920s because of the emphasis on individualized education. "In theory and practice the Gary school system both academically and vocationally has been made to fit the needs of the student rather than making the student fit the needs of an inflexible system." There were other, newer means of reaching this goal, and they were pursued by the efficiency-minded new Assistant Superintendent John G. Rossman. Appointed to replace G. W. Swartz in July 1923, who temporarily continued to direct the night school, Rossman was no stranger to the platoon plan, having worked in the system in Little Rock, Arkansas. Overflowing with energy and suggestions, he soon began flooding the teachers', principals', and supervisors' mail with informative bulletins.[57]

Beginning with the question, "How can we better meet the needs of each pupil?," the first teachers' bulletin in September 1924 included many questions and comments concerning enhancing individual abilities as well as organizational information. Principals and supervisors were soon asked to consider why so many children failed, particularly in certain schools—

Horace Mann, Ambridge, Miller, Roosevelt, and Roosevelt Annex. "Some one may be inclined to state that this is due to a particular localty [i.e., black neighborhood] but look at your diagram again. No one can offer much evidence that Virginia Street pupils are decidedly superior to those of Roosevelt Annex and yet the Annex failed practically three times as many as did Virginia Street." There was also little correlation between standard test scores and grades. The high failure rate, 19 percent, appeared to be due to a combination of student problems, particularly poor attendance, and teacher idiosyncrasies. Rossman's suggested answer: more uniform grading according to student differences and organized in average, slow, and strong groups. "All of us know that the psychology attending achievement and possible success is a very different one in its reactions than that attending failure and attempting the hopeless," he concluded, using the latest educational theory. "I have yet to hear of a case where an intelligent distribution of marks was undertaken conscientiously by the teachers, which has been attended with failure or the lowering of standards." No more than 10 percent of the students should fail. The following spring Rossman congratulated the teachers for conducting their classes "on the small group or individual basis," yet there were still too many failures.[58]

With the start of the new semester in September 1925, there was "increased attention to the individual needs of the student," as the local paper proudly informed the community. A significant change was the substitution of letter grades for the traditional practice of grading by percentages; "the change is made in accord with the general educational tendency toward more individualized instruction. It will place students more upon a separate basis than under the old percentage method." Moreover, promotions were now more by subject than grade level, and deportment would not influence the scholastic grade, but would be recorded separately. Intelligence tests were used, but the scores were only "highly suggestive," and were "not regarded as satisfactory evidence of probable success or of determining how best the child may learn." "It has become palpably absurd to expect to achieve uniform results from uniform assignments, made to a class of widely differing individuals," according to Winnetka's progressive superintendent Carleton Washburne. "Throughout the educational world there has therefore awakened a desire to find some way of adapting schools to the differing individuals who attend them." Rossman and Wirt could not agree more. The new grading system was not a magic formula for enhancing learning and reducing failures, but was to work in conjunction with increased teacher effectiveness. Responding to the question that limiting failures to 10 percent might lower standards, Rossman informed teachers that "it is a question of method in teaching, subject matter presentation and the meeting of the needs of the individual." The burden was now on the teachers to prevent loafing. All would profit by the new system, including the taxpayers, for "each pupil that is failed adds that much to the tax burden and the housing needs of the school district. Failure further deprives society of the earning powers of that particular individual, either in terms of time or unfitness." Of course, most significant was "the effect upon the child's life," but financial and social concerns had to be considered.[59]

There were various other innovations to "help" individual students. A three-hour class for non-English-speaking students over eleven, with twenty-five attending in September 1925, was established at Froebel—eleven Mexican children, five Polish, two Romanian Jews, and others from Serbia, Greece, Germany, Italy, and Russia. The next year students new to the Gary system were placed in adjustment rooms for a few weeks; "the adjustment rooms will not be for abnormal cases, disciplinary problems or special coaching work . . . school officials point out." Mentally handicapped students were filling twenty separate classes by 1928, where they would receive academic work; for nature study, music, auditorium and other special subjects they mixed with the regular pupils.[60]

If new students had problems, so did the new teachers. To facilitate their adjustment, a teacher-training department was begun in 1926. "It seems that many of these new teachers are attacked with pedological illness upon entering the schoolroom and the doses of theory and practice which have been administered through the normal or training school fails to operate satisfactorily," training director Stella Miles reported in June 1927. Six new teachers were closely monitored, given assistance, and evaluated. Of the seventeen teachers in the program since its inception, ten were considered fair and average, one was doubtful, and the others left. This program, similar to those for students, exemplified the schools' emphasis on teamwork— "creative accomplishment for each pupil, straight thinking by teacher and pupil alike were among the objectives stressed by both Mr. Wirt and Mr. Rossman. 'Our teachers, in the vast majority, have assimilated this tenet of the system and have the attitude that they are forming a team with their pupils, with the teacher as captain, to strive for everything that reacts to the welfare of the student body and which harmonizes with the objectives of the system,' " Wirt announced the following year.[61]

Some of the basic themes came together in the expanding summer-school program. Summer attendance, equalling about 50 percent of the winter enrollment by mid-decade, attracted students to academic, vocational, and recreational activities for a variety of reasons—to make up failed academic work, to take advanced classes in order to graduate early, or just to keep busy and off the streets. Rossman emphasized the efficiency side of the program, easily paying for itself by getting the students through school quicker. "Looked at in the larger sense this cost in dollars and cents is a mere bagatelle compared with the gain on the part of pupils from the standpoint of meaning that they can complete school at an earlier time, that they can begin their earning activities sooner, and that they have gained materially in the matter of self respect and the spirit of 'I can'," the Assistant

Superintendent significantly added. "And with it all there has been offered to boys and girls a very constructive occupation in a wholesome environment." By the end of the decade the shop work was curtailed in order "to obtain summer employment for as many youths in these departments as possible," but enrollment remained high in the academic courses. Efficiency and student/parent interest fueled the popularity of the summer program through the decade. Economic factors would soon curtail many programs, however, including the summer offerings.[62]

Night and day, winter and summer, Monday through Saturday, including children as well as adults, secular and religious work, educational and social activities—the school program was ever expanding into the lives of Gary's citizens. One additional example will illustrate the point. Long concerned about students' and teachers' health, the schools medical department reached optimal size by 1928 with two doctors, eight nurses, two dentists, three hygienists, one eye-specialist teacher, and one oral/deaf teacher. Students were inspected by a nurse at the beginning of each school year, and all suspicious cases were referred to the doctors. They were checked for infectious diseases, vision and hearing problems, and nits. Perhaps most serious were the students' dental problems. Health education was taught in the auditorium and nature-study classes, in addition to the work of the physical-education department. Children received free dental work, a sight-saving class was established at the Jefferson school, and special hearing classes existed at various schools. Healthy children, the community's responsibility, were assumed to be better students.[63]

In June 1929 Assistant Superintendent Rossman resigned to become superintendent in neighboring East Chicago. Wirt decided to leave the position unfilled and instead to increase the responsibilities of the nine area supervisors (auditorium, vocational, arts and sciences, welfare and attendance, libraries, kindergarten and primary, geography and history, math and commercial subjects, and teacher training), as well as assuming more authority himself. Experts from other cities would also be invited as consultants. The superintendent, in tune with the decade's dominant ethos, never ceased to improve school programs and conditions, searching for richness as well as efficiency. And to many he had succeeded. "With a population of 120,000, [Gary] has in its public schools 20,000 of the happiest, healthiest, busiest, most interested and most interesting children in America," James O'Donnel Bennett wrote in the *Chicago Tribune*.[64]

Controversy continued to stalk the Gary plan, however. Arthur Shumway, writing in *The American Parade,* a socialist magazine, described a school system which "actually gives the youth almost 24-hour-a-day and virtually six-day-a-week instruction, not only in academic subjects but in hobbies. . . . But, like all Gary, it is overrated even by outsiders, who have come to consider it a great utopian university, dominating a raw city and metamorphosing raw youngsters of ignorant laborers into juvenile savants. What it really is is a system of utilizing teachers, pupils and equipment the greatest number of hours a day, days a week and weeks a year . . . at the least possible expense, with the intention of training children broadly in the regular curriculum, the fine and industrial arts, citizenship and athletics." For others this was all to the good, but for Shumway "culture sprouted feebly from this nucleus and from the brains of the really enlightened minority among the men of wealth. Now it is being groomed and nourished as a business project." Capitalism and its educational tools were suspect in some leftist circles on the eve of the Great Depression. But for Wirt and a majority in Gary and throughout the country, connecting business and education was not only accepted, it was positively healthy. The work-study-play system was certainly in the social and ideological mainstream.[65]

During the 1920s the schools had experienced mushrooming growth—in student and teacher populations, programs, facilities, administrators—paralleling the expansion of the platoon plan nationally and continuing the attempt to offer increasing educational and social services to Gary's multifarious population. Growth was the decade's byword. Problems had emerged, such as the Emerson strike, and been settled, although not to the satisfaction of all. Racism and segregation along with nativism and economic disparities were stubborn reminders that corporate capitalism had its limits. But the general prosperity smoothed over many difficulties, convincing most that the country and its educational system, perhaps epitomized by the Gary schools, were truly the height of Western civilization. Moreover, the schools continued to be influenced by a wide variety of organizations, groups, and individuals, reflecting their central role in the city's social, economic, political, and cultural life. Now poised at the peak of their prestige and influence, the Gary schools were hardly prepared for their sudden descent on the rollercoaster ride of the depression decade.

"Busy Hour in Boyville Bank," Emerson School, ca. 1911 (unless otherwise noted, all photographs are courtesy of Calumet Regional Archives, Indiana University Northwest)

"Each child represents a different nationality at Froebel School," ca. 1913

Emerson School, 1910

Elementary classroom, Emerson School, 1911

Domestic Science classroom, Emerson School, 1910

"English Class for Foreigners," Emerson School, ca. 1916

Girls swimming in Emerson School pool, ca. 1912

Portable school in Gary, ca. 1911

Ethnic children at Bailey Branch Library, across from Froebel School, 1922
(Courtesy of Gary Public Library)

Gary Library Station at Emerson School, ca. 1911 (Courtesy of Gary Public
Library)

William A. Wirt, ca. 1920

"Gary Works" float for Loyalty Day Parade during Boys' Week, April 1923

High school class at Roosevelt School, ca. 1931

Elementary class at Roosevelt School, ca. 1931

Playground at Roosevelt School, ca. 1931

Domestic Science class at Roosevelt School, ca. 1931

Frank Sinatra at Memorial Auditorium during
Froebel strike, November 1, 1945 (Courtesy of Gary
Public Library)

Emerson School strike: students in front of Memorial Auditorium,
September 2, 1947

Social Living class, from *We Believe: Gary Public Schools Report to the Community,* June 1954

Horace Mann School, 1950

For every right or freedom our democratic way of life accords us, there is a corresponding responsibility. It is important that children learn both to follow needed directions and to cooperate in setting up and observing those regulations that are within their maturity range. As they progress in their ability to use self-control, they earn true freedom and the respect of others.

Throughout the school years, experiences are provided at each level for the growth of the child in accepting responsibility for his own behavior as well as cooperation with others.

Where a spirit of mutual trust exists, students can be guided in analyzing their own relationships.

Student government is serious business. The enrollment in our high school centers is greater than the population of many American towns.

Student Government in Action, page from *We Believe: Gary Public Schools Report to the Community,* June 1954

I pledge allegiance to the flag of the United States of America, and to the Republic for which it stands, one Nation under God, indivisible, with liberty and justice for all.

V

SURVIVAL, 1930–1940

In the spring of 1931, as winter waned and the depression deepened, newspaperman Floyd Gibbons regaled his fellow New York writers, who wondered about the meaning of Easter, with the following story about "Billy Wirt, the great schoolbuilder who lives out in Gary, Ind."

> He had thousands of kids in his schools, divided among fifty or sixty nationalities and all races, colors and creeds. Those nice school ma'ams descended on his office and wanted to know what the dickens they were going to do about their Easter school programs. Couldn't tell those Mohamedan boys and gals about the great Biblical story. Couldn't have those Chinese and Japanese youngsters taking part in things their folks wouldn't approve. Russian and Greek Easter a week or so later. It was all mixed up, this business of making Easter programs.

> Never stumped Billy Wirt though. Just called all the teachers together and this is what he told 'em—Easter means lots more than all of us think. Resurrection—that's what it means in every sense of the word. The old earth's a wakening at this time of the year. All those flowers and trees and everything on the face of this planet are springing into new life. Man's hopes spring up anew. People are better for the riddance of depressing winter. Just tell the boys and girls that and you'll have an Easter merrymaking that'll make every body [sic] happy.--Well, I saw one of those school pageants and sat between a swarthy Oriental woman and a high-cheeked Russian mother. And when their little boys came out on the stage and sang their songs, those mothers both looked so doggone happy that I wondered why the whole world doesn't adopt Billy Wirt's philosophy.

The Gary superintendent wondered the same thing. For over twenty years through the work-study-play program he had helped mold the city's heterogeneous population into a somewhat unified whole, providing an ever-increasing multitude of services for children and adults alike. He had also retained his power over school matters, despite the continuous input from a variety of organizations and individuals, including business interests, labor unions, civil rights organizations, civic groups, and the mass media. Now, as the depression worsened and entered its long winter, all of his skills, he thought, were necessary to resurrect the educational (and economic) system.[1]

Beginning the 1930s when in his mid-fifties, the superintendent could confidently look back on three decades of successful educational leadership. His popularity was still running high. His family life was finally secure. He could look forward to his remaining years as superintendent, then quiet retirement. He could write his autobiography, perhaps the long-deferred history of the platoon plan, or even devote himself to his first love, economic theory. But this was not to be. The depression created disastrous problems for Gary, its schools, and the nation, releasing new, and to Wirt most dangerous, political and economic forces throughout the land. He also had to contend with serious personal and family problems. Rather than being a fitting cap to his illustrious career, his last eight years—he died in office in 1938—would be filled with mounting problems and challenges. He struggled, somewhat in vain, to survive, little understanding the onrushing forces that engulfed his life. And just as he survived, so did his school system, tattered but intact. Wirt began the decade continuing to promote the platoon system, now more necessary than ever because of the evaporation of national publicity. Aside from Roscoe Case's detailed *The Platoon School in America* (1931), written at Stanford University with the assistance of Ellwood Cubberley, and the articles in *The Platoon School,* increasingly authored by Gary school personnel until the magazine's demise in 1939, there was little else in print. Concern over social and curricular matters now gave way to budget slashing and political infighting. A few, however, continued to remind school administrators that efficiency was the heart and soul of the platoon plan. For Case, writing in 1932, "in times like the present, when school officials are endeavoring in every possible way to maintain good schools and yet to economize, the platoon plan offers a means of not only accomplishing the thing desired, but also, however contradictory it may seem to some individuals, of permitting retrenchment and, at the same time, providing better schools." There were fewer teachers and supervisors, fewer classrooms, but also fewer student failures in platoon schools, all designed to save money. Only a handful, however, were listening.[2]

Wirt was concerned about economic savings, certainly, but he also clung to John Dewey's notion of humanizing learning. "The desirability of giving the children a chance to grow naturally and wholesomely through self-activity is no longer a debatable question," he wrote in "Making the City a Fit Place for the Rearing of Children." "The question now is how to get it done." And he had the answer. In *The Great Lockout in America's Citizenship Plants,* a booklet published in 1937, the superintendent sketched what became his final thoughts on the meaning of the Gary Plan. Filled with photographs, illustrations, charts, newspaper articles, anecdotes, and a hodgepodge of information, the publication summarized the Wirt philosophy and documented its success in Gary and throughout the country. Public schools were more important than ever because city life for children was still dangerous and debilitating: "The school can secure the time and the school can secure the activities to give children a real life and make them intelligent, industrious, reliable, and healthy. The school can thus train for its own activities, stronger boys and girls; it can teach the mastery of the tools of intelligence as well as meet the demands for industrial and social efficiency." He described the rich curriculum, the extended school day, the social activities. "By lengthening the school day the Gary School became a CHILD WORLD within the adult world of the City. By opening the School plant to adults after the day school the Gary School became also a CLUB HOUSE for the adults of the city." To the end he was an unreconstructed educational "progressive," attempting to combine the dual legacy of both Dewey and the administrative reformers. Mailing out hundreds of copies during the summer of 1937, he soon received congratulations and support from around the country. From the historian Charles A. Beard, his college acquaintance: "Thanks for the booklet. It is a grand record and we are all proud of your achievement."[3]

Wirt's educational philosophy proved most consistent, stretching back over four decades, but he was also familiar with contemporary educational trends, and problems. And he was not happy. As the depression deepened, many educators, led by a group at Teachers' College, sought to transform society through a reconstruction of the school curriculum. Suspicious of untrammeled capitalism, they preached cooperation and a planned economy. They were heartened by many of President Franklin Roosevelt's New Deal programs, although they had hoped for even more radical efforts to bring about an equitable society. Wirt, his innate economic and political conservativism rising to the fore, soon went on the attack, for he did "not believe that the fathers and mothers of the school children of America want a socialistic educational program in their schools for either school children or for adults." In a series of planned speeches, entitled "Which Way America," he voiced his thoughts and fears. "Shall we become a regimented people subject to the whims of a bureaucracy at Washington?" Schools should not propagandize "for or against the old order," he wrote in 1935. "All that I am asking is that we find out what that record is and that we be INTELLECTUALLY HONEST." The people, if properly educated, would make the correct decision.[4]

Strongly disagreeing with the educational panaceas of the social reconstructionists, Wirt connected schooling with broader economic and political forces through informing students about economic theories and history, particularly price fluctuations and depressions. In early 1932, he wrote to many publishers of United States history textbooks, suggesting revisions along these lines. More important, he began writing articles and speeches on economic themes—such as "Our Government's Responsibilities for the Present Depression," "How Can America Secure a Market?," "The Schools' Responsibility for Post-War Depression," and "How Will the Revaluation of the Dollar Operate?"—which he distributed widely to politicians, government officials, labor leaders, magazines, and newspapers. Beard welcomed Wirt's suggestions for revision of one of his own texts and informed his publisher "that Dr. Wirt's standing as a student of public affairs is such that you need have no hesitation in accepting his ideas respecting proper textbook presentation. If there is any rush, I give you a free hand to revise in cooperation with Dr. Wirt in my absence." In a letter to Wirt he recalled "the old days in Colonel Weaver's seminar" at DePauw, then added praise for the superintendent's economic theories, particularly his emphasis on the inflationary impact of wars inevitably followed by ruinous depressions. But he wondered whether it was not wise "to distinguish between historical facts and matters of interpretation and policy" in the texts. The *Gary Post-Tribune* reprinted one of Wirt's economic papers in May with the caveat that it "may be too difficult for the average reader but because of the tremendous importance of the problem facing this country we present it for the information and study of those interested."[5]

Following Roosevelt's election in November 1932, Wirt willingly offered his economic advice to the new president, but soon began to associate with a group of conservative businessmen and academics who feared a leftward drift after the inauguration. Wirt attended a series of dinners in Chicago with Professor Frederick Ogg of the University of Wisconsin, Henry Pope of Bear Brand Hosiery, W. W. Gasser of the Gary State Bank, General Robert E. Wood of Sears-Roebuck, and a number of others. They anticipated and feared rebellion from below. Simultaneously, another group concerned about preserving capitalism was forming under the name of the Committee for the Nation, also including General Wood, James H. Rand of Remington, Rand, and Wirt's old friend Edward Rumely. The Committee encouraged the National Industrial Conference Board to study money and credit, planned to prod manufacturers to increase their inventories in order to reduce unemployment, and worried about the shrinking price levels. Its major goal was the devaluation of the dollar, partially through releasing frozen bank deposits and the establishment of a free gold market. Wirt joined and was a true believer in the Committee's goals; as he wrote to Rumely, "the country is for inflation, without a doubt."[6]

While Wirt pursued his economic dreams, he continued to work with Alice Barrows and support the platoon-school organization and magazine, the latter to the tune of $2000 a year from his own pocket. Their relationship was becoming more incongruous, considering her leftwing background and leanings, but was still overshadowed by their mutual commitment to the platoon plan. Exhausted from overwork—she was still employed by the Office of Education—Barrows resigned as editor of *The Platoon School* in early 1931. She hoped Wirt would understand. "This is a parched land. And you nourish our spirits with beauty and with ideas of great vigor and originality," she assured the superintendent in late 1932. Barrows, a strong supporter of the New Deal, welcomed that Secretary of Interior Harold Ickes appointed bright, energetic people to his department, particularly in the Office of Education. She continued to support the platoon plan in her work and thoughts, however, while the platoon-school organization became further mired in debt.[7]

Representing the right and left political poles of progressive education, Wirt and Barrows had struggled to follow the same educational path. But as the depression and New Deal sharpened political differences throughout the country, they were inexorably drawn on a collision course. Wirt escalated his attacks on the New Deal through 1933 and into the following year. He continued to meet with a variety of government officials, newspaper editors, labor leaders, and business officials; and he completed a book manuscript, "The Honest Dollar," detailing his economic theories (which was never published). When Roosevelt made a move to adjust the dollar the following winter, "Wirt expressed the belief that a 50-cent dollar in terms of its old gold basis is the requirement that must be fulfilled before the commodity prices can reach the needed level."[8]

He had basically confined his remarks and publications to economic theories until the spring of 1934, when he plunged into the political cauldron. The precipitant event was a dinner party for Wirt at Alice Barrows' home in McLean, Virginia, the previous September. Present were a few of her New Deal friends: Mary Taylor, editor of the Agricultural Adjustment Administration's (AAA) *Consumers Guide;* Hildegard Kneeland, an economist in the Agriculture Department; Laurance Todd, Tass newspaper correspondent; Robert Bruere, director of the National Recovery Administration's (NRA) industrial-relations board of the textile industry; David Coyle, a member of the Technical Board of Review of the Public Works Administration (PWA). Wirt became disturbed by the dinner table talk, but waited to voice his concerns. He temper was rising. "Until the NRA [National Recovery Act] program was actually launched there was a chance to swing Roosevelt from the radical influence that surrounded him," he confided to Rumely in early March. "At the present time I do not believe that there is any such chance. . . . However, I do not believe that it is too late to successfully resist the policies of President Roosevelt and his associates. To do so will be tremendously difficult and may lead to all sorts of riots and a form of Civil War. But in my judgment, there is no other way." Having become somewhat apocalyptic, he was fortunately not alone, believing "the Committee for the Nation is the only force in America at the present time that has any chance to lead in the present struggle."[9]

Wirt's thoughts became public on March 23 when his colleague in the Committee for the Nation, James H. Rand, while testifying before the Interstate Commerce Committee of the House of Representatives, read a statement by Wirt in which he attacked the New Deal:

> The fundamental trouble with the Brain Trusters is that they start with a false assumption. They insist that the America of Washington, Jefferson and Lincoln must first be destroyed and then on the ruins they will reconstruct an America after their own pattern. . . .
>
> Last summer I asked some of the individuals in this group what their concrete plan was for bringing on the proposed overthrow of the established American social order.
>
> I was told that they believed that by thwarting our then evident recovery they would be able to prolong the country's destitution until they had demonstrated to the American people that the government must operate industry and commerce.

Wirt was most shocked by the sentiment expressed at the previously mentioned dinner party that "we have Mr. Roosevelt in the middle of a swift stream and that the current is so strong that he cannot turn back or escape from it. We believe that we can keep Mr. Roosevelt there until we are ready to supplant him with a Stalin. We all think that Mr. Roosevelt is only the Kerensky of this revolution." Stalin—Kerensky—Revolution! The idea was shocking. But this was not all. The Brain Trusters "would soon be able to use the police power of the government and 'crack down' on the Opposition with a 'big stick.' In the meantime they would extend the gloved hand and keep the 'big stick' in the background." Big stick! Suppress the opposition! Neither Wirt nor Rand revealed, yet, the names of the revolutionaries who had made these statements. When contacted by the *Gary Post-Tribune,* the superintendent had no objections to publishing his statement, for the "times are so critical that someone has to be the goat." [10]

Events quickly escalated. He was national news. The Committee for the Nation rushed into print with Wirt's pamphlet *America Must Lose—By a "Planned Economy," the Stepping Stone to a Regimented State,* which included his inflamatory charges, a discussion of economic issues, and a call to arms. The title was a takeoff on Henry A. Wallace's pamphlet in defense of government involvement in the economy, *American Must Choose.* Acting the martyr, Wirt stated, as quoted in the *New York Times,* "if it requires that I be a sacrifice to get the people to thinking about what is going on, I am willing to be one. If, after an open discussion and investigation, the American people choose the planned economy, I will co-operate in the new State. I will be an American." He volunteered to testify before Congress, but was soon enough summoned to appear before a select committee of the House of Representatives, chaired by Representative Alfred Bulwinkle of North Carolina, established on March 29, 1934 to investigate Wirt's inflamatory claims and charges. [11]

Attacks and counterattacks flew in the House. Representative Foulkes of Michigan believed Wirt's allegations were part of "a plot in which the plotters are Hitler agents in this country, hoping to discredit the social welfare and humanitarian policies of the Roosevelt administration"; "a plot in which the profiteers and grafters of the United States are readily and eagerly cooperating with Hitler tools." For the hometown crowd, the *Gary Post-Tribune* voiced its belief that "Mr. Wirt is neither a radical nor a conservative, neither a republican nor a democrat. He deals with facts and what he thinks is the meaning of those facts." According to one punster, "the country is going from bad to Wirt." He was supported by the Gary Lions and Rotary clubs. At his press conference on March 27, President Roosevelt causually dismissed the allegations: "So it seems to me that, outside of what I first mentioned, the effort to create a story out of pretty slim pickings, there is not very much to be said in the matter one way or the other. I shall go away fishing and shall not give Dr. Wirt very much thought. I don't think anybody else would. (Laughter) Question: Mr. President, are those last two sentences on the record? The President: No."[12]

Wirt received his day in the sun on April 10, when he appeared before the five-man select committee chaired by Representative Bulwinkle. "In the big caucus room, while flashlamps winked, newsreel cameras purred and squads of radio engineers and reporters elbowed through the jampacked spectators, a special committee of Representatives sat down to investigate charges of the utmost gravity," *Time* reported. Wirt immediately listed those present at the Barrows dinner party, then recounted his memory of the full three-hour conversation. Admitting that he did much of the talking, Wirt detailed the shocking statements by the other guests, particularly those referring to Secretary of Agriculture Henry Wallace and his assistant Rexford G. Tugwell. Alice Barrows said little, however, for she "tried to make it as entertaining for all of us as possible." And "was that evening entertaining?" countered Bulwinkle. "I found out what I was looking for, and that was what the main idea is," Wirt responded. "Whether I would call that 'entertaining' or 'satisfying', I don't know. It was satisfying." He also mentioned discussions with other New Deal functionaries on other occasions that had sinister overtones, but little real substance.[13]

"For two sensation-studded hours he recounted his fears to the house investigating committee, while a massed crowd followed his words," the *Gary Post-Tribune* reported. Wirt was prepared to return the following day, but the committee told him to "turn in his expense account and then go home." Wirt's supporters flooded Washington with telegrams defending the superintendent, while the Democrats continued their attack; New Deal administrator Donald Richberg, Hugh Johnson's successor as director of the NRA, summarized the official line:

A cuttlefish squirt
Nobody hurt,

From beginning to end:
Dr. Wirt.[14]

Secretary of the Interior Harold Ickes was considerably more bitter, suspicious, and alarmed, confiding in his diary on April 14: "I had learned yesterday that when a newspaper reporter called recently to interview Dr. William Wirt at his camp in Gary, Indiana, he asked Wirt if he could use his telephone. Assent being given, he was shown into a closet and when he turned the light on in there, he saw a pile of silver shirts, the uniform of a Fascist order that is attempting to be built up in the country at this time. I suggested to the President that it might be well to have an investigation made of this matter." Nothing came of this spurious revelation.[15]

A week after hearing Wirt's testimony the committee resumed its investigation by questioning the six who had been at the dinner party. Barrows, called first, admitted that she had considered the superintendent "and Mrs. Wirt among my most devoted, sincere, and loyal friends." But she denied that there was any revolutionary talk at her house that night, for Wirt "began talking on the devaluation of the dollar and talked continuously on that subject. . . . At no time during that whole evening or dinner did I hear the names of Kerensky or Stalin or Dr. Tugwell, or Secretary Wallace or the President mentioned. At no time did Dr. Wirt ask any questions." At first attempting to be charitable to Wirt, she later informed the committee, "it was inconceivable that anyone whom I had known for 20 years should so violate the principles of hospitality and friendship and bring false charges against his fellow guests and my friends." The subsequent witnesses corroborated Barrows' account of the evening's activities, denying all and accusing Wirt of dominating the discussion. With a three-to-two Democratic majority, the committee concluded in its final report that there was no evidence "showing that there was any person or group in the Government service planning to 'overthrow the existing social order' or planning or doing any of the things mentioned in Dr. Wirt's statement." The Republicans strongly dissented.[16]

Wirt's defenders and detractors quickly expressed their feelings, depending on their political beliefs. In a blunt editorial, the *Gary Post-Tribune* denied that the superintendent would lie; besides, "whatever the outcome may be the affair has shown that Mr. Wirt is a patriot and very brave man. He spoke for no selfish reason." The debate continued in Congress. Senator Connally happily proclaimed, "The Wirt myth has vanished. The Wirt bogy has been exposed. The Wirt propaganda has absolutely collapsed." Representative O'Connor, a member of the investigating committee, referring to Wirt as the "steel company's doctor," recalled the attempt to Garyize the New York City schools in order "to train the child solely so that at the age of 12 or 14 he could take a tool in his or her hand and go into a factory and perform manual labor. The Steel Trust has worked it out beautifully in Gary under Dr. Wirt." *Time* made light of the whole affair, concluding its coverage:

"The York, Pa. chapter of the Ku Klux Klan sent Dr. Wirt its commendations. But the more universal reaction to the Wirt hearing was voiced by Hostess Barrows who, recalling that the dinner was an utter failure because Dr. Wirt was a boresome 'monologist,' described the whole affair as 'perfectly absurd, perfectly ridiculous.' Miss Taylor echoed: 'Pish and piffle.'" Labor journalist Mary Heaton Vorse, writing in *The New Republic,* took the issue much more seriously. "Dr. Wirt may have seemed ridiculous to a sophisticated audience. . . . But there is no doubt that the doctor's disclosures went over big with the radio audience." She feared that, as a front for the Committee for the Nation and its conservative agenda, he was playing on the anticommunism of the masses. "He is absurd, ridiculous, anything you like, but he has not been laughed off. He is putting doubt in the minds of hundreds of thousands."[17]

And he had touched a raw nerve. The superintendent was in no mood, for example, to cross the school board when it prevented Dr. Frederick Schuman, an alleged communist, from speaking at Horace Mann school. Appearing before the American Legion in Chicago on April 30, Wirt repeated "that the plans of the 'brain trusters' are unworkable and that they can be made to work only by going the full way to communism, socialism or Hitlerism," and he received a warm reception. But one reference in the talk caused him some difficulty. He had referred to Rose Schneiderman, who was in the Virgin Islands promoting the New Deal, as the "Red Rose of Anarchy." A longtime labor activist, president of the Women's Trade Union League, and the only female member of the NRA's Labor Advisory Board, the fiery Schneiderman demanded a retraction and threatened a law suit. "Usually, I am even-tempered but occasionally I get as mad as redheads are supposed to get," she wrote in her autobiography. "At first, the only thing I wanted to overthrow was Dr. Wirt. Then I thought how F.D.R. would laugh at the idea of me, four-and-a-half-feet tall, trying to overthrow anybody, so I went to see my good friend and lawyer, Dorothy Kenyon, and asked her to file suit."[18]

Wirt issued a qualified retraction. The right rushed to his defense. Francis Ralston Welch happily supplied Wirt with a detailed statement of Schneiderman's political sins and radical connections, noting that she had been called "The Red Rose of Anarchy" for at least ten years. Harry Jung, honorary general manager of the American Vigilant Intelligence Federation, traced the nickname to her activities "on the sidewalks of New York in an anarchical syndicalist sense" in 1917 and 1918. Jung advised Wirt to obtain the assistance of Major Richard Charles, formerly connected with the American Defense Society, although "I know that he has been playing around with some Jews and since Rose Schneiderman is a Jewess, you want to watch your step." Knowingly or not, Wirt had stepped into the fascist current then running deep in the country. Schneiderman's law suit, which reached Wirt on July 17, listed his defamatory remarks and asked for a court awarded judgment of $400,000. Wirt retained counsel. The case dragged, Wirt finally apologized, and he apparently paid Schneiderman $200.[19]

Although bothered by the Schneiderman incident, Wirt nonetheless escalated his attack on the New Deal through the summer and fall of 1934. He first tried a syndicated column entitled "Which Way America," distributed by Soper Feature Service, summarizing his political and economic views. "Just as sure as God made little apples, we are headed for communism if the so-called 'brain trusters,' 'brain busters,' is a better name for them, are not literally kicked out of Washington," F. L. Soper wrote Wirt in late April. In his first article, subtitled "The Menace of Communism and Socialism," Wirt warned of the general threat from the radicals in Washington. In the second, "We Have the Right to Know," he revealed his own position: "I believe in social reform, the elimination of the abuses of capitalism, the elimination of child labor and the sweat shop. I favor the minimum wage, the maximum hour, the old age pension policies, and the elimination of the gambler's control of business and industry." He believed in change, but not "the proposed national economic planning which will place all persons under the dictatorship of politicians, and put American public opinion in a 'straight-jacket.'" Wirt expected to distribute widely his views, but by late June, Soper abandoned his syndicated column because "every newspaper office in the country is panic stricken. . . . President Roosevelt is still the hero of the hour, and being so popular, the time is not yet ripe. But, when will that time come?" Wirt, surely, had no idea.[20]

Perhaps, a column dependent on the mainstream press would not work, but he could always spread his views in person, over the radio, or through privately distributed pamphlets. He presented "Which Way America" to an enthusiastic crowd in Gary, and another paper, "Education for Citizenship," at the Morgan Park Military Academy. A West Coast lecture tour was planned for the fall of 1934 by World Celebrities, with stops in Los Angeles, San Francisco, Seattle, Portland, and at various colleges and universities. This also proved a disaster when the tour director absconded with the funds and left him stranded in Los Angeles, but he did deliver a paper at a business conference at Wellesley Hill, Massachusetts, in September.

He quickened his activities early the next year. "Dr. William A. Wirt . . . popped up again today with a warning that the nation's little red school houses are being used to spread communist propaganda," the *Gary Post-Tribune* announced on January 16, 1935. "Dr. Wirt's attack was aimed broadside at his colleagues in the teaching profession—the National Association of School Superintendents. The superintendents, he charged, are 'turning red' and using the schools to 'incite ultra-radical sentiment.'" He was particularly frightened by the influence of George Counts of Teachers College, who was questioning capitalism. These charges, with heavy documentation, appeared in "The School as an Agency for Propaganda," a thirty-five-page paper he mailed to two hundred newspapers and individuals throughout the country. "It is not that we love private enterprise so much," he concluded, "but that we love the collective-state enterprises that are offered as alternatives, less. All that I am asking is that we make up balance sheets for the several forms of social and economic orders that we can have, BEFORE WE MAKE OUR CHOICE. Then we will know what we are choosing." The dominant press still balked at printing his views, but the right wing continued to be supportive. Ernest Rheydt-Dittmer of the Germanischer Bund believed "that Dr. Wirt will continue to clear the path for better and more noble AMERICANISM as we ever could expect from any red shadow coming from RUSSIA. . . . Alas, their beastly paws reach into some of our American SCHOOLS. No! Not by any means in the city if [sic] GARY!" The Paul Reveres—"organized to promote patriotism, to advance Americanism, to combat radicalism"—were interested in distributing "your fine presentation about school propaganda," and invited Wirt to join their Advisory Board. But he maintained his independence.[21]

Wirt soon tired of his public anti-New Deal role. He preferred to concentrate on his central concern of informing the nation's children, despite the renewed interest in August 1935 of Soper Feature Service in the possibilities of selling his column. In early 1936, he issued "Keeping America Safe for Democracy," a booklet distributed to four thousand college professors, presidents, and deans, as well as to school superintendents in the larger cities. He now stressed improved citizenship training. This would entail knowledge of the causes of prosperity and depressions, which he willingly provided in another arcane discussion of economic issues. The major lesson to be learned was that "Free competition means best quality at lowest prices. Free competition means more production, more employment and higher standards of living." His faith in capitalism was unshaken, but the country seemed to follow a different drummer. So, in the end, he returned to describing his beloved school system in *The Great Lockout in America's Citizenship Plants* (1937). Widely distributed in Gary, the booklet was assigned reading to the students, and in early November 1937 it was the topic of "student orators carrying the message of Education Week before the community's service clubs and other organizations." At least there was still a captive audience at home.[22]

Although sidetracked by his struggle to save the country from political and economic ruin, the superintendent throughout the decade had to devote the bulk of his time to managing the schools. Crisis after crisis forced him to save a system he had assumed was on solid ground. Enrollment remained fairly constant, putting a heavy drain on dwindling financial resources. There were about twenty-one thousand pupils in the regular day program in 1930, with another sixteen thousand enrolled in the night school. While the day enrollment held steady throughout the decade, mirroring the city's population stagnation (somewhat over 100,000), there was some internal shifting of the student body as a greater number of teenagers remained in high school. The high school enrollment increased from five thousand to over six thousand during the decade, with the number of graduates doubling from five hundred to one thousand. The number of teachers dropped somewhat, from 615 to a low of 518 in 1932, then rebounded to reach 577 in 1940 within twenty schools. There were now six buildings with high-school enrollments— Horace Mann, Emerson, Lew Wallace (1932), Froebel, Tolleston (opened in 1934), and Roosevelt (1931). Horace Mann, located in the affluent near-west side, had over half of its 2,376 students in 1937 in the upper grades, followed by Emerson with slightly less than half. Of Froebel's 2,864 students, 743 were in the high-school grades. Lew Wallace, situated in the Glen Park neighborhood on the city's southern edge, accommodated slightly less than half of its students in the secondary grades, and the all-black Roosevelt school, with an enrollment of 2,792, had only 660 high-school students. The remaining elementary schools ranged in size from the Jefferson school with almost nine hundred, to the tiny Clark school bringing up the rear with thirty. Class and race still remained strong in influencing school attendance.[23]

As enrollment held firm, the school budget temporarily declined. The drop was not immediate, however, for the depression slowly tightened its grip in Gary and throughout the country. Both the Roosevelt and Lew Wallace schools, minus their west wings in order to save money, were opened early in the decade, each costing over $600,000, the only major construction during the depression. In early 1932, fears mounted among Glen Park parents that Lew Wallace would not be completed because some of the funds were frozen in closed banks, and their children would continue attending makeshift classes in the Glen Park Presbyterian church. School authorities promised that the building would soon be finished, however, and it was. Overall, the school budget hovered around $3 million until 1933, when it plummeted to less $2 million. While Wirt could brag to Chicago school superintendent William Bogan in April 1932 that "the work of the schools has not been curtailed in any respect," he was being rather disingenuous. The summer-school program had already been reduced, and there were cuts in the night and Saturday programs, as well as in funds for improvements, upkeep, and various other programs. But some things were temporarily sacred. In September 1931, the school board met with the Allied Council of Civic Clubs of Gary and the Lake County Taxpayers Association to discuss ways to economize. When someone suggested cutting the salaries of Wirt (then $15,000) and other administrators, board president Peter Seyl "insisted that the superintendent did not get half enough for his efforts nor as much as he might demand for his work elsewhere."[24]

Further reductions came quickly. The *Gary Post-Tribune* welcomed the cuts, arguing that "we have had our big spree and now we must pay." In June 1932, the board slashed salaries (including Wirt's) by 20 percent, reduced the school year from ten to nine months, and forced the staff to take a payless thirty-day summer vacation. As the tax base eroded, Wirt and the board naturally looked for guidance and support from the business community, especially the Gary Commercial Club and Chamber of Commerce. Additional cuts came in October with the elimination of the night and Saturday programs, which further eroded teachers' salaries. Now the schools were more like those in other cities, Wirt argued, although the longer school day and the work-study-play system continued to provide efficient educational benefits. Amid the bleak winter of 1932–33, Wirt even suggested additional salary cuts as well as closing the schools for three months to save on heating. "Even though the heavens fall our standards of education should be maintained," announced the *Post-Tribune*.[25]

The business community, obsessed with lowering taxes, welcomed the various cuts, but citizens groups soon began to be heard. In early 1933, a packed gathering of members of the Glen Park Boosters association, affiliated with the Allied Council of Civic Associations, protested the proposed closing of the Glen Park school. "The meeting was called ostensibly for discussion of the school matter, but led to general protests about poor relief, street car fares, police protection and the Glen Park pumping station." They particularly feared the superintendent's suggested winter closing scheme. "Let's tell Wirt where to get off at," Sam Shappeli shouted. "We pay for this school and we deserve more instead of less for our money." Shortly thereafter, in a crowded meeting the parent body recommended preserving the academic programs and teachers' salaries, but dropping summer classes, kindergarten, the auditorium department, and other programs. Other suggestions came from various neighborhood representatives. Finally, John Holloway defended "the present school system setup from 'harmful changes.'" Stung by the attack, Wirt publicly responded with a passionate defense of both academic and nonacademic programs. "Tours for board members through the school system during the next few weeks are to be arranged so that they can become better informed," the *Gary Post-Tribune* announced. "Wirt's unexpected defense of the school system was regarded as representing the stand he will take when next year's curtailments are determined." School auditor A. Howard Bell produced figures demonstrating that the system was financially efficient despite the richer curriculum.[26]

Debate continued concerning how much to cut, where to cut, and the virtues of the system. Teacher salaries could still be pared. Teachers were now paid partially in tax-anticipation warrants, or script, paying 6 percent interest. In May 1933, school authorities discovered they would no longer receive state school funds, totally $90,000 annually. Wirt predicted the school year might be chopped to six months or less, endangering high-school accreditation. A shrunken summer school program was still planned, despite the protest of the Gary Real Estate Board which wanted it abolished. Exuding confidence, Wirt announced in June that "the school administration has made forward strides in winning the local public to the platoon system of schooling. He believes the opposition has become a marked minority during the last several months. He believes 'figures don't lie' when it comes to proving the value of work-study-play in comparison to conventional systems." He was joined by Mrs. Frank Sheehan, president of the Dunes Federated Club, who argued that "the high cost of ignorance will be greater than any possible cost of education."[27]

As classes opened in September 1933, the budget was still problematical, depending heavily on the decision of the county board of tax adjustment concerning the maximum tax rate for schools. The school board petitioned the county board to raise the tax. But because the assessed valuation of city property had dropped from $179 million to $122 million, the rate had been reduced, and there were many tax delinquencies. Teachers now received only a six-month contract. The proposed budget contained little for the summer and night schools and nothing for Saturday school. Wirt fought to have the latter restored. In an administrative memo the virtues of the Saturday program were detailed. It offers, he wrote, "opportunity to make up academic work but most important it opens a wide field of activities to boys and girls and allows them to participate in those activities in such a way as to develop in every possible way any special interest or bent that they may have. Through its recreational program, it attracts children to the safe supervised activities of the playground and draws them away from the doubtful association of the street and alley."[28]

The winter of 1933–34 approached with little prospect of relief. But there were no further reductions, and hopes brightened in January when word arrived that the state allotment of $116,485 was on its way. Evening classes in various academic subjects were offered at Horace Mann, Roosevelt, and Lew Wallace, with a total enrollment for the year of 4,514, up somewhat from the previous year. Saturday classes were resumed in February, "another sign of depression's fading." By June, there was premature talk of restoring the ten-month school year, which was still two years off, and a nine-week summer session was planned. The schools' income had now been reduced by 44 percent, resulting in the elimination of the system's fat and much of the lean as well. To encourage taxpayer support and confidence, the Gary Principals' Association issued a lengthy pamphlet, *The Taxpayer and the Gary Public Schools,* justifying increased funding. Defending the efficiency of the Saturday and summer programs, as well as the ten-month year, the principals appealed to the citizens' interest in providing children "with wholesome, supervised activities. . . . Shops and laboratories provide work activities; playgrounds, swimming pools, auditoriums, and drawing and art rooms give not only present pleasure and recreation, but supply the sort of living in school that encourages and develops interests, the following out of which will help the adult of the coming generation better to spend his larger allotment of leisure time." Equally important was the adult education program, "dedicated to the solution of the problems connected with the efficient and economical promotion and operation of late afternoon and night school courses for the youth of Gary who, by the trend of the times, have become unemployed adults." But little was accomplished. The budget only slowly crept upward, from $1.7 million in 1934 to $2.066 million in 1936, when the ten-month year was reinstated along with other programs.[29]

Throughout the first half of the decade the system limped along, with programs slashed and salaries reduced over 30 percent, but there was one bright spot. In a bold move, Wirt launched Gary College in 1932. He continually worked to expand the school's reach and influence, and again he succeeded, despite considerable adversity. The superintendent's interest in higher education in Gary reached back to 1921 with the beginning of Indiana University's extension classes in the schools. There were fifty-five IU courses offered during the 1931–32 school year, with an enrollment of over fourteen hundred. Most popular were the English, foreign language, social science, and history courses. But Wirt was not satisfied. He desired an expanded program, an accredited junior college (perhaps even a four-year program) rather than the current arrangement with IU. The Gary schools' academic program prepared many students for college work, often in less than twelve years, and they were more likely to enter post-secondary work at a local junior college. Late afternoon and evening classes would be held in the Horace Mann school. Costs would be low, covered by a minimal tuition payment of five dollars per semester hour. "Since the high school students in the upper twenty-five per cent of our classes are young students, we have not been able to graduate them when they should have been graduated," he explained to the North Central Association for Colleges and Secondary Schools, when requesting an experiment under their supervision. "They have been too young to go away to college. Many parents could not afford to send them away from home. With college opportunities at home we can reduce the regular day school enrollment more than enough to pay the extra cost of the college to the local community."[30]

By June 1932, plans were proceeding smoothly to open in September. IU agreed to move its extension classes in the near future to neighboring East Chicago. Weighted down with increasing financial problems, the superintendent eagerly publicized this one ray of hope. As he explained to the Lew Wallace graduating class, "those who would be content to remain at home should improve their time by taking advantage of Gary's educational opportunities as represented in the Gary college. Those who cannot pay tuition will learn they can obtain the Gary college education through signing notes approved by the trustees. The Gary college is so designed as to put this educational opportunity within reach of every young man and young woman of the community." Repeating his message to Roosevelt's graduates, he underscored his determination "to give you and all other students every possible educational opportunity at the least possible expense to the taxpayers." Classes started in late September at Horace Mann school, with the college temporarily sharing space with the I.U. extension program; four hundred were expected to enroll in thirty-one subjects. In November, Wirt was elected president of the Board of Directors, and the other officers were also school administrators. Night-school director Albert Fertsch headed the college. The Board encouraged teachers to keep good students at home, rather than steer them to out-of-town colleges. "I dislike to hear the college termed a 'depression school,'" Wirt argued the following spring. "The college is not a 'depression' school. It merely chances to have been established during a period of distress."[31]

Throughout the decade enrollment held firm, with 117 in 1936, ninety-four full time, and 270 two years later. Some students--twenty in January 1935—obtained financial support from the Federal Emergency Relief Administration (FERA), for which they worked in the school library, assisted in music and physical-education classes, or did typing. One nagging problem, however, was the refusal of the North Central Association of Colleges and Secondary Schools to grant accreditation. Gary College remained on its list of "interesting experiments." A two-man team inspected the college in early February 1935 and issued a detailed report. The faculty, graduate students or college teachers from the University of Chicago, Northwestern University, and the IU extension program, were considered to be "somewhat outstanding," but little involved as a group in college activities or decisions. The teaching load was acceptable. The curriculum was somewhat lopsided, with only eight hours in the biological sciences, all in zoology, but eighty-one hours in the humanities. "On the whole, the instruction is good but not as outstanding as might justly be expected." The team found fault with record keeping, the counseling service, health service, financial arrangements, physical conditions because of overcrowding and inadequate laboratory equipment, and the administration in general. In conclusion, they believed "it should be encouraged in every possible way, but it should not be given a fallacious sense of achievement by being rated too highly." Hoping for more, Wirt continued the experiment, although he hinted in late 1936 that the college might be discontinued if a four-year college was constructed in Hammond. But this was not to be. There were thirty-nine Gary College graduates from 1933 to 1937, and twenty-nine of them continued at other colleges.[32]

Gary College shared space and its director with the much larger night-school program, which continued throughout the decade. Cut to the bone during the early years of the decade, the night program was temporarily revived by 1935 with, perhaps, six thousand or so students. New courses were begun in September, including a junior engineering course and a junior school of business, emphasizing the industrial bent of the program. Enrollment reached more than seventy-five hundred in April 1937, then plunged to about three thousand in December because of financial cuts, where it remained through the next year. But by late 1939 an enrollment of ten thousand was expected, perhaps reaching the height attained twenty years earlier. The night program struggled through the decade, offering some adults an academic or recreational respite from the gloom and hardships of the depression. "During the depression the adult education classes were reduced to the minimum," according to the program of the Third Annual Scholastic Convocation in June 1937. "Of course, this was a great mistake. Adult education facilities should have been enlarged during the depression, when so many adults were unemployed."[33]

Various programs were cut, restored, and added, but the academic schedule remained basically intact, with the platoon system maintaining its integrity. No longer in the national spotlight, Wirt and the school staff continued to concentrate on local educational matters. Combining economic savings and a traditional academic emphasis, Wirt in 1932 initiated a plan to rush some students through the elementary grades in seven years and through the high-school curriculum in three years. With the requisite number of high-school units and satisfactory scores on aptitude and achievement examinations, a select number of pupils could graduate early. Wirt estimated that the system could save approximately $150 for each early high-school graduate and $100 for each elementary student who skipped one year. "Both the three-year high school and the seven-year grammar school plans are parts of the superintendent's educational opportunity campaign," announced the local paper. The first year forty students, out of 131 juniors who were eligible, chose the three-year plan. The graduates were urged to attend college, now having the possibility of remaining at home at Gary College, or at least take the post-graduate night-school courses that were more business oriented.[34]

While Wirt pushed early graduation for those academically inclined, there were hints that the rest were falling behind. In September 1935, Isabelle Jones, supervisor of testing and measurement, sounded the alarm. The last two years, with the introduction of the nine-month school year, had seen a drop in promotions (from 87 percent in 1929 to 81 percent), an increase in failures (to 10 percent), with many conditional promotions (9 percent). "I fear we are going to see more reflections on school achievement in the immediate future in spite of the untiring efforts of directors, administrators, and teachers to maintain the usual high standards in Gary while carrying the load of the depression," she informed the superintendent. These were disturbing figures. Wirt continued to stress, however, that almost 90 percent of the high school graduates continued their education, either in college (26 percent), adult commercial education in Gary (22 percent), junior engineering work (5 percent), or other vocational training (19 percent), with the rest in general academic work in the night school.[35]

Since few were college bound and vocational training was valuable for many, in 1929 a vocational diploma was instituted. For any who had completed the regular graduation requirements, plus twelve hundred clock hours of vocational course work, they received a special certificate at graduation.

The number climbed quickly, from eighty-eight in 1929 to four hundred in 1935. Some concentrated in one area, such as forge shop, foundry, auto mechanics, drafting, and printing for boys, and homemaking arts, home economics, and art for girls. A large number specialized in band, but the greatest concentration was in general shop or work in a number of related vocational areas. "This program has proven the most potent force we have ever experienced in leading a large proportion of our boys and girls to have definite utility objective in their high school course," according to a summary of the program in 1934.[36]

The interest in vocational work was increasing, common during the depression because of the jump in enrollment of nonacademic students, but not rapidly enough for Director of Industrial Education Guy Wulfing. A long-time associate of Wirt, he still approached the superintendent warily—"I trust that you will realize that whatever I may say is inspired by a thought of service to our boys and girls and not in the least with fault finding or criticism." What bothered him was the lack of proper guidance counseling. "If the child and parent are appraised of the fact that we live in a steel manufacturing center and that perhaps eight out of ten children will have to depend on the steel industry for a future livlehood [*sic*], and then were the child to put in four to six years beating a bass drum and to have no high school shop, drawing, or industrial training, that should be his privilege, providing it can be had within [without?] restrictions or artificial barriers which we at first set up against such wild schemes." With the proper equipment and staff, Wulfing believed his department would be more competitive. In another letter to Wirt in February 1936 he was more shrill. "Thanks to our Work-Study-Play program we are improving all the time, and compared with others, the conventional school programs, we may justly sit back and be proud of our accomplishments. *But this self-satisfied attitude is the very thing I am afraid of.*" There was much success, but there was also continuing failure. "First, I would like to see steps taken to salvage some of our wreckage, especially in the high school. . . . When we set up a procedure for a three year high school program we did a splendid thing for our scholastically brilliant boys and girls, but we failed to provide a compensating program for our mentally slow and motor-minded. Many such children develop a failure complex." This charge that the program was too academic would be made by others.[37]

The next year, in a review of the industrial arts program, Wulfing listed thirty-seven shops in the high schools, including woodworking (ten), drafting (eight), general metal (four), electricity (five), machine shop (two), foundry (two), and one each of auto shop, forge, pattern shop, printing, and related technical training. "The industrial arts work has never been on a vocational basis," he wrote. Nonetheless, "during the last few years there have developed a few definitely organized trade classes operating under the Smith-Hughes law," which included machine shop (two), electricity (two), auto shop (one), general metal work (one), and printing (two). "During very recent years the shortage of skilled labor has stimulated interest in this type of work and a demand on the part of industry for such training," he added, underscoring the impact of the depression on the job market and high-school enrollment. "The best results in trade training, however, have been in connection with apprenticeship training and trade extension work for adults in connection with the night school program."[38]

The growing link between the vocational program and the job market had been underscored three years earlier, when U.S. Steel appointed Harry Matson to coordinate relations between the mill and the school system. "We feel quite sure that this arrangement is going to be very valuable to our Gary boys and incidentally will enable the schools to make more definite contributions to industry of the Calumet district," Wirt informed W. P. Gleason, General Superintendent of Gary Works. The superintendent hoped that the students would be allowed to visit the mill, along with Matson and the shop instructors, "for the purpose of better relating the practice in our shops to actual conditions and procedure in industry." The thrust for a more vocationally oriented program resulted in establishing a separate vocational diploma by 1937. Students obtaining a regular four-year degree could specialize in one of four areas—general, business, home economics, or industrial. But now there was also a two-year terminal course at the Emerson school with a vocational diploma for those over sixteen who would not complete the regular graduation requirements. There were two courses, auto mechanics and machine shop. A more extensive two-year job-training program existed at all of the high schools, with courses in metal work, printing, electricity, machine shop, and auto shop for students over sixteen. The curriculum was slowly changing, but few pupils were probably affected.[39]

Wirt struck out in all directions, including cementing closer relations with the business community, in order to obtain support, verbal and economic, for the crippled schools. He was initially wary, however, of dependence on state or possibly federal financial assistance, which was the increasing trend during the decade. But, with serious reservations, he soon compromised his principles. In late 1930, the superintendent became a member of the state branch of the blue-ribbon National Advisory Committee on Education appointed by President Herbert Hoover. Concerned about educational problems, including illiteracy, the committee initially focused on local and state responsibilities, but soon came around to supporting federal aid. Wirt followed the same path. He initially opposed even state funding, for he feared that increased taxes would only benefit downstate rural schools and lessen local control. "I would regard with rank disfavor the turning over to state officials of $21,000,000 to be used for any purpose," he informed the local Kiwanis Club. "It is a very dangerous thing. Nothing is worse than to tax people and allow alien agencies to spend the money. It is like giving a stranger license to write checks on your own bank account." As a banker, he well knew this danger. He also worked to keep politics out of state educational affairs, while criticizing Republican Governor Harry Leslie's various policies.[40]

Other issues soon emerged. There was a fear in early 1931 that Gary, with a population over 100,000, thereby classified as a first-class city, would now have an elected school board according to state law. Local politicians, both Democratic and Republican, encouraged by Wirt, introduced legislation to retain city council appointment of board members, which was successful. "The school officials, the council and citizens generally pride themselves on the fact that Gary's public schools never have been 'forced into politics,'" proclaimed the *Post-Tribune*. And the next year the paper reaffirmed its belief that "the Gary schools stand in the front rank of all schools. Much of the credit goes to Mr. Wirt and his able assistants but a large share can be credited to the absence of politics. Any interference by politicians in the affairs of Gary's schools would be extremely unpopular."[41]

The situation began to change in early 1933, however, because of escalating economic gloom, as well as the Democratic victories on the state and national levels. Newly elected Democratic Governor Paul V. McNutt removed Wirt from the state board of education, where he had served since 1927, for political and other reasons. The superintendent had rankled the powerful Indiana High School Athletic Association, for example, with his suggestion to downplay competitive athletics; in April 1931 he had even advocated abolishing the already sacred state basketball tournament, always held in Indianapolis, because of the numerous teenage drinking parties, typical in "this gin-toting age." In early 1934 he refused to answer a questionaire circulated by the state Department of Public Instruction concerning drinking and smoking among teachers. Jealous of local autonomy, Wirt argued that "the School Administration has been trying to maintain the standards of conduct becoming to teachers that the parents of Gary school children want," and therefore it was "not necessary to formulate rules of conduct." And he added, "school teachers must let partisan politicians alone, if they expect the partisan politicians to leave them alone. Men and women who enter teaching must recognize that someone else other than teachers must save the country in partisan politics, if it is to be saved." Wirt would welcome assistance, but not interference.[42]

His view of federal government involvement was perhaps more ambiguous. During the height of his attack on the New Deal in March 1934, he warned his fellow superintendents at their annual meeting in Cleveland that they should not depend on federal assistance, which would only increase taxation. Swimming against the current, for his colleagues were scrambling for the federal dollar, Wirt instead urged them to adopt the platoon plan. "In the final analysis we find that the demand for federal aid for schools is emanating from cities that do not have the work-study-play school," he concluded. Simultaneously, however, the Gary schools were receiving limited federal support. The Civil Works Administration (CWA) was even then constructing four additional rooms at the Tolleston school. Thirty-two teachers also received their salaries from the Federal Emergency Relief Administration (FERA), starting in December 1933, to conduct a variety of night classes for adults and a nursery school at the Neighborhood House for preschool children. Within a year forty-one FERA teachers were employed in a variety of functions. Over sixteen hundred adults were enrolled in sixty night classes.[43]

The conservative *Post-Tribune* welcomed all federal support: "There certainly have been enough calls on Uncle Sam's purse in the last year to justify one in subjecting any new call to the most strict scrutiny. But it does not take very long to demonstrate that this plan for money for the schools is one which thoroughly is justified. . . . We cannot permit our school system to collapse." Heavily dependent on the shrinking local tax base, the Gary schools were forced to accept limited state and federal support to continue day and night programs. Hostile to increased dependence on external funding, the superintendent was forced to compromise his principles. He was also continually distracted by a multitude of problems and pressures, particularly the growing militancy of the destitute teachers, who absorbed the brunt of the reductions.[44]

In the early 1930s, as the depression deepened, the teachers were confronted with cut after cut. They were initially confused and disorganized. Not only were salaries reduced, positions eliminated, and class sizes increased, but teachers were expected to support destitute children and their families. By late 1931, teachers were contributing to welfare funds managed by the school principals that furnished the children with shoes and other necessities. Froebel teachers donated one-day's pay a month to purchase groceries for poor children. A. Howard Bell, school auditor, was treasurer of the Gary Public Schools Central Relief Committee, and he disbursed funds allocated by the Committee on Administration of Relief and by the Payment Needs and Collections Committee. Teachers were hardly in a position to contribute significantly to the fund, however, since in January 1932 half of their salary came in the form of tax-anticipation warrants, a practice continued through the year.

The teachers soon began to organize to protect their interests. The senior teachers, represented by a committee of thirteen, were particularly disturbed when Wirt suggested in April 1932 that "the higher paid instructors should bear the brunt of pay slashes and the lower paid teachers should escape any drastic cut." The senior teachers countered that they would work for ten months but only receive a nine-month salary if the present graduated pay scale was honored. Apparently nothing came of this issue, but six months later the teachers threatened to boycott any merchants who opposed the 1933 school tax levy. Sensitive to antibusiness sentiments and to the threat of teacher militancy, the superintendent warned "that he had better not learn of public school instructors organizing for such a maneuver of any other gesture smacking of politics." The teachers were too disorganized to respond, but hovering in the wings was the Gary Teachers' Federation, loosely affiliated with the Indiana State Teachers' Association and the NEA. Regrouped sometime in the 1920s, the Federation functioned more as a social club than a union, but by mid-1933 it had enrolled 433 out of the 522 teachers in the system. It provided various benefits for its members, including a credit union and an insurance policy, and in 1931 had arranged for members to obtain a wide range of merchandise at wholesale prices from a local merchant.[45]

As wages plummeted, the Federation gathered its forces and began to raise its collective voice in muted protest. A delegation appeared before the school board in June 1933 to protest another 10 percent salary cut, but quickly caved in; the teachers were "reluctant to give up the basic salary scale for another reduction," admitted Federation president Charles Chamberlain, "but that if this is necessary the situation must be met." A more unanimous protest, with mass meetings, was launched the following year when the teachers were threatened with accepting delinquent tax warrants, payable in two years, in lieu of cash. The *Post-Tribune* sympathized with the teachers' plight and applauded them for their "fine, humanitarian service in feeding and caring for the children of Gary during the depths of the depression," yet warned that they would get more support from the business community if they shopped in the city, rather than in adjoining communities. Perhaps they "would need effective support from Gary business men some day, a support that would come from a feeling the interests of the two groups are identical." Teachers and merchants would continue to drift apart, however, as many in the business community sought to reduce their taxes. Despite their numbers, the Federation was generally helpless to protect the teachers' interests.[46]

While the teachers were most anxious to restore salaries to predepression levels or at least to establish a minimum salary scale, there were other pressing issues. In mid-1935, for example, the city council voted to fire married female teachers in order to create jobs for perceived unemployed male teachers, a common move throughout the country. Mrs. May Patterson, a school board member, was strongly opposed. The state tenure law protected the 150 tenured married women, she argued, along with 205 single women with tenure; indeed, there were only twenty married and fifteen single women without tenure. Besides, Wirt added, there were few unemployed male teachers in Gary, for the schools had always had difficulty hiring local residents. "I suppose that is explained by the lowness of teaching salaries and the counter attraction of more lucrative jobs," he believed. And the *Post-Tribune* chimed in, "the unemployed are not prepared to teach and besides if that were done it would destroy the efficiency of the school system, which would injure, not help, the children of the unemployed." So women's jobs were safe, unlike the situation elsewhere.[47]

As the depression lingered, the business community became more vocal in protesting tax increases to fund the schools. The Gary Taxpayers' Association, an arm of U.S. Steel, recommended a five-cent decrease in the proposed school tax rate for 1937. In response, teachers quickly recognized the need for a more militant union. The fact that there had earlier been a Gary Teachers' Union, Local 4 of the American Federation of Teachers (AFT), defunct for over ten years, was, apparently, long forgotten, for the Lake County Central Labor Union proposed that the teachers join the AFL in late 1934. Wirt promised that the school board would "take no steps to stop them," but the time was not ripe for them to act. Conditions would drastically change, however, by early 1937. The motivating issue was the ongoing teachers' grievance over the salary rating system adopted in 1921. Originally, supervisors could rate no more than 25 percent of the teachers in a building in the A category (with the highest salary), 40 percent in the B category, 30 percent in the C category, and 5 percent in the D category, who would be dismissed. The system was slightly altered in 1932, when only 20 percent in the A category, 50 percent in the B category, and 25 percent in the C category could be rated, with the remainder to be fired. The Teachers' Federation, incensed over the arbitrary nature of the system—which centered power in the hands of the supervisors and essentially froze the wage structure and pecking order—after a year's study, proposed in late 1936 a single salary schedule based essentially on experience rather than on a supervisor's rating. A fairer schedule, according to the Federation, would lead to the "release of the well-springs of loyalty and enthusiasm that are repressed to-day . . . and will bring us that warm understanding and fellowship in high endeavor that our mutual interests deserve."[48]

Economic conditions improved in the spring of 1937. Still, the discretionary (and low) salary schedule remained the same, leading the more militant members of the Federation to consider affiliating with the reviving AFT. Union passions ran high among the teachers, fueled by the recent organizing drive among the steel workers and the founding of the CIO. Nearly five hundred teachers, over 90 percent of the instructional force, attended an emotional meeting in mid-April. By then, however, a group of teachers had already contacted the AFT and provisionally reaffiliated as the Gary Teachers' Union Local No. 4, which quickly swelled to over one hundred members; they also joined the Lake County Central Labor Union. A majority of the remaining Federation members, who had also voted to affiliate with the AFT, were angered and in a quandary. Their attorney contacted the AFT, inquiring if it was possible to secure a second union charter. It was not, and the two sides quickly settled their differences and combined in Local No. 4, which soon included a majority of the teachers. Still affiliated with the AFL through the AFT the local received strong support as well from the local CIO.[49]

The new union quickly focused on the twin issues of increasing salaries, including acceptance of the single salary schedule, and improving working conditions. There was little question of other concerns, such as academic freedom. As one of the leaders early admitted, "so far as academic freedom in considered, I think Gary teachers are rather well off, considering the situation existing in Chicago and some other cities." Later in the year local secretary Flora Philley confidently assured the superintendent, "our teachers enjoy full freedom to discuss with their classes any subject, however controversial, in local or national affairs. . . . [W]e have, since the establishment of the Gary System, enjoyed such perfect freedom of speech in our classrooms as individuals," that no problems were anticipated. And in a promotional bulletin new members were urged to join because "the Union has the friendly support of the Mayor and the School Board. We have the backing of Organized Labor." One annoyance, however, was the state loyalty oath required of all licensed teachers. Working to have it repealed, the union was most cautious, fearing redbaiting. "We have this large foreign population," Philley explained to Wirt when requesting his support, "many of our teachers have 'foreign' names, and the *type* of *patriot* who would oppose any action *we* might take in bringing the repeal of the oath-law out into much publicity is just the type to cry 'communist' and 'propaganda peddler' at every one of them. We would have many nasty charges to meet which none of us, much less our school-heads, deserve to have thrust at us. . . . It is our plan to get this disgraceful law repealed without much thunder, if possible, at the next legislature." The superintendent, considering his politics, would hardly be sympathetic.[50]

In late April 1937, the school board worked to divide the teachers by proposing separate salary discussions according to their disciplines; "for example, history and geography teachers will send one committee, and the mathematics, gymnasium and shop instructors each will have a delegation of its own." The teachers, however, through the union, which included over half of the work force by late May, insisted on speaking with one voice. They demanded restoration of 1931–32 salaries for all school employees to be financed by a school tax levy of $1.40 on each $100 of taxable property, an increase of twenty cents. Working closely with Wirt and the school board, union members and their supporters appeared before the Lake County Tax Adjustment Board, which only raised the levy to $1.30, however. Restoration of predepression salaries was now possible. In October, the school board requested salary recommendations from the teachers, who would be divided into five categories—elementary teachers with less than three-years training (136), elementary teachers with less than an AB degree (35), elementary teachers with an AB degree (126), high-school teachers (110), and all teachers with an A or B+ ranking in 1931–32 (149).

When meeting with the school board in early December, however, representatives from four of the groups gave their "power of attorney" to the teachers' union, once again presenting a unified front; the union claimed the support of 505 of the 569 teachers. Only the higher paid A and B+ teachers appeared separately. The union next presented a detailed single salary schedule to the board, based on educational background and experience, but with no provision for success (merit) grades. Searching for external support. Flora Philley appealed to Governor Clifford Townsend and State Superintendent of Public Instruction Floyd McMurray. "The Gary Teachers' Union, Local No. 4, is putting up a desperate fight to establish a single salary schedule of pay for Gary teachers," she argued. "This, as you know, means the same pay for elementary and high school teachers with like experience and like years of training. All cities in Indiana comparable in size to Gary have this schedule. Supt. W. A. Wirt and a small group of teachers, long favored, are bitterly opposing this democratic schedule."[51]

Partial success came early the following year on January 7, 1938, when the school board passed a 2.3 percent salary increase and accepted the principle of a single salary schedule, but maintained low maximum salaries for each level of experience. Wirt calculated that 335 of the teachers would receive a raise for the coming year. Union members were incensed, for they had not been consulted and were disappointed at the projected salary figures. Union president Paul Carlson, who was not allowed to speak at the school-board meeting, immediately complained that "every principle of collective bargaining has been violated or ignored by the board." Strong support came from Mayor L. B. (Barney) Clayton and Lake County Central Labor Union president Fred Schutz. "I am convinced there is merit in the request of the Gary Teachers' union and that a few teachers are over-paid and many are under-paid," Clayton advised the school board in early March. "I therefore urge that the board of education at their next meeting give the Gary Teachers' union a full and complete hearing on their petition for a readjustment of the salaries of the teachers of Gary." The debate was escalating.[52]

A planned meeting between the union and school board was necessarily postponed because of Wirt's sudden death on March 11. The union properly memorialized the longtime superintendent: "*All children* have lost a champion whose life has been dedicated to the understanding and solution of the particular problems that limit the natural development of children in industrial centers." They then resumed their struggle with the board. In theory the board had accepted the single salary schedule, but now added an annoying rider, known as the starred maximum, which would deny automatic raises for "possibly inferior" teachers. The union was disturbed. "As union teachers, we do not condone inefficiency in our members," Flora Philley later wrote, but the "starred-maximum as teacher-discipline is a poor device at best. . . . Its presence and application in our schedule perpetuates the unwholesome morale that accompanied the old rating system. It tends to enslave the teacher to fear, suspicion, and sycophancy." Teachers whose salaries were unfairly limited were defended by the union's grievance committee.[53]

By the decade's end the union found itself in a surprisingly strong position. In the first issue of the local's newsletter, *The Gary Teacher,* appearing in October 1939, a thirteen-point agenda was outlined. "Teacher participation in school administration policies" headed the list, followed by academic and civil liberties, an improved salary schedule, a shorter school day, as well as other teacher and school issues, such as improved playgrounds; but also on the list was "support of the Better Housing program with uniform standards for all neighborhoods." Union demands were not entirely self-serving. Joining with the AFT locals in Hammond and East Chicago, Local No. 4 featured newly elected AFT president and leading progressive educator George S. Counts at their October dinner. In early 1940, union secretary Flora Philley could rightfully boast that with 70 percent of the teachers and a recent salary increase the local was most confident. "We have juggled our Superintendent"—Herbert S. Jones, Wirt's replacement—"into a position where we have collective bargaining (never using those terrible words, however) and have him boasting about the 'unity and improved morale' which he has brought about." Within a few short years the union had become a significant force in school politics due to teacher militancy, a prounion climate, local political support from a revived Democratic party, a weakened school administration, particularly with the death of Wirt, and, perhaps most important, a cooperative school board. Indeed, a strong union man, Edward T. Doyne, was elected board president in August 1939, a unique situation. Flora Philley quickly encouraged AFT secretary-treasurer Irvin Kuenzli to write to Doyne, "reminding him of his heavy obligation to labor." Kuenzli obliged.[54]

Doyne's election as board president—"although Dr. James Craig, a horrible old reactionary, was in line for the post through seniority," according to Philley—capped a political struggle starting in mid-decade for control of the school board. In 1934, as the depression deepened, the board remained safely in the hands of the business community, with holdovers P. W. Seyl, L. I. Combs, and newcomer May Patterson, a Democrat. James Craig, a doctor and a Republican, replaced Seyl the next year; and Donald Milliren, a Democrat and head of the county voters' registration bureau, took Combs' place in 1936. But the board was on the edge of a major transformation.[55]

City politics, following the national trend, shifted significantly in 1934 with the election of L. B. (Barney) Clayton as mayor, the first Democratic mayor since 1913. Within a few years the mayor began to eye the bipartisan school board, traditionally appointed by the city council. The fireworks began in February 1937, when state senators from South Bend and Evansville introduced legislation to allow the mayors of certain larger cities, including South Bend, Evansville, Fort Wayne, and Gary, to appoint the school board, as well as increase the size of the board from three to five members. Locally, influential Democrats lined up in support, while an opposition was formed by members of the city council, the school board, Kiwanis club, Emerson school parents' committee, and many others.

The conservative *Gary Post-Tribune* strenuously argued that politics had no place in school affairs, pretending that this was something new. "Has the board ever permitted politics to have any influence in the schools?" queried editor H. B. Snyder. "No, it has not. During the entire 30 years, under both democratic and republican councils, there has never been as much as a charge of political influence in the schools." And, since two of the three current board members were already Democrats, they "can remove Wirt if they think that act would benefit the Gary schools. This is not a fight between Wirt and anti-Wirt factions but an attack on the schools." Many in the city agreed. Delegations descended on the legislature, including teachers who were encouraged by their principals to oppose the bill. Rumors circulated that a new board would fire the superintendent or perhaps force him to resign. Fifteen thousand in Gary signed a petition protesting the "School Grab" bill. In response, Mayor Clayton shot back that "up to now the schools have been operated somewhat like a closed corporation." The bill became law in early March. Naturally disappointed, Wirt was buoyed up by strong community opposition. "It is most reassuring to know that the people are back of the schools," he confided to his son Franz. "That is the only protection that they have had for 30 years and now they will not be disturbed by the politicians for a long time. These things happen in school systems and of course the Washington incident entered in as well as the fact that other members of [the] family are teaching. Considering the depression and everything else we have come through very well."[56]

While satisfied, the mayor was stung by the attacks on him and continued to deny that "there will be a 'political upheaval' in the Gary school system." He finally made his school board appointments in July—Mary Schaaf, a Democrat and the Calumet Township trustee; Edward Doyne, a Republican, union supporter, and foreman in the U.S. Steel sheet and tin mills; and the three incumbents. Schaaf was not eligible, however, because she was a public employee, so Clayton appointed her husband Edward, also a Democrat and an employee of the real-estate department of the Banker's Trust Company (of which his brother was president). The board was hardly the mayor's tool, for it was slow in restoring teachers' salaries and recognizing the union, and generally deferred to Wirt. But in July 1938, Mayor Clayton named Maynard Suley to the school board, replacing the unpopular May Patterson. By appointing Suley, a Democrat whose wife was a teacher and union member, the mayor fulfilled his pledge to the union "that they should have representation on the board," according to the *Gary American*.[57]

The board now took a more independent line toward Superintendent Jones. But it was also internally divided, with the conservative Craig often in the minority, which created some turmoil. For example, in May 1939 Craig proposed that the board continue the vocational department's sales-training course for employees of Gary's retail stores, a program supported by the powerful Commercial Club, but he received no support from his colleagues. A more serious split had occurred the previous month, when three of the five members vetoed the superintendent and extended the contract of a teacher active in the union. "The superintendent took exception to the rebuff at the time, asserting in effect that the trustees had compromised him by usurping his authority as the schools' chief executive," according to the *Gary Post-Tribune*. In August, a motion by two board members to drop the Saturday, summer, and Sunday programs was defeated for lack of a majority. Clearly, the day had passed when a strong superintendent, backed by a united school board, could rule the system unchallenged. School affairs had not become more political, only less centrally controlled.[58]

Political and personal disagreements were only one additional element during the decade heightening educational controversy. Another, more long-standing problem concerned the continuing school segregation, strongly supported by white citizens but a contentious issue within the black community. The city's black population grew slowly during the 1930s from about eighteen thousand in 1930 (17.8 percent of the population) to about 20,400 in 1940 (18.3 percent of the population of 111, 719). The percentage of blacks in the school population rose from 18.6 percent to 21.1 percent during the decade, concentrated in the all-black East Pulaski (over nine hundred) and Roosevelt (about two thousand) schools, as well as the integrated Froebel school (over seven hundred, or 25 percent of the student body). There were over eighty black teachers for the thirty-seven hundred black students in 1931, climbing to ninety by the end of the decade. In an article in August 1931 in the *Crisis,* the NAACP's national newspaper, Dennis Bethea reported Superintendent Wirt's comments "that the general standard of qualification of the colored teachers was higher than that of the whites. . . . Dr. Wirt produced figures to show that there were no more failures among the colored than among the whites; moreover, that there was just as large a proportion of colored youths who went on through the high school as there is among the other groups." And Bethea added, "this was thought to be remarkable, when it is remembered that the majority of Gary people are newcomers, many from parts of the South where the school advantages are meager indeed." Six years later, in a master's thesis at Cornell University, John Foster Potts echoed these optimistic sentiments: "There is no obvious discrimination in school matters. Negro teachers are paid the same salaries as the whites and all the schools are built alike. Negroes and whites assemble together for teachers' meetings, and in every important teacher organization at least one Negro holds an office. The auditorium department of the system sponsors mixed dramatic and music contests which helps to develop good will among the races. . . . In the matter of equipment and supplies a similar policy is followed, Negroes getting their share of both."[59]

Despite these accolades, all was not well for blacks, teachers or students, within the Gary schools. They shared with their counterparts in Chicago and throughout the urban North a plethora of difficulties and handicaps, not the least of which was the stigma of segregation, although this continued to be a controversial issue within the black community. School problems mirrored the larger reality of black life in the city—crushing poverty, segregated and inadequate housing and health care, employment problems, second-rate recreational facilities, and pervasive discrimination. Hardly suffering in silence, the black community occasionally raised a muted protest, despite internal divisions and an anemic NAACP, which prevented any vigorous challenge to the most blatant forms of discrimination. But there were scattered victories, as individuals and neighborhood organizations fought for dignity and some measure of justice, often focusing on school conditions.[60]

Of immediate concern as the decade opened was the completion of the planned all-black Roosevelt school, an outcome of the successful student strike at the Emerson school in 1927, population pressures, and the black community's desire to have better high-school facilities. But the school's segregated nature continued to be a sticking point. In mid-June 1930, a mass meeting at the First Baptist Church, called by the Reverend Charles Hawkins representing the NAACP, passed a resolution opposing "the proposed segregation of races in the Gary public schools." Opposition to the resolution came from William Lorden and Charles James, who echoed the views of Marcus Garvey's Universal Negro Improvement Association (UNIA); they argued "that with the establishment of a school for both white and colored students it would tend to destroy the 'race consciousness' of the Negro children." The integrationist/separationist debate became more heated in August, when a "small riot" almost erupted at another meeting of the integrationist faction after a speaker declared "all Negroes in favor of segregated schools should go back to Mississippi."[61]

In the center of the controversy was Roosevelt Annex principal Frederick C. McFarlane, whose outspoken UNIA sentiments were thought by some to be responsible for turning the high-school boys into "nothing but hoodlums." Speaking before the local white Rotary and Lions clubs, he was applauded for his view that "intelligent Negroes no longer whimper about segregation. They have discovered that what they really want is to be free within themselves," according to the highly critical NAACP-oriented *Gary American*. "It is pitiable to see an otherwise intelligent Negro accept segregation with a lover's kiss," wrote the editor. "Our learned educator condones it—nay, begs for it." In November of 1930 McFarlane's critics attempted a student strike at the Roosevelt school, which fizzled the second day. Wirt defended the principal. The *Gary American* condemned "school strikes or any such displays of yahooism," but called for his resignation or dismissal, if a suitable replacement could be found.[62]

Discord was temporarily stilled the following April with the dedication of the impressive million-dollar main building of the Roosevelt school, which now included all grades from kindergarten through high school. The *Gary American* lavished praise on the new building, "the equal of any school building or educational center supported by public taxation in this section of the nation." "This newspaper has never approved of the separate public school for Negroes," continued the editor. "It has always believed that Negroes and whites should receive their training in the same classrooms. . . .

But if separate schools have to be established, they should be the equal of white schools in matters of equipment and efficiency of its teaching staff. In this regard the new Roosevelt high school comes up to the requirements." Proud of its elegance and all-black staff, the black community, many reluctantly, welcomed the school. McFarlane, however, was elated and emphasized that "at Roosevelt we will try to teach the Negro youth to value his own background with its African overtones. . . . The Negro is done with apology." He quoted from the poet Langston Hughes, who "wrote in substance that the Negro is proud of himself and that he has no cause to be ashamed that he knows he is beautiful, that he has no apology to offer for himself, that he will stand on his own feet, 'build his own fortresses as best he knows,' that he is glad if others are pleased and if they are not it makes no difference." The UNIA activist was not giving an inch. His appointment as principal might have surprised some, considering his controversial stance, but his separationist views coincided with Wirt's natural longstanding desire to appease the white community.[63]

McFarlane was soon putting his ideas into practice, earning him the enthusiastic support of the daily press, which believed the school formed "the substantial nucleus for a newer, better Negro community in the Steel City." The press applauded his employment of seventeen schoolboys as paid school janitors. The girls were given "instruction in expert laundry work, with equipment including white stove tubs, electric washers, mangles and other devices. Another for girls is the space set aside for instruction in housekeeping, incorporating the proper setting of tables, bed-making and so on. This includes a rollaway bed." Reminiscent of the Booker T. Washington educational philosophy, such praise for the practical approach surely rankled those who preferred a more traditional curriculum—although McFarlane certainly concentrated on academic scholarship. Criticism even came from a citizens' group organized by the Communist party, which accused McFarlane of not distributing food and clothing to needy children and of attempting to collect the book rental, which many students could not afford.[64]

As Roosevelt's population climbed to well over two thousand in early 1932, attacks on McFarlane escalated. In June he was charged with encouraging moral delinquency among the students. "An investigation revealed that the condition is attributable to several causes, one of which is lack of cooperation between principal and teachers," proclaimed the *Gary American*. "It is claimed that the principal has inaugurated a monitor system, which is nothing more than an elaborate organization of snoopers and spies whose chief duty it is to inform the principal and keep him acquainted with the movements of the teachers." He was also charged with encouraging anti-Americanism, for "foreign radical speakers have been invited to speak to the student body, and to sow the seed of hate and distrust with nobody knows what probable result to the detriment of the Negro in America." Others charged that there was a general lack of discipline. This was all grist for the opposition's mill, and the paper once again questioned McFarlane's competence. He was subtly compared with East Pulaski principal H. Theo Tatum, a strong integrationist. The *Gary American* heaped praise on Tatum, "for his excellent organization and the perfect cooperation of his entire faculty." The principal worked closely with a parents' advisory council, explaining to them "that our economic situation is quite precarious at this time," with almost half of the students' families requesting assistance. An open, fair, capable administrator, Tatum seemed the opposite of the aloof, suspicious, fanatical McFarlane—at least to the *Gary American* and its sympathetic readers.[65]

The McFarlane-Tatum controversy, symbolizing the separationist-integrationist split in the black community, took a new twist in June 1933, when McFarlane resigned to become principal of the new Paul Lawrence Dunbar high school in Dayton, Ohio. The school board quickly combined the shabby East Pulaski high school, which was not accredited by the North Central Association of Colleges and Secondary Schools, with the Roosevelt high school and appointed Tatum as principal of the grand unit-school in the heart of the black community. "Because of his quiet, unassuming manner, many people fail to appreciate the profound influence of his sane and cultured leadership," the *Gary American* crowed about the new principal. And it was correct. "With regret we wish to inform you that it will be a calamity to appoint Mr. Tatum to the Roosevelt High School," the Central District Citizens Club warned school board member May Patterson. "The majority of the parents and students strenously [*sic*] oppose the appointment. The very purpose of school will be defeated where parents, students and Principal will be at mental war." It would take a few years for this dire prediction to come true. Meanwhile, Tatum settled into his new position, changing the school's emphasis "toward the building up of the spirit of social co-operation on the part of the youth to replace that of bitterness and divisive competition which has been so evident with the adults." Teachers would now "strive to teach the Negro youth that he is an active participant in the great game of American citizenship."[66]

Tatum, his supporters, and the *Gary American* stressed cooperation with the city's white power structure—the latter praised Wirt during his political difficulties in April 1934 and invited his critics to "observe the high standard of intelligence acquired by the average student under the Wirt System"—but had difficulties with blatant discrimination. They briefly joined with a mixed group in the community to protest conditions at the Froebel school. Black students were prevented from joining in extracurricular activities, such as the band, orchestra, and student government, although they participated on athletic teams; the night school was also segregated. Perhaps most galling, they were not allowed to use the girls' and boys' swimming pools. "They have open[ed] the swimming pool here and let the white girls go swimming on Thursday and Friday," the "Colored Students of Froebel School" complained in January 1934. "The colored girls cannot go for no reason at all."

Encouraged by the local Communist party, critics voiced more complaints, and even white Froebel students were urged to "fight against discrimination. Today they have taken away the rights of the Negro student. Tomorrow they may take ours away. We must remember our future depends upon the unity of Negro and white students."[67]

The NAACP joined with the Community party in calling a protest meeting in April to question "why should the Negro student be jim crowed against the recreational activities of the school clubs, swimming pool, athletics and other intellectual activities in his district that the white youth of today take advantage of?" Froebel principal Charles Coons was equally perplexed; his suggestion was to limit the enrollment, while transferring some of the black students out of the school, if the school board believed in segregation. "We have been trying to build up in the minds of our white children *respect for the colored race,*" he informed Wirt, but this was becoming more difficult with the growing black enrollment, some of whom were in separate "chain gang" classes. "To be truly representative, the Board must carry out the mandate of the people whom it represents, and there is no mistaking that mandate so far as all that part of Gary is concerned, except the central district. The white parents of the Froebel district have as yet taken no concerted action on the policy of segregation. I am therefore not recommending any violent eradication of the colored children from Froebel school at this time," he concluded, but only curbing the black enrollment. Of course, "if the Board of Education wants to carry out a major operation on the race problem at Froebel School at this time, I shall co-operate fully in trying to make that operation a success." It did not, and Coons had to contend with the status quo, as did the black community. In July 1938 the board moved the Froebel-Roosevelt boundary north; some black children attending Froebel would now be transferred to Roosevelt, while any white children in the Roosevelt district would automatically attend Froebel. The pot would boil for another ten years in the city's only integrated school.[68]

As the community struggled to pull itself out of the depression during the decade's middle years, there was seemingly little overt concern for matters of segregation and integration, of justice and equality. The old antagonisms came to the surface in 1938, however, when controversy once again swirled around the Roosevelt principal, a sure magnet for community discontent. In early March, Principal Tatum was charged by a group of Central District residents with attempting to carry "out his avowed statement of some two or three years ago, that he will soon have all of the old teachers out of Roosevelt, and replace them with new ones." After listing various examples of the principal's perfidious behavior, the citizens wondered "how far the Board of Education is going to allow Mr. Tatum to go on in his undertakings, to provoke, to insult and fa[l]sely accuse the men and women who are misfortunate enough to be placed under him." The citizens' group was soon anticipating Tatum's resignation, but he was no quitter. Next, a group of twenty-five

Roosevelt mothers, declaring that the Parent-Teachers' Association was the principal's tool, initiated a campaign to have Tatum dismissed. Previously, he had been charged with favoring the Republicans and being anti-Roosevelt, but now political issues were not mentioned in their petition. The *Gary American*, however, strongly backing the mayor, did charge Tatum with calling "a secret session of his pet teachers to endorse the candidacy of Doctor Doty," a candidate in the Democratic primary for mayor, and with frustrating the distribution of Clayton's literature. Once in Tatum's corner, the paper was now angered because of "the numerous Republican meetings held in the auditorium of that school, and the refusal of the board or the principal, or whoever was responsible, for refusing the same auditorium to the Clayton Committee for similar meetings." The controversy demonstrated the clear shift in the black community to the Democratic party—mirroring the national trend, with, perhaps, seventy-five percent of the black vote going to Roosevelt in 1936—while a minority of professionals and others, such as Tatum, clung to their traditional Republican allegiance, to the party of Lincoln.[69]

Tatum had written, "the schools of America are dedicated to the proposition that our government can endure only through the active participation of an intelligent citizenry cheerfully working together, sharing responsibilities, and growing constantly in attitudes, appreciation, and skills. The teachers of American youth are rightfully expected to consecrate themselves to the task of developing such citizens." As the community maneuvered to force his dismissal, Tatum surely wondered how "active" the citizenry should be. Tensions heightened in late July 1938, when a law suit was filed by the Mothers' Union against the principal in the state court; they also requested a hearing before the school board. The *Gary American*, reporting on the packed, heated public meetings, refused to highlight the charges, only vaguely referring to "evidence of sexual perversion and immorality being rampant" in the Roosevelt and East Pulaski schools. Rushing to Tatum's side, the school board hired three attorneys for his defense, including J. A. Patterson, the husband of School board president May Patterson. The Mothers' Union threatened to file charges with the bar association over the possible Patterson conflict of interest. The school board next refused to debate the matter, preferring that it be handled by the court. Frustrated that the situation was dragging on, four of the mothers in January 1939 attempted to block Roosevelt's door in order to keep the teachers out, and they were arrested.[70]

In May, a delegation headed by activist attorney Milo Murray again appealed to the school board for Tatum's dismissal or demotion. They "portrayed the principal as a regular martinet, ruling his school after the manner of a Hitler, rudely denying audiences to visiting parents; 'punishing' recalcitrant members of his teaching staff; expropriating authority over the affairs of the P.T.A. and permitting immoral practices among his students."

The matter finally died with a whimper. Tatum's critics should produce more specific evidence against him, the *Gary American* finally demanded, or "out of consideration for the morale of the pupils" they should "shut up." And they did. Tatum retired from Roosevelt in 1961, a venerated educator and community leader.[71]

Tatum and his legacy survived. His ordeal highlighted the turmoil of the decade, as economic, political, and racial forces were unleashed by the advent of depression and revival. Deep rifts appeared in Gary, dividing blacks from blacks and blacks from whites, teachers from administrators, Republicans from Democrats, and capital from labor. The Roosevelt principal remained in office because he identified closely with the educational and political goals of the ever-popular superintendent, who was clearly embattled by early 1938. Wirt was shaken by the Democratic control of city government and of the newly expanded school board, the growing power of the teachers' union, the business community's intensifying reluctance to support increased school taxes, as well as by serious financial and family problems. All of his business investments, including the bank, which failed, had turned sour, and his two youngest children had developed serious health problems. He struggled to pay his bills.

One bright spot was his son Franz. For years an aloof parent, Wirt now maintained a close correspondence with his eldest, giving advice, news about family difficulties, and details about his own poverty. With little solace during his final days, he was cheered by the popular author H. G. Wells's article, appearing in the *London News-Chronicle,* praising the Gary schools. "It has not been an easy task—this acquainting the world with the advantages of the platoon school plan, obvious though they are, and some times I have thought that the work-study-play system had a greater popularity and was better understood in Europe and Asia than right here at home," Wirt confessed. "But I am less discouraged today. Comment such as that coming from Wells is indeed uplifting and fortifying. I feel I can still devote 10 years to active public service, and if, during that time, I can witness a more or less universal adoption of the Gary plan, I shall be indeed happy, and retire in contentment." Ten days later he was dead.[72]

"Death that crept up suddenly—almost without warning—today obliterated from the Gary scene the personality of William A. Wirt, founder and superintendent of the Gary schools, whose celebrated work-study-play system of child education became the steel city's gift to the world," the *Post-Tribune* announced to the world on March 11, 1938. He had recently turned sixty-four. "While the 21,000 children and young people and the 700 teachers and other employees of the schools went through the day's routine with saddened hearts and tear-dimmed eyes, a special session of the school trustees was convened . . . to draft a resolution of sorrow and arrange for a final tribute to the educator." Poor and overworked, he "died a martyr to the work to which he had dedicated his life." "There has been back-biting and criticism and political meanness now and then," the paper editorialized, "but by and large this man has been appreciated. He probably died of overwork and worry brought on by the depression and opposition, but his work has been done and whatever rewards there are in after-life for men who do the work of this world superlatively well will be given in abundance to William Wirt."[73]

Four years earlier Mary Rennels, wife of *Post-Tribune* editor H. B. Snyder, had described the superintendent, of middling height and somewhat over-weight, as looking "more like a country gentleman than a school admin-istrator. . . . he does not strike me as the sort of man to whom I would rush with an emotional tangle. I'd first want to straighten my hair, adjust my hat and order my thoughts, for it is easy to see he has no use for mud-dleheads. . . . Dr. Wirt is as impersonal as a Yogi. . . . None of his pleasures interfere with the constant working of his brain." Greatly impressed, she noted only one serious flaw, he lacked a sense of humor. Stolid and domineer-ing, emotionally distant even from his family until his last years, Wirt gar-nered awe and respect, seldom love. *The Nation's Schools* applauded him as a "courageous pioneer," but faulted his "personal inflexibilities." He was more a monument, resembling the impressive, reassuring brick facades of his beloved schools, rather than a flawed mortal. Indeed, his name would live on with the dedication of the William A. Wirt school in the Miller neighborhood the next year.[74]

The superintendent who had invented, nurtured, and dominated the fa-mous Gary school system, the only superintendent since the city's founding, was gone. A suitable replacement was necessary and needed soon. "[T]he problem facing Gary now is the selection of a superintendent who under-stands the system, believes in its success and is able to carry it on," wrote H. B. Synder. "It is no easy task and yet it can be accomplished if the members of the board of education are intent on one thing and nothing else, that is the good of the schools." The school board considered bringing in someone from the outside well versed in the system, then in April appointed as acting superintendent Herbert S. Jones, the director of social studies and a teacher in the system since 1923; he was elevated to permanent superintendent four months later. Jones would doggedly cling to the platoon plan.[75]

In June 1939 the downtown streets were lined "by proud fathers and mothers, sisters and brothers, uncles and aunts and other relatives and friends of 1,156 young men and women who, wearing mortarboard caps and gowns, marched down Broadway to Memorial auditorium for the fifth annual convocation of the graduating classes of the Gary public high schools and Gary junior college." As the members of this "record-breaking class passed into Memorial auditorium, scores of them paused to gaze reverently at a bronze bust of Dr. Wirt which stands in the lobby." Students who could dimly recall, if at all, the "prosperity" of the twenties, whose consciousness was fixed on the hardships and sacrifices of the depression years, had nonetheless survived to reach graduation and perhaps a better life now that economic recovery appeared within reach. They had clung to schooling as, perhaps, their only salvation and easily recognized the name, if not the face, of their former superintendent, as could their parents. Herbert Jones had moved into Wirt's office, but ever worked in his shadow.[76]

Although Wirt had not survived to witness the end of the decade, his school system remained as a living testimony to the vitality of his persistent vision. Former school board member May Patterson summarized the three continuing goals of the auditorium program, "the heart of the Gary system": "to develop the child as an individual by inculcating personality traits such as self-possession and poise, command of English, practice of courtesy, wise use of leisure time, and dependability. Next, to develop the child as a social being by imparting a knowledge of group action and learning to follow, as well as to lead, together with a broad attitude toward life through participation in all school activities. Then to develop the child as a citizen by bringing into being a consciousness of school, city, and world movements, respect for the rights of others and the Flag and the courtesies due it, a willingness for cooperation and an increased desire to help with the common activities of life which each day brings." Combining the main, and somewhat contradictory, curricular and extracurricular threads of progressive education—stressing the mental and physical growth of the individual in a social context—the Gary schools struggled to continue a tradition becoming increasingly unfashionable throughout the country.[77]

While praise of Wirt and his educational triumphs continued to echo throughout the city, there were rumblings of discontent. Drawing on another legacy of the progressive years, the search to improve efficiency through the results of a school survey, the school board in late November 1939 authorized an eighteen-month study of the system by a team from Purdue University. Goaded by H. B. Snyder, Wirt's eulogist and president of the conservative Gary Taxpayers' Association, which had been carping about excessive school expenditures and opposing tax levies, the board was "looking to possible economies and improvements in administrative, supervisory and tutorial practices." Of course, the survey "might disclose opportunities to effect substantial savings without in any way curtailing the educational program." Thus, as the decade faded change was in the wind.[78]

The Gary school system had survived, almost unscathed, throughout the decade. Programs had been trimmed, cut, restored, then trimmed again as the local economy, following national trends, bucked and plunged. Night, Saturday, and summer classes had been temporarily sacrificed in order to maintain the basic curriculum, which remained essentially intact. Salaries had been slashed and only slowly restored as tax revenues began to increase after mid-decade. With expanded enrollment in the high schools and neighborhood population shifts, there was a need for increased facilities, but until the decade's end the only new building was that done with federal funds.

Building maintenance also suffered. Overall, the school system looked about the same in 1939 as it did in 1930, but without Wirt at the helm.

Outwardly unscathed, the system had yet undergone significant alterations, mirroring national educational trends. No longer were the teachers docile employees. Through their union they had gained considerable unity and strength. Having achieved recognition and collective bargaining rights, teachers had become a significant and permanent force in school politics. Another vital change occurred within the business community, led by U.S. Steel and its mouthpiece the Gary Taxpayers' Association. Traditionally strong supporters of public schooling, business leaders, reeling from the effects of the depression, began to question and fight school taxes. Henceforth, the major business interests would be more concerned about their profits than upholding increased school budgets and programs; once closely allied with school officials, and, indeed, they still remained social and ideological bedfellows, many in the business community now became an entrenched opposition. At the same time state educational funding increased to about 30 percent of school revenues (up from 10 percent before 1933), lessening reliance on local property and poll taxes. Another point of friction appeared in race relations. Turmoil at the Roosevelt school would quiet down, but white-black discord at the Froebel school, continually hinted at over the years, would finally boil over within a few years. In the heavily segregated city, race would be a continual sticking point. Then, too, with the greater high-school enrollment, there were growing problems with the curriculum. It would be increasingly difficult to strike the proper balance between practical and academic subjects, particularly in the working-class schools. All of these issues and divisions would become more visible in the next decade.[79]

The major themes of Gary's school history were clearly visible during the depression years, however: the continuing commitment to maintaining and even expanding (e.g., Gary College) the schools' various programs and services, however difficult; and the plethora of influences on educational affairs, particularly the more visible role of local, state, and national political forces, business organizations, labor unions, and black interests.

VI

THE WAR YEARS, 1940–1945

Of Czech ancestory, Leonard Levenda lived with his family at 1609 Monroe in the midtown section of Gary. He had attended Holy Trinity school through the elementary grades, then entered Froebel school in 1942 for his last four years. Leonard was a good student, a member of the debate and drama clubs, quite articulate, but not particularly a school leader. Arriving at Froebel on Monday morning, September 18, 1945, at the start of his senior year, he discovered "a mob of students in the park type area there. What's going on? Them: we're not going to school. What do you mean you're not going to school? Them: we're on strike. What do you mean you're on strike? . . . So they told me what happened. So then the principal, [Richard A.] Nuzum, came out—what is this, what's this all about? They started yelling—we don't want to go to school with the blacks. They were tired of being called nigger lovers all the time."[1]

The striking students quickly chose Leonard as their spokesman to negotiate with school officials. He liked the school, believing that the teachers were "fantastic," but shared his fellow students' grievances; he also thrived in the spotlight. The strike dragged on and off during the fall, and discussions continued into the spring, with Leonard always articulating the students' changing position. He represented both the successes and failures of the Gary schools. Glib and quick witted, adept at public speaking, Leonard proved to be an academic winner. But his willingness to challenge school officials over the issue of school integration demonstrated one of the schools' weaknesses. Others would appear throughout the war years, a time of educational turmoil and survival. School officials struggled to obtain a new identity as the work-study-play system deteriorated and parents and teachers organized; there were wartime difficulties, as well as struggles over the curriculum and mounting economic problems. Once again, however, the schools managed to offer a broad array of programs, services, and courses, partially of a traditional nature and partially as a response to emergency needs. Moreover, they continued to be pushed and pulled by a variety of internal and external forces, particularly by educational experts and the needs of a wartime society.

America's public schools emerged from the ravages of the depression decade intact, but shaken. During the next decade enrollments leveled off, hovering around twenty-five million, although the elementary population would increase slightly because of the jump in the birth rate. The number of high-school graduates rose nationally, however, indicating the increasing importance of the diploma as well as family affluence. The Gary schools generally followed suit. Enrollment remained at about 21,000, while the teaching staff increased by over one hundred, to about 750. The number of high-school graduates declined, however, from 1,249 in 1940 to 1,109 in 1950, mirroring a steady drop in secondary school enrollment during the decade, with girls always outnumbering boys. During the war years jobs were plentiful in the steel mills.

If school demographics remained fairly steady, the same can not be said for the work-study-play plan, the heart of the elementary system for three decades. In late 1939, at the urging of the powerful editor of the *Gary Post-Tribune,* H. B. Snyder, the school board agreed to pay $10,000 for a survey conducted by a team from Purdue University. Survey director Frederick B. Knight, head of the Psychology Department, had only a few minor stipulations: "that the study be allowed to be carried through to completion, with all recommendations resulting therefrom to be acted upon; that the school board allow publication of the survey report, copies of which probably would enjoy a popular demand among educators over the nation." Knight was hardly lacking in confidence. Superintendent H. S. Jones, a disciple of his predecessor William A. Wirt, anticipated that some changes would be forthcoming, but "hope[d] that their recommendations will not materially affect the general organization of our program but will be suggested changes looking toward improvement in our instruction." His hopes were in vain, and his days as superintendent were nearly over.[2]

The wheels of change began to grind even before the report was concluded, as its recommendations were deliberately leaked by the staff. In December 1940 the school board began to dismantle the platoon system, slowly substituting the contained classroom in the kindergarten and first three grades. Anticipating resistance, the board also adopted a resolution "denying the right of supervisors and principals to make statements for publication concerning any administrative matter without having them approved by the superintendent before being released." The one-teacher-per-class arrangement, first introduced on an experimental basis only at the Horace Mann school, would mean that the children would no longer have separate classes for music, auditorium, or physical training, and the school day would be reduced from seven to six hours.[3]

Survey director Knight was somewhat frustrated by the natural resistance to change among many in the system. He publicly praised Wirt, but argued that "the year 1941 has an infinite number of problems that were not present 30 years ago. . . . We are trying to treat the patient, not give him nightmares. The result of our inquiry, we confidently feel, will be good for Gary, good for Purdue, good for education." Privately, he confided to newsman E. C. Rosenau in January 1941 his belief that one key to success of the new program was the role of Horace Mann principal Charles D. Lutz: "Suppose you should say to Lutz, 'Lutz, if this demonstration works well, you'll be the next superintendent.' I'll bet ten to one that things would work just as smoothly as could be. However, if you should say to Lutz, 'Here is an idea that Mr. Jones is identified with,' the thing would stick in his throat."[4]

In a letter to John Dorsey, also written in mid-January, Knight was considerably more pessimistic. "We have now relatively old people, poorly trained, who have almost a religious furvor [sic] concerning their ownership of their schools, the impropriety of the School Board being master in its own house, and the impossibility of anyone making any suggestions that involve change," he complained. The school supervisors appeared to be a serious roadblock, for they "have [been] taught the town is the perfection of the status quo and the undesirability of anything but repetition." But he found allies within the school board, the *Post-Tribune,* and the steel corporation, who were open to innovations, for they apparently desired an efficient, up-to-date school system. To Lloyd Burress, representing the mill, he complained "that we have no precedence [sic] relative to surveys to go on concerning the present situation. When the paid personnel of a school department obviously contests—often with an amazing amount of inaccuracy--recommendations and resolutions of a School Board, we have what might be called 'legal mutiny'." Despite the obstacles, Knight had faith that the public would support significant change.[5]

In late January 1941, the school board expanded the primary experiment to the Emerson, Edison, East Pulaski, and Wirt schools. The survey discovered a high retardation rate among the smaller children because of fatigue and "a tremendous amount of mental confusion." Though the illness sounded vague, the remedy was to keep the first-grade children with one teacher, while in the second and third grades the children would be with one teacher 80 percent of the time and for the remainder with the art, music, nature-study, and physical-education teachers, instead of moving from activity to activity throughout the day. The *Post-Tribune* contributed a steady barrage of positive articles on the survey's findings, featured the various team members, and argued that "educators who have their first interest in the education of our children should welcome a study which seeks to improve the benefits to our children." By mid-February, the school board tried to squelch rumors that the changes could be stopped—"Board members said they expected free discussion, but that the reorganization was a definite policy in the primary grades and was no longer a debateable [sic] issue. . . . 'I think the opposition is folding up,' [Superintendent] Jones said. 'It is to be expected that some smoldering antagonism will remain.' "[6]

The final report, when published in early 1942, included much philosophical wisdom, specific data on teachers, students, and administrators, and numerous recommendations for improving administration and teaching. Unlike the unwieldly and widely distributed earlier eight-volume GEB survey (1918), the Purdue study, with the prosaic title *Final Report: Purdue Survey Committee for the Gary Board of Education to the President and Board of Trustees of Purdue University,* was a mimeographed one-volume affair, hardly designed to attract much outside attention. In his introduction, Knight feigned ignorance of the history of the schools' internecine wars; "the present Gary Survey was, as it were, begun stone cold." Chapter one was a pep talk to the school board, advising them of their responsibility to "make the policy and then see to it that this policy is carried out," without abdicating to the superintendent, as had been the policy under Wirt. The recommendations covered a wide range of topics investigated by Knight, his two associate directors, and the ten staff members: clerical services, the school plant, libraries, secondary education, traffic safety, industrial arts and vocational education, physical education, home economics, as well as child welfare and delinquency.[7]

The survey's main thrust was to throw a bucket of cold water over local educational pretenses: "In the olden days Gary was engrossed in an important exposition and demonstration of an educational organization of great vitality and worth, i.e., the Gary 'System'. . . . It is only in your fancy, however, that the educational world is watching Gary now. Perhaps it would be wise to settle down and be just yourselves—just a good school system serving its own community as best it may." Specific problems included too much isolation and teacher inbreeding. Teacher selection should be broadened, younger teachers should be hired, and there should be increased in-service training, particularly for elementary teachers. Teacher morale would be enhanced if the school board did "not look askance at the Teacher's Union—rather make it your ally and confidant." Another hindrance to constructive change was the age and design of the major school buildings. "It has never paid (in our estimation) to keep forcing a school program to a building for the sake of proving that the original basic plan was forever right," Knight argued. "We recommend that before any other buildings of any size are planned the board take due consideration of the very creditable advances in school house architecture that have somewhat paralleled the changes in automobiles since Ford first went into production."[8]

Acquiring new buildings and new teachers was not currently practical, but other suggestions, in addition to the central issue of dropping the platoon plan in the primary grades, were put into place even before the survey's publication. First, however, was the matter of the superintendent, whose contract would expire in July 1941. While Knight and his colleagues could not explicitly recommend firing Jones, a dramatic change was obviously needed in the superintendent's office in order to guarantee progress. In April, the *Gary Post-Tribune* noted the appearance of a community-wide petition, apparently initiated by the more affluent parents of Horace Mann students, "urging the trustees to 'pick a man from outside the system, preferably from outside the city.' " The school board soon acted. They were unwilling to break completely with the past, however, and so selected Charles D. Lutz as the new superintendent at a salary of $7,000. Arriving in Gary in 1921 as a math teacher at the Froebel school, Lutz became principal of Horace Mann three years later, where he worked until 1941. His cooperation in initiating the experiment to introduce the contained classroom in the primary grades obviously signaled his flexible attitude. Fittingly, he would remain as superintendent until the next school survey in 1955 resulted in his ouster.[9]

Along with replacing the superintendent, the board drastically restructured the administrative hierarchy. The subject-area supervisors, so vital to Wirt's emphasis on academic disciplines, were replaced by grade-level supervisors, one each for kindergarten through the third grades, grades four to eight, and the high schools. Supervisors remained for home economics, auditorium, physical education, music, and industrial arts, which remained separate subjects in the elementary grades. As the scope of the supervisors' duties were changed, the principals' power and responsibilities were greatly increased, "making them directly responsible for supervision, organization, designation of teachers' duties, courses of study, curriculum plans and professional improvement in their respective buildings"—a key recommendation of the survey. "It has been proposed that the principals of the Gary schools be given wider latitude in planning and organizing an educational program in the different schools to meet the needs of the pupils," survey member B. L. Dodds concluded. The principals soon were also drawing up their schools' budgets. "In the past, the Supervisors in their respective fields had authority above the principals. 'The new plan places the emphasis on the child,' Lutz said. 'Instead of stressing subject-matter, the new supervisors will make their objective the welfare of the pupils individually.' "[10]

The board worked feverishly through the spring of 1941, rushing to make changes before the survey was published. By late May they addressed the curriculum. History and geography were to be reorganized in the elementary grades. A ninth-grade community-living course was introduced, which included such topics as "educating the young, getting a living, making a home, use of leisure time, co-operating for community welfare, local government and what constitutes good citizenship." This pleased Knight and his colleagues, who argued that "probably more reorganization and experimentation has been going on in the field of social studies in recent years than in any other field in the secondary school. Schools are experimenting with fusion courses, the organization of a sequence of work centered around social problems and processes rather than subjects fields of history, civics, and economics." An emphasis on citizenship, drawing upon recent national concerns about personal and national identity, would prefigure the Life Adjustment curriculum soon to appear as well as serve the needs of a country at war. Indeed, in the *Final Report,* issued after Pearl Harbor, Knight argued that "schools must keep in touch with life. School is life. A school system cannot operate, if it is to be real, during war times 'as if' we were at peace. In a sense school is a preparation for life in the future—for some other time than now. In a true sense school is not only preparation for next year, but it is living today. . . . All this is true in peace time; it is desperately vital in war time."[11]

One other survey recommendation piqued the interest of the school board. According to John Dorsey, a psychiatrist and member of the survey team, "unless effective preventive measures are operating in childhood severe mental disorders requiring extensive psychiatric treatment occur in adult life." In the Gary schools he found many pupils "revealing indications of significant weaknesses in the direction of mental disorder and of criminality." It was obvious to Dorsey that "any school community of its size that tries to make healthy progress without the counsel of an adequately prepared psychiatrist, sympathetic to local needs, certainly is not aware of the importance of this service. I should consider my time and energy well spent if as a result the schools engage a specially trained full-time psychiatrist whose basic training experience has been such as to permit him to see the beginnings of mental illness and crime as they are occurring every day in the schools and homes of Gary." The system had hired various professionals over the years, including Elsie Fredericksen, a psychologist, in 1929 and Harold Hulbert, a psychiatrist, in 1933, but both were part-time. Taking Dorsey's plea to heart, in July the board employed Mark Roser, a psychiatric social worker with a rich and varied background, as director of child welfare. This was the first step in creating a welfare department, with control over school attendance, guidance, testing, and mental hygiene, as well as services for handicapped children.[12]

Born in Richmond, Indiana, in 1906, Roser had attended Earlham College, then Harvard University for graduate work in social ethics and psychology; he also worked at the South End Settlement House in Boston. Next, he served as Director of the Diagnostic Department of the Norfolk Prison Colony, an experimental facility in Massachusetts, followed by a stint at a boy's school in New York City and work with the Emergency Relief Association in Syracuse. In the late 1930s he arrived at the Indiana State Prison in Michigan City, where he conducted research and supervised counseling. He met Frederick Knight at a workshop at Purdue University, who recommended him to Lutz in the summer of 1941. Until his retirement from the system thirty years later, Roser would be intimately involved in all facets of child welfare in the schools and in the city, always serving as an enlightened spirit. "My impulse to come to Gary . . . was to help individual children as we did in the prison," he later remarked. "Well, a common sense approach is if the children are hungry and have no shoes, abandoned, abused at home, they couldn't adjust to the school. And also children have various handicaps mentally and emotionally and they should be treated individually. . . . And that's what I presented myself to reach for." In Gary he found the legacy of

Wirt's creative impulse and the lingering spirit of "the city of the century": "We used to say that in Gary if you threw a stick anywhere you could grow a tree." Within a year he hired Maryalice Quick, a specialist in the behavior problems of young children.[13]

During the fall and winter of 1941, reforms were continued and clarified as the winds of change continued to blow through the superintendent's office. Two items on the top of the agenda were reduction of the school day for children (but not for teachers) and securing the principals' new authority. The former, proposed by the teachers three years before and underscored by the Purdue Survey, finally resulted in a six-hour schedule for the primary grades (one through three) and seven-and-one-quarter hours for all other grades; each class was fifty minutes long. The latter issue, however, caused more difficulty, for many of the supervisors struggled to maintain their authority. Vocational Director Guy Wulfing, for one, who had originally arrived with Wirt from Bluffton, was "in sympathy with the Survey's recommendations and believe they are intended to revitalize and improve our schools. This does not mean, however, my hundred percent endorsement," he added in a letter to school board member Glenn Rearick. In late October, the school board upheld the principals' increased power, ruling that "building principals are responsible for the conduct of the schools assigned to them, while supervisors, as 'professional specialists,' are responsible for the educational program." Supervisors would represent the superintendent and provide "leadership in the improvement of instruction."[14]

Administrative procedures and time schedules could readily be altered, but the central issue came down to the academic environment. The Purdue survey complained that the curriculum was often stultifying and the classrooms were dull: "The pupil part in too many Gary classrooms is restricted to brief recitations in answer to questions. Little opportunity is given for pupils to participate in planning the course, selecting individual projects, or do anything that involves actual problem situations." If the teachers were at fault, most, nonetheless, had job security protected by the state tenure law passed in 1927. Various subjects were not only poorly taught, but were also out of date. In February 1942 the school board created a new "social living" course for the intermediate grades (four through eight), an integration of English and social studies, and a one-year world-history course—"streamlined to provide pupils with the background to understand current problems"—was substituted for two years of ancient, medieval, and modern history in high school. All primary classes were now under the new contained-classroom plan. Still, in May Isabelle Jones, director of the educational-research department, reported that 40 percent of the twenty thousand pupils were functioning below grade level (with 6 percent above). The superintendent attributed this situation to "inadequate adjustment of the curriculum to the needs of children; poor teaching and poor administrative procedures."[15]

In addition to attributing the retardation problem to educational inade-
quacies, including overcrowded classrooms, Lutz also referred to the "social
makeup of many areas in the community." The Purdue survey had already
noted a strong correlation between the socioeconomic background of high-
school seniors and the dropout rate. Using its own American Home Scale, a
method of depicting the home environment, the survey team had discovered
that Roosevelt school had the lowest score (31.5) and the highest dropout rate
(54 percent), followed by Froebel (33 and 43 percent), Tolleston (36.5 and 41
percent), Emerson (38.8 and 43 percent), Lew Wallace (41 and 31 percent),
Horace Mann (44.4 and 17 percent), and William Wirt (45.9 and 25 percent).
Simply, the integrated central district was the poorest, with the most affluent
families living in the Horace Mann and Wirt districts. Forty percent of the
children lived in apartments, ranging from the overcrowded frame buildings
surrounding Froebel to the sumptuous brick apartments along Fifth Avenue.
Ten percent of white (and 25 percent of black) homes needed major repairs;
15 percent of white (and 21 percent of black) dwellings had no indoor
plumbing; 5 percent of white (and 15 percent of black) homes had no radio;
twice as many white homes (39 percent) were owner occupied. Yet the report
concluded: "Many of the homes of Gary seem to be blessed with the
presence of the many creative comforts of life such as the radio, telephone,
library books, etc. This condition seemed to prevail among both the white
and the negro families. There were some exceptions in both races, however, a
rather definite conclusion could be reached by saying that many of the
families of Gary are enjoying a rather wholesome standard of living." Many,
but not enough. It is always difficult to separate home from school influences
in accounting for educational success or failure. Both school officials and the
Knight team understood the necessity of exploring all sides of the situation. [16]

Little could be done about matters of wealth and poverty, but the educational system could be continually refined, particularly for the youngest
children. In September 1942 the schools began to abolish mid-year promotions, with an emphasis on automatic promotions through the third grade.
"The function of the school," according to kindergarten-primary supervisor
Elizabeth Kempton, "is to provide 'meaningful experiences' which will help
children to live co-operatively in the community." The curriculum would
become flexible, "adjusted to fit the needs of individual children." While
there was talk of expanding the contained classroom to the sixth grade, this
decision was temporarily postponed. The growing sensitivity to children was
also reflected in the deemphasis on corporal punishment, "an ineffectual and
unintelligent means of meeting problem situations"; "understanding and
treatment of children's needs should be substituted for punishment, the new
rule says." The old rule allowed principals to inflict corporal punishment
after informing the parents. [17]

Failures continued to plague the schools, however, and affected about 7
percent of the students by April 1943, an unacceptable percentage for school

administrators who anxiously sought signs of pupil (and therefore school) success. The answer, as it turned out, was simple—abolish failures. In June, the school board instituted a new policy, after a trial at the Horace Mann school: "The new plan establishes a primary cycle for grades 1, 2 and 3 and an intermediate cycle for grades 4, 5 and 6, through which children will advance at their own rate of speed." There would be no annual examinations, although students could be "adjusted" from class to class or group to group after consultation with the parents, and achievement tests would be given at the end of the third year. In the second cycle home economics and shop work would be dropped, and there would be a greater emphasis on arithmetic, reading and English, and social studies. Ideally, the teachers would devote more attention to the slower students, and they would also focus on building character. "Emotional and spiritual growth are important to understand human relationships and get along in the world," Supervisor Kempton maintained. "To give pupils an appreciation of the good, the true and the beautiful will enable them to develop their own personalities to the maximum," she asserted. The mental-hygiene movement had definitely come to Gary. Finally, in mid-1945 the "progressive promotion policy" used in the primary grades and declared a success, was extended to the fourth and fifth grades.[18]

Administrative and curricular reforms progressed amid the more mundane matters of financial exigencies and war preparations, both disquieting distractions. There were still vestiges of the depression in February 1941, as the economy slowly crawled out of its hole, and school finances remained shaky. Money for salaries was taken from the budget for the Saturday schools, which were discontinued. Various welfare programs were still in place. For example, school children, starting at the Roosevelt school, were given federal surplus commodities for their lunches, including grapefruit and apples, and the cafeterias received butter, ham, bacon, flour, rice, beans, prunes, and canned milk. The National Youth Administration (NYA) moved into new quarters in March, employing 386 young people (aged seventeen to twenty-five), about 60 percent boys. They were required to spend sixty hours a month in productive jobs, alternating with classroom work. There was racial and gender discrimination, with girls taught sewing, cooking and kitchen management, home laundering, and domestic science; and the "desire of the NYA to train Negro youths for occupations in which they can find ready employment has caused the leaders to consider the formation of classes in janitorial services, restaurant work and truck driving." By year's end nine hundred boys and 450 girls had been given training, the latter by sewing garments for the Red Cross and working in day nurseries, school kindergartens, and cafeterias. The boys were in the machine and woodworking shops.[19]

Looming over everyone, however, was the coming war. In March 1941, Superintendent Jones returned from the annual superintendents' meeting in Atlantic City with the heady news that more than three hundred school systems still had some form of the work-study-play system, at least an emphasis on good citizenship, health, and physical education. "The central theme of the convention dealt with the part of the schools in national defense," he reported. "Much was said about the training of young people for vocations after they complete their secondary schooling." In July Congress appropriated $20 million for equipment for defense-training classes, of which $67,709 appeared in Gary for industrial equipment for the Froebel school. Defense-training classes, for adults as well as high-school boys, were already functioning at the Emerson school. Industrial jobs for the trainees were becoming plentiful, as steel and allied industries geared up for war production. Students were, of course, divided by race and gender, with classes in welding and machine operation "for unemployed Negro men" at Froebel and one in machine operation "for unemployed white males" at Emerson. There were also auto mechanics, electric communications, and layout and template work at Horace Mann, as well as additional classes for apprentice carpenters begun at the request of the AFL Building Trades Council. When high-school students were taken on a tour of U.S. Steel in November during National Education Week, the boys were shown the plant, while the girls visited the auditing department.[20]

As war turned from threat to reality in late 1941, additional responsibilities were placed on the schools to control the children, assist the war effort, and boost community morale. They would once again become night community centers, with "town meetings where timely public questions will be discussed, family parties at which parents and children will enjoy movies, games and music, and drama clubs for the training of adult groups in presenting one-act plays." When the children returned from the Christmas holiday in early January 1942, they faced increased discipline. "Strict discipline is necessary for the protection of our children in the face of possible emergencies in Gary," Lutz said. "The tightening up will apply to teachers as well as pupils." There would soon be air-raid drills, defense-stamp sales, first-aid instruction, and continuing Red Cross war drives. "Teachers must not get upset over the war themselves but maintain a common sense attitude," the superintendent cautioned. While the younger children were busily engaged in school projects, many high-school boys jumped at the chance to obtain a work permit, required of all youth between fourteen and twenty-one, and obtain a full-time job. Those under eighteen could not be employed more than forty-eight hours a week, while fourteen- and fifteen-year olds could not work after 7:00 P.M. Indeed, high-school enrollment dropped from about 6,200 in 1942 to 5,800 in 1945, where it basically remained for the remainder of the decade; the number of graduates similarly declined, from 1,248 in 1941 to 1,024 five years later.[21]

Vocational training quickly increased for employable boys over sixteen and adults, who might be using the school shops twenty-four hours a day, seven days a week for arc and gas welding, foundry work, pattern layout and template making, auto repair, sheet-metal work, and machine-shop instruction. The younger boys in the wood shops would be making fifteen hundred model airplanes for the United States Navy to be used for aircraft recognition. Military training in ROTC units organized during the last war soon became compulsory for all physically fit boys starting in the tenth grade at the four largest high schools, replacing their physical education courses. By fall three thousand boys were enrolled in industrial-arts classes, although vocational director John Matthews voiced a desire to open "some of these classes to girls who have an interest in mechanical skills."[22]

Personal insecurities and family disruptions soon appeared as the most serious problems. "The war is bound to bring many maladjustments in the home life of countless families," Mark Roser argued. "Action to meet children's problems growing out of these situations is part of the added responsibility of the schools to the community." Roser obtained twelve new clerks for the child-welfare department to handle the increased load. "Their duties will be much broader than those of attendance officers," Roser said. "Their responsibility will deal chiefly in interpreting the school to parents and the home life of pupils to their teachers. . . . If a pupil appears to be unhappy, the welfare visitors will make an effort to get at the underlying cause and seek a remedy." A survey was soon completed of all families in the city, with specific data on the children. The increasing number of employed mothers, some doing shiftwork, added to the difficulty of providing a stable environment. In May the city's civilian defense council organized a child-care committee to study the problems caused by working parents. A report by the child-welfare department, released in July, found thirty-seven hundred children with both parents working, amounting to 17 percent of families with school children.[23]

In order to keep students involved in constructive activities, the 1942 summer-school program was expanded. The school board was particularly anxious that the summer program "sustain morale on the homefront in the war effort," but provided limited funding. The program included a civil-defense-training course for high-school students; home nursing and child care for junior and senior girls; food courses for boys and girls, including serving wartime meals; classes for girls in designing, making, and repairing clothes; model-airplane building for boys and girls; elementary aeronautics for boys; and musical instruction, crafts, and playground activities for the younger children. There were also a few academic courses. Enrollment eventually reached seven thousand. The food classes at the Emerson and Roosevelt schools were quite popular, as were the community-at-war courses.[24]

As the fall semester began and reorganization of the elementary grades progressed with the abandonment of the platoon plan in grades four to eight, there was heightened emphasis on matters of war and peace. High-school teachers, especially, were expected "to develop a sympathetic understanding of each pupil and a personal interest in the social problems of each child," stressing "civilian moral." Too much homework was unnecessary, cautioned high-school supervisor Russell Anderson, and students should be encouraged to take secretarial and retail-selling courses and, perhaps, a companion course in consumer education. ROTC, now compulsory for boys starting in the tenth grade, was expanded, and there were courses in civil defense. Plans were underway, starting in the winter under the national High School Victory Corps program, for three hours a day of "war training"—metal crafts, machine operation, automobile mechanics, electricity, and radio for boys, and home nursing, child care, nutrition, and home management for girls—and four hours of physical training, science, mathematics, and social problems. "Commando tactics will be used to toughen youth," physical-education director John Gilroy proudly announced. An increasing number of high-school boys joined the military, two hundred during the fall semester; the remainder were offered preinduction courses, increased guidance, and early diplomas for those entering the army or war-related work. "As far as seniors are concerned," the superintendent cautioned in January 1943, "the next semester will be turned over pretty definitely to prepare them either to enter the armed forces or industry." Social-studies classes would stress world geography, and a new required course in the twelfth grade would include discussion of "the rights and obligations of free men, the democratic process, why we are at war, paying for the war and the post-war world."[25]

The pride of the schools and the community, however, was the All-Out Americans (AOAs). Starting in early September 1942, the organization was first designed to get all of the city's elementary students in the twenty-one public and eleven parochial schools involved in a scrap drive initiated by the Junior Chamber of Commerce. Mark Roser soon took charge. The students at each school elected a major and adjutant, who together would form a citywide organization, and they were sworn in as members of the junior civilian-defense corps by the city's civil defense director Colonel Frank Gray. A twelve-year-old Girl Scout was selected as the first AOAs colonel. "Under the slogan of 'save, serve and conserve,' the children will participate in all wartime drives," Roser announced, "and strive for the top recognition for achievement in the state to win as a trophy an original brick from the chimney of Independence Hall, Philadelphia." Full of enthusiasm, within six weeks the fifteen thousand students had collected 487 tons of metal, not all of which was scrap. They also plunged into collecting old clothing for the Goodwill and silk stockings, as well as selling war stamps and bonds.[26]

The AOAs served a variety of useful functions. The children provided valuable services, including baby sitting, and thereby "are being given a feeling of security and a sense of helping." They were also kept busy and, ideally, out of trouble. "It is true that, at times, some of these student war projects will interfere with the routine of formal education," the *Post-Tribune* editorialized in January 1943. "That should not be a reason for criticism. Education is a preparation for living and unquestionably youngsters will get some knowledge from their war work that a formal curriculum could not give them nearly as well. The schools cannot be isolated from the war and, indeed, they should not be if their instruction is to have any real meaning to the students." Within a year there were twelve city-wide activity committees, including salvage, war savings, community service, war services, publicity, and patriotic services. Child care was particularly important, and the girls (and later boys) were given instruction in handling preschool children.[27]

An article in *Public Welfare in Indiana* neatly summarized the perceived impact of the AOAs: "To the city's public school teachers, pioneers in advanced educational methods, the term 'All-Out-Americans' is synonymous with citizenship training; to Gary's social agencies it means fewer 'problem' children, better adjusted adolescents, less wartime confusion among young people; and to the community as a whole the phrase connotes a generation of boys and girls who are growing up with an understanding of the society in which they later, as responsible, informed citizens, will play important adult roles." Among their many duties, the children distributed "War Workers Sleeping" signs, met with the city council to discuss a local curfew law, assisted the block-mother organization, distributed material on the Community Chest drive, "clean plate" campaign, and consumers' pledge cards, and collected records and books for servicemen.[28]

Both the AOAs and the (hardly successful) Victory Corps were designed to keep children busily engaged in patriotic endeavors, rather than indulging in unsupervised, possibly negative, activities. Nationally, the juvenile delinquency scare reached a peak in mid-1943, but continued through 1945, and reported crimes seemed to match expectations. Family disruptions appeared to be the root cause of the problem, exacerbated by working teens with too much money, while lurid reports on wild youth issued by the FBI and the United States Children's Bureau heightened expectations. Similar fears swept Gary. "Juvenile delinquency in the city is on the upgrade," the local paper announced in May 1942. Within the year there was a crackdown on "hot spots" where teenagers congregated, such as in pool rooms, drug stores, soft drink parlors, and taverns, and where they, perhaps, drank and smoked. "We do see an increased number of more nervous children and less supervised children, which are the roots of delinquency," Mark Roser announced in May 1943, and he worried about keeping children busy over the summer.[29]

An infusion of federal funds helped expand the 1943 summer program, but this was not enough. One answer was strict enforcement of a new curfew ordinance, which would prevent children under fifteen from being on the streets or beaches after 10:00 P.M. The city's youth-service board, "seeking to extend character building and recreational activities for children and young people," encouraged cooperation between the schools and the YMCA, YWCA, settlement houses, Catholic Youth Organization, and the Scouts. Overall, delinquency rates for the year seemed to have increased over those in 1942, with stealing leading the list of crimes, followed by being ungovernable, running away, mischievous behavior, sex offenses, truancy, and burglary, that is, mostly status offenses. As feared, delinquency appeared to increase during the summer of 1944, particularly for boys sixteen to eighteen who had money to spend; first, "they pass themselves off for older than they are, getting into taverns and other places of questionable character where they meet up with undesirable companions. Second, stimulated by the war hysteria, they go out to get a thrill." Many were charged with serious crimes, such as robbery, burglary, and assault.[30]

One additional solution was to keep the adolescents in school, where they could acquire skills as well as receive counseling and supervision and obtain their diploma. In September 1943, youth over sixteen who worked an eight-hour shift were still allowed to carry up to three academic subjects. About one-third of the fifty-three hundred high-school students had full or part-time jobs, with boys exceeding girls two to one. Students over sixteen could even get school credit for industrial work experience, a program designed to "help make the work-experience of high-school youth contribute to educational growth in general and to occupational adjustment in particular, to develop closer working relationships between industries and the schools, and to assist industries in meeting manpower needs." The following August, "fearing that hundreds of youths now employed at exceptionally good wages will be tempted to remain at their jobs when schools reopen next month," school officials attempted to lure those between sixteen and eighteen, estimated to number three thousand, back to the classrooms. Supported by the War Manpower Commission, administrators promised to continue the policy of adjusting class schedules for any students who worked part-time. Enrollments in September exceeded expectations, for many students seemed to be "quitting their lucrative wartime jobs or applying for part time study programs." Roser hoped that his staff could make "fuller use of the newer 'psycho-therapeutic techniques'" when counseling disturbed teens, but found them short-handed and somewhat ill-prepared to offer the "scientific friendship for each student so that each is given reassurance to live out his own individuality and develop to the fullest extent his own creativeness."[31]

Juvenile arrests continued to rise for boys (but decreased for girls), however. Fifty-five were charged in January 1945, and their crimes ranged from larceny, running away, robbery, and assault to sex offenses and burglaries. Tellingly, thirty-four were white and twenty-one black, while only 25 percent of the students were black. As the war wound down and the problems of a peacetime society were anticipated, school officials used the carrot-and-stick approach to increase attendance—make the curriculum more practical and round up the truants. High-school students, both boys and girls, were offered a "modern living" course, including home management, budgeting family income, housing problems, furnishing a home, and family relations; "consideration also will be given the place of children and the returning war veteran in the home." Many of the high-school principals (except Lew Wallace's Verna Hoke, the only female principal) requested that ROTC be made voluntary rather than compulsory, because it was quite unpopular among both the boys and the school coaches, who preferred physical education. Besides, the ROTC officers' "educational philosophy is different from the philosophy of the public schools," complained Tolleston school principal J. W. Standley. The school board partially complied in late April by making it compulsory for only two (rather than three) years starting in September 1945 until September 1946, when it would become voluntary. After all, the war was still going on.[32]

If the students had a difficult time adjusting to wartime disruptions as well as prosperity, the teachers were equally confused. They were committed to the teachers' union and increasing their benefits. Union members readily cooperated with the Purdue survey team's investigation; "this assistance largely consisted in our answering their questions honestly and fully," Flora Philley later wrote, "in a 'let the chips fall where they may' manner." The *Final Report,* in turn, urged the school board to work with the union. In June 1941, as prosperity returned, the union requested a $200 increase for each teacher and a sabbatical-leave policy. The number of teachers increased slightly during the war from about six hundred to around 640 in 1945, of whom 368 were union members.[33]

The outbreak of war put additional burdens on the teachers. They were confused and sought some direction from the superintendent and school board "in matters of 'war discipline' and in problems arising from war stimuli." "It is as if the war did not exist," according to one of the union's officers. "The war has brought up problems that are new to us and we need guidance." But one thing was clear—teachers protested having to take on new responsibilities without their consent, which would interfere with their professional responsibilities. Added duties included working in draft registration, Red Cross and nutrition projects, as well as serving on civil defense committees and promoting waste-paper campaigns. Superintendent Lutz denied that any teacher was forced to participate in these activities. Having formed a war planning board, the union complained in March that the teachers were still being ignored by school officials. The superintendent, in turn, chose to meet with one representative from each school building, but not officially with the union, prompting school board member Maynard Suley to ask, "Why not call in the union?" While union members were ruffled, they could hardly refuse to plunge into the war effort, and by May teachers were being praised for their "patriotism and professional pride" in conducting registration for the war rationing program. They also organized a victory-bond parade and conducted the campaign to collect tin cans and junk. The union was given a boost in June 1942, when it hosted the annual national meeting of the American Federation of Teachers.[34]

Patriotic duties and teaching responsibilities could not deter the teachers from their ongoing struggle to secure better wages, however, a common grievance of workers during the war. Early in the war the union proposed salary increases ranging from $200 for the lowest paid teachers to $100 for those in the top category. The school board agreed to only half of these amounts. The next year the union demanded an increase of $400 for each teacher, but again received considerably less for 1944, and the board declared this to be a "cost of living" bonus and not an increase in the salary schedule. "The union committee members reported 'great dissatisfaction' among teachers because there had been no increase in the salary schedule since Pearl Harbor," according to the *Post-Tribune*. "Many are on the lookout for better paying positions in other school systems and younger teachers are turning to other kinds of work, they said." Part bluff and part truth, the union's threats had limited, if any, effect. The teachers received only an additional $125 for 1945. They came back with another $400 request in May 1945, quickly reduced to $300, but again got only $100. There were, of course, other grievances, such as skepticism over the board's new no-fail policy—"the union warns that if the plan fails, Gary children will 'bear the scars for a long time' "—and more personal matters, such as the forced-retirement or reduced-wage policy for school employees over sixty-six. Like other workers, however, Gary's teachers were quite willing to sacrifice for the war effort, but rationally sought a higher standard of living after years of sacrifices and starvation wages.[35]

With the final victory over Japan in early August, Gary's population welcomed peace with hope mixed with trepidation; memories lingered of the depression, strikes, and violence that followed the previous war. The schools, it was hoped, could resume the business of educating students, employing teachers, and adding space, for construction had been frozen during the war. School officials, working with the United States employment service, Red Cross, and other organizations, prepared to welcome returning veterans and industrial workers. Superintendent Lutz in late August urged high-school dropouts to go back to school and successfully requested the Chamber of Commerce to encourage employers to second his request. When one thousand young people over sixteen failed to register in early September, the high-school principals agreed to write them personal letters. Former students should return not only to get more skills for themselves, editorialized the *Post-Tribune*, but also because the community "wants them to be good citizens, to be a helpful part of the community in the future. High school has much to offer them in the way of training for citizenship."[36]

Confidence that the schools could return to business as usual were quickly dashed, however, soon after classes started. On September 18, 1945, many of the white students at the Froebel school refused to attend classes, complaining of problems with the school's large black population. The strike continued periodically during the fall and resulted from racial tensions that had been building during the war in the school and throughout the city.

The city's black students, whose numbers swelled during the war, were crowded together in only four of the city's schools—the all-black Roosevelt school, with an enrollment of over thirty-three hundred in early 1944; the Froebel school, with 950 black students (41 percent of the population, with another 7 percent Mexican-American); all-black East Pulaski, with nine hundred students in grades one through eight; and the Lincoln elementary school, with an 80 percent black enrollment (314 out of 385). Only Roosevelt and East Pulaski had black teachers (with one at Froebel). Since its opening in 1931, Roosevelt had been the pride of the black community. It was not trouble free. "The Roosevelt School has all of the problems that develop in a community which has a high proportion of homes of low economic level, large families, inadequate housing and the resultant health problems which grow out of such conditions," the Purdue survey concluded. "To this must be added the unjustified but nevertheless real limitation of opportunities, vocational and otherwise, extended to the colored race." In its ranking of high schools, the survey found Roosevelt scoring lowest on the average-home-environment score and having the highest drop-out rate (54 percent). It concluded that one problem was too much emphasis on an academic curriculum; "the city wide testing program with the unfortunate comparisons of achievement of students at Roosevelt, with their limited background and environmental opportunities, with students from more favored backgrounds has made little contribution to educational progress at Roosevelt and has done possible harm." The answer was more emphasis on citizenship and "extensive work in home management, dietary and health problems plus a realistic program of vocational education in terms of occupational opportunities."[37]

The *Final Report*'s condescending attitude was hardly appreciated in the black community, which preferred to emphasize the students' responsibility to compete in the broader community. "We want our youth to have all the opportunities any other group has," advised the *Gary American,* "but at the same time, we want them to be just as fit tempermentally as well as technically as any other group." The paper did stress the need for increased vocational work and doubted that "a degree in English or the Romance languages act[s] as a prospect into industry where the future of the negro race lies." The school should upgrade its shops and improve vocational guidance. The *Gary American* clearly took one side in the longstanding split in the black community dating back to the turn-of-the century Booker T. Washington–W.E.B. DuBois feud between academic and vocational education, but was not the only voice heard. It did get the support of many whites, however, for example Earl Moore, superintendent of U.S. Steel, and Gary State Bank president W. W. Gasser, who "agreed that such training for Negro youth is vitally necessary." One galling problem was the exclusion of black schools from the Indiana High School Athletic Association (IHSA), which prevented them from playing white schools in football and basketball. Roosevelt's teams had travelled throughout the country and compiled an enviable record of seven national-negro-basketball championships between

1932 and 1940, but locally were treated "like something separate and apart." In late 1941 the IHSA voted to drop the color barrier, however, and the following February the Gary school board agreed to submit Roosevelt's application for membership. One barrier, at least, had been broken.[38]

As the war approached, Roosevelt's students and administrators were touched by the same concerns as their white counterparts. In March 1941 Principal H. Theo Tatum voiced his fears about delinquency and announced various corrective measures, such as increased teacher involvement with parents, studies of home conditions, a system of behavior guidance, and more after-school activities. A Roosevelt PTA study group, investigating health, juvenile delinquency, recreational facilities, and the cleanliness of parents and students, recommended ten-cent lunches in the cafeteria. Terry Gray was appointed assistant child-welfare director in early 1943 "to meet increasing social tensions among youth groups in the central district." He was soon concerned about late hours, lying, and stealing. Some of the problems were caused by socioeconomic conditions, others by continuing discrimination in the city; there were difficulties in including Roosevelt in the High School Victory Corps, for example. But the war provided hope that the future would be brighter. "The first thing to do is to Win the War," the *Gary American* optimistically announced in mid-1943, "and when it is Won, your posterity and mine will live in a new world—one free from Greed, Meanness, Prejudice and Hate."[39]

Among the students, however, there was considerable cynicism. "Two-thirds of the members of Roosevelt high school's graduating class, composed of 37 Negro boys and 76 Negro girls, question whether white Americans really mean to include the Negro in the post-war program of freedom of opportunity," the *Post-Tribune* informed its mostly white audience in June 1944. Drawn from a poll taken by the social-studies department, the survey was surely disturbing. The students, among the privileged minority who stayed in school until graduation, complained about their schooling; they called for more religious education, military training, and vocational classes. They could also have pointed to the terrible overcrowding, for the students were "packed into the classrooms like sardines," according to assistant superintendent Ralph Muller. Many of the first graders attended half-day classes and some in the kindergarten could only stay for two-and-one-half hours. When children throughout the city were tested at the end of the intermediate cycle (the sixth grade) in March 1944, the pupils at East Pulaski and Roosevelt scored very low, and their potential mental level was labeled "dull," the only students so designated (although 44 percent of all the students were designated "retarded"). The conditions at the Roosevelt High School are nothing short of a stench-emitting and inexcusable MESS," argued the *Gary American* at the start of the 1944 school year. "The mothers and fathers of the children who attend Roosevelt High School want action— they want remedial action—and they want it NOW!. . . They believe in

Democracy, but not the same kind of despiritualized Democracy that seems to possess those responsible for conducting Gary's school system." There was growing anger over the situation: "The neglect of school facilities for children is serious, and to bumfuddle Negro education is not only serious, but criminal."[40]

Only the black community appeared anxious about conditions at Roosevelt; yet, the situation at the Froebel school sparked wider concern because of the potential of racial conflict. An increasing minority of the students were black. They were also generally segregated within the school—while blacks could participate in sports, they could not mix with whites in dramatic activities, the band or orchestra, the swimming pools (perhaps the most galling issue, because it affected all students and because blacks had only recently been allowed to use the boy's pool), or social activities. There was a separate black Junior-Senior Social Club. The one black teacher presided over a mixed-age class of incorrigible (black) boys numbering twenty-eight in 1944. The room was described in the Purdue survey: there were forty seat-desks fastened to the floor, and "three small pictures hanging upon the dirty dingy walls of the room. An American flag was in the front of the room, upon a flag staff. . . . A phonograph was in the front of the room. It is played when the pupils behave well for several periods during the day. . . . A bust of Abraham Lincoln was sitting upon the top of one of the wooden storage cabinets. Much dust was all over the bust. . . . The walls and floor of this classroom were very dingy and black looking." Sitting at a table in the front of the room, the teacher "speaks in a loud tone of voice all the time," and has the students stand along the walls when reciting. "The pupils read aloud and are constantly reprimanded by the teacher about how they hold their books, how they speak, and their use of periods, etc." These boys appeared to be both "low in mentality" and from broken homes: "their mothers cannot discipline them at all, even the smallest chap curses his mother, yet he is only seven years old." This class, while unique, was the most glaring example of segregation at Froebel.[41]

School administrators and community leaders had long tried to turn a blind eye to Froebel's (and the city's) racial problems. In September 1939 Froebel's longtime principal Charles Coons assured the community that "boys and girls of every nationality and racial background mix and mingle here in the classrooms, laboratories, in our musical organizations, on the athletic field. They are all alike to us and they are learning to live together as good Americans." But they were not treated equally. There were danger signs by early 1943. Froebel Assistant Principal Paul Lange now "reported a growing racial antagonism between the racial groups in his school. Gangs blackmailing and intimidating other gangs of a different color were increasing. . . . The war has intensified all of these racial antagonisms and racial problems which in a measure already existed here." The race riots in Detroit and Harlem in 1943 further shook the confidence of whites and soon there were increased efforts to prevent friction in the city. The world war against fascism and racism also encouraged some to look inward, although the national civil rights movement was rather muted while fighting continued.[42]

During 1944, a flood of meetings and reports sought to heal the wounds and head off more serious racial problems. Early in the year, a confidential "Report and Recommendations on Racial Situation in Gary, Indiana" was drawn up by the Office of Community War Services in the Federal Security Agency. The agency was concerned about "racial tension of such a nature as to threaten a disturbance of war production." There were, admittedly, problems concerning recreation, education, transportation, and housing, noted the authors, which "are not at the present time dangerous or serious, but there is a considerable amount of inflammable material and every means should be taken to prevent the spark that might start a fire." The Chamber of Commerce had meanwhile appointed a fifteen-member committee to study the situation, including the mayor, *Post-Tribune* editor H. B. Snyder, the U.S. Steel superintendent, school superintendent Lutz, and six blacks, at the suggestion of the Office of Community War Services—composing the city's establishment. The committee's report appeared in August and included a "Race Relations Code," which called for an end to discrimination: "We believe that there are no superior or inferior races but that all mankind is one. . . . We believe in equality of opportunity, equal economic and cultural rewards." Without a concrete program, however, the words were hollow. More specific was a National Urban League report, "A Study of the Social and Economic Conditions of the Negro Population of Gary, Indiana," appearing in December. It stressed the pervasive and demeaning school segregation as a deliberate policy of the school board: "The most amazing yet singularly interesting bit of engineering has been done in arranging boundaries and options for school districts as they converge on the area of Negro occupancy." Both blacks and whites were handicapped by having to travel often long distances to segregated schools, except in the integrated Froebel district.[43]

Perhaps of greater significance was the work of the Bureau for Intercultural Education. In October 1944, the Rosenwald Foundation organized a conference on intergroup education and invited representatives from seven communities, including Gary. Superintendent Lutz next requested that the Bureau send consultants to work with school officials and soon a myriad of experts were traveling to the city, including Robert Havighurst and Allison Davis from the University of Chicago. They all made a point of meeting with Froebel principal Richard Nuzum. Attempts had already begun to deal with some of the school's problems; for example, the previous March about one hundred parents of both races had met to form a joint PTA, dissolving the two separate organizations that had been functioning. "Although some of the Negroes charged the whites with being foreigners and some of the whites accused the Negroes of trying to encroach upon their parent teacher organization, agreement was finally reached among the group, however, not until several white parents left," the *Gary American* reported. "It was pointed out that as parents all have the same interest in the school, that each group is only a part of the large American melting pot, and that it is in the tradition of the American way of life for various races to meet and seek some mutual solution to a ghastly problem such as the Froebel School situation has been all these years."[44]

Parents could sometimes work together, but their children remained separated, physically as well as culturally. Beginning in December, the Bureau's personnel helped establish a Committee on the Development of Democratic Living, and during the first half of 1945 three intercultural education conferences were held in Gary. At a three-day meeting for administrators in early spring the speaker, Dr. Marian Edman of the Detroit schools, "warned that the transformation of attitudes to stir up race, religious and economic hatreds can happen quickly, citing examples from Nazi Germany. . . . Education must change its emphasis to meet the social crisis of the post-war period." A similar gathering for teachers occurred in May, and a third for both administrators and teachers in August. Various community groups, led by the Anselm Forum, formed in 1931 to promote better human relations, became directly involved, as did the CIO. With the war's end there seemed cause for optimism. "Educationally, Gary has had her stormy times, especially with respect to the education of its minority group of citizens," the *Gary American* editorialized in late July. "But, little by little, the city has forged ahead in the educational field until today it is our proud boast that Gary is possessed of one [of] the finest educational systems of any city in the whole country for its size." Yet dark clouds appeared on the horizon. In concluding his discussion of racial problems in Gary, Theodore Brameld, working for the Bureau for Intercultural Education, warned that "the real task of breaking the steel ring of discrimination and segregation now gripping Copperberg [Gary] so malevolently will require all the strength of ordinary citizens as well as the finest kind of schools."[45]

The lid blew off in September of 1945. "A nationwide strike consciousness manifested itself in Gary this morning as white grade and high school pupils of Froebel school walked out of classes in a protest against Negro pupils in that institution," the *Post-Tribune* reported on Tuesday, September 18. "In a distinctly holiday mood, the strikers were orderly as a preliminary contingent of 400 gathered on the playground after walking out of classes soon after they convened. By noon, school authorities estimated the absentees included some 800 pupils, including a number of colored. . . . School officials and other observers attributed the walkout, which has been brewing for some time, to unrest coming from the war's end and the numerous strikes over the nation." While it was true that the lifting of the no-strike pledge, combined with the workers' pent-up frustrations, led to a wave of strikes throughout unionized industries in the late summer and into the fall, there were more immediate causes of the students' action. There had been a racial incident at a football game the previous weekend, the latest in a mounting string of grievances against some of the black students, many only recently having moved from the South. "You had blacks that came up from the south and they didn't know what it was like being on an equal basis with the whites and it blew their minds and they went to the extreme," Leonard Levenda, who quickly became the strike leader, later recalled. "There was no problem at all with any, as far as I know, with any black person who had lived in Gary for three or four years—they [sic] got along."[46]

By Friday, still out, and having briefly been joined by two hundred Tolleston school students, the strikers now numbered twelve hundred. They had three explicit demands: removal of all black students, replacement of principal Richard Nuzum, and the end to "using Froebel school students as 'gunea pigs' in race relation experiments." Supported by their often foreign-born, working-class parents, and, generally, the Catholic Church, the students began to see the issue more in class than racial terms, as indicated by their third demand. Their views were reinforced as the city's elite closed ranks against them. "Approximately one fifth of Gary citizens are negroes and their needs and rights and privileges must be given equal consideration with all others," declared the verbally civil-rights-conscious *Post-Tribune*. The *Gary American* reminded its readers that following the successful Emerson strike in 1927 "Gary began to see its first form of segregation on a big scale condoned by the leaders of that time." But now "things have changed." The students finally returned to classes on October 1, after a promise from the school board that there would be an investigation of the principal.[47]

Within the black community there was considerable hostility aimed at both the strikers and school officials. "Heralded the world over as a school strike by the kiddies," the *Gary American* believed that "in reality Gary is witnessing one of the most deep-rooted hate shows that could be conceived by parents with half-grown men and women acting their parts well under the tut[e]lage of hate mongers, some of them on the Froebel school staff, others too cowardly to come out into the open, and an irresponsible group of Poles, Slavs and what-have-you with their second papers in their hands less than two decades. This hate show has been given momentum because the duly constituted authorities have been what they call 'patient' instead of positive. . . . THIS IS NO TIME TO COMPROMISE." The *Gary American* lashed out at the strikers with a less than subtle attack on their immigrant roots, its antiforeign diatribes revealing both anger and helplessness. The black community could express its feelings that "American hypocrisy makes it quite possible for any sort of scum from Europe or elsewhere whose skin is not black to cash in on his fairer skin and to gain opportunities and rights that are basely denied purely American citizens of color," but could hardly present a unified front. The problem was the lack of a strong organization.[48]

The NAACP chapter, having previously been active, was now only a paper organization. "We are deeply concerned over the present school situation in Gary," national secretary Walter White wrote to chapter "president" Alfred Hall in late September. "It is hoped that the Gary Branch of the NAACP is vigorously protesting any moves which are being made to completely segregate Negroes in the Gary public schools." A month later, with no action from Hall, White vented his feelings of frustration, warning that "no branch of the NAACP, especially in a critical area like Gary, can be permitted to remain inactive." But Noma Jensen, representing the national office, sadly reported to White that "the Gary Branch is practically non-existent at least as far as their [*sic*] influence in community matters is concerned. . . . The Gary Branch is commonly referred to as the 'Republican Club.'" There were similar student strikes in Chicago and New York City, sparked by the Gary situation. "In all three instances the strikes broke out in areas where there is a heavy concentration of foreign-born—Italian, Hungarian, Polish, Spanish, etc.—largely an economically insecure group," Jensen informed White. "Undoubtedly, they provide a fertile field for Fascist-minded Americans, who are bent upon dividing our people." Secretary White rushed to the city, met with H. B. Snyder and other local leaders, and even tried to organize a rally featuring singer Paul Robeson and Supreme Court Justice Frank Murphy. He reiterated the common wisdom "that most of the trouble has been caused not by Southern whites, but by Serbian, Polish, Lithuanian and other foreign born Catholic groups." The national office could offer its help, but without a functioning local branch the NAACP was rather ineffectual.[49]

The National Urban League (NUL) rushed in to fill the void. Under the auspices of the Community Relations Project for Interracial Social Planning, the national office had targeted Gary as one of its seven pilot cities, and its research team had issued a report in December 1944, "A Study of the Social and Economic Conditions of the Negro Population of Gary, Indiana." Concerned about the strike situation, in mid-October J. Harvey Kerns was sent from the national office to meet with a newly formed local NUL board dominated by H. B. Snyder and Roosevelt principal H. Theo Tatum, Kerns discouraged the board from "participation in the highly controversial school strike, my reason being that the League was too new . . . and to involve an infant agency in so highly controversial issues at this time would certainly be an unfortunate beginning." In early November the board hired Joseph Chapman to head the Gary office, which was formally established in mid-December. Born in Saint Louis, during the war Chapman had become coordinator of personnel for the Curtiss-Wright Corporation in his native city, then forced by the government to hire more black workers. His civil rights background proved valuable as he cautiously became involved in school affairs, which continued on their rocky road.[50]

The students had returned to school in early October, 1945 trusting that the investigation of Principal Nuzum would result in his removal. Three outside experts studied conditions at Froebel, then issued their report, which exonerated the principal: "The evidence leads to the conclusion that, considering the conditions under which Mr. Nuzum has worked in Froebel school, he has been an effective administrator." With Nuzum's return (he had taken a leave during the investigation) a sigh of relief swept much of the city. "The chief lesson to be learned from this local disturbance is the importance of having public officials who try to do the right thing," voiced the editor of the *Post-Tribune*. "From the start the board of education took the stand it had a job to do and it did it without fear or favor." But the white students were not about to give up. Strike leader Levenda charged Nuzum with promoting racially mixed parties, repeated the call for citywide integration, and threatened to renew the strike. The parents were also becoming more shrill; at a meeting one parent declared "we are fighting the Civil Liberties, the Communists, the Urban League, the Jewish League, the CIO, the PTA, and the Men's Forum as well as a lot of other organizations who have no interest in Froebel. This is a matter between us and the school board and this could have been settled a long time ago if the outsiders had kept out of it." The walkout resumed on October 29 and continued until November 12. With so many high-school pupils on strike, perhaps 70 percent, the school soon cancelled the football season.[51]

"Leaden skies today had a silver lining and damp cold winds blew heart-stirring melodies for thousands of teen-age devotees of the King of Swoon who came by plane this morning from New York City to croon Gary bobby-soxers and their boy friends into a democratic attitude on the race relations problem," the *Post-Tribune* greeted its evening readers on November 1. Frank Sinatra, then touring the country to promote civil rights, had been invited by the Anselm Forum. Before the concert he met with representatives from the high schools and various youth groups, but not with the strikers, who refused to attend. At the end of a most enthusiastic concert, with the girls' screams almost drowning out his voice, Sinatra warned the students "against the nazi technique of divide and conquer," and requested the strikers to return to school "as a favor and I shall be grateful to you." He then met privately with Leonard Levenda and even invited him to come to New York for further talks. The student leader refused.[52]

As Levenda later recalled, "the thing with Sinatra was that he thought he could come over and sing a song and say go back to school and we'd go back to school. He may have meant well but we had problems here, that was, you're entertaining people, you don't know what is going on, you want to get involved, fine, spend six months, get involved." The Sinatra visit was exciting and garnered the city additional national publicity. But the local paper admitted, "there is no reason to think Frank's speech had much effect on his hearers or will help get the strikers back in school." However, "it is true that the Froebel strike has ceased to be a local issue and has become an American issue." *Life* magazine was more cynical. Quickly dismissing the striking students and their parents—"Goading on these childish grievances were parents who feared competition for their steel-mill jobs from Gary's increasing Negro pupulation"—the magazine took Sinatra no more seriously. "Frankie was deeply earnest at the high-school meeting. First he sang some songs. Then he made some vague references to the American Way of Life and the Hot Dog. When it was all over, Frankie had failed. The strike was still on," the article facetiously concluded.[53]

Additional celebrities soon arrived for an antistrike rally, including Edna Ferber, Carl Sandburg, Bill Mauldin, and Clifton Fadiman. Indeed, articles filled the press nationwide, generally condemning the strikers. As the black *Michigan Chronicle* remarked, "the scandalous action of the Gary, Indiana, high school students who went on strike to protest the presence of Negro students at the high school and the riot between white and Negro students of a New York high school last week cannot be ignored. Here is young America going crazy on the race issue at the very moment in our national history when we are celebrating a great victory over the enemies of democracy." With little resolution in sight, some of the Froebel parents met in Indianapolis with C. T. Malan, the state superintendent of public instruction, to request his intervention. They were disappointed. While still demanding Nuzum's removal, they were willing to accept an integrated school if they could be guaranteed "relief from overcrowding and tensions and bad conditions." With the parents growing increasingly lukewarm and with no prospect of a settlement in sight, the students agreed to go back to school on Monday, November 12. To Levenda, "we were being sold down the river by our own parents, not my parents personally, but by the parents' group. And this was terrible. . . . They sold out their own kids."[54]

The strike was over, but nothing had been resolved. And the issues remained muddled. The *Gary American* celebrated the victory, yet worried that "as a last resort, these hate mongers have changed their course to fit their nefarious pattern. 'Full freedom for the Negroes' is the cry subtlely [*sic*] suggest[ed] to the unsuspecting, but are actually looking toward further trouble. They now advocate a consolidation of forces against the north side— a trap that only a few fools cannot see. The Negroes, with only a few exceptions, are not going to give ground to the Spahalaskis, Lochs and whathave-you's." Competition continued in the Froebel district between poor whites and blacks. Joseph Chapman, an outsider, had a different perspective. "I thought there was more to it than racism," he later reminisced. "The thing that struck me most was that the Froebel area was largely populated by people of first and second generation. . . . And they felt that they were people of less status than anybody. Actually, I became very sympathetic towards those people."[55]

Others took a more psychological approach. Mark Roser, with a background in social psychiatry, emphasized that "with but two exceptions, all of these boys have extreme personality problems, such as instability, hostility, shyness or a history of aggressive behavior." He recognized their "*lack of status.* Their behavior is very largely motivated by efforts to gain attention, exhibitionism, offset by frequent quarreling and rebellious behavior. . . . The expressions of their Negro hostility arouses in them at the same time a deep fear of retaliation on the part of negroes." James Tipton, in his published study of the strike, *Community in Crisis* (1953), repeated these observations: "They were unhappy in their relations with other boys and girls as well as with teachers and principal. This spurred them to try to build more satisfactory pictures in their own minds of what their status was, with other young people particularly, and with those adults whose opinions counted with them. They were driven to become attention-seekers, 'zoot-suiters,' extremists in behavior, speech, and appearance." Tipton also stressed the students' "inferior social position." "These white boys and girls, and their foreign-born parents . . . had apparently been quite resigned until just recently to their inferior position in relation to other Central City [Gary] whites. They could accept their lot more easily in the knowledge that they were not at the bottom of the ladder, for the Negroes were standing firmly on that rung." But recent signs of integration at Froebel appeared most disruptive. Tipton and Roser are surely correct in hitting upon the personal and class dimensions of the situation, for the strikers, a majority of the older white Froebel students—living in a "slum area," according to a report to the Anselm Forum—felt threatened by various social dislocations as the war ended and the future appeared uncertain. They wanted, above all, a fair chance and signs that they were not being treated unequally. They now called for citywide school integration.[56]

It would take time, however, for many to accept even symbolic integration throughout Gary. One stumbling block was the school superintendent, who believed "the community won't stand for doing away with segregated schools. People in Central City [Gary] believe in segregation. If allowed to vote, 80 per cent would vote for segregated schools." Perhaps. But there were other forces emerging. In December, a variety of organizations, including the Urban League, Chamber of Commerce, CIO, Central District Business Men's Bureau, and the Civil Liberties Committee, formed a coordinating agency on interracial problems. They met with Mayor Joseph Finerty to discuss the issues. "Many leaders of the city are recognizing the untenable position of the Board of Education in standing firm for non-segregation at Froebel School and yet maintaining a policy of segregation in all other high schools in the city," concluded a report on the situation to the Anselm Forum. The city's pulse quickened when rumors circulated of a threatened strike in March. "Froebel students were reported balloting yesterday and today on a proposal to give the student committee which directed last fall's strike the authority to call another at the school," the *Post-Tribune* reported on January 5, 1946. The students were still grumbling about unfair treatment.[57]

The solution to the problem lay in the hands of the five school board members, a mixed lot scarcely ready to make their mark on history. The president was Cloyce Bowers, a druggist, Democrat, and member of his local Eagles lodge. Michael Lobo, a thirty-seven-year-old management employee of U.S. Steel, also a Democrat, and a Catholic, was the board's vice president. The treasurer was the Reverend Newton Fowler, pastor of the Westminster Presbyterian Church in the Tolleston neighborhood and a political maverick without party affiliation. The two newest members, appointed in July 1945, were Mrs. Uno T. Hill and Daniel Kreitzman. Hill was the most liberal member of the board, a Democrat and former social worker, who was active in the League of Women Voters. Kreitzman, in contrast was a Republican, Shriner, assistant manager of the local power company, and the outgoing president of the Chamber of Commerce. Soon to join the board, replacing Bowers in July 1946, was William Stern, who furthered its liberal tilt. Stern was a contractor, a Democrat, a director of the Chamber of Commerce, president of the Gary Council of Social Agencies, and, perhaps most important, a member of the Anselm Forum with a strong interest in civil rights. These six would shoulder the burden of school integration, but for the moment moved crabwise toward their goal. As the Reverend Fowler confided to James Tipton, "the board had agreed at last that a policy of nonsegregation for all schools was both desirable and necessary," but "they were unwilling to make such an abrupt change as opening all schools at once to eligible Negro pupils would be." They feared possible violence from the white community.[58]

During January and February of 1946 the various community groups jockeyed for position. The Committee of Thirteen, the white, prostrike parents group in the Froebel district, was reconstituted as the Eleventh Subdivision Civil Club and promised to work through the Froebel PTA. In mid-February, however, the club again demanded Nuzum's removal, without satisfaction. Tempers were once again rising. Working diligently for a satisfactory resolution was Joe Chapman of the Urban League. "We have established a relationship, that is, the local League and these dissatisfied parents, and we are talking over very frankly racial issues," Chapman informed the national office on February 20. "Through this same group the Executive has established a relationship with a small group of Negroes [*sic*] students and White students (former strike leaders), and through the two we believe the League is going to make a significant contribution in solving the Froebel problem and prevent a strike." The NUL executive director had convinced Leonard Levenda and Mary Balas, the girls' strike leader, to meet privately with a handful of black students and work out their differences. Additional incentive came from the school board, which threatened to expel any striking students.[59]

Finally, on March 2 the *Post-Tribune* announced, "white and colored students of Froebel school today issued a joint statement declaring a permanent truce between racial groups and pledging themselves to follow the

American way of living together." They were not finished, however: "We are firmly convinced that the question is not completely isolated in all aspects but is also definitely involved in citywide educational practices in Gary. We strongly urge the board of education to issue a statement and policy providing for the enrollment of all students, regardless of race, creed or color, to attend whatever institution is located in the zone of their residence." Taking a firm stand for citywide integration, the students deftly put the school board on the defensive. They also supported an interracial council named the Gary Unity Assembly, composed of parents, students, and teachers, to work out problems at Froebel. Sanity seemed to have come to the central district; "my impression is that the students of Froebel school are becoming the most tolerant in the whole city," Mark Roser asserted. The *Gary American* was elated: "Froebel high school is once more the scene of light-hearted bobbysoxers, whose main concern these days is the chances of Froebel's thinlies in the Spring track events. The spectre of race hate, suspicion and mutual distrust between Negro and white students, has been dissolved. The repeat performance of the strike which made Gary the northern counterpart of Biloxi, Miss., has been called off."[60]

The spotlight continued on the school board. Human-relations workshops were held into the summer sponsored by the League of Women Voters, Urban League, YWCA, and other organizations. The superintendent remained doubtful: "If we make a move to open all schools to Negroes, it may mean we'll have complete segregation instead. Watch what I tell you." But school integration resolutions were voted by the Gary Council of Churches, the League of Women Voters, the Gary Teachers' Union, and the Civil Liberties Union, as well as the persistent Anselm Forum. The impasse was broken during a secret meeting organized by Fisk University president Charles S. Johnson, a prominent sociologist, held at the Rosenwald Foundation in Chicago in early July. Present were H. B. Snyder, Tatum, Superintendent Lutz, newly appointed school board member William Stern, and Chapman. Lutz emerged from the meeting with a firmer commitment to integration. In any case, with a little more pressure on the board members, particularly Hill, Stern, and Kreitzman, a policy statement favoring integration was passed on August 27: "Children under the jurisdiction of the Gary public schools shall not be discriminated against in the school districts in which they live, or within the schools which they attend, because of race, color, or religion." Ever cautious, the board decreed that the policy would not be implemented until September 1947, allowing time for community acceptance. "The policy means," Lutz warned, "that some negro children eventually may be assigned to schools now exclusively white and some white children may be transferred to schools that are chiefly negro." However temporizing, the policy was a breath of fresh air for many. "Last night the Board of Education, in solemn session, enacted the non-discrimination policy, long fought over, and much feared," the Anselm Forum's Reuben Olson informed Manet Fowler of the Urban League. "History was written last night. . . . From the housetops of the world Gary has been blasted as a hateful town. Now let it be commended for its belated courage in educational democracy."[61]

Success, on paper, had been achieved, but would integration be accomplished smoothly? However painful, the Froebel strikes may have been ultimately beneficial. For Tipton, "the strikes, especially the threat of a third strike, forced school and community authorities to face up to the necessity of revising school policies in a democratic direction as quickly as possible." But, although integration was now accepted in the Froebel district, "school and community leaders anxiously awaited the reaction of residents of those other sections to the new policy." They would find out in September 1947.[62]

The Gary schools had emerged from the war years tattered, but somewhat recognizable. The work-study-play system was only a shadow of its former self, having succumbed to the criticisms of the Purdue survey and the loss of will by school administrators who wanted to appear modern. Educational change took a variety of forms, including implementation of the contained classroom, a new promotion policy, and increased powers for the building principals. The war had some influence, particularly on the high-school curriculum, as there was increased concern over such issues as the meaning of citizenship and the need for a more practical course of study. Students threw themselves into the war effort by forming the High School Victory Corps and particularly the All-Out Americans, which worked to organize the home front. As the students attempted to demonstrate their hard work and patriotism, ripples of fear swept the city that juvenile delinquency, fueled by the new prosperity and lack of parental control, was on the rise. There was an increased move to keep the kids in school, particularly as the war wound down. The key issue became the meaning of democracy. Matters of segregation and integration, visible since the early days of the school system, took center stage when the frustrations of the white students at the Froebel school spilled over, touching off citywide turmoil. The forces promoting racial harmony, led by the city's white elite and black community, seemed arrayed against the midtown immigrant population, which felt itself to be an integrated island surrounded by a segregated sea. The members of the Anselm Forum and the Chamber of Commerce, despite a commitment to human rights, could, perhaps, feel confident that in promoting school integration their children would remain in white schools because of continuing neighborhood segregation. At any rate, Gary's schools once again found themselves in the national spotlight, a glaring example of what the war had been fought for and against. And the city seemed to vindicate itself.

With the war's end, and their democratic image now forged in the crucible of racial conflict, the Gary schools were prepared to enter the postwar era of growth and prosperity. But the issues of equality and educational achievement plagued the school board, administration, teachers, parents, students, and the community in general. And they would continue to search for harmony and consensus, for the schools still played a major role in the city. Pursuing its long-established role, the educational system hoped to provide various programs and services to the young and assurances to the adults that the schools were a vital part of urban life. They were increasingly influenced by various local and national groups, however, which used the schools as a touchstone for their own concerns and interests. The shrinking power of the superintendent may have opened the door for greater external pressures. Moreover, state funding had been raised to almost 40 percent of the local school budget. The war had certainly expanded ties between Gary and the outer world, and this trend would continue.

VII

POSTWAR PROBLEMS, 1945–1950

Stanley Kohn arrived in Gary in 1940 to work in the advertising department at H. Gordon & Sons, one of the city's leading downtown department stores. A graduate of the University of Chicago, Kohn became interested in the public schools in 1945 when his son began attending kindergarten in the old Miller elementary school. "I would visit there and he was in the classroom in the basement of the school right next to the coal burning boiler, and kids, forty of them, were sitting on the floor, concrete floor, which was rather upsetting to me to see the condition of it," he later recalled. Kohn joined the Miller-Wirt PTA and quickly discovered that the school tax levy was frozen and there had been no school construction for some years. In order to put pressure on the school board to raise the levy and begin construction, as well as institute other improvements, the Miller parents combined with other PTAs throughout the city in early 1946 to form the City-wide Parents' Council. Kohn took a leading role in the new organization and became its second president.[1]

The Council soon found itself challenged by the Gary Taxpayers Association, controlled by U.S. Steel and headed by *Post-Tribune* editor H. B. Snyder, and the Chamber of Commerce, which resisted higher taxes. During the depression Gary's business elite had begun actively to oppose, for the first time, increasing school and other taxes, as profit concerns definitely took priority over their civic considerations. No longer were many business leaders economically confident, or quite so socially conscientious, despite the return of prosperity during the war. The teachers had organized in the late 1930s, the students had formed the AOAs during the war, the administrators worked together, and the business community was unified through the Gary Taxpayers Association and the Chamber of Commerce—it was time for the parents to find a collective voice. The educational harmony under Superintendent Wirt, having begun to disintegrate during his last years, was now clearly shattered. Interest-group politics predominated during the postwar years, as each group struggled to gain the advantage, bringing into sharper focus the variety of forces, personalities, and organizations that continually influenced school matters. But the factions partially came together to find a solution to the nagging problem of racial segregation. Meanwhile, the schools continued to offer a broady array of courses and programs to Gary's children.

In late August 1946, the school board had approved a broad integration policy for the city's schools to go into effect in September 1947 in the elementary grades. It remained to be seen, however, how easily this could be accomplished. As the National Urban League's Manet Fowler wrote later in the year, "on its own, Gary's struggle continues, the issue has been drawn, and purely local allegiances sworn. But with an American population estimated as 80 percent white (25 per cent foreign-born and 20 per cent colored); with one of 'the largest foreign-born white populations per total population of any city in the United States'—and with no larger percentage of Negroes shown by any large city north of the Mason and Dixon line—this struggle, this issue, and these allegiances, must be of more than local concern. For the Nation, let it be said, it is more than heartening news today that there stand brave citizens of the republic in this town, who recall, without sympathy or yearning, an unimaginitive past in race relations—and to that past will bear no returning."[2]

School officials well understood the sensitive nature of their new policy and struggled to promote and improve intercultural relations—among students, parents, and throughout the community—as the deadline drew near. Intercultural workshops for teachers and administrators had already been conducted during the first half of 1946, and Democratic Living Committees had been established in each of the schools, coordinated by a Central Committee. The Central Committee formed three subcommittees: one on school boundaries, one on transfer policies, and a teachers' committee which would handle community outreach. The latter supplied speakers for almost 150 community groups during the year. Various community organizations, including the Urban League, Anselm Forum, League of Women Voters, and the YWCA, continually worked to promote racial harmony. The school board's desegregation policy appeared hopeful to many, but one sour note was sounded by Anselm Forum member Melville Thomas.

In an unpublished paper done for a class at Gary College, Thomas pointed out that "the policy pertains to the schools only, and not to the city itself. Specifically, a Negro child may be allowed to attend an all-White school in a section of the city if he lives in that district, but under the city laws, no Negroes are permitted to live in certain sections of the city and consequently can not be allowed to attend the school there. In this respect, the hands of the school board are tied, and any solution to discriminatory practices of this sort will have to come as a result of a greater cooperation between the schools and the city government." Thomas also feared that discriminatory policies within the schools would continue, for segregation and racial hostilities were deeply ingrained in the community. His pessimism was not widely voiced, however, at least not publicly, for few whites appeared to share his vision of the city's entrenched segregation.[3]

Signs appeared early that the new policy would, indeed, not be quietly accepted, particularly in the Emerson school district, the site of the 1927 school strike. "A petition protesting against 'past, future or present' zoning of the Emerson school district to include any territory south of the Wabash tracks, or the admission of 'any persons other than members of the Caucasian race' from attending Emerson school" reached the school board in mid-November 1946. The petition seemingly contained the names of 90 percent of the district's taxpayers. Prointegrationist forces, including the school board, teachers' union, *Post-Tribune,* Anselm Forum, Gary Council of Churches, and the American Veterans Committee, quickly closed ranks and branded the petition 'as undemocratic, un-American, and un-Christian." Emerson had been all white since 1927, but it was obvious that it would soon receive a few dozen or so black students who lived on the city's east side. The newly formed Emerson Parents and Taxpayers Club tried to organize anti-integrationist parents throughout the city, with little luck; still, one impassioned member labeled the school board, city council, and mayor "nigger lovers" who were "10 times worse than any negro." Having little support, however, the parents became quiet, biding their time.[4]

The school board members had been dragging their feet about formulating a specific integration policy. As September approached they became energized. Hopes brightened in the spring when the integrationist candidate for mayor, Eugene Swartz, won the Democratic primary by a slim margin against his anti-integrationist opponent (Swartz would win in November against the Republican candidate who refused to back the school board), and when black doctors were finally admitted to practice in the city's Methodist and Catholic hospitals, an important victory for the black community. So, in late June 1947, the board redrew the attendance boundaries for nine of the city's eighteen grade-school districts. Still cautious, however, they mandated that only children from kindergarten through the sixth grade would be affected by the new neighborhood-school policy. Child-welfare director Mark Roser calculated that only 139 black children would be attending six previously all-white schools. No white students would be going to black schools, however, despite the board's ruling "that no transfers to others schools, contrary to the new policy, shall be made by reason of race, color or religion." The racial division between East and West Pulaski schools would also end, and black students in the intermediate grades at Froebel would finally be able to swim with whites, enter the band classes, and join the Junior Dramatic Club. There were contingency plans if there was overt student resistance: the *Post-Tribune* would use the word truant rather than striker, "firmness without appeasement would be the policy," and "there would be no more such blunders as bringing Frank Sinatra to plead with the students who stayed away from school, now that the new ruling is law."[5]

"City schools opened today with no untoward incidents, except in the Emerson district," the *Post-Tribune* greeted its readers on Tuesday, September 2, 1947. Black students attending five of the schools (including one at Horace Mann) found no organized opposition, but the thirty-eight young newcomers who cautiously entered the Emerson school were met by about two hundred white students who refused to mix with them. Superintendent Charles Lutz immediately threatened to punish all striking students under sixteen as truants; those over sixteen would be suspended and, therefore, ineligible for athletics. Roser, appearing at a strike rally in a local park, cited the new Indiana antihate law that made it a felony to associate together to spread hatred by reason of race, color, or religion. Nonetheless, the next day more than half of the school's 1,750 students were absent, including a large number of high-school pupils who were not directly affected. True to his word, on Thursday the superintendent suspended the older students and disbanded the football team. When the strike continued on Friday, H. B. Snyder editorialized in the *Post-Tribune:* "The people of the Emerson district have been spending a lot of time making a mountain out of a mole-hill. Why, if the menace of the negro is so threatening, has there been no trouble in any other school district? . . . They have stirred up a cauldron of ill-will which can become a lasting poison if it is not countered with a realization they have made a mistake." About six hundred high-school students had already been expelled, and when readmitted they would be barred from extracurricular activities. Having previously learned their lesson during the Froebel strike, school officials were now not about to equivocate.[6]

By the week's end, as the strike continued, both the supporting and the opposing forces gathered strength. Large crowds of adults and children had been milling outside the Emerson school and intimidating the black pupils, who were protected by the police. On the other side were a variety of community groups, this time led by the churches. Monsignor John Sullivan, dean of the Gary deanery of the Catholic Church, issued a strong denunciation, and he was supported by the Gary Council of Churches, Council of Church Women, and Ministerial Association, as well as the Bar Association, Chamber of Commerce, and the steelworkers union. The latter threatened to expel any members whose children continued to strike: "It is sickening to come to Gary and see members of the CIO participating in a shameful, anti-democratic and subversive demonstration," United Steelworkers district director Joe Germano announced. "The situation is deplorable because the union in Gary is so strong and could have prevented it." A mass meeting on Friday night at the YWCA attracted representatives from twenty civic groups. National publicity, as well, ran strongly against the strikers. "The forthright action of the superintendent of schools in Gary, Ind., in disciplining several hundred students for their refusal to sit in classrooms with negroes is in the best American tradition," ran the editorial in the *New York Times.* The police chief, mayor, assistant superintendent, and child-welfare director met nightly to plan their strategy. They in turn conferred often with H. B. Snyder, the superintendent, and other community leaders.[7]

Facing such strong and united resistance, the strike began to lose momentum early the following week. A handful of Tolleston school students, briefly induced to join the walkout, were immediately threatened with punishment. By the end of the second week over 80 percent of the students had returned to their classes; many of the parents had lost heart when threatened with truancy violations, and a few were served with warrants. With a sigh of relief, the *Post-Tribune* reported on Monday, September 15, "conditions at Emerson school were practically normal today, following two weeks' disruption caused by a mass truancy." School athletics would soon be reinstated. The established white community had closed ranks to defeat the strikers, with the steelworkers, Chamber of Commerce, and local churches—perhaps strange bedfellows—being particularly adamant. They were joined by the traditional civil rights organizations. "There were times during the school strikes when some school administrators and community leaders were convinced that all was lost," the close observer of school affairs James Tipton concluded. "But there was sufficient energy, intelligence, confidence, and teamwork among the group as a whole for them to win out in the end. They won by gaining the support and cooperation of an increasing number of citizens, by asking for and using the advice of outside, objective observers, by redoubling their efforts when all seemed hopeless, and by refusing to be permanently vindictive toward their opponents." Congratulations came from various quarters. But there remained questions about what the future offered. "The most hopeful sign from Gary is that progressives have united to enforce a liberal policy," Paul Klein wrote in *The Nation*. "Also important, the bigots have been compelled to conduct the fight on the liberals' level, with legal and political weapons. But the fight is not yet won, and Gary cannot afford to relax."[8]

Conspicuously absent during the struggle were the NAACP as well as the Urban League; indeed, the black community was mostly silent, letting the whites fight the battle. The NAACP remained moribund. "We are very much disturbed over the fact that during this crisis the NAACP Branch in Gary apparently did not find it necessary to activate itself by holding meetings, etc.," the national office informed Gary president Alfred Hall. "We sincerely hope that as a result of this second disturbance in the school system you will organize a strong education committee composed of representatives of Negro and white groups and will activate the membership to a broad comprehensive education program within the framework of the NAACP." Activity was still a few years off, however. As for the Urban League, executive secretary Joseph Chapman had been in the thick of the struggle since his arrival two years before, but now preferred to stay on the sidelines. "Sometimes no action is maybe the best action," he later noted. "At least as far as my injecting myself into it. I knew their attitude and it was a large white conservative element. Just a little more American as I said than the Froebel [population] but enough American to know that they didn't want them over there. I thought maybe the less said the better." Once the strike was over, Chapman met with some of the Emerson parents to encourage them to accept the situation.[9]

The Emerson strike was lost with or without the black community's opposition, but there was one issue that sparked much interest: the appointment of a black member to the board of education. In June 1946, anticipating a vacancy on the board, representatives from thirty-seven black civic and church organizations submitted three names to the board. Mayor Joseph Finerty named William Stern, a strong voice for civil rights. During the Emerson strike the board was shorthanded, for Michael Lobo had resigned, and decisions were essentially made by the three integrationists, Stern, the Reverend Newton Fowler, and Mrs. Uno Hill. Finally, in June 1948 Mayor Swartz appointed John Davies to replace Lobo. Davies was an employee of the Gary Railways, a former commander of the Glen Park American Legion, whose views on race issues were unknown. The Reverend Fowler's seat was also vacant. Pressure came from various groups and interests, including the Chamber of Commerce, which was most concerned about the school tax levy. "Many individuals not living in the Central District are of the impression that the citizens south of the Wabash tracks are not too concerned over the present school board appointment that is to be made in the near future," the *Gary American,* a dominant voice in the black community, remarked in late August. "Apparently they got this false impression because there are no pressure groups constantly asking [for an] audience with the mayor to present him weekly [with requests] about a representative being placed on the board from this area, as have the other sections of our city."[10]

Finally, in March 1949, "after months of procrastination," the mayor appointed the Reverend J. Claude Allen, identified by the *Post-Tribune* as a "midtown Negro churchman." Allen had arrived in Gary in 1934 as pastor of the Israel Colored Methodist Episcopal Church (CME); in 1946 he was appointed executive secretary of the department of mission and church extension of the national CME Church. The *Gary American* was ecstatic: "The announcement today of the appointment of Rev. J. Claude Allen to the School Board has won the respect for the mayor of nearly every citizen in the Central District. . . . There will be lots of opposition to the appointment from the other sections of the city, (mainly Tolleston) but we want the mayor to know: That for every friend he loses in these districts, he picked up two out here." Another color barrier had been crossed.[11]

Race relations had taken a turn for the better, but following the Emerson imbroglio, and even with the eventual appointment of the Reverend Allen, a variety of problems persisted—the continuing education of the students and community concerning intercultural relations, serious overcrowding in the black schools, and the nagging problem of a deeply segregated city. Only the first two were directly confronted. A City-wide Democratic Living Committee was organized during the 1947–48 school year, which worked with personnel from the Bureau for Intercultural Education and the teachers to promote "democratic living." When integration was extended to seventh graders the following year, there was increased need for intercultural education, but a lack of funds forced the withdrawal of the Bureau, which had been in the city for some years.

Various curricular changes were introduced, however: "(1) A unit on anthropology was included in upper grade science; (2) Units in social problems in senior high school were organized to teach better human relations; (3) Units in tenth grade English had definite objectives in understanding and tolerance; (4) In all grades, free and directed lists of material were made available to further understanding." Experimental courses were also started at various schools. Yet, as one study concluded in 1949, there remained serious integroup problems; "the prejudice, misinformation, scapegoating, and false generalizations which underlie strained race relations in Gary are factors which must be recognized in remedial and preventive educational efforts in all of the Gary schools." There were also lingering ethnic, religious, and class frictions. Individual efforts by teachers and principals were important, but there was no overall program or approach. The city nonetheless glowed with pride when, in February 1948, Mrs. Eleanor Roosevelt, representing the United Nations' human rights commission, presented Superintendent Lutz with the Bureau for Intercultural Education's special intercultural citation. Joining Lutz to accept the award was H. B. Snyder.[12]

With little leadership from above, intercultural relations drifted as the black enrollment continued to rise, reaching sixty-seven hundred in 1949, 34 percent of the student population (compared to 22 percent in 1940). The vast majority of the black students were crammed into a few increasingly crowded schools. By late 1947, the only children in the city attending for only a half-day were in the first and second grades at the Roosevelt school, where the average elementary classroom had forty-four children. (Part of the problem resulted from a fire in October 1946 that destroyed seven portable buildings adjacent to the school that housed the shops and a small gym.) The next year the school had more than one thousand students over its rated capacity. Despite the overcrowding, children within the district were prevented from attending other schools. Indeed, in September 1949, city councilman Terry Gray formally protested to the school board when his two children were denied permission to attend the new school at Twenty-sixth Avenue and Virginia Street. Besides the situation at Roosevelt, Gray complained "that the strict adherence to attendance of schools in the district, only applied to the Negroes. Whites living in Roosevelt district have the privilege of enrolling in any school in the city, while Negroes are kept strictly within the defined boundaries." In agreeing with Gray, the *Post-Tribune* pointed out that what the councilman was "seeking was a true integration program, instead of a sham, double-standard program, which applied to Negroes solely." But there would be no relief.[13]

One additional problem continued to linger—the nature of the Roosevelt high-school curriculum. There had long been a debate over the need for more vocational courses and programs, although the small high-school enrollment continued to focus on academic subjects. Once again, in late 1949, H. B. Snyder raised the question why the Roosevelt students were not getting beter training in the trades, for there were few classes and they were poorly taught and equipped. "Horace Mann has a first class equipped printing shop; Froebel has a machine shop that has everything; Roosevelt has nothing—but cast offs, and not enough for anything." Snyder, in an editorial, cast the blame on longtime school principal H. Theo Tatum: "Maybe one day the head of the institution will see the need for teaching for the masses instead of the classes and get the equipment to teach the graduates how to earn an honest living without having to get additional training." Rather than blaming the school board or superintendent for giving the school castoffs or employers for discriminating against black workers, the *Post-Tribune* editor found it comfortable to attack Tatum. This was somewhat odd, for the paper had long supported the principal, and Snyder had worked intimately with him in the Urban League and other organizations. But the long shadow of Booker T. Washington continued to hover over educational thinking in the steel city.[14]

The large number of black students and the flamboyant nature of race relations made the Gary schools somewhat unique. In other ways they experienced educational problems common throughout the country following the war. "America's public school system is confronted with the most serious crisis in its history," *New York Times* reporter Benjamin Fine announced in 1947. He then proceeded with a list of horrors: "Main bulwark of the democratic way of life, the schools have deteriorated alarmingly since Pearl Harbor. Teacher morale is at the lowest it has ever been. . . . Public confidence in the schools has dropped sharply. . . . School buildings are in need of repair. School supplies and equipment are lacking. Overcrowded classrooms have increased at an alrming rate. . . . Teachers are deserting the classrooms by the tens of thousands." And the answer: "I believe that if the community, if society itself, can be made aware of how serious the school situation is, greater financial and moral support will be forthcoming." Perhaps conditions were not everywhere this bad, but educational problems seemed endemic in the nation's cities.[15]

In Gary the overriding consideration was the strained school budget, which was linked to two particular issues—the need for additional space and increased salaries. There was, however, no community consensus on what should be done. In early January 1946 the school board began to focus on the need for more classrooms. One obvious hurdle was the growing opposition of the business community to an increased budget, now more than a decade in the making; board member Dan Kreitzman suggested that "representatives of big taxpayers will be taken on tours of the schools to see for themselves the inadequate housing provided for school children." It was not that the enrollment was escalating, for it was not—the overall enrollment hovered around twenty-one thousand throughout the decade—but population shifts within the city caused overcrowding at some schools, for example Roosevelt, while Emerson and Horace Mann had surplus rooms and small classes. To prepare for anticipated increased enrollments on the city's east, west, and south sides, the board adopted a ten-year building plan in mid-May. Assistant Superintendent Ralph Muller, appearing before the Kiwanis soon after, explained why there was a growing space problem: the birth rate was rising (as indicated by the increase in the kindergarten enrollment), there had been no new buildings since 1931, the abandonment of the work-study-play plan created a need for more classrooms, and many of the older portables needed replacing.[16]

While the board naturally looked to the increasingly recalcitrant business community for support, a surprising, and most valuable, alliance was building between the board and parents throughout the city. In March, at the instigation of Stanley Kohn and the Miller PTA, parent groups from nineteen school districts formed a City-wide Parents' Council, adopting the slogan "children cannot speak for themselves." Their major goal was an increase in the property-tax rate to provide money for new schools. Gary appeared to have the lowest urban property valuation in Lake County. After meeting with the superintendent and his assistant, the Council agreed to ask the school board for a special sixty-cent school-building levy to fund a projected $4 million school construction program. The Council's tactic was to exert continued pressure on individual board members.[17]

As school opened in September 1946, overcrowding was expected at the Edison, Tolleston, and (black) East Pulaski schools, where the first three grades were shifted to the (white) West Pulaski school. But trouble was already brewing over the school board's proposed budget of $3.5 million and an increased tax levy. Organized to oppose the budget were the business heavyweights—the Chamber of Commerce, Gary Industrial Foundation, Real Estate Board, and especially the Gary Taxpayers Association, the steel corporation's mouthpiece. In late August, H. B. Snyder, *Post-Tribune* editor and president of the Taxpayers Association, "told the board that the association would fight the special levy to the end that it be entirely eliminated. Failing in this, he said, the association would file a remonstrance with the state tax board." Perhaps even more influential was the Association's executive secretary, M. W. Madden, a CPA who intimately knew the details of the school budget and who attended all of the board's budget meetings. Arrayed against these titans were the newly formed City-wide Parents' Council and its allies, left mavericks such as attorney Mario Tomsich and Dr. Frank Neuwelt, the Lake County Communist party, as well as the teachers' union, and AFL and CIO representatives. Nonetheless, the board voted to increase the school tax levy and add a special twenty-cent building levy, not exactly what the parents had desired, but a start.[18]

No sooner was the first round over than squabbling began concerning the increased tax rate which would have to be approved by the Indiana Tax Board. City-wide Parents' Council president John Schoon wrote to the tax board in mid-October, presenting the Council's case. "We have been told that it is unusual for a group of taxpayers to promote HIGHER taxes," he informed Peter Beczkiewicz of the board. "Therefore, it is our desire to put in writing before you, why we are backing the Gary Board of Education in their requests for higher taxes in 1947. . . . We discovered that the schools were hampered by lack of funds . . . that our children were in overcrowded classrooms . . . that education facilities were lacking . . . that the school system was bonded to its legal limit . . . and that every attempt to pay off the full amount of the bonds was met with refunding and efforts to obtain additional funds were thwarted by interests desiring to maintain a constant tax rate." In late November, the state board upheld the tax increase.[19]

Parents' and school administrators' dreams of school expansion were given a decided boost in March 1947 with the publication of a survey of Gary's school buildings. Some months earlier the school board had requested that the Committee on Field Services of the University of Chicago conduct a thorough survey of the city's school buildings and assess future needs. In a lengthy report, the survey team discussed national and local population predictions (projecting an enrollment of twenty-five thousand by 1960), summarized the current utilization of school facilities, presented a history of school construction, and evaluated the eight unit schools and twelve elementary schools and their sites. All of the schools had various shortcomings, including unsanitary and inadequate facilities, poor lighting, cramped space, and fire hazards. The report recommended numerous major and minor construction projects, as well as other structural improvements, costing a little more than $3 million over five years. There was immediate need for additions to the Edison, Wirt, and Lincoln schools and a new school on Twenty-sixth Avenue.[20]

Within two months the school board, waxing enthusiastic, adopted a two-year, $2 million building program to include four new elementary schools. In July it proposed a 1948 school budget of slightly over $6 million, compared to about $3.5 million in the current year, but reduced the building budget by $250,000. School administrators once again called upon the City-wide Parents' Council to raise its voice in support of the budget and an increased tax levy and asked H. Theo Tatum, representing the United Council of Negro Organizations, to support them. At their late August meeting the board once again heard from W. M. Madden of the Taxpayers Association, however, who opposed the projected $2.06 tax levy, which the board reduced to $2.00. Frank Blackwell, welfare chairman of the CIO, originally sided with the parents, then backed the Madden "plan so long as it did not effect the wage increases voted school employees nor hinder the school building program." The increased budget looked safe until the steel corporation requested a reduction of its property assessment in the fall. "If this plea is approved by the State Tax Board it would mean that the schools would receive $340,000.00 less next year and would put an absolute stop to any new buildings until 1950," the City-wide Parents' Council informed the membership, which was encouraged to protest to the tax board. "Write to the State Tax Board that we represent the parents of children whose very education is being periled by this belated action." The struggle would continue.[21]

In January 1948, the board of education voted $1.240 million in school-building bonds, upon the approval of the city council, to fund seven building projects, including a new school at Twenty-sixth and Virginia. There was a slight snag, however, when two councilmen from Glen Park protested that no new schools were planned for their neighborhood, a common refrain from the burgeoning south-side community. The City-wide Parents' Council immediately launched a telephone campaign to back the bond issue. They were successful. But within a few months the parents were requesting another twenty-cent increase in the school-building tax levy; they also protested that the board was concentrating on expanding the larger schools, particularly Tolleston, Wirt, and Edison, while neglecting to build smaller schools. The parents' council focused on the students' needs for facilities, but it did not neglect curricular matters. For example, the parents heard a lecture on "Sex Education in the Home and at School" and agreed to increase the schools' social-hygiene programs.[22]

The school board voted another property-tax-rate increase in late July, over the protest of M. W. Madden that it should "make a 'genuine effort' to hold the school rate down to a reasonable level." The board also accepted a twenty-cent increase in the building levy. "Business interests of the city, tax experts and property owners, both large and small, are 'calling for a halt,' " H. B. Snyder announced in his editorial, "and since the school board is leading the way in the tax increase procession it seems that here is a fitting place to start." The *Post-Tribune* editor was obviously perturbed that he and his friends were no longer dictating school policy, and he cautioned against municipal bankruptcy. Strongly supported by the parents, the board refused to heed Snyder's warning and passed the increased levy.[23]

The struggle was not over, however, for the Gary Industrial Foundation submitted a petition, signed by one thousand taxpayers, protesting the property-tax increase. So the parents' council once again requested that the state tax board hold its hearings in Gary in order to give the Gary parents a chance to be heard—"We have just started the building program this summer . . . and are building the very minimum . . . CLASS ROOMS ONLY. Some of our high schools do not have gymnasiums, auditoriums or cafeteria spaces nor do we propose to build them now. With soaring building costs, the 20¢ levy is proving woefully too little." The parents were seconded by the teachers' union, which "chided Chamber of Commerce members for their failure to take more interest in the schools—except at tax time. [Union president William] Swan contended that the schools are in the condition they are in today because businessmen have neglected their duty towards the schools." When the schools opened in early September, the parents' and teachers' arguments were underscored by serious overcrowding at the Roosevelt, Froebel, Pulaski, and Edison schools; kindergarten classes in Miller were held in the Duneland Village housing project for lack of regular school space. A few weeks later the state tax board accepted the increased building tax.[24]

While the parents' council continued to be interested in a variety of issues, including a series of lectures on "Peoples of Different Races, Creeds and National Origins," the business community remained more narrowly focused. In late October, after the tax increase had been passed, the Gary Taxpayers' Association was still attempting to get the rate reduced. Trying a different tack, the Chamber of Commerce discussed conducting an investigation of the school administration after accepting a report by Harold Phipps, the chairman of its tax research committee. "Phipps charged that attempts by school officials to explain the plight of the Gary school system and its building needs have been little more than 'propaganda to prepare the public for an additional tax allotment to the schools next year.'" Arguing that the schools were not being used efficiently, Phipps defensively concluded "that school officials have employed the use of mass psychology in inducing people to believe that the Chamber and other groups are against good education and expansion of the school system. 'This is wrong,' he said, explaining that 'first the school officials must use what they have at hand to the best of their ability.'" Another member suggested that the Chamber study the educational standards of Gary's high-school graduates. Despite the report of school auditor A. Howard Bell, a longtime employee, that Gary's per-pupil costs were the lowest of the eight largest school systems in the state, in early 1949 the Chamber nonetheless delegated its educational committee to "examine the program of education and the use of school plant facilities so that recommendations may be made to the public on questions of administration and expansion of the school city."[25]

With the increased funding, despite the business community's obstructionist tactics, the school board continued to construct a few new schools and add on to others. After the completion of the school at Twenty-sixth and Virginia, whose students were all black, high priority was placed on building a new elementary school in Glen Park and expanding the Pulaski school. Still, school administrators admitted that school overcrowding would continue, partially because there were delays in getting building materials. The parents' council happily announced in late July, however, that sixty-one new classrooms would be ready by the start of the new semester. It also congratulated the school board on projecting a cut of eight cents in the tax rate (soon reduced to four-and-one-half cents), although the budget would increase by

$500,000; the difference would partially be made up by another increase in the state's contribution. There was also a drop in capital outlay for new buildings. "Overcrowding will be the rule in most Gary schools this fall," the *Post-Tribune* announced on September 6, 1949, "in spite of the $1,500,000 investment this year in new buildings." But the situation was uneven, with the Emerson, Horace Mann, and a few other schools underenrolled, and the blacks' schools, particularly Roosevelt, bursting at the seams. Almost one-third of Roosevelt's thirty-five hundred students were now attending only half-day classes, a particularly disturbing situation to councilman Terry Gray and attorney Milo Murray. Overall, with a pupil/teacher ratio of 31:4, Gary had the highest average among the state's eight largest cities. There was, certainly, cause for alarm, as the next decade would increasingly demonstrate.[26]

As the parents, school board, and business interests battled over increased school funding, another element in the educational equation were the teachers. Having been rather quiescent during the war, the teachers' union began to reassert itself by early 1946. During the latter half of the decade AFT membership would increase from 368 in 1945 to almost five hundred in 1949 (out of a total teaching force of 690). With such a clear majority, the union was in a strong bargaining position. In early March 1946, the union began its campaign for a 20 percent salary increase, which would include raising the minimum levels at all salary ranks, as well as giving each teacher a $700 boost. The board agreed to raise the minimum and maximum schedules, but voted to grant the teachers only $250 each. There was soon a growing fear that, because the salaries remained generally low, new teachers would be reluctant to come to Gary, particularly men; the school board also refused to grant veterans credit for their wartime experience. There were still twenty vacancies as of August 1, mirroring the national teacher stortage. The board was forced to hire teachers with little or no experience and some with less than four years of college; increasingly, the newer teachers were graduates of Gary's high schools.

Another issue was the no-strike provision in the AFT constitution passed in 1916 because of the belief that public employees should not strike. With the war's end, however, and strike fever sweeping the country, teachers could hardly remain immune; strikes, or strike talk, broke out in Detroit, Saint Paul, Minneapolis, Pontiac, and Flint. During the 1946 AFT convention, the Executive Council voted to open the topic for debate during the next year. Along with many locals throughout the country, Gary's members voted to recommend removal of the no-strike pledge: "Local #4 needs this recognized weapon on defense. We may not have to employ it, but to defend our gains the time may come when we may have to use it." They were in the minority, however, and the no-strike clause was upheld at the 1947 convention. Nonetheless, scattered locals continued to strike, and the Gary union would theoretically cling to this final straw for many years.[27]

Strikes were, possibly, the ultimate weapon. For now, however, talk would have to suffice. In March 1947, the teachers' lobby succeeded in getting the state government to increase its school aid, including teachers' salaries, but this was not enough, and the next month the union demanded a 30 percent salary hike from the school board. The local also objected to the board's policy of requiring teachers to spend a day going door-to-door taking the school census, but at a mass meeting a majority of the members voted to cooperate with school officials. " 'I think our teachers will be more tolerant with their pupils, now they have seen at first hand the kind of homes the children come from,' said Asst. Principal Frank Albright of Froebel school." When the board, in late May, discussed teacher raises in the neighborhood of $700, the union protested, as it did when it received word that all teachers would have to get their bachelors' degree within a few years and those with a four-year degree would have to take an additional five hours of study every four years. Joining with the much smaller, but still active, Gary Teachers' Federation (NEA), the AFT local came back with a proposal for a $960 raise for each teacher and a suggestion for an in-service professional program. A settlement was finally reached, with the teachers accepting a smaller raise than they had demanded and the board agreeing that the professional-training requirement would be voluntary.[28]

As the teacher shortage continued, Superintendent Lutz touted the virtues of teaching in Gary, using the argument that the city "has a progressive school system that is willing to try new ideas." More specifically, teachers had one of the best salary schedules in the state, he argued, with salaries starting at $2,500 and going to $4,500 for eighteen years of experience and a master's degree; there was a generous sick-benefit plan; and the nine subject-area supervisors provided expert assistant to new teachers. But this was surely not enough. The union once again requested a sabbatical leave program, an issue earlier dropped with the outbreak of war. The board came back with an increase of 25 percent in sick benefits. Then, in April 1948, the AFT demanded a pay raise of 15 percent for all teachers with more than five-years' experience in Gary. This was not all, for the local also suggested "reduction of the class loads to an average of 25 pupils per teacher, a lessening of clerical work and routine record keeping, additional equipment necessary in all departments to establish activity programs, establishment of sabbatical leaves, employment of coaching teachers for slow pupils, and establishment of in-service training programs to help encourage and orient newly recruited teachers."[29]

The union's proposal favoring increases for only the experienced teachers rankled board members and school administrators, already pressured by space shortages and attacks from the business community. Moreover, abandoning their short-lived alliance with the teachers' union, the much smaller teachers' federation agreed to settle for a more limited raise for all teachers. Primary- and elementary-school supervisor Bernice Engels then announced that because of the shortage of elementary-school teachers, caused by the low starting salaries, in the fall high-school teachers would "have to be shifted down to teach younger children." Next, in June the board refused to pass a salary increase, substituting instead a thirteen dollar monthly cost-of-living bonus for all licensed teachers and administrators. Dejected, the union reluctantly accepted this small bone.[30]

The following April, however, the union announced that it would be asking for "substantial wage increases," and united with the AFT locals in neighboring East Chicago, Hammond, and Whiting to obtain a uniform wage scale. In Gary, the requested wage increase would average about $525 per teacher. This was too much for M. W. Madden of the Gary Taxpayers' Association, who offered his services to the board and recommended that any increase not start until February 1950. Enraged, the union's finance committee suggested "that economy measures be taken by school officals and any savings be utilized to make base salaries of Gary teachers 'comparable with teachers salaries in other Indiana communities of like size.'" Specifically, the union suggested discontinuing summer, Saturday, and night-school classes, as well as adult education, and reducing the school year from ten to nine months. Next, although the union did not officially condone strikes, the local threatened to begin a "work stoppage" on Monday June 6, less than a week before the end of the semester, if there was no "satisfactory agreement on salaries."[31]

The teachers were promised support from the AFL-affiliated Lake County Central Labor Union. But on June 1 the union's executive board "called off plans for a 'sit-down' strike," after obtaining a promise of higher salaries depending upon the amount of the state distribution of school funds. A month later the teachers accepted a $300 pay increase, which partially included the previous year's bonus. The higher starting salaries helped attract new teachers, and there was only a small shortage by mid-August, despite the attempt to hire only teachers with four-year degrees. At the year's end, although higher salaries would always head the agenda, union president William Swan was also complaining "that the schools have been fooling the public with a lot of circus activity that looks good to the general public but actually is selling the children short." Promising an investigation of school affairs, the union was specifically concerned about the teachers' multifarious duties, including "sponsorship of classes and clubs, endless reports, too much clerical work, register class activities, selling of tickets, [and] student council affairs." Teachers should teach, period. The school board welcomed the study.[32]

The school board was continually short of funds, and thereby hampered in its efforts to accelerate the building program and raise salaries, because of its essential dependence on the local tax base as well as some, albeit increasing, funding from the state based on enrollment. The later accounted for about $1.5 million in 1950, roughly one-third of the total budget (not including new buildings), slightly less than the state average. There was some assistance from the federal government, but, as usual, only for specific projects. Attempts throughout the decade to pass a general federal-aid bill for education were continually thwarted for a variety of reasons. Congress did, however, continue the Lanham Act, passed originally in 1940 as a war measure to assist defense workers in a variety of ways, until the end of the decade. The Gary schools received $21,665 in late 1945 for child-care programs at three neighborhood locations. At the same time they acquired free war surplus, including shop machinery and machine tools for the Froebel and Emerson vocational programs. Under another program the vocational department received some support in 1946; and there was additional money for teaching job-related courses to veterans. The *Post-Tribune* strongly supported federal aid in 1948. Referring to the bill sponsored by Republican Senator Robert A. Taft, it argued that "this proposal of federal help isn't just a school matter. It is tied up with national defense, with our hope for an intelligent and strong America." It would be another seventeen years, however, before federal aid would become a reality. In the meantime the Gary schools would limp along, with continual money worries as school officials altered the curriculum.[33]

The war's end brought an outpouring of interest in education. " 'Securing the peace' was the theme of citywide visiting day," the local paper announced on November 14, 1945. "School leaders emphasized that parents will be welcome any time during the week to witness normal class routine and special events prepared in accord with continuing themes, including finishing the unfinished tasks of the war, improving economic well-being, building sound health and developing good citizenship." These broad areas, grouped under the rubric of life-adjustment education, would increasingly guide school policies. Direction came from a series of national and regional conferences starting in June 1945, and the appointment by the Commissioner of Education of a National Commission on Life Adjustment Education for Youth two years later. The "new" thrust—there were definite precedents nationally and in the Gary schools, somewhat accelerating in the 1930s—would emphasize vocational, health, and family-living elements in the high-school curriculum, as well as increased child-welfare services for all students. In his 1949 report, child-welfare director Mark Roser, whose educational role continually expanded, summarized the need for "constructive help to the individual child so that he can mature into an independent, self-respecting and creative democratic citizen. To achieve this aim children must have wise and happy adults to guide them. They must have educational experiences which have meaning for them." "Adjustment" and "practicality," hardly novel ideas, would increasingly become the guiding terms.[34]

Various practical curricular reforms were soon implemented. Science courses starting in the fourth grade would include a unit on steel production and information on the atom bomb, and there was a new high-school course on the "Problems of Democracy," a fixture in other cities for a few decades. The Chamber of Commerce, representing "merchants and industrialists who expressed a common feeling that the schools have been falling short in preparing high school people for jobs in stores, banks and industrial plants immediately upon their graduation," pushed for additional business-oriented courses. Standing behind the Chamber were Gary's economic powers, including U.S. Steel, Gary National Bank, Gary Trust and Savings Bank, and the power company. School officials agreed to survey local businesses in order to gauge their future employment needs, then train students in these areas. As for the schools' industrial-arts program, an integral part of the original Wirt system, each of the eight high schools had woodworking and drawing, and most had metal and machine shops; Roosevelt had building techniques and general shop; Horace Mann had courses in electricity; Emerson, one of the two vocational centers, had foundry and auto-mechanics; and Froebel, the other vocational center, had foundry and welding. Additional vocational courses were offered to adults, particularly veterans, in a cooperative arrangement with various AFL trade unions. Adult-education programs were expanded in 1948, with an increased emphasis on apprentice training (as the interest in academic subjects waned). At the Froebel school workers from U.S. Steel could take a variety of night courses—boilermaking, pipe fitting, bricklaying, welding, foundry, machine shop, carpentry, patternmaking, instrument repair, and electricity. Both labor and capital were thus served.[35]

More broadly, beginning in July 1946, school administrators placed greater emphasis on "pupil guidance to the end that individual children shall be helped in the areas of social adjustment and health improvement as well as in study achievement." They were, once again, concerned about individualizing instruction in order to curtail student failures, thereby adjusting the students to a life of purported success. What about juvenile delinquents, society's failures? Roser, along with neighboring school-attendance officers, desired more cooperation from the juvenile court so that the offenders could be kept in school. But, at least in Gary, delinquency seemed to be decreasing in 1946, particularly for the more serious offenses of burglary, larceny, and auto theft, although the national scare continued. There seemed to be "more stabilization in the home, a stabilization that was lacking during the war." Students who acted out in school might be referred to the juvenile court, but this number also declined over the latter half of the decade as other measures were used by Roser and his staff.[36]

Another "at-risk" group were handicapped children, who also came in for special consideration. In early 1947, the child-welfare department cooperated with the Indiana Association for Crippled Children and the Campbell Friendship settlement house to open a special school in the latter's building in the heart of the midtown neighborhood. The association would furnish two teachers, the settlement house would provide the space, and the schools would pay for the materials and supplies. Perhaps twenty emotionally handicapped students could be accommodated. The following year Roser hired a handicapped-children's specialist, who began planning a specialized class-room to be built in the Goodwill Industries building. There was also home schooling for those unable to attend classes for physical or emotional rea-sons, totaling 166 students during the 1948–49 school year. Because of a recent law, the state would now provide reimbursement for any additional expenses for the disabled.

Then, in September 1948, a school for physically handicapped children was opened in the Norton Park community center. Under the direction of the child-welfare department, the school was also a cooperative venture of the state welfare department, the Lake County chapter of the Indiana Society for Crippled Children, the Cerebral Palsy Parents Advisory Council, and the Lake County Medical Society. "Isolated, unhappy children, some of whom had never played with other children, have been changed in a few short weeks into happy, contented persons," Mark Roser remarked about the sixteen children attending the school. The students were provided with occupational therapy, speech work, physiotherapy, and academic work, while the parents were offered counseling. Finally, as the decade ended, another school for "slow learners" was opened in the pavilion in North Gleason Park on the city's south side. As one of the system's "Friendship Schools," its aim was to provide: "(1) tasks geared to the level of children's ability . . . and (2) a close and accepting relationship between teacher and student; (3) a permissive and noncompulsory atmosphere." The children were eager to attend, Roser averred, "and in many instances patterns of hostility and delinquency have been dropped."[37]

The child-welfare department's multifarious duties attested to the growing emphasis on specialized services for various groups of troubled and handi-capped students, that is, those who have "abnormal adjustment problems to school work or to the community." Indeed, this was potentially no small number. While the department referred only thirty-nine pupils to Gary's Mental Hygiene Clinic in 1948–49 for a variety of offenses—poor achieve-ment, agressiveness, anxiety, stealing, hostility, and even immaturity—Roser estimated "that 45 per cent of our children are hampered by emotional problems severe enough to cause physical symptoms." After all, Roser was hired because of the Purdue survey's emphasis on the schools' need for a clinical psychologist. Using his background to good advantage, the director steadily increased his department's services, adding more testing, home visits, and case conferences. Students had difficulties for a variety of reasons. Some were "mentally defective or retarded in intelligence," particularly in the Central District, others had a strong vocational bent, and still others had pressures at home—"the only boy in an Italian family, living with father, mother, and paternal grandparents, has been so loved, watched, and doted upon that he has had little chance to do things for himself. At school he could not study without the teacher's individual help. Helping him grow up be-comes a joint responsibility of family and of school personnel." There were also the white and black children arriving from the rural South, "with its distinctive cultural patterns," who became "confused in the North where other cultural patterns prevail." Slowly, the schools were adjusting their programs, for "today's children face a world of new insecurities which calls for bold action on the part of the total community," Roser remarked in his department's 1949 report. "Provisions must be made for more adequate measures of individual attention as well as a renewed vision and courage to alter educational patterns as they become meaningless to larger numbers of children."[38]

The schools were increasingly demonstrating their practical nature, suiting the perceived needs of children and community alike. During the 1947 first annual educational fair, booths and exhibits at the various schools were designed "to demonstrate to parents and the community at large what Junior Gary gets for the tax dollars invested in education." What "Junior Gary" continued to get were more socially oriented courses. For example, the Gary social-protection committee demanded that the schools begin teaching family living and sex, for it appeared that a "study of 50 delinquency cases showed nearly complete lack of such training in the home." The *Post-Tribune's* H. B. Snyder strongly favored "family living" courses. "Young people want to know how to get along in marriage and how to make [a] home," he argued. "They want preparation for family living. And much of this training can and should be provided through the schools, working in co-operation with the parents." Material on getting along with people could be offered in the various physical education, hygiene, science, and home economics courses, but much more controversial was sex education, still under discussion as the decade ended.[39]

In planning for their future, Gary's students were also expected to worry about their career plans. Additional guidance counselors were added to the high schools in 1948, and they immediately began planning a tour of the steel mills, cementing their relationship with the city's number one employer. "There has not been, however, as close liaison in the past between schools and industry as would be beneficial to both," lamented the local newspaper. "It is not a matter of 'selling' the steel industry to our young people. It's just a matter of making them thoroughly acquainted with the employment possibilities, the career possibilities which are present here at home." Naturally, school officials believed the schools should also improve their contacts with other regional industries. Whether the increased work of the guidance counselors was particularly beneficial is questionable, for the vast majority of the students, particularly boys, left school once they turned sixteen and found work. All minors (under eighteen) needed a work permit issued by the Child Welfare Department and the Vocational Supervisor's office after September 1948. There were still stringent regulations for those under sixteen, who could only work during the daytime and in certain jobs; they could not be employed in manufacturing plants, for a messenger service, or in hazardous occupations, and boys were forbidden from employment in bowling alleys, pool rooms, or billiard parlors. But there were plenty of other job possibilities, particularly for white children. More than seven hundred work permits were issued from September 1948 to September 1949, most for those sixteen and over. For the majority, schooling was only a short respite from family and work responsibilities.[40]

Students were in an anomalous situation, for they were part of the world, yet had to be sheltered from it. In May 1948, the high-school-student councils and the All-Out Americans sponsored a mass parade down Broadway, involving two thousand pupils, to demonstrate support for "the United Nations appeal for aid to the destitute children of the world." They were no strangers to hunger and poverty in the world. At the same time some adults tried to shield them from the sordid influences of comic books. The national comic-book scare was touched off in 1948 by the heated charges of Frederic Wertham against crime comics, and soon there were calls for censorship around the country. In Gary, in the spring, the City-wide Parents' Council launched its campaign against comic books and movies harmful to children. Working with the mayor and Child Welfare Department, the parents were successful in eliminating thirty comics from the newsstands. But the scourge was not over. A "second crop of objectionable comics [began] appearing on Gary newsstands, as bad or possibly worse," in the fall, raising the ire of the Knights of Columbus. The Catholic organization urged the mayor "to ban 'objectionable, undesirable and evil' comic books and indecent literature from being distributed in the city," specifically "books which glorify murder, burglary, sex, kidnapping, arson, assault with deadly weapons or other nefarious activities." The mayor promised to comply. The scare soon died down, but was revived in the early 1950s.[41]

While the Gary schools were often embroiled in local issues and controversies, they were never immune from state or national political and legal decisions. Take, for example, the controversy over religion in the schools. Years earlier, to still the debate, Superintendent Wirt had established the program of released time for religious instruction, and the churches had willingly organized their separate weekday schools. But the depression had forced them to close. In 1930, with Wirt's blessing, religious instruction moved back into the schools and included trained Protestant teachers, hired and paid by the church-school board of education, offering courses to both elementary and high-school classes. Moreover, beginning in 1934, Catholic priests were teaching Bible Study courses for English credit in the high schools; and the Sisters of the Poor Handmaids of Jesus Christ offered religious classes to the younger students, using "any methods or means, any topics, text books, charts or teaching aids at their disposal dealing with the religious education program." All supplies were furnished by the public schools. Sectarian religious instruction was common throughout the nation's schools and certainly found fertile ground in Gary.[42]

These programs were continued through the war, with classes for Catholic children offered at Horace Mann, Froebel, Emerson, Jefferson, and East Pulaski. The Gary Council of Churches, now supervising the Protestant teachers, temporarily curtailed most instruction, then in September 1943 reinstituted classes in grades four through six in all of the schools. At the same time, the city's ministers, in order to promote "closer co-operation between the public school and the churches in their religious education programs," held receptions for the public school teachers. They were encouraged by a recent state law legalizing voluntary religious instruction in the schools. Then, in December, the mayor's youth-service board, fearing that the growing youth lawlessness was caused by a lack of religious influence, invited forty Protestant, Catholic, Orthodox, and Jewish clergymen to visit the schools. "Co-operation of the schools in this non-denominational effort to 'sell' the churches of the community to its junior citizens was pledged by Supt. Charles D. Lutz at a meeting with the youth board and ministers," the *Post-Tribune* reported. By the war's end, and into the postwar years, the city's political, religious, and educational leaders were working closely together. As the *Post-Tribune* later remarked, "Gary long has been recognized in Protestant circles as the pioneer community in religious education."[43]

The religious-secular educational alliance came to a crashing halt in March 1948. The Supreme Court, in an eight-to-one decision in the *McCollum* case, ruled that an Illinois law permitting released time for religious instruction was unconstitutional; as Justice Hugo Black declared, public schools could not be used "to aid any or all religious faiths or sects in the dissemination of their doctrines and ideals." The *Post-Tribune* recorded on March 9, "Weekday religious education is continuing in the Gary public schools today as school officials and church leaders seek to determine the full effect and extent of the U.S. Supreme court decision yesterday barring the use of tax-supported school facilities for religious instruction." Both church and school officials tried to postpone the inevitable. But in June the school board, its members professing their belief in religion, ruled that because of the court decision there could be neither religious use of school property nor released time for religious instruction during school hours, and teachers could not promote religion. The board also denied the Gideon Society's request to distribute bibles through the schools. A thirty-year era had come to a sudden end. The schools, after all, were not immune from the law of the land.[44]

Another change was in the wind, marking the further disintegration of the Pax Wirt. Gary College, founded during the depths of the depression, was an additional sign of the former superintendent's ability to accomplish the seemingly impossible. He had always hoped to make the schools as all-inclusive as possible, touching the broadest section of the city's population and offering a wide variety of courses and services. Gary College was his pride and joy, and it survived his demise, depression, and war. In October 1945, there were 293 students enrolled for Monday night classes, slightly below projections, perhaps, because of the merchants' new policy of staying open on the first night of the week. The influx of veterans boosted the enrollment to 950 the next year. But the continuing expense, along with other problems—the drain on school resources and personnel—prompted the school board to invite Indiana University to return to the city in early 1948. With the university offering extension courses in a variety of subjects, there seemed little reason for continuing Gary College, which was merged with the university the following June; classes were now offered at Seaman Hall rather than at Horace Mann school. Over eighty-six hundred students had taken classes during the college's sixteen years as an appendage of the school system. In late 1950 it was finally dissolved. But it had served its purpose—to provide Gary's population with college-level courses conveniently and at minimal cost.

Service to the community remained the watchword of school officials as the decade ended, even as programs and policies continued to change. "Doors of the public schools will be thrown open next week to the community so that parents and taxpayers may discover how and what Gary children are being taught and how well the city is providing for the educational development of the younger generation," the *Post-Tribune* reported on November 1, 1949. " 'It was felt by the Education week committee that "living democracy" adequately expresses the citizenship goal of the public schools as teachers, students and parents work day after day in bringing philosophy and practice closer together,' said Dr. Lee Gilbert of Emerson school, chairman of the week." Parents and representatives from civic and social organizations were invited to witness a school board meeting, "demonstrating the great variety of problems that come to the board for a solution. Board members will sit around a table on the platform and talk into microphones so that the audience can follow the business." The board surely hoped to gain the sympathy and support of a broad segment of the population, for it was about to enter a decade of significant growth and change.[45]

School board members, administrators, teachers, students, parents, and the community at large had watched the schools survive numerous problems during the latter half of the decade. There was never consensus, but coalitions formed, interest groups organized and pressured, and there was finally a temporary resolution of most issues. The curriculum remained flexible, with an attempt at some balance between academic and vocational programs and an overall practical bent. Racial desegregation became official board policy, and there was some interest in promoting intercultural programs, but the city's entrenched de facto segregation prevented any widespread student integration. During the next decade this problem would remain intractable. Similarly, there would continue to be problems concerning inadequate facilities, as the student population grew and shifted geographically. The modest amount of school building following the war made some dent in the situation, but as the decade ended some schools were bursting at the seams, while others, those on the north side, had room to spare.

The prime issue was money. The budget was always too limited, although not limited enough to suit the business interests, led by U.S. Steel, which continually attacked and questioned any tax increases. The parents, in contrast, represented by the City-wide Parents' Council, joined by a variety of community groups and individuals, were relentless in lobbying for more taxes. This rift between the parents and the business community, having originated during the depression, would continue to mark school politics. Another aspect of the factional split was the teachers' growing consciousness, as both teachers' organizations, led by the dominant AFT local, continually demanded higher wages and other benefits. The postwar years had brought no answers, only more educational questions and dilemmas. They would continue as the number of students, teachers, and schools quickly climbed during the 1950s. And, once again, there would be a call for reform, administrative and otherwise, starting at the top.

There were new starts as well as important educational continuities during the postwar years. The schools pursued their primary goal of offering a multitude of courses, programs, and services to the community, with a new twist here and there because of fresh local and national trends. Children were perceived to need a more socially and economically relevant curriculum as well as extracurricular activities. Moreover, various pressure groups, both within and without the school system, attempted to enhance their influence. Economic issues—wages, taxes, the school budget—were paramount, but other concerns were also visible, for example religious, cultural, political, and legal matters. The school board and superintendent were increasingly swayed by these forces, as state and national intervention mounted. The Gary schools were swimming in a larger and larger sea.

VIII

CONTINUITY AND CHANGE, 1950–1960

In 1955, Betty Balanoff, along with her steelworker husband and four (white) children, moved from Chicago to midtown Gary. The children enrolled in the Froebel school, still housing grades K–12, and Betty, a born activist, quickly became a leader in the PTA. With a predominantly black enrollment, Froebel's twenty-five hundred or so working-class students, heavily concentrated in the elementary grades (there were only 102 graduates that spring), were overflowing the classrooms. As she later remembered: "Froebel School became so crowded that the first four grades were put on half-day shifts. Portables, World War II quonset huts, were added to our campus. Rental property was used, and in spite of this some children housed in Froebel's main building had their desks in one of the larger halls. Class sizes were large. I recall that my second grader was in a class with forty-five students, and the same teacher who taught all their subjects in the morning had another group of similar size in the afternoon. . . . None of the Froebel children were allowed to take their books home because the books, too, were used by two sets of children."[1]

Balanoff was eager for the school board to construct new schools, as were parents throughout the city confronted with similar circumstances. But—and this was quite unique—she also joined with her colleagues in the interracial Froebel PTA to have a new school built in Norton Park, located in an integrated neighborhood. After much resistance from the school board, the parents secured a new integrated school. Their agitation proved successful, highlighting the persistence of race and class as concerns during the 1950s. There were, of course, other issues, as the Gary schools struggled to survive swelling enrollments, administrative squabbling, structural changes, teacher activism, and various political pressures. By 1960, they would scarcely resemble Wirt's fabled work-study-play system, so carefully erected decades earlier.

The demise of the platoon plan would change the schools during the decade, but there were also important continuities with their history. School authorities still sought to maintain a plethora of courses and services, keeping the educational system a vital aspect of community life, directly for the children and more indirectly for the rest of society. Moreover, the educational establishment felt pressure from many sources, local, state, and national, which worked diligently to shape school matters. Schools were, after all, the touchstone for society, representing the values and aspirations, however conflicting, of its organizations and citizens.

Growth was both the bane and the blessing of the decade. Gary's population grew from 134,000 to almost 180,000 from 1950 to 1960; the black population almost doubled, from thirty-nine thousand to over sixty-nine thousand. The schools' enrollment more than kept pace, jumping from twenty-three thousand to over forty-one thousand. (Nationally, public school enrollment climbed from 25.5 million to 36.3 million.) Even more striking was the leap in the black enrollment from over eight thousand to about twenty-three thousand, more than half of the schools' total by the decade's end. The rising birth rate, combined with a large high-school drop-out rate in the working-class schools, meant that most of the students were concentrated in the elementary grades (thirty-two thousand in K–8 in 1960); high-school graduates only increased from 1,109 in 1950 to 1,483 in 1959. The number of teachers almost doubled as well, rising from 780 to almost fourteen hundred. School building always lagged behind enrollment pressures, but the number of schools did go from twenty-two to thirty-six. While other cities were losing businesses and population to the burgeoning surburbs, Gary remained a thriving, although highly segregated, community, the economic and cultural center of northwest Indiana.[2]

The burden of coping with the escalating student population, along with multifarious other educational problems, was thrust upon the appointed school board, the usual mixture of five of Gary's middling citizens—a street-car executive, contractor, druggist, black minister, a sheet metal worker, and community activist. During the next ten years the membership would change without altering the influence of these interests. Gary's elite had long abandoned direct control of the city's institutions. In August 1950, Mayor Eugene Swartz appointed Joseph Luckey, a longtime clerical employee of American Bridge and president of his United Steelworkers' union local, to replace William Stern. The mayor, a "reform" Democrat, noted that he desired U. S. Steel to have some representation and that Luckey is "very acceptable to the corporation, and comes highly recommended by the manager of the bridge plant." The *Post-Tribune* had mixed feelings about the mayor's action: "The appointment of Joseph Luckey to succeed Stern appears to be a good one so this is not a case where an incapable appointment results from political considerations. However, it would seem to be good sense to keep men on the job when they have shown considerable above average ability in serving the public. For it should be noted that the building era is continuing and there is still need for the kind of ability for which Stern [a contractor] was praised." Three years later Chris Retson, a CPA, replaced Arlie Premo as the third Democrat, and Charles Daugherty, a Republican, attorney, and director of the YMCA, took Emery Badanish's place on the board, without stirring controversy. Then, in 1955, Mrs. Robert Standley, past-president of the Horace

Mann Parent-Teacher Council, a Republican, and graduate of Emerson school, succeeded John W. Davies. Standley, a school activist, was the first woman on the board since Mrs. Uno Hill ended her term in 1949. The next year the Reverend Robert Penn, pastor of the First Baptist Church, assumed the black seat on the board, replacing Bishop Claude Allen. As the decade ended the school board, with some balance and little divergence of opinion, continued to steer the schools among the rocky shoals of budgetary constraints, uncontrolled growth, curriculum concerns, and administrative squabbles.[3]

The board's primary concern was juggling numbers—enrollments, budgets, schools, supplies, teachers, salaries, and the like. New schools were continually on the planning board—indeed three were projected in early 1950—although it appeared that class sizes hovered around the national average, about thirty-one in the grade schools and twenty-five in the upper grades. In some schools, such as Froebel and Roosevelt, classes were considerably larger. The school budget rose to $6,358,915 for 1950–51, which included $1,561,290 from the state general fund. Reducing the school day to seven hours (8:30 A.M. to 3:30 P.M.), starting at the Tolleston school, another blow at the old Wirt system, appeared to save some money. The one-teacher-per-class plan now appeared to be superior to the work-study-play system but could not be implemented in every school because of a lack of classroom space. Even with the addition of a twenty-one room wing to the multiracial Pulaski school (black, white, and Puerto Rican), school principal Robert Greer declared that the "housing problem can only be solved by the use of the platoon system. . . . Most of the non-academic classes will be double-size." School board members generally received community support, although the *Post-Tribune* characteristically put them on notice as the decade opened that they should not conduct business in executive sessions—"decisions on matters of interest to the general public or concerning the use of public funds ought not to be reached in star chamber meetings."[4]

The budget climbed for 1951–52, despite the persistent opposition of the Gary Taxpayers' Association. Building plans also continued apace, although there were serious material shortages and government restrictions on new construction sparked by the Korean War; in November 1951 a Defense Production administrator announced that another fifteen thousand tons of steel would be available for emergency school construction in Gary early the next year. Soon there was a $5 million five-year building program, an attempt to keep up with the mounting birth rate. The City-wide Parents' Council proposed that the money be raised from another increase in the school-building levy, rather than by selling school-building bonds which would be paid by the next generation. " 'We pay half and leave the other half for others to pay,' Emery Badanish, school board treasurer, commented. 'Why not let others who will use the buildings in years to come help pay for them?' " The bonds were issued.[5]

School schedules as well as funds could also be juggled, for various reasons. After five years of complaints and threats from the North Central Association of Colleges and Secondary Schools high-school classes were reduced from seven to six per day in mid-1952, but each class was now to meet for fifty-five (instead of fifty) minutes, thereby conforming to the association's requirement as well as state standards. Outside pressure was always telling, despite the argument in Gary "that the children in this industrial city should be in school for longer periods of time than is the general practice." Implementation, however, would prove difficult because of overcrowding and would be delayed until 1957. At the same time the school year was reduced from forty to thirty-eight weeks, the standard among adjoining school systems. In this case, however, change came from within, for the teachers' union threatened to demand overtime if the forty-week year continued. The *Post-Tribune* applauded the reduction: "One argument used to be that the longer school year kept youngsters off the streets and out of mischief or trouble for that much longer. It isn't a very good argument; education shouldn't be urged as a disciplinary program or custodial plan. Perhaps we should be doing much more in the way of planned recreation in the summer months, or in the provision of play areas. But if there is a problem, we ought to solve it along those lines and not just by keeping youngsters in classrooms for two extra weeks." Feigning concern for the teachers, children, and their parents, the paper was, perhaps, more concerned about fiscal issues.[6]

As pressures mounted from various directions—the teachers and parents, the state, the North Central Association, business interests—another voice emerged, the local Democratic machine, then in control of city government. "Upsetting Gary's traditional separation between politics and education, Mayor Peter Mandich and his city controller [Metro Holovachka] undertook to lecture board members and executives last night on how the city's schools should be operated," the local paper reported in July 1952. Mandich, elected the previous fall, appeared to be repeating the sins of Mayor Barney Clayton fifteen years earlier. "Using school data for 1948–49, Holovachka made various comparisons to support his contention that Gary schools were overspending. He maintained especially that the schools were spending too much for supervision." The mayor and the controller recommended cutting school clerks, supervisors, and physicians, as well as reducing the night program; they also criticized the "high" salaries for teachers and principals and thought the building program too grandiose.[7]

"Your offhand method of running the schools is pretty marvelous," Superintendent Charles Lutz responded. "I couldn't run your job and I question if you could run mine." Hardly designed to appeal to the party's rank-and-file, the city administration's strategy was perhaps designed to win over the business community, which was increasingly concerned about continuing charges of graft and corruption at City Hall. Tensions heightened in August when, upon the recommendation of the Gary Taxpayers' Association, the school board cut the tax rate by five cents. George Chacharis, characterized as "a City Hall spokesman and fuel supplier," but in fact the power behind the mayor and soon-to-be-appointed controller, lashed out at M. W. Madden, president of the Taxpayers' Association, for representing "nobody but the steel company and The Post-Tribune." But he also charged that the superintendent ran the school board and criticized the bloated school budget. In response, Stanley Kohn, of the City-wide Parent Teachers Council, praised the board and its new budget. School politics were once again making strange bedfellows.[8]

When school opened in September 1952, the verbal war proceeded, and school officials grappled with mounting enrollments. Despite two new elementary schools, three classes from Lew Wallace were housed in the Forty-Third Avenue Presbyterian Church, some Roosevelt children found themselves in the basement of the Lutheran Church at Twenty-Fifth and Harrison as well as in the American Legion hut, and the Galilee Baptist Church provided space for opportunity classes from Froebel. A few schools had forty to fifty pupils in a room. The board planned additional construction projects. "Gary's second largest industry and probably its most important is the city's public school system," the Post-Tribune bragged in November during National Education Week, using its common business metaphor. "Its 25 education factories, built at a cost to the taxpayers of nearly $15,000,000 today serve more than 25,000 children." As a sign of this boom, in July 1953 the school board passed a record budget of $8,927,875 (later reduced by $220,000), and raised the tax levy by thirty-five cents.[9]

In September 1953, the overcrowding continued, with students now using rooms in the Stewart House, a settlement house in the heart of the black community, Galilee Baptist Church, Ivanhoe Gardens housing project, and the American Legion hut. Schools in the Miller-Aetna neighborhood, and within the Froebel and Roosevelt districts, still had the worst problems. In July 1954, the board approved of two new elementary schools in Miller-Aetna, but in the meantime considered housing the overflow students in the Chapel of the Dunes Church, Bethel Lutheran Church, and the Duneland housing project, despite parents' objections that these rooms were too cold and damp. The board also attempted to raise the 1955 budget to $9 million, then quickly lowered it by $400,000 upon the pro forma protest of the Gary Taxpayers Association, which continued to flex its muscles. The cut necessitated reductions in adult education, school recreation programs, and summer school. Further complications developed late in the year when the state tax board cut over seven cents from the city tax rate for schools. School board president Charles Daugherty accused school administrators of making a poor presentation to the tax board, yet another example of a growing rift between the school board and the superintendent.

A financial crisis loomed in June 1955, when unexpected tax delinquencies forced the school board to borrow almost $500,000 to meet operating expenses for the next month. This stopgap solution was not designed to correct the more serious issue of a continuing budget shortfall, however, for the city's assessed valuation had not appreciably increased, thereby forcing the board to attempt once again to increase the tax rate, a joyless task. The *Post-Tribune's* H. B. Snyder suggested attracting new businesses to the city, while M. W. Madden of the Taxpayers Association counseled stricter tax collection; neither desired increased taxes. The continuing budgetary squeeze, as well as other problems, made it obvious by the fall that some heads would have to roll, and they would not be the school board's.

Superintendent Charles Lutz had been appointed in 1941, following closely upon the heels of the highly critical Purdue survey; over the years he had received the board's support and an ever-increasing salary. He was unanimously reappointed to another five-year term in April 1952. Late the following year, however, a note of rancor appeared in school board–superintendent relations. Some board members charged that Lutz refused to allow "many persons" to appear before the school board. Perhaps coincidentally, the board now also began serious consideration of an external survey of the schools' buildings and curriculum, despite administration feelings that such a study be conducted by the system's professional staff. The board had a nagging suspicion that the system was old fashioned and the superintendent inadequate to cope with new problems and challenges. Perhaps the twentieth century was passing them by.[10]

Individuals and community groups were asked to contribute their ideas. The City-wide Parents' Council soon responded, recommending "that the proposed survey be conducted by an outside group of professionals well qualified in education and not be a commercial firm; that the survey scrutinize the building program, curriculum, school business procedures, administration procedures and teaching standards." Indeed, "the parents were emphatic in their expression of dissatisfaction with the teaching methods in the schools, and with the 'product' of the schools." They were particularly disturbed about the perceived low academic level of the high schools. In May 1954, the board, with broad support, hired the Public Administration Service (PAS) of Chicago, a private, nonprofit consulting firm, to conduct a survey, at a cost of $31,500. Another study by outside experts, another scientific measure of the schools' successes and failures was on the drawing board.[11]

Led by five core investigators, assisted by team members and advisors, including Earl McGrath, the former United States Commmissioner of Education, the PAS spent a year in Gary collecting data and composing a final report. Released in September 1955, the *Post-Tribune* touted the report as "unquestionably the most important book published this year so far as the people of Gary are concerned. . . . These are matters on which the whole community, not just the school board, must make up its mind. But we shouldn't reach a decision until we have thoroughly assimilated the report." Ignoring such sage advice, the board quickly requested the resignations of

the superintendent and Assistant Superintendent Ralph Muller. Both refused, although Muller later changed his mind. Lutz was appointed a consultant to the board for the remainder of his contract. Edison school principal
Clarence Swingley was named interim superintendent. The board was anxious to implement the report's basic recommendations: "the establishment of
a higher standard of education in Gary, the strengthening of industrial arts,
vocational and technical training, increased emphasis. . . of systematic educational, physical and financial planning." Obviously, the superintendent was
considered a major impediment to achieving these goals.[12]

Compared to its two predecessors, the GEB study and the Purdue survey,
the PAS report was more succinctly written, cogently argued, and, perhaps,
based on a better grasp of the facts and figures. Attractively presented, with
numerous informative tables and maps, the report was designed to convince
through evidence and reason and to avoid the philosophical asides that larded
the Purdue survey. It was divided into six parts—Gary's history, educational
problems, instructional programs, administrative organization, school-building needs, and school finances. In the introduction the authors struck a note
of sobriety, expressing their sensitivity to the students' ethnic, racial, and
economic diversity; indeed, "large sections of the city are highly congested
and provide an exceedingly unfavorable environment in which to rear children." The answer, connecting with the schools' longstanding approach to
educational matters, was that "the school system should in every way possible attempt to compensate for local social and homelife deficiencies by
offering a broad and well-planned program of activities, instruction, and, in
many cases, remedial work." Considering the industrial nature of Gary and
its neighbors—U. S. Steel alone employed over twenty thousand—the report
was quick to emphasize the schools' need for vocational programs, although
the community naturally needed "doctors, teachers, lawyers, engineers, and
many others. Clearly the school program should provide ample opportunities
for preparation for further professional education as well as terminal work for
those who will complete their formal training in the Gary public schools."
And, overall, the program should be "designed to equip all students for good
citizenship and a satisfactory adjustment to social and economic life."[13]

The authors paid the obligatory homage to William Wirt and the work-
study-play system, then argued that although much of the original plan had
been haphazardly abandoned, there had been no systematic attempt to
substitute a new organizational structure. What, specifically, were the consequences of this lack of planning? There appeared to be fewer students
going on to college—perhaps 25 percent of the high-school graduates (compared to 40 percent nationally)—despite the drop-out rate of close to 40
percent, somewhat above the statewide average. This was disturbing. And
what of the remaining students who found local employment? Employers
complained that they were poorly prepared, frequently indifferent to the job,
and lacked self-discipline. High-school students appeared to have normal

mental ability but generally scored low on standardized achievement tests, particularly in American history, English, mechanics, and physics. The high drop-out rate, particularly from "those schools whose students are from the poorer economic group and who may be expected to enter the unskilled labor market," notably Roosevelt and Froebel, could perhaps be mitigated by an increase in vocational programs. "In general, it may be stated that the Gary school system program in vocational education is almost nonexistent, in spite of the fact that the community provides greater opportunity for conduct of such a program than almost any other area in the United States."[14]

Another difficulty exacerbating many of the problems was the persistence of the eight unit-schools (Kindergarten through grade twelve), enrolling over half of the city's students; the remainder were in a variety of schools, some K–3, K–5, K–6, and even K–8. There appeared to be too many high schools, the elementary students in the unit-schools were shortchanged by a lack of competent administrators, and facilities were inadequate for both the younger and older students. The report recommended switching to a uniform elementary–junior high–senior high (6-3-3) plan, then becoming standard throughout the country because of the growing popularity of the junior-high school. There would be a need for only four senior-high schools, as well as a new vocational and technical high school (possibly the converted Froebel school). The platoon plan in the lower grades should also be dropped, which would only entail eliminating the auditorium period and reducing physical education from five to two periods a week; the students would then be spending the bulk of their time in the contained classrooms. There was great need for additional elementary schools, well constructed, to relieve the current and projected overcrowding as well as to provide the requisite facilities for the new organizational structure.

Change was not possible, however, without cohesive leadership and direction. In recent years the school board and superintendent had been at loggerheads, with the superintendent generally not fulfilling his duties and responsibilities. Then, too, the school principals appeared to have too much power, preventing any uniformity of programs—a product, it apeared, of the recommendations in the earlier Purdue survey. "In its purely administrative aspects," the report continued, "the process of decentralization and pseudo democratization has diffused responsibility and watered down the exercise of administrative authority and leadership. Increasingly, administrative action has come to be symbolized by appointing a committee to study something rather than by making a decision." Clearly, greater administrative efficiency and control, including budgetary matters, were necessary, but unlikely because of the superintendent's shortcomings—"Within the school system there is little evidence of vigorous action or leadership. For the public there is only talk of the low cost of public education in Gary."[15]

Overall, the report was highly critical, laying the blame for problems at the feet of the superintendent as well as the school board, other administrators, the teachers, and even the taxpayers. Yet, it closed on an upbeat note: "Bleak though these prospects may appear, there is no reason for unleavened pessimism. Gary is at the hub of an area whose present and potential concentrations of industrial and commercial wealth are enormous. . . . Such qualities as these justify confidence that this community can and will do what is necessary to give its children the kind of educational preparation they need to become useful and productive members of an increasingly complex society."[16]

The PAS report, clearly and forcefully presenting a blueprint for a modern, efficient, productive, "successful" school system, was quickly taken to heart by the school board upon the urging of the *Post-Tribune*. "If the school board accepts the findings and recommendations of the Public Administration Service's survey, it has the duty to proceed promptly with implementing those recommendations," the paper editorialized. "That can only be done, it is clear from the report, by putting new leadership in command of the school administration," which was already a fait accompli. "The whole undertaking will be costly to the taxpayers. But there will be no protest over the cost if we give Gary's youth the right education. The eventual cost to the city will be much greater if we don't." Editor H. B. Snyder, long an exponent of limited school budgets, but now not wanting to seem obstreperous, was changing his tune. Within a few weeks the board discussed converting Froebel to a vocational high school, changing the plans of two proposed new elementary schools to conform to the report's recommendations, and revamping the business department.[17]

Soon all of the city was swept up in educational matters. The study's director, Wendell Schaeffer, discussed the report with the City-wide Parents' Council, and he was consulted by the school board on various matters. The board eagerly welcomed suggestions from parents, teachers, and the entire comunity in a show of democratic zeal. Perhaps inevitably, educational matters became an issue in the fall 1955 mayoral election. Republican candidate Emery Badanish, a former school board member, berated the board for firing Lutz, an obvious political act. "Since that infamous night of Sept. 23, suspicion, mistrust, misgiving, apprehension, and anxiety have covered Gary like a pall," he proclaimed. "For days little groups of people gathered on street corners, in office building corridors, in grocery stores, in restaurants trying to piece together an explanation to find some meaning in what on the surface seems to be a meaningless act. The people of Gary are still searching for the answer." But it was simple; to Badanish this was creeping communism: "We have witnessed how politically controlled schools have become the communistic indoctrination centers in Europe. It was by little infringements, by storming the battlements one at a time, taking over a department here, cutting down an opponent there. That is exactly what has been taking place before our eyes in the last four years." In his desperation, Badanish had hoped to tar Mayor Pete Mandich with the board's nefarious conduct. Not even the strongly Republican *Post-Tribune*, never known to defy the era's anticommunist crusade, could buy this smear, however, for there was "utterly no evidence that politics had anything to do with the PAS survey or the action pursuant to it." Mandich easily won reelection.[18]

Under Acting Superintendent Swingley, the school system continued to grow, with the approval of five new elementary schools by the board in December. Most sensitive to the need for community input, the board, unsure of the type of construction to be used because of the PAS recommendations, requested advice from parent-teacher groups, the Chamber of Commerce, and the Gary League of Women Voters; it was later decided the schools would include neither auditoriums nor gymnasiums. The PAS continued to make recommendations, soon summarized in a fifty-one-page report, particularly concerning the schools' financial affairs. But not all of the PAS suggestions were followed. Responding to parent fears, the board promised in March 1956 that no high schools would be closed or converted to junior highs, at least not for another four or more years.

Most significant, however, was the employment in February of a new superintendent, Alden Blankenship, after an exhaustive search. With a doctorate in education from Teachers College, Columbia University, and prime administrative experience as school superintendent in Oak Ridge, Tennessee (1943–46), and most recently as superintendent in Tacoma, Washington (1950–56), Blankenship was warmly greeted when he finally arrived in late June. The search had involved the school board's Citizens Advisory Committee, originally appointed the previous year, which included a sampling of the city's diverse power elite—the assistant general superintendent of U.S. Steel, newspaper editor H. B. Snyder, executive secretary of the Urban League Clifford Minton, and various union representatives—as well as PAS project-supervisor Ream Lazaro.

Lutz's removal and Blankenship's appointment buoyed optimism in Gary that the schools would now have fresh, dynamic leadership, but all were not so pleased. In early November 1955, the *Post-Tribune* warned that the National Commission for the Defense of Democracy Through Education of the National Education Association (NEA), formed in 1941, was contemplating an investigation of the PAS report and its consequences upon the request of the Indiana City and Town Superintendents Association and the Upper Mississippi Valley Superintendents Association to the American Association of School Administrators. There were a variety of complaints about the PAS survey team: "teachers, the Superintendent, and others in administrative positions had been little consulted"; "the survey group had had no official meetings with the Board as a whole"; "school files, even desks, of officials were examined in the absence of the administrators"; "numerous statements were generalizations not supported by fact, some seemingly deliberately false and others false by implication and innuendo." In essence, the report was biased and unfair, leading to the arbitrary and heavy-handed removal of the superintendent and assistant superintendent. The NEA National Commission appointed a Special Committee of seven educators to investigate these charges, chaired by Virgil Rogers, dean of the College of Education, Syracuse University.[19]

The Special Committee seemingly conducted a thorough investigation, although it was unable to interview the school board, which directed them to meet with the PAS staff, the new superintendent, and others. In its rather lengthy report issued in June 1957, the committee was critical of both the PAS report and the school board. Much of the PAS report appeared fair, but some sections were definitely slanted against the administration. Many statements were vague, others misleading, often giving the impression that Gary's school problems were unique, or had not been seriously considered by the administration; other conclusions were based on sloppy research. Perhaps the report's most egregious error was to call for the superintendent's dismissal, a most unusual conclusion in a school survey. There were also problems with the report's other recommendations. In short, the Special Committee concluded: "(a) The PAS report contains some stinging and professionally obnoxious references that were certainly unnecessary . . . . (b) The PAS report, in contrast with the earlier [Flexner and Purdue] reports, is poorly documented and lacks much of the supporting data that should be present in a professional survey report. (c) The PAS report manifests a philosophy that regards education as merely one of the many functions of government in which efficiency is virtually an end in itself." Moreover, the superintendent and assistant superintendent were treated shabbily, and in the future the school board should act with respect and fairness towards its administrators.[20]

The Defense Commission's findings appear to have had little effect in Gary, although the PAS immediately charged that the report consisted of "misrepresentations, inaccuracies, half-truths and opinions open to question." Professional reputations were certainly at stake. What was most important, however, was for the new superintendent to continue to grapple with the immediate issues of school overcrowding and financial exigencies. Blankenship began with a flurry of activity in July 1956, starting with a reorganization of the finance department, one of the PAS's prime recommendations, and rushing completion of five new schools. Everyone, it seemed, was now anxious to support the new administration. There was, for example, no opposition to the school board's approval of an increased school-building levy, for new schools were vitally needed; during the coming year the board would have to rent fifteen community locations to house the overflow students. Moreover, there was no protest in late August when the board adopted a whopping $13.577 million budget and increased the tax levy. Three months later six more schools were planned, although the superintendent cautioned that they must be efficiently, perhaps uniquely, designed.[21]

Overcrowding continued to be the central problem in 1957. Blankenship calculated in March that almost four thousand were attending part time, fifteen hundred were in rented facilities, and another ten thousand were in overcrowded classrooms. Perhaps one answer, following the PAS's suggestions, was to build separate junior-high schools, and five were planned over the next four years. Again in late August, there was no protest to another budget increase and construction of more elementary schools. But Blankenship complained that additional teachers and administrators were needed, including fifteen more instructors for the handicapped and emotionally disturbed, three speech and hearing therapists, and five vocational-education teachers. As budgetary demands escalated, however, it became obvious that the cooperative climate could not last. In November, the new Gary branch of the Lake County Taxpayers Association, representing business interests, launched its remonstrance with the state tax board against the increased tax rate. Profits once again took precedence over community harmony.

Despite the evident needs, a deepening recession increased tax delinquencies and forced a postponement of the board's building plans in early 1958. The crisis worsened when it became apparent that the opening of eight new schools over the next two years, and the continuing enrollment glut, would necessitate hiring two hundred new teachers for about $680,000. One hope was federal funding for school expansion, but the Commissioner of Education ruled that Gary was ineligible because it was financially solvent. Blankenship announced in May that the board would have to borrow $1.5 million to meet current expenses, a proposal immediately challenged by the Lake County Property Owners and Taxpayers Association. Since there appeared to be a continuing income shortfall into the foreseeable future, the superintendent called for increased state support (currently 19 percent of the schools' income, an unusually low figure), as well as federal aid. To attract the latter, Orval Kincaid, subdistrict director of the steelworkers union, and City-wide PTA president Harold Johnson testified in Washington in October. They were supported by Congressman Ray Madden, a Democrat, and Indiana Senator Homer Capehart, a Republican, but to no avail. Simultaneously, local parents were battling the Chamber of Commerce, backed by the Property Owners and Taxpayers Association, before the State Tax Board over a reduced tax levy. Kincaid "called the efforts to cut the budget a disgrace. 'Intentionally or unintentionally, directly or indirectly, the Communists are being aided and abetted by those people who try to cut the education of our children,' he said. . . . He said the Russians are doing a better job of educating their children than we are." The steelworkers' organizer could sling mud as well as anyone.[22]

As the decade ended the schools' seemingly intractable financial and overcrowding problems persisted. The future appeared bright, however, in March 1959, when a gala celebration greeted the opening of six new elementary schools. Appearing together at the dedication were Lawrence Derthick, the United States Commissioner of Education, I. W. Abel, secretary-treasurer of the United Steelworkers of America, and Thomas W. Hunter, general superintendent of U.S. Steel's Gary Works. Derthick, whose son was assistant principal of the Lew Wallace school, was currently reviewing the school-system's application for $2 million in federal aid. Despite the outward show of unity, by the summer controversy continued over increases in the school budget and proposed tax levy. Once again the higher rate was supported by the City-wide Parent-Teacher Council, the League of Women Voters, and the Central Labor Union, among others. The county board of tax review, prodded by the Lake County Property Owners and Taxpayers Association and the Chamber of Commerce, cut the proposed school budget in October. But this time, upon the school board's appeal, the State Tax Board reinstated the higher tax rate, allowing for an increased budget.

Financial matters were unusually complicated because of the lingering national steel strike. Begun in mid-July, when the union and the steel companies could not agree on a new contract, the steelworkers in Gary (and nationally) were out of work until early November. The average steel worker lost about $2,000. Since many temporarily moved away to find other work, the fall enrollment was below the projected number of forty-one thousand, relieving for now the overcrowding. The low enrollment was also somewhat of a problem, for the amount of state aid was based on the number of students at the end of October.

Throughout the 1950s the strained school budget, continually increasing because of the mounting number of students, administrators, teachers, and programs, was under attack from the business community. Since the depression, business groups and organizations, led by U.S. Steel, had put tax considerations before the public schools' financial needs as articulated by the school board and its allies. This was not unusual. According to a 1958 article, "in many American communities there are local taxpayer associations. These groups are especially concerned about the steadily rising property taxes and often try to bring pressure on local government agencies to reduce their budgets. Nearly one-half of the superintendents indicated that they had been subjected to pressures from these organizations. In addition, one-third of the superintendents reported that individuals influential for economic reasons in their communities had demanded that educational costs be lowered." Nonetheless, these same business leaders basked in high esteem, as the schools worked hard to promote a respect for capitalism and groom the students for their future roles as workers and consumers in the economic system. In turn, the Chamber of Commerce, the main voice of the business community, attempted to influence school matters, particularly the curriculum.[23]

Indeed, the business community faced little opposition, other than in budgetary and related matters, in wielding its influence. Nowhere was this more evident than in the attack on the scourge of democracy and freedom, the feared communist menace. Most segments of the community, committed to capitalism and demonstrating scant regard for the First Amendment, rallied with little hesitation to the anticommunist banner. The cold war had begun as the ashes of World War II were still smoldering, and by 1950 the Red scare was rapidly heating up. "Principals of Gary high schools were alerted today by Supt. Charles D. Lutz to watch out for any attempt to circulate among students a communist-inspired petition calling on the government to ban the use of atomic weapons," the *Post-Tribune* informed its readers in June 1950, about a year after the Soviet Union had detonated its own atom bomb. "Such a petition was circulated Friday in Washington high school, East Chicago, by a group of students suspected of having had communist propaganda training." When classes started in September school authorities went on the offensive, supporting a veterans-sponsored "Sell Democracy" day. High-school supervisor Frank Albright assured Gary's citizens that all teachers had signed a state loyalty oath, and "in department meetings of teachers, there are frequent discussions of democratic attitudes and improved methods of teaching how to put democratic ideals into practice. . . . 'We place the emphasis on home and family living, good citizenship, democratic living and appreciation of American culture and international understanding.'" In addition, teachers and students, starting in the fifth grade, were soon studying the textbook "Survival under Atomic Attack." Safety classes concentrated on civil-defense techniques and first-aid training, and civil-defense drills became routine. Children were tatooed on their side with their blood type to facilitate identification during a nuclear attack or other disaster.[24]

Democracy, revered in theory, was more problematic in practice. When, in July 1952, the local Progressive party, a remnant of the Henry Wallace presidential campaign of 1948 and popularly considered a Red front, attempted to reserve the Froebel school auditorium for a speaker, the school board denied the request. Threats of violence had come from the American Legion and Veterans of Foreign Wars, stiffening the board's natural reluctance. Ever vigilant, school authorities believed they had nothing to hide from anticommunist probers. In January 1953 Superintendent Lutz welcomed the Senate Internal Security subcommittee, then proposing an investigation of "Red influence in the nation's high schools and colleges. . . . 'From the best information I have,' Lutz said, 'there is no cause for suspicion of Communist influence in any of the Gary schools. If there is any, we want to know about it.'" Again in September, he assured the local Kiwanis club that teachers had taken a loyalty oath for the past thirty years; "un-official investigations are made to determine whether prospective teachers have communistic tendencies," he continued, "and if they are found to have some, we do not hire the teachers." The national Red scare necessarily had a chilling effect on Gary's teachers and classrooms, and the threat of attack disturbed the children, but administrators would not admit that there were overt problems. And by mid-decade the fear seemed to be subsiding. In any event, Gary was spared the virulent redbaiting that seriously infected other school systems at the time and society generally.[25]

Facing little ideological opposition, the business community eagerly cooperated with the schools, continuing an alliance that had been nurtured since the system's founding. Rather than call for more vocational instruction, which was offered on the job, business leaders "urged the schools to put more stress on teaching students 'know-how' of concentration and the correct methods of analyzing problems." During the first annual Business-Education (B-E) Day sponsored by the Chamber of Commerce in May 1951 all of the teachers were expected to tour Gary Works, Gary Sheet and Tin Mill, and assorted other businesses in the city and surrounding communities. A week later there was E-B Day, with the businessmen now visiting the schools. The next year, however, the local CIO Industrial Union Council complained to the school board that the program was an "attempt by industrial interests to educate the school teachers of this area in pro-management relations." It requested that "in the event the school teachers are allowed to attend conferences and tours directed by pro-management leaders during taxpayers' time, we of the CIO want a like amount of time to present to the teachers pro-labor viewpoints on various issues." The unionists, having a strong local base, made a telling point. The following year the board planned a program of cooperation between business, industry, the teachers, as well as labor, now renamed B-L-E Day, although still sponsored by the Chamber and with seemingly little variation from the former B-E Day.[26]

In June 1955, the Chamber of Commerce launched its own study of the Gary schools as part of its national effort to profile school problems and needs. Included on the Chamber's five subcommittees were ex-school-board-member William Stern, Clifford Minton of the Urban League, former superintendent Charles Lutz, and other educational notables. Within a month its report was finished. Recognizing the pressing need for new schools, the Chamber called for more state support and the collection of delinquent taxes, but for neither federal aid nor increased local taxes. The report also supported night-school programs for adults, and urged "that the education program during the normal school age be deliberately attuned to the changing nature of society and such necessary abilities as the wise and rewarding use of leisure time, the desire as well as ability for wide reading, and the basic ability of adequate self-expression."[27]

Perhaps more indicative of the Chamber's concern, however, was its request a few months later for increased vocational programs, following the PAS report's conclusions. The Chamber recognized that local businesses would have to cooperate with the schools and that even state and federal funding might be necessary to insure an adequate vocational program. It soon launched a survey of the city's employment needs, mailing questionnaires to about fifteen hundred local business, industrial, and professional employers. Only 138 finally responded, and their views were, perhaps, surprising. The Chamber reported in late August 1956 that "the best interests of Gary will not be served by the transformation of Froebel into a technical-vocational school for the whole community"; indeed, the employers desired improving the teaching of the basics—reading, writing, and arithmetic—although they supported expansion of shops in the schools and were even willing to pay higher taxes for an improved technical-vocational program. But "it was shown in the survey that the fastest growing type of educational requirement was in the field that asked [for] some type of college training." So much for the PAS report. The school board was slow to react, although it seemed to concur that there should be more emphasis on the three Rs.[28]

Support for a vocational-technical high school came not from business, but from organized labor. Returning from the annual convention of the National Vocational Education Association in St. Louis in late 1956, the steelworkers' Orval Kincaid was enthusiastic about that city's new $7 million vocational high school, just what Gary needed. But the steel city, because of the opposition of the business community, was not ready for such an expense. In late 1957, however, the school board did institute a cooperative vocational program in the Emerson, Horace Mann, and Froebel high schools that offered students over sixteen a new schedule: a half day of classes, including two academic subjects and one vocational class, and a half day of work in the community. Emerson would specialize in salesmanship, Horace Mann would concentrate on office work and record keeping, and Froebel would offer certain industrial trades. This was far from a vocational program, but, perhaps, it was a start. A new *Gary Curriculum Guide* adopted the following year contained plans for technical-training shops at all of the high schools, including appliance repair, auto mechanics, and electronics, but they were not introduced. Ten years later an expansive Career Center was finally opened, eventually fulfilling the hopes for a complete vocational program.[29]

Rather than support vocational instruction, the Chamber of Commerce in 1958 repeated its demand for more emphasis on reading, spelling, and simple mathematics in the elementary grades. More important, the Chamber continued to oppose increased school budgets and taxes, while insisting that it believed "that every Gary youth has the right to receive the highest quality education possible and shall continue to strive for the maximum use of the resources of our community to attain this end." When in November 1958 the Chamber once again petitioned the State Tax Board to cut the budget, Rabbi Carl Miller of Temple Israel charged that it was being "penny-wise and intellectually foolish." But the pattern had been set years before, and the business community, in Gary and throughout the country, would not diverge from its chosen path of educational efficiency and frugality.[30]

Gary's business leaders, united in the Chamber of Commerce, attempted to flex their muscles, but they did not always go unchallenged. The parents, through the City-wide Parents' Council, presented a strong opposition regarding school financial matters. Of course, many were themselves in business or the wives of businessmen, but they were somehow able to switch roles, sometimes opposing their spouses, when their children's welfare was at issue. In any case, the organized parents never wavered in their goal to expand the school system as fast as possible, providing adequate, if not the best, facilities, teachers, and educational programs. They were usually a strong ally of the school board and school administration, and they normally cooperated with the Chamber of Commerce.

Hoping to gain some leverage in the appointment of new school board members, the City-wide Parents' Council in early 1950, joined by the Chamber of Commerce, Council of Churches, American Association of University Women, League of Women Voters, and the United Council of Negro Organizations, formed a committee to lobby the mayor. The committee wanted to narrow the mayor's choice to its own list of five names. Oddly, the steelworkers union and the Junior Chamber of Commerce refused to participate. Mayor Eugene Swartz, reluctant to have his hands tied, politely declined the offer. Next, the civic committee suggested that the mayor consider eight qualifications for future board members; tellingly, qualification number seven noted that a candidate "must realize that the school board is a policy-making board, and that the program of the schools shall be directed by the administration staff."[31]

Parents and civic organizations were generally frustrated when attempting to gain political power, but the former appeared to have more luck in discussing, if not quite in influencing, other matters. For a few years, starting in 1950, representatives of the parents met with teachers and administrators in a series of workshops to discuss curricular and other matters, as well as to mix informally. As one report concluded, the workshop experience "improves human relations and promotes personal understanding among teachers, parents and administrators." While ceaselessly working to increase the schools' budget, the City-wide Parents' Council was simultaneously involved in a variety of educational issues—"the school curriculum, parent-teacher relations, individual differences in children, an expanded physical education program, a shorter school year, parents' problems in child training, citizenship development, parent education, . . .federal aid to education, and the value of workshops." Home-school relations were often discussed. The parents even became involved in civil defense. In 1952 they participated in the organization of the city's elementary-school districts into a block-warden system.[32]

By mid-decade, the City-wide Parents' Council had branched out to discuss health service, personal guidance, recreation, and adult education. Discipline and delinquency continued to be controversial issues, and there was an emphasis on the spiritual training of the children in the home as well as increased teacher-parent cooperation. One heated topic was whether or not the City-wide Parents' Council should affiliate with the National Congress of Parents and Teachers (PTA), although many individual parent-teacher associations were members. In January 1958, the Council voted not to join, then changed its name to the Gary Citywide Parent-Teacher Council as a demonstration of unity with the teachers. Later in the year, with renewed vigor, the Council organized a letter-writing campaign to Arthur Flemming, secretary of Health, Education, and Welfare: "Parents are asked to tell Flemming, in their own words, the Gary story of 11,000 poorly housed children in substandard schools. This means that one of every four children is attending classes in makeshift rental quarters, wooden portables, overcrowded classrooms, and converted basement rooms, the PTA Council said." The parents and teachers hoped to snag $2 million in federal funds. As the decade ended, and despite the aggravated shortage of funds, the Council optimistically planned a $15 million school-building program.[33]

Often having similar goals, parents and teachers managed to cooperate throughout the 1950s, but the latter continued to feel the necessity of also working through the union. A strong voice for teacher interests since its revival in the late 1930s, the Gary Teachers Union (AFT) worked diligently to protect its members' interests, particularly economic ones. Membership kept pace with the increasing number of teachers, climbing from about four hundred in 1950, to 550 in 1955, to over eight hundred by 1960, a clear majority of the teaching staff. Throughout the 1950s unions nationally continued to hold their membership, while succumbing to anticommunism and accommodation with business, symbolized by the AFL-CIO merger in 1955, and the AFT was no different. The Gary local, situated in a strongly prounion city, was perhaps one of the more successful. Flora Philley's election as president in early 1950 prompted Irvin Kuenzli, AFT Secretary-Treasurer, to write that "Local 4 has worked toward and made great progress in attaining the highest professional standards not only in relation to working conditions for teachers but also in promoting many phases of educational welfare of children and youth." Philley responded that her election "was a case of handing the 'willing horse' one more dirty job," but she worked diligently to invigorate the membership.[34]

As its first priority, the union continued to demand higher salaries, a common refrain throughout the decade. In May 1950, shortly afer the salary scale was frozen for another year, the union protested to the school board "the undemocratic way in which it settled the salary question." It next asked to see the school budget and requested overtime pay for teachers attending conferences or meetings after school as well as compensation for the two-week Christmas holiday. The union gained little satisfaction. Some teachers were paid for a five-day retreat in September with administrators, however, where they discussed training "children in the democratic way of life." To get into the spirit, the camp would be "strictly a first name affair," instructed the superintendent, "with old clothes and [a] camping atmosphere the order of the day."[35]

Discussions of democracy for children and teachers were uplifting, but they did not put food on the table. In January 1951, the union asked for more than the recently announced $150 pay increase. Three months later, facing a recalcitrant school board, the union lowered its demand for an increase, which the board still did not meet. The board's new $250 pay hike was unacceptable, and if upheld the union would demand a shorter school year and Christmas pay. After classes started in September the teachers were still grumbling. The next spring they repeated their request for more money or a school year reduced by two weeks. Pleading for cooperation, board member John Davies told a teachers' meeting that "we all want good teachers and good teacher relations. . . but we must consider children and parents as well as teachers. Remember, the school board does not run the schools, it sees that they are run." The teachers turned a deaf ear. In June they were finally victorious, receiving both a raise and a shorter school year.[36]

The union next requested four additional paid holidays, which according to the superintendent would shrink the school year to less than the 180-day legal minimum set by the North Central States Association of Colleges and Secondary Schools. The board agreed to two more paid holidays, despite the opposition of Superintendent Lutz: "Parents want their children in school. The point I am making is this—it is worth something for children to be with teachers or isn't it?" Salaries inched up for the next two years, but always fell short of the union's demands; and there were additional grievances concerning sabbatical leaves and extending the retirement age from sixty-six to seventy. Finally, in April 1955, the union voted to strike unless a satisfactory settlement was reached with the board. "A strike by the teachers is not a strike against the school board," argued the conservative *Post-Tribune*. "It is a strike against the school children." The teachers' action was averted, however, when a compromise was reached with the board.[37]

Soon after arriving in early 1956, and confronted by a nagging teacher shortage, Superintendent Blankenship fought for increased salaries. The system had to remain competitive. Yet there were also budgetary considerations. When the superintendent cautioned that there would be no raise for 1958–59, the union demanded another two-week reduction in the school year. Teacher morale was very low, warned Ann Maloney, the union's executive secretary, and the turnover high, which Blankenship denied. About this same time an article in the local paper boasted that the "teachers' individual initiative is encouraged. Opportunities are plentiful for professional staff members to contribute ideas thru [sic] professional association, individual building staffs, curriculum study groups and advisory council to [the] superintendent." The teachers were not so optimistic. When the school board voted another raise in April 1959, the union again protested its inadequacy. As a sop to the teachers, who had been complaining about the proliferation of administrators, the board agreed that the latter would get no raise for the coming year. As the decade closed the union–school board adversarial relationship had been firmly set. The teachers were by no means

radical, only concerned about protecting their interests, financial and otherwise. Most, surely, were dedicated to the profession, yet believed they could
not do their job without more money and autonomy.[38]

The teachers were not alone in struggling to protect their interests while
remaining part of the city's educational family. The black community had its
own grievances and concerns centered around the fight for improved schooling within an integrated system. They were frustrated on both counts. In
1951, 85 percent of the schools were segregated, and 83 percent of the 8,406
black children were attending all-black schools. Ten years later 90 percent of
the schools were highly segregated, and 97 percent of the 23,055 black pupils
were in eighteen predominantly or exclusively black schools with primarily
black teachers and administrators. By mid-decade 90 percent of the black
teachers, composing 26 percent of the teaching force, were in all-black
schools. One persistent problem was overcrowding, particularly in the Roosevelt school district. In early 1950, many children attended only half days or
were housed in rented facilities. Two kindergarten classes met in the basement of community church, where "the plasterboard ceiling leaks, the windows are all painted so that no natural light comes in, the insulation is so
poor that the children are exposed to constant drafts. The cement floor is so
damp and cold that the PTA bought carpeting for the children to sit on. There
is but one toilet stool available." As new elementary schools opened, the
situation eased somewhat.[39]

The school board had adopted an integration policy in 1946, followed by a
statewide plan three years later, and had made some moves to implement it,
but without much success. Child Welfare Director Mark Roser, strongly pro-
civil rights, believed segregation was effectively over. Of course, he argued in
1950, "all children must attend the school in their district unless such
attendance will cause the child undue hardship," in which case his office
could issue a transfer. Above all, "boundary changes to avoid segregation
calls *[sic]* for definite and unyielding school leadership with the courage to
apply consistent vision of democratic goals. . . . School leadership must
implement distant democratic goals with energy, conviction, and realism to
make these steps in the process real in the immediate situation." Roser was
idealistic. Based on the concept of the neighborhood school, the policy did
not address the issue of geographical segregation, then increasing.[40]

Moreover, the theory was often breached in practice—at least this was
assumed within the black community. In late 1949 the leadership of the local
National Association for the Advancement of Colored People (NAACP),
currently being revived, suspected that plans for adding to the all-black
Pulaski school were motivated by the desire to siphon black students from
the still volatile Emerson school. "Our Gary Inter-cultural policy and the
new state non-segregation in schools law will be simple scraps of paper if
'flattering priorities' for providing needed, but late facilities in present
NEGRO SCHOOLS are continued in order to keep negroes from being

integrated into the schools of the city," local president Edna Morris informed the national office. Many in the black community would continue to be wary.[41]

By mid-decade, however, a gloss of optimism covered school interracial matters. In May 1954, the day after the Supreme Court's *Brown* decision declaring school segregation unconstitutional, the *Post-Tribune* bragged that the decision followed desegregation in Gary by more than seven years. "The program of eliminating gradually segregation in the city's schools has now been completed," according to Superintendent Lutz. Mark Roser was equally jubilant, arguing that intercultural education was no longer necessary because "in 1954, cultural differences among children are taken as a matter of course, and those differences are absorbed in the teaching process aimed to provide proper educational development of each child's unique personality." While not perfect "the Gary Schools have successfully established a basic policy of Human relations on which future achievement can be built." Even a National Urban League (NUL) study the following year, despite finding pervasive student and teacher segregation as well as a hint of racial gerrymandering of school boundaries, congratulated the board of education and school administrators "for their efforts in eliminating discriminatory practices in the school system."[42]

Clifford Minton, local NUL executive secretary, was not so sanguine. Having started with the Urban League in Little Rock, Arkansas, in 1940, Minton had most recently headed the organization in Cleveland, then arrived in Gary in 1949 to replace Joseph Chapman. The local NUL board of directors, headed by *Post-Tribune* editor H. B. Snyder, was cautious and had to be continually cajoled into action by the executive secretary. Minton's was a subtle yet strong voice for civil rights. To Warren Banner, NUL director of Research and Community Projects, who authored the Gary study, he critically suggested that "the gradual changes which have taken place from year to year came almost inspite of rather than because of interest and leadership on the part of top school administrators. In most cases positive changes have been effected in proportion to the extent they were warranted by expediency." Minton feared that Superintendent Lutz, a particularly wary administrator, would use Banner's praise to justify further inaction. The NUL executive secretary welcomed, even took some credit for, Lutz's removal in late 1955: "We remained in the background, but to put it mildly, our interest and influence on this development was significant," he bragged to NUL Executive Director Lester B. Granger.[43]

Minton served on the search committee for a new superintendent and influenced the hiring of Alden Blankenship. "When we boiled it down and we interviewed all these people—when it boiled down to Dr. Blankenship—I interviewed him so that I was asked to check up on his background to see how compatible it would be to a racial situation in Gary," he later recalled. "I knew more about Dr. Blankenship than anybody else on that committee," he continued, because of his Urban League connections, particularly in Springfield, Massachusetts, where Blankenship had previously been superintendent. For the remainder of the decade, aside from specific problems that surfaced from time to time, Minton focused on six main issues: the segregation of school districts and the placement of new schools, the integration of teaching staffs, equal access for blacks to all school facilities, the hiring of additional black employees in the school system, the expansion of vocational programs, and the employment opportunities of high-school graduates. Overall, while Minton believed he had a good relationship with Blankenship and the school board (he was a member of its advisory committee) little was accomplished in furthering school integration because of the practice of clustering the new elementary schools near the older segregated schools; few new schools would draw both black and white students. "Now we could have made and there was from time to time something said that was in the paper but we just simply didn't have the horses—we could have made a stronger protest but that's just about what it really added up to," he concluded years later.[44]

Lesser issues could be confronted, however, and produce occasional victories. The "black" seat on the school board remained secure with the appointment in July 1956 of the Reverend Robert Penn, pastor of the First Baptist Church, who replaced Bishop J. Claude Allen. Perhaps more significantly, the next month Walter E. Wiley, principal of Carver school for the past five years, was named elementary supervisor. The first black supervisor, Wiley symbolized progress after years of struggle and frustration. He soon moved on to become director of research for the school system.

Some racial friction existed in two schools with white faculties on the west side where the black population was expanding. According to some of the black parents, Minton informed Blankenship in March 1957, "evidence of subtle and overt teacher-pupil resentment to the increase of Negro enrollment in the school population has not and is not being met with positive leadership and planning conducive to the development of good human relations[,] attitudes and citizenship." Some months later, after more correspondence, the superintendent assured the NUL leader "we are making progress in the schools even though we do not have all of the answers. In our school curriculum, we are emphasizing the likenesses of people of different races and creeds and the fact that it is the individual rather than his race, color or creed which is important." Racial barriers were being attacked, but "we still have some schools with an all-white or an all-negro population. Changes will come slowly in certain areas of the community," he optimistically concluded.[45]

Reporting to the national office soon after receiving Blankenship's reply, Minton weighed the credits and debits of the situation. Blacks served on the school board and in administrative jobs, he noted, there was no overt segregation of school facilities, white parents and black parents as well as teachers cooperated, and there was growing community sensitivity. On the negative side, however, he stressed "the potent influence of the 'residential ghetto' on the integration process and the exceedingly limited approaches toward modifying this pattern of both public and voluntary organizations and agencies." New schools were constructed in segregated neighborhoods, and black teachers were still assigned to predominantly black schools. Still, concerned about the city's image, he concluded "that we are heartened by the progress made on the integration process in the Gary School System during recent years and [that] is still being made."[46]

If segregation proved intractable, perhaps the black students' vocational choices could be improved, another of Minton's goals. One strategy was to increase participation in the schools' Cooperative Vocational Education Program which placed students in clerical and sales training programs in various stores, such as F. W. Woolworth. In early 1959, Minton informed his board of directors that despite the apparent willingness of leading employers to begin hiring blacks, *"we have no knowledge of any Negro students now or ever being enrolled in the Distributive (Sales) and Business Education (Secretarial-Clerical) Sections of the Cooperative Vocational Education Program."* There was continued widespread discrimination by the downtown merchants, but change was coming. Since few black students graduated from high school—only 256 from Roosevelt in 1959—it appeared reasonable to focus on job training, although in this case the emphasis seemed to be on jobs for girls.[47]

Another continuing source of friction was teacher segregation and school hiring practices. In 1959, the League discovered that in an advertisement of current teaching vacancies certain positions were secretly designated as being for whites while others were for blacks. In an interview the director of personnel "admitted that this was the first occasion on which 'apparent racial designations' were used to describe the location of specific vacancies," and promised it was an aberration. Perhaps so. But teacher segregation continued. "There is little if any evidence to show that systematic efforts are being made to encourage or to implement a policy of teacher integration in the majority of our public schools," one report concluded late in the year. "Contacts with school principals indicate that the vast majority of them have a traditional segregated orientation and that little if any guidance or suggestions have been given them on this matter." As the new decade opened the Midtown Citizens' Committee, representing the black leadership, publicly questioned why "some 5 or 6 of the 36 schools have token faculty integration—in most cases these schools have only one or two teachers of the 'other race.'" The administration continued to promise progress.[48]

Racial friction in the Emerson school, the historic hot spot in the system, and prolonged segregation finally goaded the black community to launch a frontal assault. In 1962, in *Bell v. School City of Gary,* the NAACP charged: that the school board and superintendent had a "constitutional duty to provide and maintain a racially integrated school system"; that segregation was deliberate; and black schools had "unequal facilities in all respects, including, but not limited to over-crowded and larger classes, and unequal recreational facilities." The suit, one of the first in the North, which the NAACP lost, capped a decades-long struggle to achieve equal schooling in Gary. The plaintiffs could not prove that school segregation was designed by the school board, rather than a product of neighborhood segregation; moreover, in building ten new schools in the Central District the school board had apparently shown good faith in trying to cope with the population explosion. The judge's decision was upheld by the Seventh Circuit Court of Appeals. School segregation was a perplexing problem, one that would be exacerbated as the student population became progressively more black over the next three decades.[49]

Black students were mostly restricted to separate schools, but otherwise shared with the rest of the student population a changing educational structure and curriculum throughout the 1950s, particularly after mid-decade. The final blow to the work-study-play system came in late 1956. As his first major order of business, Superintendent Blankenship called for full use of the contained classroom in the elementary grades in order to improve the students' basic skills. "The big advantage is to have a smaller number of pupils, not over 30, in a class so that special help can be given children who need it," he informed the teachers in early September. "This can not happen when the classes are too large and the teacher has a different group of pupils every hour." The newer elementary schools were designed for contained classes; the unique Marquette school in Miller, for example, was composed of nine separate buildings, with ten classes for the lower grades and twelve rooms for grades four through six. Some parents protested the changes, arguing that "the Wirt system was 'tailored more to the individual,' while the present system is 'tailored more for the mass.'" They were fighting a losing battle, however. When school opened in September 1958 all but six elementary schools had the new arrangement.[50]

The secondary program was also in a state of flux. Starting in 1958 high-school graduates needed eighteen academic units, two above the state requirement. A new curriculum guide was also issued, and put greater emphasis on science and math courses. Pressure had come from the National Science Foundation and the federal government since 1950 to increase these areas; the Soviet launching of Sputnik, the first artificial satellite, on October 4, 1957, only heightened the fear of American inferiority. "A year before the Russian Sputniks hurtled skywar," the *Post-Tribune* reported, "School Supt. Alden H. Blankenship realized that Gary schools should afford better opportunities for students in the fields of science and mathematics," but not to the detriment of other programs. Facilities were inadequate, however, and science teachers scarce. The science curriculum was rather traditional, and course enrollment was limited to the more academically inclined, while the majority of students huddled in the classes and courses for the average and below average. There appeared to be a growing number of electives, ranging from arts and crafts, commercial art, machine calculation, and general music to senior math, world problems, and advanced science. French, Spanish, and German were available, starting in the seventh grade, but not Russian, which was vetoed by state authorities. There were now 136 high-school courses, something for almost everyone.[51]

The schools had never concentrated strictly on academic matters, however, and they were not about to start neglecting the plethora of programs and activities that had been accumulating over the years. Students' interests and problems of whatever shape or size would be addressed. "Advocates of a more narrow and intellectual type of curriculum have reacted sharply to Sputnik and the Soviet challenge by demanding more specialized attention to science, mathematics, and purely academic studies," R. Freeman Butts of Teachers College wrote in 1958. "But the necessity for a broadened curriculum to embrace the values of organized knowledge, of scholarship, of social welfare, and of personal competence has increasingly been accepted by the educational profession and by the public generally." For those with a military bent the ROTC program operated at four of the high schools. The medical department started the decade with two physicians, ten nurses, two special teachers, two dentists, two dental hygienists, two dental clerks, and one secretary. It would grow over the next two years, supplying the elementary students with a broad range of medical and dental services.[52]

Keeping the children busy and out of trouble continued to be a high priority, as it had been since the city's early years. Those in grade school, members of the ten-thousand-strong All-Out Americans (AOAs), initially organized during the war, began the decade with a citywide cleanup campaign. The schools were heavily involved, with the English classes writing papers on "Let's Make Gary a Clean City," the social studies classes discussing the importance of a clean city, and the science classes studying community health. Older students were more difficult to control. Students at Wirt high school, in the Miller neighborhood, admitted that they were often bored, which caused the boys to visit the pool hall and the girls to gather "for a hen party" or stay home. To school authorities drinking and reckless driving seemed increasingly prevalent student pastimes. The school board emphasized that the responsibility lay with the home, church, and civil authorities, as well as the school. Adding a more somber note, Police Chief Millard Matovina "declared that the same kind of report on the status of young people could have been written 30 years back. Young people now are no better or no worse, he holds."[53]

Child Welfare Director Mark Roser complained that "the present situation places too heavy a burden on schools to prevent the spread of a wayward life." There were too few school counselors, not to mention the shortage of juvenile officers, probation workers, and welfare department caseworkers, he argued, and the lawless nature of many of the city's adults encouraged similar behavior among the young. The particularly brutal murder of a high-school teacher, Mary Cheever, the previous year had inflamed many in the community, particularly the female teachers, who continued to agitate against corrupt politicians and organized crime throughout the decade. The *Post-Tribune* had an even broader view of the problem: "From coast to coast the kids are running wild. It's high sport for youngsters to beat up innocent people, to shoot and even kill each other in well-generaled gang wars, to fill city streets with terror and violence." The answer: "Youngsters need companionship and organized, disciplined group activity in healthful surroundings. Delinquency can spring up when any of the elements basic to normal growth are missing." Parents had to exercise more supervision, particularly monitoring their children's leisure hours. "Movies and radio, welcomed by parents as outlets for youthful enthusiasm, unfortunately tend to warp those impulses into unhealthy channels. Most experts agree that movie-radio emphasis on crime is doing grave damage to impressionable minds." Teachers seemingly took on added responsibilities in late 1952. According to the schools' TV-Radio Committee, they were supposed to start advising the students on their selection of radio and television programs through use of a weekly bulletin.[54]

Delinquency, with its many causes—poverty, indulgent parents, urban crime, lack of recreational facilities, the evil influences of the mass media, few support services, dropping out of school, and gangs—continued as a disturbing problem. In late 1953, Roser feared the rate was rising because of "the breakdown of law enforcement," compounded by "the bad example of citizenship set by the community." Three years later he was more upbeat, reporting that many Gary teachers found the majority of youth were now "more appreciative of democratic controls" and "easier to discipline." The delinquency scare was, perhaps, ebbing as the decade ended, but would never die out. There was always a new fear. For example, in 1959 the school board banned secret clubs in the high schools, believing them to be undemocratic and a threat to student morale.[55]

School authorities, Mark Roser in particular, realized that the schools' power was limited and that there were many other influences on children in the city, for good and evil, but this did not prevent them from continually trying to extend their reach. They could not admit defeat. Delinquency, broadly conceived, was one challenge, handicapped children were another. In 1950, the welfare director calculated that 7 percent of the students had physical disabilities, others were mentally retarded, a large number were slow learners, and "every classroom, on the average, has one child who is emotionally ill, four who are severely handicapped emotionally, eight so disturbed that they should have special care." There were twenty-four special teachers. The child-welfare director would soon be calling for a new Family Service Agency to deal with family problems, including poverty, violence, and single parenthood. He was particularly worried about malnutrition—afflicting an estimated 5 percent of the students in 1959—and other medical problems that led to truancy, learning problems, and misbehavior.[56]

There was particular need for increased facilities for "retarded" students, despite a claim by the state director of special education that Gary had more students in special-education programs than any other Indiana community. Slow learners were attending classes at the Stewart Settlement House, the North Gleason Park pavillion, and the Tolleston Library, as well as in various elementary schools. Even brain-damaged children, previously in a school run by the Parents' Council for the Retarded Child, now came within the school board's jurisdiction. State funding for special classes, in addition to the standard appropriation based on daily attendance, was welcomed, but fell short of what was necessary. Roser estimated that perhaps 10 percent of the students were so "slow" they could not finish the fifth grade.

A considerably larger group of students had more mundane, but nonetheless troubling, problems. "Child welfare officials take a personal interest in children whose personal difficulties are reflected in their behavior," the *Post-Tribune* reassured its readers just before Christmas 1952. "Conferences are held with teachers, principals and parents and of course with the children involved to help them solve their own problems. When necessary the cases are referred to the school psychological personnel to be taken to the Mental Hygiene clinic. The welfare workers last month dealt with 526 children who were behavior problems." Mark Roser had expanded the counseling program a decade earlier and carefully nurtured it. Now, with the growing popularity of psychotherapy and increased fear of adolescent maladjustment, personal counseling took on added importance. "Trained counselors in each of the high schools help teen-agers to understand themselves and the adjustments they must make to meet complex social and economic situations in school and in later life," the paper reported a few months later. "By the time the child enters the seventh grade, he may need help with the more serious problems of entering adolescence." There was both individual counseling and group guidance in the homerooms and general classrooms. "Today they spare the rod and help the child to become a happy adult in the Gary schools."[57]

While discussion was emphasized, corporal punishment was still possible. There had to be an adult witness, however, and the parents needed previous notification. Generally, the parents approved, but Melvin Wise, president of the Roosevelt High School parents' council, was most critical: "Formerly. . .students who violated the rules had to wash windows or floors or something like that. Now we use counseling only. If a good talking to failed, then I would say use major punishment for the grade school pupils. I don't think its proper for the high schools." Wise's belief in counseling was strongly supported by Superintendent Blankenship, who recommended in

1957 that the dental program be cut but that two additional psychologists be hired.[58]

The schools' social-service program, including counseling, was not new, but continued to grow during the 1950s along with the rest of the system. By the end of the decade Gary's educational establishment retained a familiar cast, yet had been changing in numerous ways. There was an attempt to create greater uniformity throughout the system with rigorous administrative plans and controls, and the schools more nearly resembled their counterparts throughout the country. School board member Alice Standley, herself a product of the Wirt system, remarked in 1959 "that several years ago, 'it was like visiting a different country' to go from one Gary third grade class into another such class. The vast differences no longer exist."[59]

Much credit went to Superintendent Blankenship, whose contract was renewed for another four years, a move applauded by the Citywide Parent-Teacher Council. He had enriched the curriculum, expanded the vocational program, increased the number of counselors, built thirteen new schools, and added to the special-services program. "Much progress has been achieved both in reorienting the system to meet the needs of the times and in expanding it to care for the mounting school population," the daily paper editorialized. "Blankenship has demonstrated his ability in detailed planning on the one hand and in providing a high type of educational leadership on the other hand." Parents, teachers, community leaders, and the school board concurred. And yet difficulties remained: "The problems of overcrowded schools, overworked teachers and not enough money to provide satisfactory room for each child still plague Gary school leaders, as they do school people in most sections of the country."[60]

The Gary schools had managed to shake off much of their legacy, more and more resembling urban school systems throughout the country in structure and content. "A few cities, notably Detroit, have retained the 'platoon system' by which children go from room to room during the day," Martin Mayer reported in 1961, "receiving instruction in their native language and history-geography in their 'home room,' and moving through the school to work in arithmetic, science, the Beautiful Arts and perhaps, these days, a foreign language." Detroit clung to the past, but the steel city retained only a few platoon schools because they were still too overcrowded to convert to the regular plan. Otherwise, school officials were struggling, with much difficulty, to establish what would become the standard elementary–junior high–senior high (6-3-3) model. There was as yet no uniformity, however, because of demographic, historical, and other factors. There were many standard elementary buildings for grades K–6, including the sixteen new schools opened from 1956 to 1960, but there were other schools with grades 6–12, 5–12, 7–12, 3–9, and even one K–12 holdout (Emerson). There did not yet exist a single junior high.[61]

As the buildings and organization changed so did the personnel. Everett Spaulding, hired by Wirt in 1910 as a teacher in the Emerson school and serving as its principal since 1917, finally retired in 1952, a year after music supervisor Melvin Snyder, who had begun in 1907, started collecting his pension. Spaulding was followed two years later by school auditor A. Howard Bell, who had opened a drugstore in Gary in 1906, then was employed by the superintendent five years later to manage financial affairs. Physical-education director Jack Gilroy had also joined the system in 1911 and finally bowed out in 1956. The same year Bernice Engels, initially the arithmetic supervisor and later elementary supervisor, a relative newcomer who had arrived in 1923, joined Gilroy in retirement. And there were numerous others.

They had devoted many years to working in and defending the Wirt system, only to see it gradually dismantled after his death. Did they lament its passing? Did they struggle to salvage any of its features? There is little evidence that there was much of a fight. Guy Wulfing, who had followed Wirt from Bluffton and was industrial-arts supervisor and physical-plant director for many years, retired in 1945 and was interviewed when he returned to the city in 1953. He uttered something of a lament: "He thinks that where 'progressive education' or the 'Wirt system' failed was due to having teachers spread themselves too thin, and assigning teachers for various activities for which they were not specifically trained." Wirt's dream was certainly ambitious. Two decades after his death the educational system still tried to accomplish much, but in a more conventional form and setting.[62]

During the 1950s the schools experienced a confusing mix of overcrowding and expansion, conflict and optimism, the influence of politics and expertise, racial difficulties, and various scares. Pressure for reform came from a variety of interests and individuals, including the business community, parents, teachers, civil rights organizations, politicians, and other interested parties. The 1955 PAS survey, and the reaction to it, demonstrated that school officials and the community were still dependent on the advice of outside experts as a spur to change. But this was only one among numerous influences on school affairs, as the system continued to serve as a symbol of competing fears and aspirations for today's students and tomorrow's citizens. The plethora of programs, new and old, were another testimony to the schools' traditional wide reach into the lives of the young. The legacy of the depression years was also much in evidence, as the teachers' union continued to flex its muscles and the corporate community balked at increased school taxes, while easily maintaining a high profile among administrators, teachers, and students alike.

There was a strong emphasis on children and the family throughout the decade, particularly in the middle-class suburbs, but also in the central cities. Schools were important, providing various programs and services, but they had to act in concert with the parents. This was continually stressed in Gary. Earlier in the century Superintendent Wirt had greatly expanded the schools' hours and activities because he assumed—a popular belief among reformers at the time—that poor and immigrant parents were unable to provide a healthy environment for their children. Such views were now outdated, although there was still much suspicion of poor families, as well as a sincere concern for children's well-being. Thus the continuing need for health, counseling, social, and other services. This thrust was reinforced by the growing belief in individual treatment, a concept dating back thirty years. Perhaps, even more would have been attempted in the 1950s if resources had been more plentiful and overcrowding had not caused so many difficulties.[63]

The Gary schools had survived over fifty years of growth and development, storm and strife, years of fortune and years of famine. Once in the forefront of educational change, they entered the 1960s huddled in the middle of the institutional pack along with most city school systems. Were the students better off in a more conventional setting compared to their parents and grandparents who had experienced the famous platoon plan in the elementary grades? Surely the work-study-play system was richer and more stimulating, but it was also, perhaps, hectic and confusing to those who struggled to sit still in overflowing auditoriums, were jostled by bigger kids in the hallways, and put in exceedingly long days.

Schools accomplish various functions, perhaps conflicting, including keeping kids under supervision for long periods of time, teaching basic skills, encouraging students to learn and think, instilling patriotism, promoting conformity, providing social and recreational activities, offering medical care, a healthy diet, and other amenities, preparing workers, as well as reinforcing the economic status quo. The Gary schools continually sought to do these and other things throughout their history. The changing structures and curriculum; the continual struggle among groups and individuals to influence the schools; the ongoing economic problems; the role of outside forces; the waxing and waning of racial strife—all attested to the importance of schooling in Gary (and throughout American society). Children were important, but they were only one factor in the educational equation. And whether they liked or disliked school, whether they graduated or dropped out early, whether they learned much or little, whether they obtained job skills or not was, perhaps, of lesser importance. Above all the schools were a fact of life in Gary and elsewhere, a prime feature of the urban landscape. They served as a magnet for the community's manifold hopes and frustrations. They were never the sole creature of the school board or the superintendent, not even one as powerful as Wirt.

"Education is an integral element of the society and culture of which it is a part," R. Freeman Butts wrote in 1958. "Educational institutions are influenced by the other institutions, ideas, and beliefs of a society, and education in turn helps to shape the social and intellectual character of a people. American education is no exception. It reflects the way of life of the American people, their customs and traditions, their aspirations and beliefs, and

their common values and differences." This was certaily true in Gary during
the first half of the twentieth century. But the schools also reflected somewhat conflicting goals and interests in the city and throughout society.
Schools were most important, and, perhaps for that reason, consensus never
existed.[64]

AFTERWORD

Gary's public schools have changed greatly since 1960, yet remain much the same. Similar shaping forces and influences have been in evidence: parents, teachers, community groups, business leaders, civil rights organizations, state educational and political authorities, federal bureaucrats, and educational professionals. All subsequent superintendents have been involuntarily replaced by the school board, following in the footsteps of Superintendents Jones and Lutz. Racial factors have continued to loom large, but for somewhat different reasons, as the complexion of the students, teachers, administrators, school board, and staff has become progressively darker. One noticeable change for some years was the presence of numerous federal grants, and other examples of federal intervention, which sparked a plethora of new programs. This money has declined during the 1980s. The schools continued to offer a broad array of services to the students, however, carrying on a tradition that had its roots in the early decades of the century. As for the students, they still occupy their seats, cheer on their sports teams, hassle the teachers, and most even manage to graduate from high school (about 75 percent), despite the daily presence of armed police in the larger schools. There has been growth and decline. But are the schools overall better or worse than they were thirty, fifty, or seventy years ago? I would not venture a guess.

The schools experienced a steady growth in population during the 1960s, reaching a peak of about forty-eight thousand students by the decade's end. Then the enrollment began steadily to drop. By the fall of 1988 there were slightly over twenty-seven thousand children attending classes in forty-four school buildings, with about equal numbers in the elementary and secondary grades. This drop-off mirrored national trends in urban school districts. As the population swelled, then shrank, it was readily becoming obvious that there were more and more minority children. In 1969, over three-fifths of the students were Afro-American (thirty thousand), another 4,397 were Spanish-surnamed, and the remainder were Caucasian (slightly over thirteen thousand). Ten years later there were over twenty-eight thousand black students, about eighteen hundred Spanish-surnamed, and the remainder, or about twenty-three hundred, were white. In 1988, over twenty-five thousand black children occupied their school desks, another nine hundred or so were Spanish-surnamed, and the rest, perhaps five hundred, were white or Asian. That is, over 98 percent of the students are currently nonwhite.

While the enrollment has declined, the number of school personnel has managed to remain fairly constant, following similar national trends. There were 1,687 teachers in 1979, and there remain about one hundred less today. The number of adminstrators has actually increased by twenty or so, while there are still a large number of paraprofessionals and other nonteaching staff. The budget, naturally, has soared, jumping from $61 million in 1979 to over $100 million ten years later. Despite overall cutbacks during the 1980s, federal funding still managed to increase slightly, climbing from about $6 million in 1979 to $7.6 million by the end of the decade. As a percentage of overall expenditures, however, the federal share has shrunk considerably.

The schools have not changed much in function or purpose, although a number of innovations, simmering on the back burner for some decades, were finally adopted. In 1962, at the time of yet another study, this one conducted by the Bureau of Educational Research and Service from Ohio State University and entitled *A Plan for Housing Gary's Public Education Program,* there were three junior high/middle schools planned. The report, like its predecessors, encouraged the school board to adopt a 6-3-3 structure. Following the completion of the West Side High School in 1968, the only new regular high school built since World War II, three older schools became junior high/middle schools (Froebel, Tolleston, and Edison). By 1988 there remained six middle schools and five high schools, in addition to the twenty-nine elementary schools. Moreover, also completed in 1968 was the Technical-Vocational Career Center, a large building offering half-day trade training for high-school students. This was another innovation long advocated by professional educators, and one increasingly popular throughout the country.

As the Gary schools fully entered the mainstream, the administration eagerly sought federal grants in order to expand the programs. By 1966 the money was flowing, to the tune of $2.4 million during the year, from various programs: Title I for disadvantaged students, Title II for books and other learning aids, Head Start for preschool children, Title III of the National Defense Education Act for improvement in science and foreign languages, as well as smaller initiatives. With an increasing enrollment of poor black children and a shaky local tax base because of white flight, combined with the growing problems of U.S. Steel, the schools experienced a mounting reliance on outside funding. Superintendent Gordon McAndrew (1968–79) was particularly zealous in expanding programs through obtaining additional funds, for example from the Model Cities program. He also signed a contract with a private company, Behavioral Research Laboratories (BRL), which took over the Banneker elementary school in the early 1970s. Employing paraprofessionals and using teaching machines, with a guarantee of increasing student skills, BRL quickly garnered the hostility of the teachers union as well as many others. When it became obvious that the students were not performing better, the contract was cancelled, although individualized instruction appeared to be popular and the school continued to be experimental.

The teachers union, AFT Local No. 4, has consistently been a strong influence on school matters, particularly regarding teachers' welfare. Charles Smith became the union's president in 1962, and the following year a one day strike, the local's first, marked a new stage in teacher militancy. Subsequent strikes under Smith and his successor Sandra Irons (1970–   ) over salary matters and a variety of other issues during contract negotiations have established the union as an important player in school politics. The parents have also been most important, in the PTA and various ad-hoc organizations over the years. During a particularly trying time in 1971–72, when school funds were depleted and it appeared the school year would be very short, the Coalition to Save Our Schools was organized. Including a broad cross section of parents and community leaders, the Coalition worked closely with school administrators to put pressure on the state legislature to increase its funding, which occurred, and the schools were saved.

The parents, white, Hispanic, and black, also became very involved in school affairs in the 1960s when integration became a burning issue. There were various hot spots. The Horace Mann school, for one, long the elite high school, experienced racial strife late in the decade. Busing black children to Glen Park's previously all-white schools, particularly Lew Wallace and Bailly Middle School, in the mid-1960s resulted in considerable contention, fueled by the election of Richard Gordon Hatcher in 1967, the city's first black mayor. And as the number of black students increased in the early 1970s, tensions reached the breaking point. Within a few years, however, white flight had emptied the schools of most white children, thereby eliminating overt racial problems. Simultaneously, there was an increasing number of black teachers and administrators. A struggle over bilingual education, moreover, marked the increasing presence of Spanish-speaking students.

By the mid-1980s, the Gary schools closely resembled their counterparts in every other northern city: overwhelmingly black, plagued with academic problems, occasionally violent, having an essentially automatic promotion policy, and marked by sporadic academic, athletic, and social successes. The back-to-basics scare, combined with the state's vigorous emphasis on accountability and more academic work, has recently forced the schools into greater testing and increased graduation requirements. While the drop-out rate remains surprisingly low, about 25 percent, it is unclear what these new constraints will mean, since many of the students have academic difficulties. The curriculum has continued to change, blown by the winds of educational fashion and the interests of the textbook publishers. While there has been a strong commitment to helping the slower students in various ways, with mixed success, a magnet elementary school for the gifted and talented has attracted those anxious for an accelerated academic program. And the opening of a secondary school for performing arts in the Emerson building has garnered much attention. A new superintendent, Betty Mason (1988–   ), and a recently expanded seven-member appointed school board continue to cope with the ever-present problems of limited budgets, troubled students, disgruntled teachers, and aging buildings. As society's racial and economic problems continue, the schools will be hard pressed to improve their success rate, except for a select minority. Perhaps a return to the old work-study-play plan would make the elementary schools at least more interesting, if not actually increasing the students' academic, cultural, and social skills. Perhaps.

A NOTE ON SOURCES

Any study of the Gary schools during their first five decades must begin with the William A. Wirt Manuscripts in the Lilly Library at Indiana University, Bloomington. Luckily, Wirt appears to have kept almost everything that crossed his desk, including correspondence, reports, and publications. The Wirt Manuscripts are particularly rich in material covering the period 1907–30. The William A. Wirt and Mildred H. Wirt Papers at the Calumet Regional Archives (CRA), Indiana University Northwest, Gary, richly supplement the Wirt Manuscripts, particularly for the last decade of his life, and include Mildred's school materials. Also housed at the CRA are numerous smaller collections and scattered documents, photographs, and publications, including the Guy Wulfing Papers, the Stanley Kohn Papers, and the Clifford Minton Papers. All of my files, notes, transcripts of interviews, correspondence, and other research materials have been deposited at the CRA.

Unfortunately, there are very limited official records of the Gary public school system, other than those contained in the Wirt Manuscripts and Papers. The manuscripts of school board minutes, housed at the School Service Center, Gary, are very brief and without much importance. Except for an early report by Wirt—"The School Town of Gary," *First Annual Report of the Board of Trustees of the Town of Gary, Ind. . . .for the Year Ending Dec. 31st, 1908* (Gary, 1909)—neither the superintendent nor the school board ever issued an annual report. School board activities, and so much else pertaining to educational matters, must be pieced together from the files of the daily newspapers, located on microfilm at the Information Center, Gary Public Library: *Northern Indianian* (1906–09), *Gary Daily Tribune* (1908–21), *Gary Evening Post* (1909–21), *Gary Evening Post and Daily Tribune* (1921–22), *Gary Post-Tribune* (1922–60). Also on microfilm are the files of the black weekly newspapers: *Gary Sun* (1923–29) and the *Gary Colored American/Gary American* (1927–46, 1948–51, 1956–60). The newspapers have been of immeasurable value in my study.

Information on the rise of the teachers' union was obtained from the Gary Teachers' Union, AFT Local No.4, files located at the union's office in Gary, and the American Federation of Teachers Papers, Archives of Labor History and Urban Affairs, Wayne State University, Detroit. For details on issues of segregation and civil rights I consulted the NAACP Papers, Library of Congress; the National Urban League Papers, Library of Congress; and the Gary Urban League Papers, University of Illinois-Chicago Library, Chicago. Also helpful were the Abraham Flexner Papers, Library of Congress, and the

General Education Board Papers, Rockefeller Archives Center, North Tarry-town, New York.

Various publications by Wirt and others were most helpful: Wirt, "Industrial Work in Public Schools," *The Platoon School,* 6 (December 1932):13–16 (reprinted from *The Twenty-third Biennial Report of the State Superintendent of Public Instruction [Indiana] for the School Years Ending July 31, 1905 and July 31, 1906* [Indianapolis, 1906], which contains excellent photographs missing in the reprint); Wirt, "Gary Schools," in Frank Heighway, *Educational Report of Lake County Schools* (Crown Point, Ind., 1913), 14–20, 60–61; Wirt, *The Great Lockout in America's Citizenship Plants,* part 1 (Gary, 1937); William P. Burris, *The Public School System of Gary, Ind.,* United States Bureau of Education, Bulletin, 1914, no. 18 (Washington, D.C., 1914); Roscoe D. Case, *The Platoon School in America* (Stanford, Calif., 1931); John and Evelyn Dewey, *Schools of To-Morrow* (New York, 1915); Randolph Bourne, *The Gary Schools* (Boston, 1916, new edition Cambridge, Mass., 1970); Abraham Flexner and Frank Bachman, *The Gary Schools: A General Account* (New York, 1918), and the other seven volumes of the GEB study; Flora Philley, *Teacher Help Yourself* (Gary, 1948); F. B. Knight et al., *Final Report: Purdue Survey Committee for the Gary Board of Education to the President and Board of Trustees of Purdue University* (n.p., [1942]); James H. Tipton, *Community in Crisis: The Elimination of Segregation from a Public School System* (New York, 1953); National Urban League, "A Study of the Social and Economic Conditions of the Negro Population of Gary, Indiana," mimeo, December 1944 (ms in CRA); William C. Reavis et al., *Survey Report: School Buildings and Sites, Gary, Indiana* (Chicago, 1947); Wendell Schaeffer et al., *The Public School System of Gary, Indiana* ([Chicago], 1955); National Commission for the Defense of Democracy through Education of the National Education Association of the United States, *Gary, Indiana: A Study of Some Aspects and Outcomes of a General School Survey* (New York, June 1957); Warren Banner, *A Study of the Social and Economic Conditions in Three Minority Groups* (New York, 1955). In addition, there are many valuable articles in *The Platoon School.*

Hundreds of articles were published dealing with the platoon plan in Gary and elsewhere into the 1930s. Thereafter, the Gary schools only seemed to attract outside notice during a crisis or peculiar event. Copies of some of these articles and publications can be found in the Wirt Papers and Wirt Manuscripts. For a listing of many of these various publications see: James A. McMillen, *The Gary System: A Bibliography* (University of Rochester Library, Rochester, N.Y., January 31, 1917); [Mabel Tinkham], *Bibliography: Publications Concerning the Gary Public Schools* ([Gary], October 1, 1917); Velma Ruth Shaffer, *The Gary System: A Bibliography, 1916–1935* (mimeo, School of Library Service, Columbia University, N.Y., 1935). More recently, in 1984 David Lerner produced an updated "Bibliography of the Platoon School Plan," a copy of which is in the CRA. Consult also "A Note on

Sources" in Ronald D. Cohen and Raymond A. Mohl, *The Paradox of Progessive Education: The Gary Plan and Urban Schooling* (Port Washington, N.Y., 1979), 184–188. There are two invaluable histories of Gary that were most helpful: James B. Lane, *"City of the Century": A History of Gary, Indiana* (Bloomington, Ind., 1978), and Raymond A. Mohl and Neil Betten, *Steel City: Urban and Ethnic Patterns in Gary, Indiana, 1906–1950* (New York, 1986). Complete documentation for both primary and secondary sources may be found in the notes.

NOTES

Preface

1. Lawrence A. Cremin, *The Transformation of the School: Progressivism in American Education, 1876–1957* (New York, 1961, paperback ed. 1964), viii, 155; Ellwood P. Cubberley, *Public Education in the United States: A Study and Interpretation of American Educational History* (revised and enlarged ed., Boston, 1934), 530. Cremin has recently somewhat modified his view of progressive education, but not by much; see *American Education*, vol. 3: *The Metropolitan Experience, 1876–1980* (New York, 1988).

2. Callahan, *Education and the Cult of Efficiency: A Study of the Social Forces That Have Shaped the Administration of the Public Schools* (Chicago, 1962), vii, 131; Kliebard, *The Struggle for the American Curriculum, 1893–1958* (Boston and London, 1986), 98.

3. For an earlier statement of my historiographical views see Ronald D. Cohen and Raymond A. Mohl, *The Paradox of Progressive Education: The Gary Plan and Urban Schooling* (Port Washington, N.Y., 1979), chap. 8.

1. Establishing the System

1. *Gary Daily Tribune*, June 1, 1909.

2. William A. Wirt manuscript speech, 1926, 3–4, William A. Wirt and Mildred H. Wirt Papers, Calumet Regional Archives, Indiana University Northwest, Gary, Indiana (hereafter cited as Wirt Pps.).

3. Ibid., 8–9. On Weaver see Merle Curti, "A Great Teacher's Teacher," *Social Education*, 13 (October 1949):263–266, 274, who was particularly liked by Wirt's classmate the historian Charles A. Beard. For William Morris and his influence in the U.S. see Eileen Boris, *Art and Labor: Ruskin, Morris, and the Craftsman Ideal in America* (Philadelphia, 1986).

4. Wirt manuscript speech, 1926, 17, Wirt Pps.

5. William A. Wirt, "Industrial Work in Public Schools," *The Platoon School*, 6 (December 1932):12 (originally published in *The Twenty-third Biennial Report of the State Superintendent of Public Instruction (Indiana) for the School Years Ending July 31, 1905 and July 31, 1906* [Indianapolis, 1906])—only the original has the illustrations, which are most interesting; Wirt, "A School Year of Twelve Months," *Education*, 27 (1906–07):619–622.

6. Wirt, "Industrial Work in Public Schools," 14–15; Lawrence Cremin, *The Transformation of the School: Progressivism in American Education, 1876–1957* (New York, 1964), 135–142.

7. *Gary Post-Tribune*, May 13, 1922; "Minutes of Meetings of the School Board of the Town of Gary, Lake County, Indiana," I, 9, 17, manuscript in Service Center, School City of Gary, Gary, Indiana; *Northern Indianian*, September 21, 1906; W. R. Curtis to C. O. Holmes, September 25, 1906, William A. Wirt Manuscripts, Lilly Library, Indiana University, Bloomington, Indiana (hereafter cited as Wirt Mss.). On the city's founding see James B. Lane, *"City of the Century": A History of Gary, Indiana* (Bloomington, Ind., 1978), 27–48, and Raymond A. Mohl and Neil Betten, *Steel City: Urban and Ethnic Patterns in Gary, Indiana, 1906–1950* (New York, 1986), 10–25.

8. Holmes to Wirt, November 5, 1906, Wirt to Holmes, November 7, 1906, Wirt Mss.; Bluffton *Evening News*, November 8, 1906.

9. David Tyack and Elisabeth Hansot, *Managers of Virtue: Public School Leadership in America, 1820–1980* (New York, 1982), 116–120 and chap. 11.

10. Wirt to Board of Education, December 15, 1906, Holmes to Wirt, December 20, 1906, Holmes to Wirt, January 21, 1907, Wirt Mss.

11. Guy Study, "The Work of William B. Ittner FAIA," *Architectural Record*, 57 (February 1925):99, and 97–124; Marie Anderson Ittner, "William B. Ittner: His Service to American School Architecture," *American School Board Journal*, 102 (January 1941):30–31, 101. On the Saint Louis schools, which influenced Wirt in many ways, see Selwyn K. Troen, *The Public and the Schools: Shaping the St. Louis System, 1838–1920* (Columbia, Mo., 1975).

12. Holmes to Wirt, March 29, 1907, Wirt Mss.

13. On the European trip see Wirt to Holmes, May 13, 1907, Wirt Pps. *Northern Indianian*, September 13, 1907; *Gary Post-Tribune*, November 24, 1953; Melvin Snyder, "Music in the Early Years of the Gary Schools," 5, unpub. ms. in files of the *Post-Tribune*, Gary, Ind. On German schooling see James C. Albisetti, *Secondary School Reform in Imperial Germany* (Princeton, N.J., 1983).

14. *Gary Post-Tribune*, June 3, 1956, B7; Gertrude Ogg Fife, "Gary's First High School," unpub. ms., copy in author's possession; Snyder, "Music in the Early Years of the Gary Schools," 3.

15. *Northern Indianian*, January 24, 1908, April 17, 1908, May 29, 1908, July 3, 1908, July 10, 1908. For the Chicago schools see David Hogan, *Class and Reform: School and Society in Chicago, 1880–1930* (Philadelphia, 1985), particularly chap. 4 on vocational schooling.

16. *Gary Daily Tribune*, September 10, 1908, December 14, 1908, December 15, 1908, December 18, 1908; *Northern Indianian*, December 18, 1908; Ronald D. Cohen and Raymond A. Mohl, *The Paradox of Progressive Education: The Gary Plan and Urban Schooling* (Port Washington, N.Y., 1979), chap. 5. For other examples see Michael W. Homel, *Down from Equality: Black Chicagoans and the Public Schools, 1920–41* (Urbana, Ill., 1984); Judy Jolley Mohraz, *The Separate Problem: Case Studies of Black Education in the North, 1900–1930* (Westport, Conn., 1979); Vincent P. Franklin, *The Education of Black Philadelphia: The Social and Educational History of a Minority Community, 1900–1950* (Philadelphia, 1979).

17. President [Holmes] to Mr. Muzzall, December 14, 1906, Wirt Mss.; Clifton J. Phillips, *Indiana in Transition: The Emergence of an Industrial Commonwealth, 1880–1920* (Indianapolis, 1968), 389; and see David Tyack and Michael Berkowitz, "The Man Nobody Liked: Toward a Social History of the Truant Officer, 1840–1940," *American Quarterly*, 29 (Spring 1977):34.

18. [Wirt] to Muzzall, January 2, 1909, Wirt Mss.; *Gary Daily Tribune*, September 30, 1908, October 15, 1908, November 18, 1908, November 19, 1908.

19. *Gary Daily Tribune*, February 8, 1909, February 22, 1909, February 24, 1909.

20. Ibid., March 11, 1909, October 13, 1909, October 21, 1909; Ray to Wirt, January 19, 1910, Wirt Mss.

21. *Gary Daily Tribune*, July 1, 1910; Ray to Wirt, June 27, 1910, Wirt Mss. On the connection between poverty and truancy in Chicago see Hogan, *Class and Reform*, 110–113.

22. For different interpretations of the purposes of kindergartens see Michael S. Shapiro, *Child's Garden: The Kindergarten Movement from Froebel to Dewey* (University Park, Pa., 1983); Marvin Lazerson, *Origins of the Urban School: Public Education in Massachusetts, 1870–1915* (Cambridge, Mass., 1971), 72–73; Hogan, *Class and Reform*, 79–82.

23. *Gary Daily Tribune*, September 10, 1908, October 8, 1909, January 13, 1910, January 14, 1910; Wirt to Principals, January 6, 1914, Wirt Mss.

24. *Gary Daily Tribune,* December 9, 1908; *Gary Evening Post,* November 8, 1909. For the national context see Clarence A. Perry, *Wider Use of the School Plant* (New York, 1910), chap. 2; William J. Reese, *Power and the Promise of School Reform: Grass Roots Movements during the Progressive Era* (London and New York, 1986); Lazerson, *Origins of the Urban School,* 206–223.

25. *Gary Daily Tribune,* January 14, 1910; *Gary Evening Post,* January 24, 1910, September 15, 1910.

26. *Gary Daily Tribune,* June 12, 1909, July 24, 1909, July 27, 1909, August 13, 1909, November 11, 1909; Wirt to Playground Association of America, June 21, 1909, Wirt Mss.

27. Joseph Lee, *Constructive and Preventive Philanthropy* (New York, 1910), 138–139; Dominick Cavallo, *Muscles and Morals: Organized Playgrounds and Urban Reform, 1880–1920* (Philadelphia, 1981); Hogan, *Class and Reform,* 69–71; and for a more critical appraisal Cary Goodman, *Choosing Sides: Playground and Street Life on the Lower East Side* (New York, 1979); David Nasaw, *Children of the City; At Work and at Play* (New York, 1985).

28. *Gary Daily Tribune,* November 24, 1909, April 2, 1910.

29. Wirt, "The School Town of Gary," *First Annual Report of the Board of Trustees of the Town of Gary, Ind. . . . for the Year Ending Dec. 31st, 1908* (Gary, 1909), 51–52, 56–57, 68.

30. *Gary Daily Tribune,* April 5, 1909, May 29, 1909, June 7, 1909.

31. *Gary Daily Tribune,* September 13, 1909, September 28, 1909; "Minutes of the Meetings of the School Board," II, 71, 78, 261–262.

32. Sargent to Wirt, June 23, 1908, Wirt Mss.

33. Klingensmith to Wirt, July 17, 1909, Netherton to Wirt, March 16, 1909, Wirt to Netherton, April 22, 1910, Wirt to Wahl, April 22, 1910, Elizabeth Kan (?) to Lucie (Huston ?), August 18, 1908, Wirt Mss.

34. Wirt to Charles L. Sawyer, March 4, 1909, Wirt to Robert Steed, June 28, 1909, Wirt Mss.; *Gary Evening Post,* January 19, 1910, June 3, 1910; *Gary Daily Tribune,* May 4, 1910, May 10, 1910, May 11, 1910, July 13, 1910.

35. *Gary Daily Tribune,* December 20, 1909.

36. *Gary Daily Tribune,* April 27, 1910, June 23, 1910; Wirt to Bruce, December 9, 1910, Wirt Mss.

37. *Gary Evening Post,* February 24, 1910; John Dewey, *The School and Society* (paperback, Chicago, 1956 [original rev. ed. 1915]), 132–133.

38. Wirt, manuscript speech, 1926, 18, Wirt Pps; Dewey, *School and Society,* 29; Hogan, *Class and Reform,* chap. 4; Harvey Kantor, "Vocationalism in American Education: The Economic and Political Context," Harvey Kantor and David B. Tyack, eds., *Work, Youth and Schooling: Historical Perspectives on Vocationalism in American Education* (Stanford, Calif., 1982), 26–36; Harvey Kantor, *Learning to Earn: School, Work, and Reform in California, 1880–1930* (Madison, Wis., 1988). See also Arthur G. Wirth, *Education in the Technological Society: The Vocational-Liberal Studies Controversy in the Early Twentieth Century* (Scranton, Pa. 1972).

39. *Gary Daily Tribune,* May 26, 1910, December 30, 1911, January 12, 1912; David I. Macleod, *Building Character in the American Boy: The Boy Scouts, YMCA, and Their Forerunners, 1870–1920* (Madison, Wis., 1983), 81 and passim.

40. Buffington to Wirt, February 1, 1910, Wirt to Buffington, February 3, 1910, Wirt Pps.; *Gary Daily Tribune,* February 19, 1910.

41. Wirt to Buffington, February 3, 1910, Wirt Pps.; Cohen and Mohl, *Paradox of Progressive Education,* 20–22.

42. *Gary Evening Post,* October 4, 1909; *Gary Daily Tribune,* October 13, 1909.

43. *Gary Daily Tribune,* June 23, 1910.

44. On school board consolidation see David B. Tyack, *The One Best System: A History of American Urban Education* (Cambridge, Mass., 1974), 126–167.

45. Helen Langan to Wirt, September 8, 1910, Wirt Mss. For a comparison of schools in another mill town see Margaret Byington, *Homestead: The Households of a Mill Town* (Pittsburgh, 1974 [orig. ed. 1910]), 119–122.

2. In the Schools

1. Ray to Wirt, October 2, 1911, Wirt Mss.
2. *Gary Daily Tribune,* August 22, 1910, September 1, 1910, September 6, 1910.
3. *Gary Daily Tribune,* April 6, 1910, September 3, 1910, September 23, 1910; Robert H. Bremner, ed., *Children & Youth in America: A Documentary History* (Cambridge, Mass., 1971), II, 813; "What American Cities Are Doing for the Health of School Children," Russell Sage Foundation, Dept. of Child Hygiene, Pamphlet no. 101 (New York, 1911), 3–13.
4. "Minute Book, Health Board, City of Gary, Dec. 19, 1909–Jan. 25, 1911," 12–15, ms, Calumet Regional Archives; *Gary Daily Tribune,* February 9, 1911, March 14, 1911, December 6, 1911. On the history of school dentistry see Steven L. Schlossman, JoAnne Brown, Michael Sedlak, *The Public School in American Dentistry* (pamphlet, Santa Monica, Calif., April 1986).
5. *Gary Daily Tribune,* September 3, 1910, March 22, 1911, May 26, 1911, June 27, 1911.
6. *Gary Daily Tribune,* October 6, 1910, July 13, 1911, September 12, 1911.
7. *Gary Daily Tribune,* September 21, 1910, September 27, 1910, October 19, 1910.
8. On Brown see Ronald D. Cohen and Raymond A. Mohl, *The Paradox of Progressive Education: The Gary Plan and Urban Schooling* (Port Washington, New York, 1979), chap. 3. On the recent literature on progressive child saving see Ronald D. Cohen, "Child-Saving and Progressivism, 1885–1914," in Joseph M. Hawes and N. Ray Hiner, eds., *American Childhood: A Research Guide and Historical Handbook* (Westport, Conn., 1985), 273–309; LeRoy Ashby, *Saving the Waifs: Reformers and Dependent Children, 1890–1917* (Philadelphia, 1984).
9. *Gary Evening Post,* February 17, 1912.
10. *Gary Daily Tribune,* February 12, 1912, February 26, 1912, April 17, 1912, April 30, 1912.
11. *Gary Daily Tribune,* July 2, 1912, April 16, 1913, January 13, 1914; Wirt to Amos Butler, December 18, 1912, Ray to Wirt, June 28, 1912, Wirt Mss. See also David Nasaw, *Children of the City: At Work and at Play* (New York, 1985).
12. "Civic Development at Gary," *The Iron Age,* March 24, 1910, 673; *Gary Daily Tribune,* December 3, 1910.
13. Rheta Childe Dorr, *A Woman of Fifty* (New York, 1924), 204; Wirt to Dorr, May 5, 1911, Wirt to Dorr, May 10, 1911, Wirt Mss.; Dorr, "Keeping the Children in School," *Hampton's Magazine,* 27 (July 1911):57–59, 64; *Gary Daily Tribune,* June 19, 1911.
14. Wirt to Theiss, January 17, 1912, Wirt Mss.; Theiss, "A School Built on Play: How They Solved the Public School Problem in Gary, Indiana," *Pictorial Review,* June 1912 (reprint), 2, 8. See also John Franklin Bobbitt, "The Elimination of Waste in Education," *The Elementary School Teacher,* 12 (February 1912):259–271. See also Wirt, "Scientific Management of School Plants," *American School Board Journal,* 42 (February 1911); Wirt, "Newer Ideals in Education: The Complete Use of the School Plant," Public Education Association of Philadelphia, *Study, No. 37* (Philadelphia, 1912).
15. *Gary Daily Tribune,* November 22, 1911; William P. Burris, *The Public School System of Gary, Ind.,* United States Bureau of Education, Bulletin, 1914, no. 18 (Washington, D.C., 1914), 36–37; Burris to Wirt, February 3, 1914, Wirt Mss.
16. *Gary Daily Tribune,* January 4, 1912, April 4, 1912, November 12, 1913, December 10, 1913; Emerson School, "Notes to Visitors" (pamphlet, 1911), 10.

17. Roscoe D. Case, *The Platoon School in America* (Stanford, Calif., 1931), 23; *Gary Daily Tribune,* February 12, 1912.

18. Wirt, "The Place of the Public School in a Community Program for Child Welfare," *The Child,* 1 (July 1912):11, 15; Wirt, "Gary Schools," in Frank Heighway, *Educational Report: Lake County Schools* (Crown Point, Ind., 1913), 15; Hendrick, "Children of the Steel Kings," *McClure's Magazine,* 41 (September 1913):63; Wirt to Hendrick, May 9, 1913, Wirt Mss.

19. Wirt to Albert Jay Nock, October 20, 1913, Wirt to L. B. Hays, November 7, 1913, Wirt Mss.; Nock, "An Adventure in Education," *American Magazine,* 77 (April 1914):27–28; *Gary Evening Post,* July 20, 1912.

20. *Gary Daily Tribune,* June 7, 1911, July 19, 1911, August 19, 1911, August 23, 1911, September 15, 1911, September 16, 1911.

21. E. J. Buffington to Wirt, February 7, 1912, Septmber 3, 1912, December 31, 1913, Wirt Mss.; *Gary Daily Tribune,* November 17, 1911, March 6, 1912, March 23, 1912, July 13, 1912, July 17, 1912, August 10, 1912, August 14, 1912, September 18, 1912. U.S. Steel had donated the YMCA building, costing $260,000, the Gary Hospital, as well as other buildings to the community. It was generous, but not overly so.

22. Edward J. Ward, *The Social Center* (New York, 1913), 336; *Gary Evening Post,* September 15, 1910. See also Clarence A. Perry, *Wider Use of the School Plant* (New York, 1910); William J. Reese, *Power and the Promise of School Reform: Grass Roots Movements during the Progressive Era* (London and Boston, 1986).

23. *Gary Daily Tribune,* November 30, 1910, December 16, 1910, January 23, 1911, September 18, 1911; "Report of Emerson Night School, 1911–12," Wirt Mss.; Raymond A. Mohl and Neil Betten, *Steel City: Urban and Ethnic Patterns in Gary, Indiana, 1906–1950* (New York, 1986), chaps. 5–7.

24. *Gary Daily Tribune,* December 30, 1911, January 12, 1912, July 17, 1912, August 31, 1912.

25. *Gary Daily Tribune,* September 18, 1912, February 1, 1913, February 14, 1913, December 26, 1913; *Gary Evening Post,* October 3, 1913.

26. *Gary Daily Tribune,* January 18, 1912, February 18, 1914, March 11, 1914.

27. *Gary Daily Tribune,* January 4, 1911, June 21, 1911, February 17, 1913; *Gary Evening Post,* May 28, 1913.

28. *Gary Daily Tribune,* August 5, 1913, August 26, 1913.

29. *Gary Evening Post,* December 2, 1914, December 3, 1914; *The Gary Evening Schools* ("Prepared by the Editorial Staff of the Eagle Magazine," Gary, n.d.), 1.

30. G. W. Swartz, "Gary Public Evening Schools—School Year 1914–191[5]," 7, Wirt Mss.

31. *Gary Tribune,* October 26, 1914, April 2, 1915; Swartz, "Gary Public Evening Schools—School Year 1914–191[5]," 2, 11, Wirt Mss. See also Public Evening Schools, "Catalog: Courses of Study, 1914–1915," (pamphlet, Gary, 1914).

32. *Gary Daily Tribune,* October 1, 1910, November 19, 1910, February 6, 1911, October 17, 1911, May 22, 1912. On the difference between class and race in public schooling see Ira Katznelson and Margaret Weir, *Schooling for All: Class, Race, and the Decline of the Democratic Ideal* (New York, 1985).

33. *Gary Daily Tribune,* October 26, 1912, July 18, 1913, September 19, 1914, December 10, 1914; Burris, *Public School System of Gary,* 40; Swartz, "Gary Public Evening Schools—School Year 1914–191[5]," 2, 6, Wirt Mss. On early immigrant attitudes towards blacks and the argument that segregation was fostered by the city's elite see Mohl and Betten, *Steel City,* 51–55.

34. G. E. Wulfing, "Can the Administration Department of a School System Serve as a Laboratory for the Vocational Training of Children?," *American School Board Journal,* (August 1912, reprint):2; Wulfing, "Plan and Purpose in the Gary Vocational Schools," Wisconsin Teachers' Association, *Proceedings,* 61 (1913):121; *Gary Daily Tribune,* March 22, 1912, October 2, 1912.

35. Wirt to Charles A. Greathouse, June 7, 1913; Wulfing to Wirt, November 5, 1912, Wirt Mss.; *Gary Daily Tribune,* May 29, 1913, May 31, 1913. On vocational education for girls see John Rury, "Vocationalism for Home and Work: Women's Education in the United States, 1880–1930," *History of Education Quarterly,* 24 (Spring 1984):21–44.

36. G. W. Swartz, "What Gary, Indiana, Is Doing Industrially," Northwestern Wisconsin Teachers' Association, *Proceedings of the 1914 Convention* (1914), 62; Wirt to Frank F. Heighway, January 16, 1914; Wulfing to Wirt, January 30, 1914, Wirt Mss. On vocational education see also Harvey Kantor, *Learning to Earn: School, Work, and Reform in California, 1880–1930* (Madison, Wis., 1988); Herbert M. Kliebard, *The Struggle for the American Curriculum, 1893–1958* (Boston and London, 1986), 128–152.

37. *Gary Daily Tribune,* August 11, 1913.

38. *Gary Evening Post,* May 9, 1913; *Gary Daily Tribune,* January 22, 1914.

39. *Gary Daily Tribune,* November 20, 1912, May 26, 1913.

40. Wirt to Nock, October 22, 1913, Wirt Mss.; *Gary Daily Tribune,* November 13, 1913, November 19, 1913.

41. *Gary Daily Tribune,* March 20, 1914, April 15, 1914, April 17, 1914; Wirt to Brickley, February 27, 1914, Wirt Mss.

42. *Gary Daily Tribune,* September 11, 1914, September 15, 1914, September 22, 1914.

43. "Complaints Made to School System Committee," ca. 1913, Wirt Mss.

44. Englehart to W. A. Cain, August 29, 1912; Wirt to Englehart, September 7, 1912, Wirt Mss.; *Gary Daily Tribune,* June 19, 1912, June 20, 1912, July 3, 1912, May 14, 1913, February 12, 1914, February 13, 1914, February 14, 1914.

45. *Gary Daily Tribune,* June 7, 1913.

46. *Gary Daily Tribune,* February 19, 1914, April 30, 1914, May 28, 1914, June 11, 1914, October 1, 1914.

47. *Gary Daily Tribune,* August 14, 1913, October 14, 1913, October 28, 1913; Wirt to J. M. Avann, January 14, 1914, Wirt Mss.

48. Wirt to E. A. Hotchkiss, January 9, 1914; Wirt to T. W. Metcalfe, May 4, 1914, Wirt Mss.; *Gary Daily Tribune,* July 10, 1914, December 1, 1914; Cohen and Mohl, *Paradox of Progressive Education,* 36–40.

49. Wulfing to Wirt, January 30, 1914, February 9, 1914; Klingensmith to Wirt, February 10, 1914, February 11, 1914, Wirt Mss.

50. Wirt to J. L. Harmon, May 14, 1914; Klingensmith to Wirt, May 27, 1914, October 28, 1914, October 29, 1914, November 9, 1914, Wirt Mss.

51. Swartz to Wirt, November 21, 1914; Brickley to Swartz, January 9, 1915; Klingensmith to Wirt, January 11, 1915, Wirt Mss.

52. *Gary Daily Tribune,* August 12, 1914, January 15, 1915, January 28, 1915; *Gary Evening Post,* September 2, 1914; Ray to Wirt, December 29, 1914, Wirt Mss.

53. Wirt to W. B. Ittner, November 7, 1914, Wirt Mss.; *Gary Daily Tribune,* January 27, 1915, February 4, 1915.

3. Time of Troubles

1. Annie Klingensmith, "Monthly Report for November and December [1916]," Wirt Mss. For housing conditions in this neighborhood see Elizabeth Hughes and Lydia Roberts, *Children of Preschool Age in Gary, Ind.,* U.S. Dept. of Labor, Children's Bureau, Bureau Publication no. 122 (Washington, D.C., 1922), 7–29; Raymond A. Mohl and Neil Betten, *Steel City: Urban and Ethnic Patterns in Gary, Indiana, 1906–1950* (New York, 1986).

2. See the tables in Ronald D. Cohen and Raymond A. Mohl, *The Paradox of Progressive Education: The Gary Plan and Urban Schooling* (Port Washington, N.Y.,

1979), on pp. 177–178, 182. Enrollment figures are approximate because the sources differ.

3. *Gary Daily Tribune,* March 5, 1917.

4. John F. Carr, "A School with a Clear Aim," *World's Work,* vol. 19, 12364; Wirt to Interlaken School, August 3, 1916, Wirt Mss.

5. E. A. Spaulding to Wirt, February 23, 1917, Wirt to Spaulding, March 2, 1917, Wirt to Mrs. J. Rosenbaum, May 9, 1917, O. P. Pitts to Wirt, September 7, 1918, Rumely to Wirt, October 13, 1919, Wirt to George Foland, May 20, 1925, Wirt Mss.; *Gary Daily Tribune,* April 11, 1917, April 13, 1917, July 30, 1917, July 9, 1919, October 21, 1919.

6. *Gary Daily Tribune,* March 25, 1915, August 14, 1915, September 18, 1915, November 22, 1915, August 28, 1916, May 19, 1917, June 22, 1917.

7. Roscoe D. Case, *The Platoon School in America* (Stanford, Calif., 1931), 26–27; *Gary Daily Tribune,* February 22, 1916; Wirt to William Davidson, November 26, 1917, Wirt to C. E. Chadsey, January 10, 1918, Wirt Mss. For a sampling of the literature see W. J. McNally, *The Gary School System* (pamphlet, *Minneapolis Tribune,* November 1915); The Committee on Education, The Cleveland Chamber of Commerce, *Gary? A Contribution to the Present Discussion Regarding the Educational Features of the Public School System of Gary, Indiana* (pamphlet, [Cleveland, 1915]). On the struggle in New York see Cohen and Mohl, *Paradox of Progressive Education,* chap. 2. For a listing of published articles consult James A. McMillen, *The Gary System: A Bibliography* (University of Rochester, N.Y., Library, January 31, 1917); Velma R. Shaffer, *The Gary System: A Bibliography, 1916–1935* (mimeo, Columbia University, School of Library Service, 1935).

8. *Gary Daily Tribune,* September 1, 1917, June 10, 1916; *Gary Evening Post,* April 1, 1918; Dewey to Wirt, November 12, 1919, Wirt Mss.

9. *Gary Daily Tribune,* September 28, 1916; John Adams, "The School as a Social Centre," Conference of Educational Associations, *Report* (London, 1918), 121, and 119–128 passim; John Adams, *Modern Developments in Educational Practice* (New York, [1922, originally published in Great Britain]), 191; J. H. Putnam, "Modern Educational Movements," *Educational Review* 55 (April 1918):287; Mrs. Paul Tillard to Wirt, May 10, 1920, Wirt to Tillard, June 9 (?), 1920, Wirt Mss. See also Wirt, "Progress in Education through School Administration," Dominion Educational Association, *Proceedings of the Ninth Convention of the Association,* Jan. 31–Feb. 2, 1917 (Ottawa, 1917), 65–78; R. J. W. Selleck, *English Primary Education and the Progressives, 1914–1939* (London, 1972), 42; Neil Sutherland, *Children in English-Canadian Society: Framing the Twentieth-Century Consensus* (Toronto, 1976), 215–220.

10. Scott Nearing, *The New Education* (Chicago, 1915), 82–83. And on Nearing see Scott Nearing, *The Making of a Radical: A Political Autobiography* (New York, 1972).

11. John Dewey to Wirt, May 10, 1914, Wirt to Dewey, May 14, 1914, Wirt Mss.; John Dewey, "A Policy of Industrial Education," *The New Republic,* 1 (December 19, 1914):12.

12. John Dewey and Evelyn Dewey, *Schools of To-Morrow* (New York, 1915), 176, 185, 252.

13. Bourne, "Schools in Gary," *The New Republic,* 2 (March 27, 1915):198–199 (quote); "Communities for Children," ibid. (April 3, 1915):233–234; "Really Public Schools," ibid. (April 10, 1915):259–261; "Apprentices to the School," ibid. (April 24, 1915):302–303; "The Natural School," ibid. (May 1, 1915):326–328; Bourne, "Some Social Implications of the Gary School," *The American Teacher,* 4 (June 1915):82–85; Bourne, "The Gary Public Schools," *Scribner's Magazine,* 60 (September 1916):371–380; Bourne, *The Gary Schools* (Boston, 1916, new ed. Cambridge, Mass., 1970), 45–

46; Bourne to Wirt, September 29, 1915, Wirt Mss. See also Bruce Clayton, *Forgotten Prophet: The Life of Randolph Bourne* (Baton Rouge, La., 1984), 141–159 and passim for Bourne's life and ideas.

14. Floyd Dell, "Were You Ever a Child: A Discussion of Education," *The Liberator,* 1 (November 1918):22. That the Gary Plan made strange bedfellows see Cohen and Mohl, *Paradox of Progressive Education,* 10–34.

15. Ueland to Wirt, August 18, 1914, Wirt to Ueland, August 20, 1914, Wirt to the Principals and Teachers, January 31, 1916, Wirt to Ueland, January 12, 1916, Wirt Mss.; Elsa Ueland to Raymond Mohl, September 19, 1973, October 20, 1973 (copies in author's possession); Elsa Ueland to Ronald Cohen, June 2, 1974 (original in author's possession).

16. Ueland to Mohl, September 19, 1973 (copy in author's possession); Ueland to Cohen, June 2, 1974 (original in author's possession); McNally, *The Gary School System,* 36; Elsa Ueland, "The Teacher and the Gary Plan," *The New Republic,* 7 (July 1, 1916):220.

17. Jesse B. Sears, *The School Survey: A Textbook on the Use of School Surveying in the Administration of Public Schools* (Boston, 1925), xi–xii; Rick Ginsberg, "Analyzing School Surveys: Chicago, 1897–1964" (Ph.D. dissertation, University of Chicago, 1983); 1–13; Raymond E. Callahan, *Education and the Cult of Efficiency: A Study of the Social Forces That Have Shaped the Administration of the Public Schools* (Chicago, 1962), 112–120; David Tyack and Elisabeth Hansot, *Managers of Virtue: Public School Leadership in America, 1820–1980* (New York, 1982), 160–167.

18. Abraham Flexner, *The Modern School* (rev. ed., New York, 1921), 4; Ronald F. Movrich, "Before the Gates of Excellence: Abraham Flexner and Education, 1866–1918" (Ph.D. dissertation, University of California, Berkeley, 1981); on the Lincoln School see Lawrence A. Cremin, *The Transformation of the School: Progressivism in American Education, 1876–1957* (New York, 1964), 280–291.

19. Abraham Flexner to Jean Flexner, May 5, 1915, Abraham Flexner Papers, Library of Congress; Flexner to Wirt, June 23, 1915, Wirt to Flexner, July 8, 1915, Wirt Mss.; Leonard Ayres to Flexner, September 14, 1915, General Education Board Papers, Rockefeller Archive Center, North Tarrytown, N.Y. (hereafter cited as GEB Papers). For a brief discussion of Ayres and the Cleveland survey see Edward M. Miggins, "The Search for the One Best System: Cleveland Public Schools and Educational Reform, 1836–1920," David D. VanTassel and John J. Grabowski, eds., *Cleveland: A Tradition of Reform* (Kent, Ohio, 1986), 151–153.

20. Flexner to Charles Judd, January 21, 1916, Lee Hanmer to Flexner, February 11, 1916, GEB Papers; Movrich, "Before the Gates of Excellence," chap. 6.

21. Flexner to Anne Flexner, March 10, 1916, Flexner to Anne Flexner, May 10, 1916, Flexner to Anne Flexner, June 6, 1916, Flexner Papers; Flexner to George Strayer, May 17, 1916, GEB Papers.

22. Flexner to Courtis, August 15, 1916, (emphasis in original), Flexner to Courtis, May 23, 1917, GEB Papers.

23. Annie Klingensmith to Joseph [*sic*] Bachman, December 6, 1917, Wirt Mss.

24. Flexner to Frank Spaulding, February 28, 1918, Wirt to Flexner, March 6, 1918, Wirt to Flexner, April 6, 1918, GEB Papers; Flexner to Wirt, April 9, 1918, Wirt to Alice Barrows Fernandez, October 8, 1918, Wirt Mss.

25. Flexner and Bachman, *The Gary Schools: A General Account* (New York, 1918), 21, 87, 105, 195, 198, 200, 204–206.

26. Julius Sachs, "The Gary Schools," *Columbia University Quarterly,* 21 (April 1919):117; Henry Holmes to Flexner, January 8, 1919, GEB Papers; Bachman to Flexner, June 12, 1919, GEB Papers; Flexner, *I Remember* (New York, 1940), 255. See also Henry W. Holmes, "The Gary System Examined: A Review of the Report by the General Education Board of the Schools of Gary, Indiana," *Review of Reviews,* 59

(June 1919):611–617; "The Gary Survey," *The Elementary School Journal,* 19 (January 1919):330–335; Movrich, "Before the Gates of Excellence," 198–201.

27. *Gary Evening Post,* September 24, 1918; A. P. Melton to Wirt, March 31, 1919, Wirt to Bessie Stern, February 2, 1920, Wirt Mss.; Wirt to Mrs. Willard Straight, May 31, 1920, Wirt Pps.; Wirt, "Plain Facts about the Rockefeller Foundation Survey of the Gary Schools," ca. 1919, mimeo, Guy Wulfing Papers, Calumet Regional Archives, 1, 23. On the importance of testing and age grading see David L. Angus, Jeffrey E. Mirel, and Maris A. Vinovskis, "Historical Development of Age Stratification in Schooling," *Teachers College Record,* 90 (Winter 1988):211–236.

28. *Gary Daily Tribune,* December 17, 1915, December 28, 1915; Wirt to Paul Blakely, June 19, 1916, John B. DeVille to Wirt, November 18, 1919, Wirt Mss.; Cohen and Mohl, *Paradox of Progressive Education,* 62.

29. *Gary Daily Tribune,* August 18, 1917, August 28, 1917, November 21, 1917, June 3, 1918, October 1, 1918; William Grant Seaman and Mary Elizabeth Abernethy, *Community Schools for Week-Day Religious Instruction: Gary, Indiana* (Gary: Board of Religious Education, 1921), 5–28; Walter A. Squires, *Week-Day Religious Instruction: The Gary Plan of Church Schools* (Philadelphia, [1919]), 9–10; "The Gary Schools of Religion," *Religious Education,* 14 (August 1919):276–277.

30. Squires, *Week-Day Religious Instruction,* 17, 24; "Gary Schools of Religion," *Religious Education,* 277; Seaman and Abernethy, *Community Schools for Week-Day Religious Instruction,* 27; *Gary Daily Tribune,* February 12, 1916, May 29, 1919.

31. Wirt to Judge Elbert H. Gary, January 9, 1916, E. H. Gary to Hearst, November 15, 1917, E. H. Gary to Wirt, December 19, 1917, Wirt Mss.

32. Upton Sinclair, *The Goslings: A Study of the American Schools* (Pasadena, Calif., 1924), 291; Charles Burns to Geo. Sheehan, September 24, 1917, Sheehan to P. J. Brady, September 29, 1917, Wirt Mss.

33. Wirt to Samuel Gompers, February 11, 1916, Gompers to Wirt, February 19, 1916, Gompers to Wirt, August 30, 1916, Wirt to Gompers, September 28, 1916, Wirt Mss. While the AFL was the center of the organized labor movement at the time, it was not particularly anticapital; for a good recent study see Foster Rhea Dulles and Melvyn Dubofsky, *Labor in America: A History* (4th ed., Arlington Heights, Ill., 1984), chaps. 11–13.

34. Wirt to Judge Gary, October 10, 1916, Wirt to E. J. Buffington, October 11, 1916, Wirt Mss.

35. Wirt to R. D. Chadwick, May 12, 1915, Wirt to Max Loeb, November 20, 1915, Wirt Mss.; *Gary Daily Tribune,* May 14, 1915, October 12, 1916; William E. Eaton, *The American Federation of Teachers, 1916–1961: A History of the Movement* (Carbondale, Ill., 1975), 15–16.

36. *Gary Daily Tribune,* April 25, 1916, April 28, 1916, April 27, 1917, May 11, 1917, May 8, 1919, May 9, 1919; notes of a Teachers' Federation meeting beginning "At a regular meeting of the Teachers Federation, April 10," [1917], Wirt Mss. Among the recent accounts, one of the best on the role of the teachers' union in Chicago is Julia Wrigley, *Class Politics and Public Schools: Chicago, 1900–1950* (New Brunswick, N.J., 1982).

37. Clara Keopka to E. Miles Norton, June 19, 1916, and accompanying resolution, June 15, 1916, Geo. Sheehan to P. J. Brady, September 29, 1917, Wirt Mss.; *Gary Daily Tribune,* December 31, 1918, November 25, 1919, December 1, 1919. On the bread-and-butter nature of teacher unions see Wayne Urban, *Why Teachers Organize* (Detroit, 1982).

38. David M. Kennedy, *Over Here: The First World War and American Society* (New York, 1980), 53–59; Lewis P. Todd, *Wartime Relations of the Federal Government and the Public Schools, 1917–1918* (New York, 1945); William J. Reese, *Power and the Promise of School Reform: Grassroots Movements during the Progressive Era* (Boston, 1986), 238–249.

39. *Gary Daily Tribune,* June 16, 1916, March 30, 1917, April 9, 1917; Lillian Wald to Wirt, January 11, 1917, Wirt Mss.

40. *Gary Daily Tribune,* September 14, 1918, October 25, 1918, April 10, 1919, April 30, 1919; Wirt to Walter J. Parsons, April 22, 1918, Wirt to War Department, Committee on Education and Special Training, February 10, 1919, Wirt Mss.

41. *Gary Daily Tribune,* April 13, 1917, May 12, 1917, January 31, 1918, February 4, 1918, June 28, 1918, July 1, 1918, July 12, 1918; *Gary Evening Post,* January 9, 1918; Secretary to the Superintendent to Anna Matties (chairman, Lake Co. Committee on Educational War Propaganda), August 9, 1918, Wirt Mss.

42. *Gary Daily Tribune,* October 9, 1917, March 19, 1918, May 9, 1918, May 10, 1918; Wirt to *Gary Daily Tribune,* May 11, 1918, Wirt Mss. See also David Tyack, Thomas James, Aaron Benavot, *Law and the Shaping of Public Education, 1785–1954* (Madison, Wis., 1987), 172–173.

43. *Gary Evening Post,* March 31, 1915; *Gary Daily Tribune,* April 2, 1915, See Mohl and Betten, *Steel City,* chap. 6, for a thorough discussion of immigrants and education in Gary; and John Bodnar, *The Transplanted: A History of Immigrants in Urban America* (Bloomington, Ind., 1985), chap. 7.

44. *Gary Daily Tribune,* January 13, 1917, September 10, 1918; *Gary Evening Post,* September 17, 1917.

45. *Gary Daily Tribune,* August 9, 1919; Estelle M. Sternberger, "Gary and the Foreigner's Opportunity," *Survey,* 42 (June 28, 1919):480–482; Wirt to *The Arkansas Democrat,* November 18, 1919, Wirt Mss. On the steel strike and disruptions at the time see Mohl and Betten, *Steel City,* chap. 2. See also Maxine Seller, "The Education of the Immigrant Woman, 1900–1935," *Journal of Urban History,* 4 (May 1978):307–330.

46. *Gary Daily Tribune,* July 12, 1918, September 19, 1918; Sternberger, "Gary and the Foreigner's Opportunity," 482.

47. Frank Bachman to Charles Richards, August 11, 1916, Annie Klingensmith to Wirt, Report for September 1916, Wirt Mss.; *Gary Evening Post,* September 29, 1916; "The Model Schools of Gary, Indiana," *Crisis,* 13 (January 1917):121. And Mohl and Betten, *Steel City,* 49–56.

48. Petition to the School Board, [October 2, 1917], Petition to Charles S. Coons, March 1, 1918, Wirt Mss. For a discussion of developing segregation in Chicago's schools at this time see Michael W. Homel, *Down from Equality: Black Chicagoans and the Public Schools, 1920–41* (Urbana, Ill., 1984), 17–22; and on the deplorable conditions in segregated southern schools for black children see James D. Anderson, *The Education of Blacks in the South, 1860–1935* (Chapel Hill, N.C., 1988).

49. Petition to Charles S. Coons, March 1, 1918, Coons to Wirt, March 25, 1918, Wirt Mss.

50. *Gary Daily Tribune,* July 13, 1918; *Gary Evening Post,* January 10, 1919; [Swartz], "The Colored Situation," attached to J. E. McCoughtry to Swartz, September 25, 1918, Swartz to J. E. McCoughtry, September 27, 1918, Wirt Mss.

51. Swartz to Wirt, October 28, 1918, October 30, 1918, Wirt to C. E. Hawkins, December 12, 1919, Wirt Mss.; *Gary Daily Tribune,* September 3, 1919.

52. Guy Wulfing to F. F. Heighway, December 10, 1918, E. D. Simpson to Wirt, January 20, 1919, Wirt Mss. John F. Potts, "A History of the Growth of the Negro Population of Gary, Indiana" (MA thesis, Cornell University, 1937), 10.

53. *Gary Daily Tribune,* January 15, 1915, January 27, 1915, January 28, 1915.

54. J. B. Sleezer to Wirt, June 1, 1915, Wirt Mss.

55. Sleezer to Wirt, June 29, 1916, Wirt Mss.; *Gary Daily Tribune,* September 15, 1915; Flexner and Bachman, *The Gary Schools,* 177.

56. Wirt to Sleezer, May 17, 1917, Sleezer to Wirt, June 26, 1917, Wirt Mss.

57. Sleezer to Wirt, June 26, 1917, Horace Ellis to Ada Dunsing, June 25, 1918, Wirt Mss.; *Gary Daily Tribune,* April 25, 1918. Unfortunately, there are no extant

reports from Sleezer for 1918–1920. For recent, imaginative studies of the nature and meaning of child labor at the time see David Nasaw, *Children of the City: At Work and at Play* (Garden City, N.Y., 1985); Viviana A. Zelizer, *Pricing the Priceless Child: The Changing Social Value of Children* (New York, 1985).

58. *Gary Daily Tribune,* January 2, 1919, January 14, 1919, February 6, 1919; Wirt to Jas. Cullerton, January 20, 1919, Wirt Mss.

59. *Gary Daily Tribune,* April 18, 1919, June 19, 1919, July 25, 1919, September 13, 1919; "Report to J. G. Collicott of Indianapolis on Working Permits," December 27, 1918, Wirt Mss.

60. *Gary Daily Tribune,* January 21, 1919, January 24, 1919, January 31, 1919, February 4, 1919; *Gary Evening Post,* April 5, 1919.

61. *Gary Daily Tribune,* August 10, 1917, September 12, 1918; Wirt to Division of Psychology, Medical Department, War Department, January 29, 1919, Wirt Mss.

62. Annie Klingensmith, Monthly Report, November 1, 1916, Klingensmith to Wirt, March 12, 1918, Marvin Fuller to Superintendent, January 3, 1918[19], Wulfing to Fuller, January 9, 1919, Wirt Mss. Detailed reports from Klingensmith and Swartz, as well as from various principals, are scattered throughout the Wirt Mss.

63. Wirt to Klingensmith, July 9, 1919, Klingensmith to Spaulding, July 11, 1919, Wirt Mss.

64. Nora Lockridge to Wirt, November 24, 1917, Wirt Mss.

4. Flush Times

1. Cohen interview with YJean Staples Chambers, July 22, 1985, copy in Calumet Regional Archives.

2. *Gary Post-Tribune,* February 1, 1924, January 2, 1926, September 1, 1927.

3. Wirt to Frank Hatfield, March 3, 1923, Wirt Mss.

4. *Gary Post-Tribune,* September 29, 1922, December 15, 1927; Wirt, "Ways and Means for a Closer Union between the School and the Non-School Activities— Abstract," National Education Association, *Addresses and Proceedings of the Sixty- First Annual Meetings, July 1–6, 1923,* 61 (Washington, D.C., 1923), 445–447; Wirt, "Some Features of Time Distribution at Gary, Indiana," National Society for the Study of Education, *24th Yearbook,* part 2: *Adapting the Schools to Individual Differences* (Bloomington, Ill., 1925), 39–40; Wirt, "School Days Then and Now," *Journal of Education,* (June 17, 1926):662–663; Wirt, "Opportunities of the Platoon School," ms. notes on a speech delivered in Cleveland, Ohio, Feb. 1929, 7, Wirt Mss.

5. *Gary Post-Tribune,* May 29, 1924; Roscoe D. Case, *The Platoon School in America* (Stanford, Calif., 1931), 26–35, 49.

6. John Amid, "Some Children Have All the Luck," *Collier's,* 73 (February 9, 1924):15; Carleton Washburne and Myron M. Stearns, *Better Schools: A Survey of Progressive Education in American Public Schools* (New York, 1928), 247 (much of the section on Gary is taken from the Amid article). On Washburne see Lawrence A. Cremin, *The Transformation of the School: Progressivism in American Education, 1876–1957* (New York, 1961), 295–298.

7. Alice Barrows, "First National Conference on the Work-Study-Play, or Platoon Plan," U.S. Office of Education, *Bulletin,* 35 (1922):1–16; John J. Tigert to Wirt, January 13, 1923, Tigert to Wirt, December 13, 1924, Wirt Mss.

8. Charles Spain to Alice Barrows, March 17, 1925, Wirt to Barrows, January 31, 1927, Barrows to Wirt, February 5, 1927, Wirt Mss.: Case, *Platoon School in America,* 269–270.

9. Barrows to Wirt, September 9, 1927, Wirt to Barrows, November 17, 1927, Wirt to Barrows, November 26, 1929, Barrows to Wirt, January 4, 1930, Wirt Mss.; *Gary Post-Tribune,* March 5, 1929. On Barrows see also Ronald D. Cohen and Raymond A. Mohl, *The Paradox of Progressive Education: The Gary Plan and Urban Schooling* (Port Washington, N.Y., 1979), 27–28.

10. Wirt to William McAndrew, January 17, 1924, Wirt Mss.

11. Robert L. Reid, ed., *Battleground: The Autobiography of Margaret A. Haley* (Urbana, Ill., 1982), 210; Margaret A. Haley, "The Factory System," *The New Republic,* 40 (November 12, 1924):19; Upton Sinclair, *The Goslings: A Study of the American Schools* (Pasadena, Calif., 1924), 102; Don C. Rogers and C. E. Lang, "A Comparison of the Chicago Double Schools, the Gary System, and the Detroit Platoon Plan," *Chicago Schools Journal,* 6 (April 1924):281–295; Illinois State Federation of Labor, *Weekly News Letter,* 10 (July 26, 1924):2–4; George S. Counts, *School and Society in Chicago* (New York, 1928), 177–184; Julia Wrigley, *Class Politics & Public Schools: Chicago, 1900–1950* (New Brunswick, N.J., 1982), 160–163.

12. On Gary in the 1920s see James B. Lane, *"City of the Century": A History of Gary, Indiana* (Bloomington, Ind., 1978), 105–129. See also Edward A. Krug, *The Shaping of the American High School,* vol. 2: *1920–1941* (Madison, Wis., 1972).

13. *Gary Post and Tribune,* July 31, 1922.

14. "Survey of 241 Continuation School Pupils," February 18, 1921, Sleezer to Wirt, June 27, 1921, Wirt Mss. See also Edna H. Edmondson, "Juvenile Delinquency and Adult Crime: Certain Associations of Juvenile Delinquency and Adult Crime in Gary, Ind.," *Indiana University Studies,* 8, 49 (June 1921); E. M. McDonough, "Organization and Administration of a Continuation School," *Industrial Arts Magazine,* 10 (June 1921):203–206; Franklin J. Keller, *Day Schools for Young Workers: The Organization and Management of Part-Time and Continuation Schools* (New York, 1924).

15. *Gary Post and Tribune,* January 10, 1922, November 4, 1922; Sleezer to Wirt, June 26, 1922, Report on Mary Wassel, January 24, 1923, Wirt Mss.

16. Sleezer to Wirt, June 22, 1923, Keziah Stright to Wirt, June 26, 1923, Wirt Mss.; *Gary Post-Tribune,* December 5, 1922.

17. *Gary Post-Tribune,* November 17, 1923, February 16, 1926; John G. Rossman, "What Gary Is Doing for Its Children," *Teachers College Record,* 27 (December 1925):291.

18. Swartz to Wirt, February 9, 1920, Wirt Mss.

19. *Gary Post and Tribune,* September 13, 1921, September 22, 1921.

20. Albert Fertsch, "Evening School Activities in Gary, Indiana," *National Education Association Journal,* 13 (December 1924):332–333; Fertsch, "Adult Education From the Viewpoint of a City," National Education Association, *Proceedings of the Sixty-Sixth Annual Meeting,* July 1–6, 1928, 66 ([1928]), 270.

21. Charles Coons, "Notice," October 23, 1921, Wirt to Mrs. Jacob Smith, February 9, 1922, Wirt Mss.; *Gary Daily Tribune,* February 17, 1921. On Americanization in the city see Raymond A. Mohl and Neil Betten, *Steel City: Urban and Ethnic Patterns in Gary, Indiana, 1906–1950* (New York, 1986), chaps. 2, 5, 6; and John F. McClymer, "The Americanization Movement and the Education of the Foreign-Born Adult, 1914–25," in Bernard J. Weiss, ed., *American Education and the European Immigrant: 1840–1940* (Urbana, Ill., 1982), 96–111.

22. *Gary Post-Tribune,* November 22, 1927; Wirt to Fertsch, March 21, 1928, Wirt Mss.

23. *Gary Post-Tribune,* November 22, 1927; Swartz to F. W. Roe, July 26, 1918, Arthur Smith to My dear friend, October 1, 1919, Wirt Mss.

24. Benjamin Burris to Wirt, April 14, 1923, Wirt Mss.

25. *Gary Post-Tribune,* September 8, 1927.

26. *Gary Post and Tribune,* April 5, 1922.

27. *Gary Post-Tribune,* May 11, 1925 (quoting from the *Gary Works Circle*); *Gary Post and Tribune,* May 20, 1922, June 15, 1922.

28. *Gary Evening Post,* June 17, 1920; *Gary Daily Tribune,* March 11, 1920; *Gary Post-Tribune,* September 10, 1925.

29. Charles Coons to Wirt, January 16, 1922, Wirt Mss. On the AFT in the 1920s see William E. Eaton, *The American Federation of Teachers, 1916–1961* (Carbondale, Ill., 1975), 18–37.

30. *Gary Post-Tribune,* July 2, 1924, October 7, 1925; Mathew Woll to Wirt, February 13, 1925, Wirt to Woll, February 18, 1925, Alice Barrows to Wirt, December 2, 1925, William Green to Wirt, November 5, 1929, Wirt to Green, November 13, 1929, Wirt Mss. In 1925, however, suspicious of economic efficiency, a shrunken AFT passed a resolution at its annual convention to initiate a study of the platoon system "among its constituent locals and to combat efforts to use this educational experiment toward ends which are not definitely of an educational character." The Commission on Educational Reconstruction, *Organizing the Teaching Profession: The Story of the American Federation of Teachers* (Glencoe, Ill., 1955), 215. On organized labor in the decade see Foster Rhea Dulles and Melvyn Dubofsky, *Labor in America: A History* (4th ed., Arlington Heights, Ill., 1984), 233–250.

31. For population figures see Cohen and Mohl, *Paradox of Progressive Education,* 177; John Foster Potts, "A History of the Growth of the Negro Population of Gary, Indiana," (MA thesis, Cornell University, 1937), 14, 16. For a comparative study of increasing school segregation in Chicago and the reactions of the black community see Michael W. Homel, *Down from Equality: Black Chicagoans and the Public Schools, 1920–41* (Urbana, Ill., 1984).

32. *Gary Daily Tribune,* January 13, 1921, January 17, 1921, April 11, 1921. See also Mohl and Betten, *Steel City,* chap. 3.

33. A. F. Smith to Wirt, April 18, 1921, "Program of Topics under consideration by Peoples' Committee in connection with certain practices in vogue and attempted in the Gary Public School System," September 29, 1921, Wirt Mss.; *Gary Post and Tribune,* July 22, 1921.

34. *Gary Post and Tribune,* November 18, 1921, February 7, 1922; Albert Fertsch, "Colored Trade School at Gary, Ind.," *School Life,* 7 (November 1921):65.

35. *Gary Post-Tribune,* January 31, 1923; E. E. Ramsey to Wirt, April 11, 1923, W. C. Hueston to Wirt, September 6, 1924, Wirt to Hueston, September 11, 1924, Wirt Mss.; L. Campbell to State Dept. of Education, January 22, 1922[3], Series G-62, NAACP Papers, Library of Congress (hereafter cites as NAACP Pps.).

36. James Weldon Johnson to T. J. Wilson, February 14, 1923, William Smith to National NAACP, August 30, 1925, Walter White to William Smith, September 3, 1925, Series G-62, NAACP Pps.

37. *Gary Post-Tribune,* September 26, 1927, September 27, 1927, September 28, 1927, September 30, 1927; "Negro Students in a Gary High School," *School and Society,* 26 (October 8, 1927):453.

38. *Gary Colored American,* December 22, 1927.

39. James Weldon Johnson to Wirt, September 29, 1927, Series D-56, NAACP Pps.; *The (Gary) Sun,* October 8, 1927; *Chicago Daily News,* October 1, 1927, quoted in *Chicago Defender,* October 8, 1927. See also R. L. Bailey to James Weldon Johnson, October 1, 1927, Series D-56, NAACP Pps.

40. "The Gary School Strike," *School and Society,* 26 (October 29, 1927):563; G. Victor Cools, "Gary's High-School Strike," ibid., 26 (November 26, 1927):686.

41. *The (Gary) Sun,* November 11, 1927; *Gary Colored American,* December 15, 1927.

42. Edward M. Bacoyn to National Office, December 12, 1927, Series D-56, NAACP Pps.

43. Edward M. Bacoyn to James Weldon Johnson, January 4, 1928, Series D-56, NAACP Pps.; *Gary Colored American,* January 5, 1928, January 12, 1928. For another view of the Emerson strike see Mohl and Betten, *Steel City,* 58–59.

44. Edward M. Bacoyn to William T. Andrews, August 13, 1928, Series D-56, NAACP Pps.

45. *The Sand Dune,* 1932 (Yearbook of East Pulaski High School), 7.

46. H. Theo Tatum, "Annual Report of Virginia Street School, Session, 1926–1927," June 14, 1927, Tatum, "Annual Report of Virginia School, Session 1927–1928," June 2, 1928, 2–3, 8, Wirt Mss.

47. *Gary American,* September 7, 1928; R. L. Bailey to James Weldon Johnson, October 1, 1927, Series D-56, Walter White to A. C. Bailey, Series D-57, NAACP Pps. In his MA thesis, "The Organization and Administration of the Typical Gary School Center" (MA thesis, Columbia University, 1928), Tatum does not mention the segregated schools or any race problems.

48. Jacob L. Reddix, *A Voice Crying in the Wilderness: The Memoirs of Jacob L. Reddix* (Jackson, Miss., 1974), 109; *The (Gary) Sun,* November 4, 1927, November 11, 1927, November 18, 1927, January 6, 1928. On the UNIA in Gary see Judith Stein, *The World of Marcus Garvey: Race and Class in Modern Society* (Baton Rouge, La., 1986), 242–246; Mohl and Betten, *Steel City,* 81–83.

49. *Gary American,* June 21, 1929, June 28, 1929.

50. Wirt to Milton Fairchild, October 5, 1920, Wirt Mss.; Mohl and Betten, *Steel City,* 156–158.

51. Mary Abernethy to "Dear Friend," October 1, 1923, "Gary Public Schools" scrapbook, vol. 1, Indiana Room, Gary Public Library, Gary, Ind.; *Gary Post-Tribune,* January 21, 1924, June 4, 1931.

52. *Gary Post-Tribune,* July 23, 1925, June 4, 1931; G. W. Swartz to Wirt, March 9, 1923, Wirt to Mary Abernethy, August 29, 1923, Wirt Mss.

53. John Rossman, "Principals-Supervisors Bulletin No. 27," November 24, 1926, Gary Klan #123 to Wirt, March 11, 1927, Wirt Mss.

54. Wirt to Lieut. Colonel David H. Biddle, March 27, 1922, Wirt Mss.; *Gary Daily Tribune,* January 17, 1921; *Gary Post and Tribune,* March 15, 1922; *Gary Post-Tribune,* May 2, 1923.

55. *Gary Post-Tribune,* March 23, 1923, May 2, 1923, November 22, 1924, September 9, 1927. For the argument that the commercial courses for girls were much more important than the vocational classes for boys, at least in California, see Harvey Kantor, *Learning to Earn: School, Work, and Vocational Reform in California, 1880–1930* (Madison, Wis., 1988), esp. chap. 7.

56. Guy Wulfing to Wirt, May 20, 1924, Wirt Mss.

57. *Gary Post-Tribune,* September 9, 1927.

58. "Principals and Supervisors Bulletin No. 12," October 14, 1924, "Teachers Bulletin No. 15," April 3, 1925, Wirt Mss.

59. *Gary Post-Tribune,* September 8, 1925, October 8, 1925; "Some Forward Steps, Gary Public Schools, 1923–1928, Part B," 6, Wirt Mss; "Teachers' Bulletin No. 12," January 5, 1926, Wirt Mss.; A. H. Bell, "The Work-Study-Play Program: An Analysis of the Gary Program and Its Cost," paper delivered before the Eighteenth Annual Meeting of the National Association of Public School Business Officials, Columbus, Ohio, May 23, 1929 (pamphlet in Gary Public Library, Gary, Ind.). Carleton W. Washburne "Introduction and Summary," National Society for the Study of Education, *Adapting the Schools to Individual Differences,* 24th Yearbook, part 2 (Bloomington, Ill., 1925), x. See also Eugene Smith, *Education Moves Ahead: A Survey of Progressive Methods* (Boston, 1924); Krug, *Shaping of the American High School, 1920–1941,* 141–144; David L. Angus, Jeffrey E. Mirel, Maris A. Vinovskis, "Historical Development of Age Stratification in Schooling," *Teachers College Record,* 90 (Winter 1988):224–226.

60. *Gary Post-Tribune,* September 4, 1926; "Some Forward Steps, Gary Public Schools, 1923–1928, Part B," 3, Wirt Mss.

61. *Gary Post-Tribune,* September 4, 1928; Stella Z. Miles, "Second Annual Report, Teacher Training Department," June 15, 1927, Wirt Mss.

62. "Principals-Supervisors Bulletin No. 13," October 8, 1925, Wirt Mss.; *Gary Post-Tribune,* July 3, 1929.

63. O. B. Nesbit, "Health Work in the Public Schools," *The Journal of the Indiana State Medical Association,* 21 (November 15, 1928):483–489; Elizabeth Ames, "Opportunities in a Work-Study-Play Organization for Health Instruction," *Platoon School,* 4 (September 1930):132–135.

64. *Chicago Tribune,* December 8, 1929.

65. Arthur Shumway, "Gary, Shrine of the Steel God," *The American Parade,* 3 (Jan.–March 1929):29.

5. Survival

1. *Gary Post-Tribune,* April 8, 1931. This is possibly a true story, but no one, not even his oldest colleagues, called him "Billy" Wirt. He was always Mr. Wirt or Dr. Wirt.

2. Roscoe D. Case, *The Platoon School in America* (Stanford, Calif., 1931); Case, "The Platoon School and the Depression," *School Executives Magazine,* October 1932, 63. See also, Charles Spain, "Keep Frills—Save Money," *School Life,* 18 (March 1933):122. For the survival of one platoon system see Jeffrey Mirel, "Politics and Public Education in the Great Depression: Detroit, 1929–1940" (Ph.D. dissertation, University of Michigan, 1984). And David Tyack, Robert Lowe, and Elisabeth Hansot, *Public Schools in Hard Times: The Great Depression and Recent Years* (Cambridge, Mass., 1984).

3. Wirt, "Making the City a Fit Place for the Rearing of Children," *The Platoon School,* 4 (March 1930):11; Wirt, *The Great Lockout in America's Citizenship Plants,* part 1 (Gary, 1937), 22 (part 2, if written, was never published); Charles Beard to Wirt, November 14, [1937], Wirt Pps. See also Wirt, "One Teacher or Many," *The Platoon School,* 5 (March 1931):6–16.

4. Wirt, "Which Way America: Should Educators Be Alarmed," ms. [1934], Wirt, "The School as an Agency for Propaganda," ms. 1935, 5, Wirt Pps. For the conservative reaction of other "progressives" during the 1930s see Otis L. Graham, *An Encore for Reform: The Old Progressives and the New Deal* (New York, 1967).

5. There are copies of these papers and Wirt's correspondence in the Wirt Pps; and also William A. Wirt, "Addresses on Currency and the Depression (1932–1934)," bound volume of mimeographed papers in the Indiana Room, Gary Public Library; Charles A. Beard to Mr. Nelson, March 31, 1932, Wirt Pps.; Beard to Wirt, June 8, 1932, Wirt Mss.; *Gary Post-Tribune,* May 4, 1932.

6. Edward A. Rumely to Wirt, January 26, 1933, Wirt Mss.; Wirt to Rumely, May 5, 1933, Wirt Pps.; Joseph E. Reeve, *Monetary Reform Movements: A Survey of Recent Plans and Panaceas* (Washington, D.C., 1943), 55–56; Arthur M. Schlesinger, *The Coming of the New Deal* (Boston, 1958), 198–199; Herbert M. Bratter, "The Committee for the Nation: A Case History in Monetary Propaganda," *Journal of Political Economy* (August 1941):531–553.

7. Alice Barrows to Wirt, October 26, 1932, Wirt Mss. See also Ronald D. Cohen and Raymond A. Mohl, *The Paradox of Progressive Education: The Gary Plan and Urban Schooling* (Port Washington, N.Y., 1979), chap. 1, for a thorough discussion of Barrows and Wirt.

8. *Gary Post-Tribune,* January 16, 1934.

9. Wirt to Edward Rumely, March 12, 1934, Wirt Pps.

10. The statement appeared in the *New York Times* and other papers and is reprinted in William A. Wirt, *America Must Lose—By a "Planed Economy", the Stepping-stone to a Regimented State* (New York, 1934), 33–35; *Gary Post-Tribune,* March 23, 1934. See also John J. Healy, "William A. Wirt and the Bulwinkle

Investigation of 1934," (MA thesis, Indiana University, 1960), which is strongly pro-Wirt.

11. *New York Times,* March 25, 1934.

12. U.S., *Congressional Record-House,* 73rd Cong., 2d sess., 1934, March 27, 5561; *Gary Post-Tribune,* March 26, 1934, March 27, 1934; *Complete Presidential Press Conferences of Franklin D. Roosevelt* 25 vols., (New York, 1972), vol. 3, 266.

13. *Time,* April 23, 1934, 15; U.S., Congress, House, *Hearings before the Select Committee to Investigate Charges Made by Dr. William A. Wirt,* 73rd Cong., 2d sess. (Washington, D.C., 1934), 19.

14. *Gary Post-Tribune,* April 10, 1934, April 11, 1934; the Richberg quote is in George Wolfskill and John A. Hudson, *All but the People: Franklin D. Roosevelt and His Critics, 1933–39* (New York, 1969), 101.

15. *The Secret Diary of Harold L. Ickes: The First Thousand Days, 1933–1936* (New York, 1953), 160.

16. *Hearings before the Select Committee to Investigate Charges Made by Dr. William A. Wirt,* 38, 39, 48; U.S., Congress, House, *Investigation of Certain Statements Made by One Dr. William A. Wirt . . . Report* 73rd Cong., 2d sess., May 2, 1934, H. R. 1439, 4.

17. *Gary Post-Tribune,* April 19, 1934; U.S., *Congressional Record-Senate,* 73rd Cong., 2d sess., 1934, April 17, 6737; U.S., *Congressional Record-House,* 73rd Cong., 2d sess., 1934, April 17, 6785; *Time,* April 23, 1934, 15–16; Mary Heaton Vorse, "Behind Doctor Wirt," *The New Republic,* 78 (April 25, 1934):299–300. See also, "A Word About Wirt," *The Nation,* 138 (May 2, 1934):495–496; Edmund Wilson, *Travels in Two Democracies* (New York, 1936), 103–111.

18. *Gary Post-Tribune,* April 30, 1934; Rose Schneiderman (with Lucy Goldthwaite), *All For One* (New York, 1967), 209.

19. Francis Ralston Welch to Wirt, May 4, 1934, Harry A. Jung to Wirt, May 5, 1934, Jung to Wirt, August 10, 1934, Copy of Schneiderman v. Wirt, July 1934, along with Wirt's notes, Wirt Pps.

20. F. L. Soper to Wirt, April 21, 1934, Soper to Wirt, June 26, 1934, Wirt, "Which Way America: We Have the Right to Know," Wirt Mss.

21. *Gary Post-Tribune,* January 16, 1935; Wirt, "The School as an Agency for Propaganda," ms. 1935, 35, Edwin Hadley to Wirt, February 15, 1935, Wirt Pps; Ernest Rheydt-Dittmer to Wirt, February 10, 1935, Wirt Mss. There were also letters from members of the Silver Shirt Legion and the League Against Communism.

22. Wirt, *Keeping America Safe for Democracy* (Gary, 1936), 23; *Gary Post-Tribune,* November 9, 1937.

23. The enrollment figures in Gary followed national trends; see Tyack, Lowe, Hansot, *Public Schools in Hard Times,* 144–149; Jeffrey E. Mirel and David L. Angus, "The Rising Tide of Custodialism: Enrollment Increases and Curriculum Reform in Detroit, 1928–1940," *Issues in Education,* 4 (Fall 1986):101–120.

24. Wirt to William J. Bogan, April 15, 1932, Wirt Mss.; *Gary Post-Tribune,* September 9, 1931. And for comparison with the situation in Detroit see Jeffrey Mirel, "The Politics of Educational Retrenchment in Detroit, 1929–1935," *History of Education Quarterly,* 24 (Fall 1984):323–358; Mirel, "Politics and Public Education in the Great Depression: Detroit, 1929–1940."

25. *Gary Post-Tribune,* April 18, 1932, January 28, 1933.

26. *Gary Post-Tribune,* February 22, 1933, March 25, 1933, March 29, 1933, April 7, 1933.

27. *Gary Post-Tribune,* June 7, 1933, August 23, 1933.

28. "Saturday School in Gary," [October 1933], 3, Wirt Mss. The state had long controlled property tax rates for local schools, depriving the community school board

of any initiative or flexibility; moreover, economic conditions dictated the value of taxable property, the basic source of school revenues. There was also a small state allotment, primarily based on student enrollment.

29. *Gary Post-Tribune,* February 22, 1934; Gary Principals' Association, *The Taxpayer and the Gary Public Schools* (Gary, June 1934).

30. Wirt to Doctor J. J. Edmonson, March 11, 1932, Wirt Pps.

31. *Gary Post-Tribune,* June 17, 1932, June 21, 1932, April 8, 1933.

32. "GARY COLLEGE, Inspection by A. J. Brumbaugh and John L. Seaton, February 8–9, 1935," 4, 12, ms copy in School Service Center, Gary.

33. Program of the "Third Annual Scholastic Convocation," June 16, [1937], Bernice Engels Papers, Calumet Regional Archives.

34. *Gary Post-Tribune,* May 27, 1932. See also Charles Lutz, "Pupil Achievement in Platoon and Non-Platoon Schools," (MA thesis, University of Chicago, 1932).

35. Isabelle V. Jones to Wirt, September 10, 1935, mimeo, Wirt Pps.; *Gary Post-Tribune,* April 13, 1937 (all figures rounded off).

36. "Technical and Trade Training in the Gary Public Schools," [1934], 3, Wirt Mss.

37. G. E. Wulfing to Wirt, mid-1930s, Wulfing to Wirt, February 5, 1936 (emphasis in original), Guy Wulfing Papers, Calumet Regional Archives; Mirel and Angus, "The Rising Tide of Custodialism," 101–120.

38. [Wulfing], "The Place of Industrial Arts in the Gary School Plan," [1937], Wulfing Pps.

39. Wirt to W. P. Gleason, December 13, 1934, Wirt Mss.; Supervisors of the Gary Public Schools, *Choosing Your Life Work: A Message to Gary Boys and Girls* (pamphlet, 1937).

40. *Gary Post-Tribune,* November 26, 1930; Tyack, Lowe, Hansot, *Public Schools in Hard Times,* chap. 3.

41. *Gary Post-Tribune,* February 5, 1931, March 3, 1932.

42. *Gary Post-Tribune,* April 24, 1931, February 6, 1934; Wirt to ?, February 5, 1934, Wirt Pps.

43. *Gary Post-Tribune,* March 7, 1934.

44. Ibid.

45. *Gary Post-Tribune,* April 13, 1932, October 12, 1932; Flora A. Philley, *Teacher Help Yourself* (Gary, 1948), 23.

46. *Gary Post-Tribune,* June 8, 1933, March 6, 1934.

47. *Gary Post-Tribune,* August 14, 1935, August 16, 1935; [Wirt], "Gary Public Schools Bulletin—July, 1935. "Data Concerning Employment of Teachers From June 1930 to June 1935," 12–13, mimeo, Wirt Pps. See also Lois Scharf, *To Work and To Wed* (Westport, Conn., 1980) and Winifred Wandersee, *Women's Work and Family Values, 1920–1940* (Cambridge, Mass., 1981).

48. *Gary Post-Tribune,* October 16, 1934; Flora Philley, Chairman, Single Salary Schedule Study Committee, "Arguments for Single Salary Schedule," December 8, 1936, Gary Teachers' Union MSS, Local #4, Gary, Indiana; Philley, *Teacher, Help Yourself,* 6–30. High-school teachers were also paid more than elementary teachers, a traditional discrepancy.

49. *Gary Post-Tribune,* April 13, 1937, April 14, 1937; Thomas Hurley to American Federation of Teachers, April 17, 1937, American Federation of Teachers Papers, Archives of Labor History and Urban Affairs, Wayne State University, Detroit, Michigan (hereafter cited as AFT Pps.). See also Foster Rhea Dulles and Melvin Dubofsky, *Labor in America: A History* (4th ed., Arlington Heights, Ill., 1984), 278–300. There was some opposition to joining the AFT, mostly among teachers from Emerson and Horace Mann, the more elite schools; they maintained their mem-

bership in a small chapter of the Gary Teachers' Federation. The Federation was "a useless appendix," according to Flora Philley, "causing us now and then an abdominal *malaise,* but nothing more." Philley, *Teacher, Help Yourself,* 32.

50. *Gary Post-Tribune,* April 19, 1937; Flora Philley to Wirt, November 3, 1937, Philley to Wirt, November 14, 1937, Gary Teachers' Union MSS; "Why Join the Gary Teachers' Union Local No. 4," Bulletin 5, n.d., AFT Pps. For a discussion of the concerns of the other AFT locals, including academic freedom, see The Commission on Educational Reconstruction, *Organizing the Teaching Profession: The Story of the American Federation of Teachers* (Glencoe, Ill., 1955), 38–47.

51. *Gary Post-Tribune,* April 27, 1937, December 7, 1937; "Proposed Salary Schedule, Submitted by Gary Teachers' Union Local No. 4," December 1, 1937, AFT Pps; Flora Philley to M. Clifford Townsend, November 7, 1937, Gary Teachers' Union MSS; Philley, *Teacher, Help Yourself,* 37–53.

52. *Gary Post-Tribune,* January 7, 1938, January 8, 1938, January 13, 1938, March 3, 1938; Philley, *Teacher, Help Yourself,* 59.

53. Gary Teachers' Union, Local No. 4, "A Resolution of the Passing of Superintendent William A. Wirt," March 12, 1938, Gary Teachers' Union MSS; *Gary Post-Tribune,* April 29, 1938; Philley, *Teacher, Help Yourself,* 94–95.

54. *The Gary Teacher,* 1, 1 (October 1939):2, copy in AFT Pps; Flora Philley to Herbert Cole, February 24, 1940, Gary Teachers' Union MSS; Philley to Irvin Kuenzli, August 30, 1939, Kuenzli to Edward T. Doyne, September 7, 1939, AFT Pps.

55. Flora Philley to Miss Herstien, August 30, 1939, AFT Pps.

56. *Gary Post-Tribune,* February 18, 1937, February 26, 1937; Wirt to Franz Wirt, March 6, 1937, Wirt Pps. Wirt's brother-in-law Orville Fisher taught at Froebel and his sister Mrs. Lulu Roberts taught at Jefferson school at the time.

57. *Gary Post-Tribune,* April 12, 1937; *Gary American,* July 15, 1938.

58. *Gary Post-Tribune,* May 10, 1939.

59. Dennis Bethea, "The Colored Group in the Gary School System," *Crisis,* 38 (August 1931):282–283; John Foster Potts, "A History of the Growth of the Negro Population of Gary, Indiana" (MA thesis, Cornell University, 1937), 47. For background information on the black community see Elizabeth Balanoff, "A History of the Black Community of Gary, Indiana, 1906–1940" (Ph.D. dissertation, University of Chicago, 1974); Raymond A. Mohl and Neil Betten, *Steel City: Urban and Ethnic Patterns in Gary, Indiana, 1906–1950* (New York, 1986), 48–90. See also Michael W. Homel, *Down from Equality: Black Chicagoans and the Public Schools, 1920–41* (Urbana, Ill., 1984); Tyack, Lowe, Hansot, *Public Schools in Hard Times,* 176–185.

60. For a recent study of the NAACP's legal strategy at the time, which focused on segregated schooling in the south, see Mark V. Tushnet, *The NAACP's Legal Strategy against Segregated Education, 1925–1950* (Chapel Hill, N.C., 1987), chaps. 2–5.

61. *Gary American,* June 28, 1930, August 2, 1930.

62. *Gary American,* October 11, 1930, November 22, 1930.

63. *Gary American,* April 18, 1931; *Gary Post-Tribune,* April 21, 1931. Interestingly, in 1936 Wirt prevented Langston Hughes from speaking at the Roosevelt school because of "his communistic beliefs. . . . Dr. Wirt declared a number of citizens had complained against the young writer's appearance because they believed his program would consist of a discussion of communism and atheism in addition to reading of his poetry." He appeared at the Croatian Hall, sponsored by the Trinity Baptist Church. *Gary American,* January 24, 1936.

64. *Gary Post-Tribune,* September 29, 1931; *Gary American,* December 5, 1931.

65. *Gary American,* June 4, 1932, June 18, 1932, September 24, 1932, October 15, 1932. Jacob Reddix, a teacher at the Roosevelt school, later recalled that "under McFarlane's leadership, the faculty launched a crusade to improve the scholarship at

Roosevelt High School. . . . McFarlane devoted his time to individual instruction for the students at Roosevelt High School." Jacob L. Reddix, *A Voice Crying in the Wilderness: The Memoirs of Jacob L. Reddix* (Jackson, Miss., 1974), 109–110.

66. *Gary American,* June 16, 1933; *Gary Post-Tribune,* May 8, 1934; A. J. Butler, President, Central District Citizens Club to Mrs. James Patterson, June 10, 1933, Wirt Mss.

67. *Gary American,* April 6, 1934; Colored Students of Froebel School to Dear Sir, January 18, 1934, Leaflet entitled "Students of Froebel! Demand Equal Rights for Negro Students," ca. February 1934, Wirt Mss.

68. *Gary American,* April 6, 1934; Charles Coons to Wirt, February 16, 1934, Wirt Mss.; Board of Trustees, School City of Gary, "Minutes of School Board Meetings," July 14, 1938, vol. 7, 383, Service Center, School City of Gary.

69. *Gary American,* March 4, 1938, April 22, 1938, May 6, 1938. See Harvard Sitkoff, *A New Deal for Blacks: The Emergence of Civil Rights as a National Issue,* vol. 1: *The Depression Decade* (New York, 1978), chap. 4.

70. H. Theo Tatum, "Education for Democratic Living," *National Educational Outlook among Negroes,* 19 (March 1938):23; *Gary American,* August 26, 1938.

71. *Gary American,* May 26, 1939, June 2, 1939.

72. *Gary Post-Tribune,* February 1, 1938.

73. *Gary Post-Tribune,* March 11, 1938, March 12, 1938.

74. Mary Rennels, "Dr. and Mrs. William A. Wirt of Gary and What They are Like in Their Home," *Chicago Daily News,* April 7, 1934; "William A. Wirt," *The Nation's Schools,* 21 (May 1938):17.

75. *Gary Post-Tribune,* March 16, 1938.

76. *Gary Post-Tribune,* June 14, 1939.

77. Workers of the Writers' Program of the Works Projects Administration, *The Calumet Region Historical Guide* ([Gary], 1939), 179.

78. *Gary Post-Tribune,* November 25, 1939.

79. I have been influenced by the work of Jeffrey Mirel on the 1930s; see his publications cited above and his review of Tyack, Lowe, Hansot, *Public Schools in Hard Times,* in *Educational Studies,* 16 (Summer 1985):156–164. See also for state-wide issues James H. Madison, *Indiana through Tradition and Change: A History of the Hoosier State and Its People, 1920–1945* (Indianapolis, 1982), 281–283.

6. The War Years

1. Interview with Leonard Levenda, Merrillville, Indiana, July 8, 1982, in possession of the author. He would later graduate from the American Academy of Dramatic Arts in New York City, majoring in acting, directing, and radio. He credited the auditorium department at Froebel with his inspiration to go into drama. *Gary Post-Tribune,* March 29, 1949. A full discussion of the Froebel student strike appears below. Parts of this chapter originally appeared in Cohen, "World War II and the Travail of Progressive Schooling: Gary, Indiana, 1940–1946," in Ronald K. Goodenow and Diane Ravitch, eds., *Schools in Cities: Consensus and Conflict in American Educational History* (New York, 1983), 263–286; and Cohen, "The Dilemma of School Integration in the North: Gary, Indiana, 1945–1960," *Indiana Magazine of History,* 82 (June 1986):161–184.

2. *Gary Post-Tribune,* November 25, 1939; H. S. Jones to Richard Welling, November 27, 1940, Wirt Pps.

3. *Gary Post-Tribune,* December 5, 1940.

4. *Gary Post-Tribune,* January 16, 1941; F. B. Knight to Erwin C. Rosenau, January 16, 1941, Erwin C. Rosenau Papers, Calumet Regional Archives.

5. F. B. Knight to Dr. John M. Dorsey, January 16, 1941, Knight to Lloyd F. Burress, January 16, 1941, Rosenau Papers, Calumet Regional Archives.

6. *Gary Post-Tribune,* January 22, 1941, February 10, 1941, February 18, 1941.

7. F. B. Knight, R. B. Stewart, R. J. Greenly, *Final Report: Purdue Survey Committee for the Gary Board of Education to the President and Board of Trustees of Purdue University* (n.p., [1942]), 1, 5.

8. Ibid., 33–34, 41, 44.

9. *Gary Post-Tribune,* April 11, 1941.

10. Ibid., April 23, 1941, May 29, 1941; Knight et al., *Final Report,* 212. Supervisors were dropped for social studies, commercial subjects, arts and sciences, English and foreign languages, and handwriting.

11. *Gary Post-Tribune,* May 22, 1941; Knight et al., *Final Report,* 26, 189. See also Edward A. Krug, *The Shaping of the American High School,* vol. 2: *1920–1941* (Madison, Wis., 1972), chap. 13; Herbert M. Kliebard, *The Struggle for the American Curriculum, 1893–1958* (Boston, 1986), chap. 9 on Life Adjustment; and James B. Lane, *"City of the Century": A History of Gary, Indiana* (Bloomington, Ind., 1978), 208–215, for Gary during the war.

12. Knight et al., *Final Report,* 37, 40. For background on the mental hygiene movement see Hamilton Cravens, "Child-Saving in the Age of Professionalism, 1915–1930," in Joseph M. Hawes and N. Ray Hiner, eds., *American Childhood: A Research Guide and Historical Handbook* (Westport, Conn., 1985), 415–488.

13. Interview with Mark Roser, Beverly Shores, Indiana, September 16, 1980, in possession of the author. For a critical interpretation of his work at the Norfolk Prison Colony see David Rothman, *Conscience and Convenience: The Asylum and Its Alternatives in Progressive America* (Boston, 1980), chap. 11.

14. *Gary Post-Tribune,* October 21, 1941, October 29, 1941: G. E. Wulfing to Glen[n] Rearick, May 20, 1941, Guy Wulfing Papers, Calumet Regional Archives.

15. Knight et al., *Final Report,* 202; *Gary Post-Tribune,* February 2, 1942, May 28, 1942.

16. *Gary Post-Tribune,* June 2, 1942; Knight et al., *Final Report,* 269, 338; Raymond A. Mohl and Neil Betten, *Steel City: Urban and Ethnic Patterns in Gary, Indiana, 1906–1950* (New York, 1986), 72.

17. *Gary Post-Tribune,* September 2, 1942, September 8, 1942.

18. *Gary Post-Tribune,* June 9, 1943, August 23, 1943. On the history of social promotion and individual progress see David L. Angus, Jeffrey W. Mirel, Maris A. Vinovskis, "Historical Development of Age Stratification in Schooling," *Teachers College Record,* 90 (Winter 1988):227–232.

19. *Gary Post-Tribune,* March 27, 1941

20. *Gary Post-Tribune,* March 3, 1941, September 12, 1941.

21. *Gary Post-Tribune,* October 14, 1941, January 8, 1942. See also John Morton Blum, *V Was for Victory: Politics and American Culture during World War II* (New York, 1976); I. L. Kandel, *The Impact of the War upon American Education* (Chapel Hill, N.C., 1948).

22. *Gary Post-Tribune,* September 4, 1942.

23. *Gary Post-Tribune,* February 13, 1942. See also Karen Anderson, *Wartime Women: Sex Roles, Family Relations, and the Status of Women during World War II* (Westport, Conn., 1981), 189–212; D'Ann Campbell, *Women at War with America: Private Lives in a Patriotic Era* (Cambridge, Mass., 1984), 75–111.

24. *Gary Post-Tribune,* May 28, 1942.

25. *Gary Post-Tribune,* September 3, 1942, October 28, 1942, January 19, 1943, February 8, 1943; Richard M. Ugland, " 'Education for Victory': The High School Victory Corps and Curricular Adaptation During World War II," *History of Educa-*

tion Quarterly, 19 (Winter 1979):435–451. See also, Ugland, "Viewpoints and Morale of Urban High School Students during World War II—Indianapolis as a Case Study," *Indiana Magazine of History,* 77 (June 1981):150–178.

26. *Gary Post-Tribune,* September 15, 1942; "Gary's 'All-Out Americans,' " *Public Welfare in Indiana,* 54 (February 1944):6–10.

27. *Gary Post-Tribune,* November 17, 1942, January 23, 1943.

28. "Gary's 'All-Out Americans,' " *Public Welfare in Indiana,* 10.

29. *Gary Post-Tribune,* May 8, 1942, February 18, 1943; James Gilbert, *A Cycle of Outrage: America's Reaction to the Juvenile Delinquent in the 1950s* (New York, 1986), chap. 2.

30. *Gary Post-Tribune,* August 19, 1943, March 7, 1944, September 20, 1944.

31. *Gary Post-Tribune,* August 16, 1944, September 5, 1944, December 14, 1944; C. A. Jessen, "School-Work Programs For High-School Youth," *Education for Victory,* 3 (April 20, 1945):8. The types of jobs for youth varied according to age and gender, ranging from being newsboys to working in groceries, bowling alleys, steel mills, and restaurants for boys; girls worked in private homes or stores. Many of the younger children were found to be working without permits and after 7:00 P.M. "Employment Survey of Gary Public School Pupils, Age 14 to 18," Container 45, Gary, Indiana, Research File VI, D, National Urban League Papers, Library of Congress, Washington, D.C. (hereafter cited as NUL Papers).

32. *Gary Post-Tribune,* February 1, 1945, April 25, 1945.

33. Flora Philley, *Teacher Help Yourself* (Gary, Indiana, 1948), 76.

34. *Gary Post-Tribune,* December 12, 1941, March 25, 1942, May 7, 1942.

35. *Gary Post-Tribune,* April 19, 1943, May 24, 1944. On labor during the war see Nelson Lichtenstein, *Labor's War at Home: The CIO in World War II* (New York, 1982).

36. *Gary Post-Tribune,* September 12, 1945.

37. Knight et al., *Final Report,* 180. The East Pulaski school was adjacent to the "white" West Pulaski school and, because of space problems, one kindergarten composed of black children used a room in the West building. It was, however, under the direction of the black principal of East Pulaski.

38. *Gary American,* March 15, 1940, June 7, 1940, September 13, 1940, September 27, 1940.

39. *Gary Post-Tribune,* February 3, 1943; *Gary American,* June 4, 1943.

40. *Gary Post-Tribune,* June 17, 1944, September 6, 1944; *Gary American,* September 8, 1944, September 29, 1944; Isabelle Jones, "Evaluation Report at End of Intermediate Cycle," Bulletin P-20, July 31, 1944, ms in Container 45, Gary, Indiana, Research File VI, D, NUL Papers.

41. Knight et al., *Final Report,* 317–319; Theodore Brameld, *Minority Problems in the Public Schools: A Study of Administrative Policies and Practices in Seven School Systems* (New York, 1946), 199.

42. *Gary Post-Tribune,* September 6, 1939; Charles D. Lutz et al., "A Discussion of the War Employment Situation in Gary, The Needs of Working Mothers, and a Plan for Extending School Services through the Use of Lanham Funds," [1943], 4, Container 45, Gary, Indiana, Research File, VI, D, NUL Papers; Harvard Sitkoff, *The Struggle for Black Equality, 1954–1980* (New York, 1981), 12–13.

43. Office of Community War Services, Federal Security Agency, "Gary, Indiana, Report on Racial Situation," February 14, 1944, Container 24, Gary, Indiana, Research File, VI, A, NUL Papers; James H. Tipton, *Community in Crisis: The Elimination of Segregation from a Public School System* (New York, 1953), 27; National Urban League, "A Study of the Social and Economic Conditions of the Negro Population of Gary, Indiana," mimeo, December 1944, 24, ms in Calumet Regional Archives.

44. *Gary American,* March 3, 1944. On the Bureau for Intercultural Education see

Nicholas V. Montalto, *A History of the Intercultural Educational Movement, 1924–1941* (New York, 1982).

45. *Gary Post-Tribune,* March 13, 1945; *Gary American,* July 20, 1945; Brameld, *Minority Problems in the Public Schools,* 218, and chap. 7.

46. *Gary Post-Tribune,* September 18, 1945; interview with Leonard Levenda, July 8, 1982.

47. *Gary Post-Tribune,* September 21, 1945; *Gary American,* September 21, 1945. For a detailed discussion of the strike see Tipton, *Community in Crisis.* Tipton was in Gary working for the Bureau for Intercultural Education during the strike.

48. *Gary American,* September 28, 1945, October 12, 1945.

49. Walter White to Alfred Hall, September 24, 1945, White to Hall, October 22, 1945, Noma Jensen, "Report on the Investigation of the Gary Branch of the NAACP," [1945], [Jensen], "School Strikes in Gary, Chicago, and New York," [1945], (published as "What's behind These School Strikes?" *The Nation's Schools,* 36 [December 1945]:24–25), Walter White to Paul Robeson, October 29, 1945, School Incidents, January–October, 1945, Container 501, Series A, General Office File, 1940–1955, NAACP Papers.

50. J. Harvey Kerns to Eugene Kinckle Jones, October 12, 1945, Container 25, Gary, Indiana, Research File, VI, C, NUL Papers. See Jesse Thomas Moore, *A Search for Equality: The National Urban League, 1910–1961* (University Park, Pa., 1981), which is weak on this period; and Guichard Parris and Lester Brooks, *Blacks in the City: A History of the National Urban League* (Boston, 1971), esp. 313–317, which is more detailed.

51. *Gary Post-Tribune,* October 25, 1945; Tipton, *Community in Crisis,* 56.

52. *Gary Post-Tribune,* November 1, 1945, November 2, 1945.

53. *Gary Post-Tribune,* November 3, 1945; interview with Leonard Levenda, July 8, 1982; *Life,* November 12, 1945.

54. *Michigan Chronicle,* October 6, 1945; *Gary Post-Tribune,* November 8, 1945; interview with Leonard Levenda, July 8, 1982.

55. *Gary American,* November 2, 1945; interview with Joseph Chapman, Gary, Indiana, December 1, 1981, in possession of the author.

56. [Mark Roser], "Some Conclusions from the Study of the Personalities in the Strike," [September 25, 1945], ms in Guy Wulfing Papers, Calumet Regional Archives; Tipton, *Community in Crisis,* 69–71; "An Analysis of Factors Causing the School Strike at Gary, Indiana," ms in Anselm Forum, "Press Reaction to Gary's School Troubles over Integration . . . Aug.–Sept. 1945," scrapbook, Indiana Room, Gary Public Library, Gary, Indiana.

57. Tipton, *Community in Crisis,* 77–78; "An Analysis of Factors Causing the School Strike at Gary, Indiana," ms in Anselm Forum, "Press Reaction to Gary's School Troubles over Integration . . . Aug.–Sept. 1945"; *Gary Post-Tribune,* January 5, 1946

58. Tipton, *Community in Crisis,* 89.

59. Joseph Chapman to Lester Granger, February 20, 1946, Container 91, Gary, Indiana, Research File, VI, F, NUL Papers.

60. *Gary Post-Tribune,* March 2, 1946, March 4, 1946; *Gary American,* March 8, 1946.

61. Tipton, *Community in Crisis,* 99–100; *Gary Post-Tribune,* August 28, 1946; Reuben Olson to Manet Fowler, August 29, 1946, Container 24, Gary, Indiana, Research File VI, C, NUL Papers.

62. Tipton, *Community in Crisis,* 110–111.

7. Postwar Problems

1. Interview with Stanley Kohn, Gary, Indiana, November 20, 1980, in possession of the author.

2. Manet Fowler, "Spotlight Still on Gary," *American Unity,* 5 (January 1947):7. And see August Meier and Elliott Rudwick, *Along the Color Line: Explorations in the Black Experience* (Urbana, Ill., 1976), 359–363.

3. [Melville Thomas], "Racial Discrimination in the Gary Public Schools," 3–4, ms in Anselm Forum, "Press Reaction to Gary's School Troubles over Integration . . . Aug.–Sept. 1945," scrapbook, Indiana Room, Gary Public Library, Gary, Indiana; Dana Whitmer, "Proposed Extension in the School and Classroom Programs of Intergroup Education in the Public Schools of Gary, Indiana" (Ph.D dissertation, Ohio State University, 1949), 32.

4. *Gary Post-Tribune,* November 13, 1946, December 2, 1946; James H. Tipton, *Community in Crisis: The Elimination of Segregation from a Public School System* (New York, 1953), 113–116.

5. *Gary Post-Tribune,* June 25, 1947; S. Andhil Fineberg, "What Happened in Gary," September 26, 1947, 2, ms in Anselm Forum, "Press Reaction to Gary's School Troubles over Integration," Scrapbook, Indiana Room, Gary Public Library.

6. *Gary Post-Tribune,* September 2, 1947, September 5, 1947.

7. *New York Times,* September 6, 1947, September 9, 1947; Tipton, *Community in Crisis,* 133–142.

8. *Gary Post-Tribune,* September 15, 1947; Paul Klein, "The Gary School Strike," *The Nation,* 165 (October 4, 1947):336; Tipton, *Community in Crisis,* 143–147, 180.

9. Gloster B. Current to Alfred Hall, September 16, 1947, folder 1946–1955, Gary, Indiana, Branch File, 1940–1955, NAACP Papers; interview with Joseph Chapman, Gary, Indiana, December 1, 1981, in possession of the author.

10. *Gary American,* August 27, 1948.

11. *Gary American,* March 4, 1949; *Gary Post-Tribune,* March 4, 1949. Mayor Swartz made two more appointments in July 1949: Emery Badanish, a Republican and Miller pharmacist, replacing Kreitzman; and Arlie Premo, a sheetmetalworker, union leader, and a Democrat, replacing Mrs. Hill.

12. Whitmer, "Proposed Extension in the School and Classroom Programs of Intergroup Education in the Public Schools of Gary, Indiana," 36–38; Gladys Pierce, "Intercultural Relations, Gary, Indiana," (M.E. thesis, Indiana University, 1950), 51.

13. *Gary Post-Tribune,* September 30, 1949.

14. *Gary Post-Tribune,* November 11, 1949.

15. Benjamin Fine, *Our Children Are Cheated: The Crisis in American Education* (New York, 1947), 1–2, 10.

16. *Gary Post-Tribune,* January 9, 1946.

17. *Gary Post-Tribune,* March 27, 1946.

18. *Gary Post-Tribune,* August 28, 1946.

19. J. Schoon to Peter Beczkiewicz, October 19, 1946, Stanley Kohn Papers, Calumet Regional Archives.

20. William C. Reavis et al., *Survey Report: School Buildings and Sites, Gary, Indiana* (Committee on Field Service, Dept. of Education, University of Chicago, March 1947); *Gary Post-Tribune,* March 29, 1947.

21. *Gary Post-Tribune,* August 29, 1947; "Urgent! Concerning the Future of Gary Schools," October 24, 1947, Stanley Kohn Papers, Calumet Regional Archives.

22. "Gary's City-Wide Parents Council Newsletter," June 14, 1948, Stanley Kohn Papers, Calumet Regional Archives.

23. *Gary Post-Tribune,* July 28, 1948.

24. *Gary Post-Tribune,* August 10, 1948; Stanley Kohn to Walter Klege, August 27, 1948, Stanley Kohn Papers, Calumet Regional Archives.

25. "News Letter—Gary's City-Wide Parents Council," October 20, 1948, Stanley Kohn Papers, Calumet Regional Archives; *Gary Post-Tribune,* December 21, 1948, January 25, 1949.

26. *Gary Post-Tribune,* September 6, 1949.
27. Executive Board Local #4 to Irvin Kuenzli, December 5, 1946, AFT Pps.; William E. Eaton, *The American Federation of Teachers, 1916–1961* (Carbondale, Ill., 1975), 143–151; The Commission on Educational Reconstruction, *Organizing the Teaching Profession: The Story of the American Federation of Teachers* (Glencoe, Ill., 1955), 99–102.
28. *Gary Post-Tribune,* May 24, 1947.
29. *Gary Post-Tribune,* April 14, 1948.
30. *Gary Post-Tribune,* May 19, 1948.
31. *Gary Post-Tribune,* April 7, 1949, April 25, 1949, May 10, 1949.
32. *Gary Post-Tribune,* December 9, 1949.
33. *Gary Post-Tribune,* May 15, 1948; Gilbert E. Smith, *The Limits of Reform: Politics and Federal Aid to Education, 1937–1950* (New York, 1982).
34. *Gary Post-Tribune,* November 14, 1945; Child Welfare Services, "Report," 1949, 1, ms in Indiana Room, Gary Public Library; Diane Ravitch, *The Troubled Crusade: American Education, 1945–1980* (New York, 1983), 64–68; Herbert M. Kliebard, *The Struggle for the American Curriculum, 1893–1958* (Boston, 1986), 240–258; Robert L. Hampel, *The Last Little Citadel: American High Schools since 1940* (Boston, 1986), 43–53.
35. *Gary Post-Tribune,* December 31, 1945, March 25, 1946.
36. *Gary Post-Tribune,* July 1, 1946, March 12, 1947.
37. *Gary Post-Tribune,* November 12, 1948; Child Welfare Services, "Report," 1949, 19–20, ms in Indiana Room, Gary Public Library.
38. *Gary Post-Tribune,* November 26, 1947; Child Welfare Services, "Report," 1949, 1–2, 9, 23–24, ms in Indiana Room, Gary Public Library.
39. *Gary Post-Tribune,* April 24, 1947, May 23, 1947, November 24, 1948.
40. *Gary Post-Tribune,* November 27, 1948. The Gary schools were, perhaps, ahead of other school systems in introducing the new programs. According to Robert Hampel, "Employment of guidance counselors and school psychologists, together, is an example of conservative reform. The counseling ranks increased faster than the student population in the 1950s and early 1960s. . . . School psychology also expanded rapidly in the 1950s." *The Last Little Citadel,* 51. On the dubious value of guidance counselors for job placement, at least in the 1920s in California, see Harvey Kantor, *Learning to Earn: School, Work, and Vocational Reform in California, 1880–1930* (Madison, Wis., 1988,) chap. 8.
41. *Gary Post-Tribune,* May 17, 1948, December 14, 1948; James Gilbert, *A Cycle of Outrage: America's Reaction to the Juvenile Delinquent in the 1950s* (New York, 1986), 91–101.
42. *Gary Post-Tribune,* June 4, 1931 (John Wolever, "U.S. Studies Church School Development Here since 1914"); Roman Witowski, "Plans of Religious Instruction for Christian Children Attending Public Schools" (BA thesis, Dept. of Education, University of Notre Dame, February 1944), 37.
43. *Gary Post-Tribune,* September 29, 1943, December 2, 1943, March 9, 1948.
44. *Gary Post-Tribune,* March 9, 1948, June 23, 1948; Ravitch, *The Troubled Crusade,* 32, and on church-school issues see 29–38.
45. *Gary Post-Tribune,* November 1, 1949.

8. Continuity and Change

1. Elizabeth Balanoff, "The Gary School Crisis of the 1950s: A Personal Memoir," *Indiana Magazine of History,* 83 (March 1987):66–67. On Gary during the decade see James B. Lane, *"City of the Century": A History of Gary, Indiana,* (Bloomington, Ind., 1978), 242–266.

2. See Kenneth T. Jackson, *Crabgrass Frontier: The Suburbanization of the United States* (New York, 1985), chaps. 13–14.

3. *Gary Post-Tribune*, August 25, 1950.

4. *Gary Post-Tribune*, March 18, 1950, August 10, 1951. For a discussion of budget planning see Charles D. Lutz, "Long Range and Annual Budgeting in Gary," *American School Board Journal*, 120 (June 1950):23, 82.

5. *Gary Post-Tribune*, March 13, 1952.

6. Ibid., March 31, 1952, June 10, 1952.

7. Ibid., July 9, 1952.

8. Ibid., July 9, 1952, August 29, 1952.

9. Ibid., November 15, 1952.

10. Ibid., October 28, 1953.

11. Ibid., January 22, 1954.

12. Ibid., September 20, 1955, September 24, 1955.

13. [Wendell Schaeffer *et al.*], *The Public School System of Gary, Indiana* ([Chicago], 1955), 3, 4.

14. Ibid., 17.

15. Ibid., 30, 31.

16. Ibid., 195.

17. *Gary Post-Tribune*, September 26, 1955.

18. Ibid., November 4, 1955, November 11, 1955.

19. National Commission for the Defense of Democracy Through Education of the National Education Association of the United States, *Gary, Indiana: A Study of Some Aspects and Outcomes of a General School Survey* (n.p., June 1957), 6.

20. Ibid., 28.

21. *Gary Post-Tribune*, July 6, 1957.

22. Ibid., November 12, 1958.

23. Neal Gross, "Local Pressures on the Public School Superintendent," in George Z. F. Bereday and Luigi Volpicelli, eds., *Public Education in America: A New Interpretation of Purpose and Practice* (New York, 1958), 138.

24. *Gary Post-Tribune*, June 19, 1950, September 6, 1960; JoAnne Brown, "A Is for Atom, B Is for Bomb: Civil Defense in American Public Education, 1948–1963," *Journal of American History*, 75 (June 1988):68–90. And see Diane Ravitch, *The Troubled Crusade: American Education, 1945–1980* (New York, 1983), chap. 3.

25. *Gary Post-Tribune*, January 13, 1953, September 23, 1953; Lane, *"City of the Century,"* 241. For the political situation in the Chicago schools see Mary J. Herrick, *The Chicago Schools: A Social and Political History* (Beverly Hills, Calif., 1971), 296–298; for the problems in higher education Ellen W. Schrecker, *No Ivory Tower: McCarthyism and the Universities* (New York, 1986); and for the Red scare in general David Caute, *The Great Fear: The Anti-Communist Purge under Truman and Eisenhower* (New York, 1978). A (too) optimistic account of the decade is William L. O'Neill, *American High: The Years of Confidence, 1945–1960* (New York, 1986).

26. *Gary Post-Tribune*, March 16, 1951, May 15, 1952.

27. Ibid., June 25, 1955.

28. Ibid., August 31, 1956.

29. W. Lynn McKinney and Ian Westbury, "Stability and Change: The Public Schools of Gary, Indiana, 1940–70," in William A. Reid and Decker F. Walker, eds., *Case Studies in Curriculum Change: Great Britain and the United States* (London and Boston, 1975), 38–40.

30. *Gary Post-Tribune*, September 30, 1958, November 13, 1958.

31. Ibid., March 27, 1950.

32. Dana P. Whitmer, "Camp Workshops Give a Glow to In-Service Education," *The Nation's Schools* (April 1952), n.p. (reprint); *Gary Post-Tribune*, May 24, 1952.

33. *Gary Post-Tribune,* September 25, 1958.

34. Irvin Kuenzli to Flora Philley, March 29, 1950, Philley to Kuenzli, April 10, 1950, AFT Pps. There continued to exist a Gary Teachers Federation, affiliated with the NEA, but it was quite small and often cooperated with the AFT local.

35. *Gary Post-Tribune,* May 10, 1950, June 26, 1950.

36. Ibid., March 12, 1952.

37. Ibid., January 14, 1953, April 30, 1955.

38. Ibid., August 20, 1958.

39. Ibid., January 25, 1950. In 1955 there were only about 100 Mexican-American and 75 Puerto Rican children in the schools and one Mexican-American teacher.

40. Mark C. Roser, "Administrative Techniques in Establishing School Boundary Lines," *American School Board Journal,* 120 (May 1950):25.

41. [Edna Morris to National Office, ca. October 1949] accompanied by newspaper clipping from *Gary Post-Tribune,* September 28, 1949, "Pulaski Addition Is Given Priority: Work Will Start This Year; Glen Park School Delayed until 1950," folder 1946–1955, Gary, Indiana, Branch File 1940–1955, NAACP Papers.

42. *Gary Post-Tribune,* May 18, 1954; Mark Roser, "Gary Public Schools and Democracy," *INFO,* Anniversary Edition, 2 (March 1954):10, 37; Warren M. Banner, *A Study of the Social and Economic Conditions in Three Minority Groups, Gary, Indiana* (New York, 1955), 81.

43. Clifford Minton to Warren Banner, June 3, 1955, Container 97, Gary 1955, Affiliate File D, I Administrative Department, NUL Papers; Minton to Granger, January 24, 1956, Container 97, Gary 1956, ibid.

44. Interview with Clifford Minton, October 19, 1982, Gary, Indiana, copy in author's possession.

45. Minton to Alden Blankenship, March 5, 1957, Blankenship to Minton, December 3, 1957, Gary Urban League Papers, University of Illinois at Chicago Library, Chicago, Illinois.

46. Minton to R. Maurice Moss, December 5, 1957, ibid.

47. Minton to Members, Gary Urban League Board of Directors and Advisory Council, January 20, 1959 (emphasis in original), ibid.

48. Charles Graves to Minton, November 12, 1959, "Special Factors Re: Teacher-Integration in Gary Public Schools to be Considered at the December Meeting of the Midtown Citizens' Committee," December 4, 1959, "For Information of Midtown Citizens' Committee Members, Gary Public Schools, 1960," January 1960, ibid.

49. See Max Wolff, "Segregation in the Schools of Gary, Indiana," *Journal of Educational Sociology,* 36 (February 1963):251–61; John Kaplan, "Segregation Litigation and the Schools—Part III: The Gary Litigation," *Northwestern University Law Review* 59 (May–June 1964):121–70. And, more generally, Kaplan, "Segregation Litigation and the Schools—Part II: The General Northern Problem," *Northwestern University Law School,* 58 (May–June 1963):157–214; Frank I. Goodman, "DeFacto School Segregation: A Constitutional and Empirical Analysis," *California Law Review,* 60 (March 1972): 275–437.

50. *Gary Post-Tribune,* September 4, 1956, November 14, 1957.

51. *Gary Post-Tribune,* January 23, 1958; McKinney and Westbury, "Stability and Change: The Public Schools of Gary, Indiana, 1940–70," 24–31; Ravitch, *The Troubled Crusade,* 228–232.

52. R. Freeman Butts, "Basic Features of American Education," in Bereday and Volpicelli, eds., *Public Education in America,* 12.

53. *Gary Post-Tribune,* May 16, 1950, May 18, 1950.

54. Ibid., May 18, 1950, June 7, 1950; Lane, "City of the Century," 247–253; James Gilbert, *A Cycle of Outrage: America's Reaction to the Juvenile Delinquent in the 1950s* (New York, 1986), chaps. 8–10.

55. *Gary Post-Tribune,* October 19, 1953, March 23, 1956; and see William Graebner, "Outlawing Teenage Populism: The Campaign against Secret Societies in the American High School, 1900–1960," *Journal of American History,* 74 (September 1987):411–435.

56. *Gary Post-Tribune,* May 19, 1950.

57. Ibid., December 22, 1952, April 1, 1953.

58. Ibid., November 22, 1954.

59. Ibid., October 28, 1959.

60. Ibid., November 13, 1959, November 16, 1959.

61. Martin Mayer, *The Schools* (New York, 1961), 9–10.

62. *Gary Post-Tribune,* November 24, 1953.

63. On children in the 1950s see Charles E. Stickland and Andrew M. Ambrose, "The Baby Boom, Prosperity, and the Changing Worlds of Children, 1945–1963," in Joseph M. Hawes and N. Ray Hiner, eds., *American Childhood: A Research Guide and Historical Handbook* (Westport, Conn., 1985), 533–585.

64. R. Freeman Butts, "Basic Features of American Education," in Bereday and Volpicelli, eds., *Public Education in America,* 1.

INDEX

Abel, I. W. 222
Abernethy, Mary, 60, 100
Adams, John, 50–51
Adult education: early development of, 11–12; expansion of, 31–33; during W.W. I, 65–67; in 1920s, 86–89; in 1930s, 135–36
Albright, Frank, 200, 223
All-Out Americans, 168–69, 234
Allen, J. Claude, 192, 212, 231
American Federation of Labor, 62, 92
American Federation of Teachers, 64, 142, 145. *See also* Gary Teachers' Union
Americanization, 11–12, 23, 31–33, 34–36, 60–61, 66–68, 88–89
Anderson, Russell, 168
Andros, Mike, 25–26
Attendance: law regarding, 9
Attendance officer. *See* Truant officer
Auditorium, 16, 42–43
Ayres, Leonard, 55

Bachman, Frank, 55–58 *passim*
Bacoyn, Edward, 96–97
Badanish, Emery, 211, 212, 218
Bailey, A. C., 99
Balanoff, Betty, 210
Balas, Mary, 183
Balinski, Louis, 25
Ballou, Frank, 57
Banner, Warren, 230
Barrows, Alice, 53, 57, 61, 81–83, 123–27
Beard, Charles A., 122, 123
Beczkiewicz, Peter, 196
Bell, A. Howard, 132, 140, 198, 238
Bennett, James O'Donnel, 106
Bethea, Dennis, 147
Black community: in segregated evening classes, 36–37; reaction to 1927 Emerson strike, 95–99; population in 1930s, 147; and Froebel strike, 178–79, 181; and 1947 Emerson strike, 191–92; and schools in 1950s, 229–33
Black students: segregation of, 8, 36, 68–71; at Froebel school, 68–70; enrollment of, 92, 147, 193, 229, 241; during W.W. II, 172–85. *See also* Emerson school; Froebel school; Roosevelt school; Segregation; Integration
Black teachers, 71, 92, 147, 229
Blackwell, Frank, 196
Blankenship, Alden, 219, 220–21, 228, 230–31, 233, 236, 237

Bluffton, Ind., 1–5 *passim*
Bogan, William, 131
Bourne, Randolph, 52, 56
Bowers, Cloyce, 183
Boyville, 25
Brameld, Theodore, 177
Brennan, John, 20
Brickley, S. J., 6, 15, 40
Broche, F. J., 88
Brown, Willis, 25–26, 29
Bruce, William, 17
Bruere, Robert, 124
Budget: in 1930s, 131–34; in 1940s, 195–98; in 1950s, 212, 214, 221; in 1980s, 242
Buffington, E. J., 18–19, 30–31, 63
Bulwinkle, Alfred, 125, 126
Bureau for Intercultural Education, 176, 177, 193
Burns, Charles, 62
Burress, Lloyd, 159
Burris, Benjamin, 94
Burris, William P., 28, 36
Business community: and schools in 1920s, 90–91; and schools in 1930s, 132, 141–42; and schools in 1940s, 187, 194–98, 202–3; and schools in 1950s, 221, 222, 224–25
Butts, R. Freeman, 234, 239

Cain, William A., 19, 30, 42
Caldwell, Otis, 55
Campbell, Lewis, 94
Capehart, Homer, 221
Carlson, Paul, 144
Case, Roscoe, 80, 121
Chacharis, George, 214
Chadsey, Charles, 56
Chamber of Commerce. *See* Business community
Chamberlain, Charles, 141
Chapman, Joseph, 179, 181, 183, 184, 191–92, 230
Charles, Richard, 128
Charlton, Mrs. R. M., 24
Chase, Adele M., 48, 78
Cheeks, Alberta, 97
Cheeks, Earline, 97
Cheever, Mary, 235
Child welfare, 162–63, 164, 203–5, 236
Chiles, Cree, 71
Churchill, Thomas W., 43